Pushing The Limit

Pushing The Limit

Try Anything For One More Day

Gary J. Mello

Library of Congress Control Number:		2010918571
ISBN:	Hardcover	978-1-4568-3330-5
	Softcover	978-1-4568-3329-9
	Ebook	978-1-4568-3331-2

This book was printed in the United States of America.

To order additional copies of this book, contact:
Xlibris Corporation
1-888-795-4274
www.Xlibris.com
Orders@Xlibris.com
89553

CONTENTS

INTRODUCTION

Before you begin on this journey, find your quiet spot, the one place, you reserve for yourself, shut off all the lights, and block out any noise or interference. The darker the better. Read this tale as if it was about yourself or a family member. Light a single candle which will last this tale. Read this entire book in one sitting. I am the hamster running within my cage turning my wheel to power the movie screen to allow you a front row seat to my story. Allow yourself an open mind during this process. This has the best effect to cleanse.

I must race to get this story out of my head before it disappears. I am in a complete mental breakdown mania brought on by a miscommunication with my doctor. This is a slight mishap on both our parts, a miscalculation, a total drug interaction, with the worst possible side effects that can occur. My mind is being erased. This is a total race against the clock. Dementia is happening. Death is following me, and he wants my immortal soul.

The government has not approached me in any way, shape, or form to follow up on any of my training that has been paid for by the American people. I haven't asked either, nor have I committed myself to do so. My blood, sweat, and tears have also paid for it. I have paid my dues as a fully trained United States Marine. I have gone through their standard thirteen-week boot camp, well, fourteen-week training period if you count the receiving week also, but nothing prepares you for my life's tale of woe. I have become a soldier now and have brought myself back from pure self-destruction and drug use as a child only to be put out to pasture. For some reason, my being positive for the human immunodeficiency virus has hindered their belief that I could be combat effective or even a part of their organization whatsoever. Today I'm a 100 percent disabled veteran. I agree, but you be the judge.

I joined the Marine Corps to be the best. To be the guy who smartened up in the eyes of my family and overcome the odds of bad judgments and wrongdoings. I wanted a future that didn't involve drugs, cops, judges, lawyers, and maybe the chance of rotting away in some prison. My path was very dark, and I wanted to see the world. I wanted more than a quickened train's ride to my possible death. I may have died in combat, but any true Marine doesn't fear his own death after they have been trained, or so I was told. Nope, that's not an option at all. We were trained to kill and not to be killed anyways. What makes the grass grow? Blood, blood, blood. What do we do? Kill, kill, kill. That's just one of the many little gems you pick up during training. If you're a movie buff as I am, you will also hear this chant in the movie *Full Metal Jacket.* Trust me; it is not the only thing the Marine Corps teaches. You're taught plenty of other stuff also, but for some reason, the blood and death sticks around a whole lot longer than simply learning how to blouse your trousers above your boots.

During my younger years, I was considered snot-nosed and a little punk. I was quick to fight and defy the rules. Actually, you know what; I was a great kid in my youth before I started drinking and taking drugs. I had gone to a Catholic school from kindergarten till the eighth grade, played basketball, football, baseball, and I even was a fucking Cub Scout for that matter. My downfall was definitely the drugs, drinking, and total anarchist behavior. I had learned early in life you had to fight for what is yours, whether it is money, food, clothes, drugs, or anything else for that matter. You also had to fight to protect your things. Growing up poor with four brothers by a single mother, you may have a glimpse of understanding where I'm coming from. It is just like I feel as if I'm fighting with my mind to get the words out right now. Fighting my mind to get them out and also fighting for those of us who have been shit on and spit at for what seems like all our lives. It is time for my words to be seen and heard. This is my side of the sandbox, and no, you can't cross my line without getting your hands bloody. Hoorah!

When I entered the Marine Corps in Boston's main hub, I did reveal to the gunnery sergeant what kind of environment I was raised in. All my chips were on the table, and they said yes. "No worries, son, we'll make a Marine out of you anyways. So never mind all your bad deeds, and get your ass over in that line. You're going to Paris Island, boy." Just getting to this moment was an achievement beyond belief. I had fucked up plenty as a kid: drug arrests, assaults, breaking and entering, drunken disorderly. I was a crack addict by the tender age of thirteen, an alcoholic, a high school dropout, and let's not forget, a model citizen. Oh yes, my recruiter told me exactly how to answer their questions in Boston. Everything you've done in the past was a mistake and it was only experimental. How convenient it was to be coached into the meat grinder called the United States Marine Corps.

Obviously they knew I was just involved in an assault and battery with the New Bedford Police Department. A total scandal if I may say so myself, but that's another story all in itself. I will leave that one alone. Nope, you know what? Fuck 'em! I'm saying it anyways. This is my story, let them write one if they deny what transpired. It was an early Friday night when they beat the hell out of me with their sticks and Mace for several hours. It was a five on one, and they felt it necessary to pummel me in the police station while handcuffed. I had been smashed so many freaking times by different officers I lost count. What I don't know anymore is their names, but they know exactly what they did to me and who they are. I'll leave it at that. My head was swollen so badly the next morning I looked like the elephant man. My mom had come to pick me up from the downtown station when the bail bondsman released me early the next morning. I could tell I looked bad because she had a shocked look on her face when I came into her vision. She screamed actually, "Oh my god!" There were a few other choice words spoken to the people on duty at the station, but I will not repeat them because I love my mom and she need not remember this. Well, Mom was pissed, that's about all I can say. She drove me over to the hospital to be checked out, and the nurses were stunned also. I was severely concussed and had multiple contusions covering my arms and legs. I also heard that two of the officers were being treated as well for their injuries, but I was glad to have put two of them there along with me at that time. It was a simple case of hero cop overstepping his authority that began the whole nightmare of travels.

My younger brother Brian had been pulled over for turning around into a parking lot, but he traveled several yards up a one-way street to enter the lot. I had asked the officers' permission to walk up several blocks to an older brothers' apartment around the corner. He said, "Yes, by all means, go. Get out of the streets already, we told you before to find somewhere to hang out earlier." I had been stopped earlier in the evening hanging out with an older friend of my brother Kevin. We were told to get home and quit lingering around on the streets at night. That was our daily routine: to get out of work and hang out all night smoking grass and drinking on the avenue. Nothing new to be told to get lost or else, so we did without incident. So with that in mind, I asked to leave because I didn't want them to treat my younger brother differently knowing I was in his vehicle. I began to walk up the sidewalk, and another police officer arrived on the scene only to grab me from behind and punch me in the face screaming, "Where the hell you going?" I looked into this officer's face and realized he was black, and I called him a sucker-punching nigger. Totally uncalled-for remark, but hey, that is just what he was in my eyes. Well, when I went to break free of his hold on me, he hit me again. I turned in the direction of my younger brother and told him one more time, "Brian, it's on." He hit me a third time, only this time I was being choked from behind by his partner. That's when I lost it. I punched this cop right in the face, smashing his glasses into his eye. That's the first guy who was being treated at the hospital with me. The next cop who was choking me from behind was hit when I swung my elbow backward to break free of his grasp so I could breathe. I must have connected good because I heard him scream, "He broke my nose." So that's the other officer being treated this morning with me.

So what happened next, I was swarmed on by at least five cops tackling me to the ground including one kneeling on my head. While I was pinned to the ground, I was kicked in the face from the cop whose nose was supposedly broken. He managed to break my cheekbone with that cheap shot. So that's why when you look at me now, my left eye is slightly lower than my right one; it had healed wrong. I was handcuffed extra tightly then muscled into the paddy wagon, and my inner rages were far from over. I began screaming and smashing my body against the doors to get out because I knew they just arrested me for nothing and they had bashed me. I was pissed. After about nine or so full hits into the doors with my shoulders, I fell backward and was trying to get up for another run at it when the door slightly opened and one of the officers emptied a nice fresh dose of Mace right into my face. I wasn't able to shield myself because I was cuffed, and it burned like hell. The air in the wagon was no longer breathable at all when they shut the doors again. I was going to suffocate and they didn't give a rat fuck about it. They hopped into the cab of this traveling cage on wheels without any concern. The officer in the driver's seat sped up and hit the brakes constantly along the way to the north end station so I would be tossed around the back like a rag doll hitting off the walls.

Once we arrived to the station, I was snatched out the back by two of them and thrown to the ground. I couldn't breathe or see, but I managed to sneak a breath and a peek of an incoming wall while being led inside. They smashed me off the left side of the door opening in turn, splitting my bottom lip open from the impact. Once inside I was forced over a desk face forward, cuffed behind my back with two officers holding me down. That's when I was beaten atop my head with their sticks at least five hits from three of them each and also several extras from the original cop who started the whole thing. He was screaming, "You little motherfucker. When I say you're under arrest, you fucking comply." I was screaming faggot, pussy, pig, no-balls-having motherfuckers repeatedly during their barrage of strikes. I was egging them to hit me more because they hit like girls and wouldn't have the sand to fight fair one-on-one without their badges or without these cuffs on. Well, that just enraged them more, so I got a few extras. When they got out their rage and finally sit me upright in a chair, my face was swollen and bleeding quite a bit. Right then I noticed a female cop walking by the room where they had just preformed their brutal attack on me and asked her with a bit of a smart-ass kind of tone, "Hey, Officer, what's with all the police brutality?" She kindly stepped into the room and gave me a nice billy club strike to the jaw for asking. What a fucking bitch, I thought. Really nice woman there, the tender, loving, caring type, I'm sure. So anyways, that was that. Off I was brought to the downtown station and thrown into a cell to await the bail bondsman. No need for medical attention, no need for anything but a "fuck you" and "suffer, you little prick." Several hours went by, like about six of them, before my mom picked me up to take me to the hospital.

I was ordered to report to court the following Monday, so my mother took pictures of me all beaten and bashed beyond recognition. When I arrived to court and showed these pictures to the judge, I was told to get them the fuck out of his courtroom and those were his exact words. I was charged with assault on police officers and resisting arrest. They wanted to charge me with all this shit and put me in prison over this, so when it came to my pretrial, I brought along my recruiter to speak on my behalf. He told them that I had gone back to high school to get my diploma and was already within the Poole program scheduled to join the Marine Corps upon graduation. Now at the time, I was young and scared when I think back on this occasion because I was facing somewhere in the neighborhood of two to seven years if convicted. I agreed to take the judge's advice and leave it all alone, and he would allow me to enter the Marine Corps. No harm, no foul. Well, that's bullshit because that is still on my criminal record, and them cops never got convicted for their misuse of force if I think about it now. In fact a red flag goes up advising them not to approach me alone if I was being arrested ever again.

But hey, it's water under the bridge to me these days. I have other fish to fry. The city of New Bedford got theirs a year or so later when the police beat the hell out of a black guy almost similar to my encounter, but the cops ended up going a bit too far on this beating and the poor guy died in his cell. If you look this up, you will see I'm not lying about his ordeal. The man's family sued the city for millions of dollars and won their case. My only regret is that when they had done this to me, I should have pursued my case further and punished them cops for what they did. Maybe that man would still be alive today if I had done so. I live with this now, and it hurts me. All I can do now is say a silent prayer for that man's family and say sorry. Sorry for not speaking up about when they did it to me. Sorry for your loss.

That is just a taste of some of the guilt I feel when I look back on my own life and write about my past. There were a lot of other things done to me and that I have done that I'm not particularly proud of, but this is not the time. You will read this book and totally understand the true meaning of forgiveness, suffering, pain, and sacrifice. I just hope you enjoy my life story and what it takes to live it for me. So let's take a walk in my shoes and my head for a while. I promise this tale will not only have you crying but it will also have you look into your own life and wonder what can you do today to change the path you are on and to possibly be who you always wanted to be before time runs out.

Now as for Paris Island, South Carolina, that was a definite wake-up call if there ever was one. You fly in on a commercial express plane with a few other Marine hopefuls and just pray you're not in over your head. We dare not speak to one another in fear of there being some reprimand when we reach the island. Who knows for sure who may be watching and listening. We were told to shut the fuck up. So off to the island we went without our moms to wipe our noses, without our teenage prom queen, without any fucking clue why we joined up other than in my case it had to be a better life than the one I was leading. Shit, it was only four hours ago that I was having my final day of freedom. I had just partied all night with some black chick I met at a bar doing blow, drinking, and getting laid before I put all this shit ass life behind me. No more beatings from a drunken old man called your father. No more drugs, no more failing in life, no more fighting with my brothers over food or clothes. It was a blessing to leave and never look back in my eyes. I was going to be a Marine. The word *Marine* just sounded so much better than *army, air force, navy,* or *Coast Guard.* For me, I wanted the best training and the toughest if I was going to fight and possibly die in some third world country. Yes, I was ready to be pushed beyond my limits physically and mentally and ask for more. Whatever they could dish out, I could take. Anything was better than being a cook or a roofer or working for some sleazy drug-dealing bastard who used kids to turn a profit, also in the process making them addicts.

The next step was the absolute right one to take. I was going to prove them all wrong, all those teachers, judges, court officials, and maybe even a few family members who didn't think I would amount to shit. I had quit school during my senior year to find a job that paid more than working as a dishwasher or a farmer's helper. The school thing just wasn't any fun to me, I felt as if I could do better without the hassle of being there. You heard the story before from someone, Mom raised five boys on her own, and she worked three jobs just to keep a roof over our heads. Dad split when I was nine to pursue some new pussy. I hated him for that. I had to seek a job, and at a very young age, I think I was eleven. That was just to be sure I had money in my pocket for food or some candy from the store that we walked to several miles away. I would also ride along with my older brothers who had paper routes in their youth. I was always picked to do the dead-end dirt road with two vicious dogs. These dogs definitely weren't shy to bite if you happened to be peddling. I remember doing this very young actually. My bike was always my shield and a few rocks helped. Imagine being shorter than the dogs, and they worked as a team. I was screaming and crying before you knew it. I was lucky not to get bitten very hard. Yes, they did mouth me a few times and it hurt. I swear them dogs loved to attack then let you go.

I remember having to grab someone else's bike when mine was busted or they didn't want to go at all. Sometimes you got lucky and scrounged enough parts in the yard or the junkyard to put together a bicycle and get it functioning to make life easier. Hitchhiking worked well also, but that happened in my teens. There is a saying, "If only I knew then what I know now, I would have never stuck my thumb out for a ride at all." Come to think of it, the cops still haven't caught that serial killer who was leaving dead prostitutes on the surrounding highways. I was just a kid then and I was unaware of such things at the time. Like I said, if I knew then what I know now, I probably would've chopped off my own thumb before hitching a ride. But hey, we are talking Rochester, Massachusetts. Here, it wasn't some busy-assed city like Boston. It was very quite in our town. You almost had no chance of being abducted as a child in such a small town where everyone knows everyone's business. Well, I was never taken, and that's a good thing. I really think our justice system absolutely sucks when a kid can be bashed the way I was and some sick fuck that kills prostitutes is still free roaming around out in the world. They should focus more on stuff like that rather than throwing their weight around—well, that's my opinion anyways.

I got a job also to contribute and to help ease the strain on my mom. Maybe it was to lessen the guilt for us growing up without any real parental supervision or guidance. The closest thing we got to authority after our father bailed on us was and has always been the police department for doing something stupid. As for the guidance, that came in the form of a belt beating, a two-by-four smash, a wooden spoon throttling, a wooden stick, a broom, or anything moms could grab to smash you when you were acting a fool. Dad was more of a drunken-comes-home-and-whack-your-kids kind of guy with a belt and occasionally be yelling around your mom. But hey, that's all water under the bridge also.

There was a time when a friend and me broke into the little league concession stand in the center of town and were caught in the act. The whole reason we broke into it is unclear, but I'm sure it was for candy or maybe some money for smokes, maybe even for kicks. Either way, we got nabbed red-handed using a long stick through the twelve-inch square window to try and snare the cash box. One of the neighborhood moms drove up on us while returning from the woods because the first cash box we snatched turned out to be a cleverly disguised first aid kit. We thought we hit pay dirt only to discover upon opening this thing it was filled with Band-Aids and gauze. We ended up doing community service for that ordeal. I remember being picked up by the police chief of Rochester along with my buddy and we had to scrape old paint from the fire station. I remember being up on a twenty-foot ladder scraping away when a bunch of bees or hornets came flying out after me, stinging the shit out of me, so I hurried down the ladder halfway and jumped to safety. In the process of getting away, I must have nudged the ladder because it fell also. Just my luck though, it had smashed the one police car I think the town had at the time, breaking the top lights and scratching the hood pretty badly. The chief wasn't pleased at all. He had us fill potholes in the parking lot for the rest of the day, and that was it. We got off easy if I think about it. I think the chief was so disgusted with us he just let us go away.

Oh yeah, I did tell you I was smoking, right? Oh yes, indeed, my first cigarette came when I was ten. But even worse still, I had already smoked pot with an older person when I was nine. I was also introduced to cocaine at the very tender age of thirteen. We are not talking sniffing the stuff, we are talking mixing it with water and some baking soda and heating it until it becomes oil, then allowing it to harden. Putting it in a soda can form it into a pipe with some ashes and smoking it. Lo and behold, you're a free baser now. Thanks, friend of mine. As you can see, things were pretty tough growing up. Nothing like being an addict all during school, in and out of trouble because it's no fault of your own, you just got addicted. Believe me, once this happens, you will become a very nasty individual to feed your monkey called addiction. That and the fact you're reckless in your youth. The combination of the two is totally a bad situation. Well, it was normal for us growing up to be stereotyped within our community as being the wild Mello boys. Friends of mine today have told me their parents wouldn't allow their children, meaning them, around us. They didn't know what went on with us, but they had an idea, so who could blame them? So I grew up kind of an outcast from normal society at a very young age and only hung out with other troublemakers and addicts.

Well, tough shit I say to that, and I'm tough enough to be a Marine. I was schooled very well in the art of self-defense growing up wild and pretty much on the streets. Mom never knew half the stuff we did as kids, and she may never know. If she reads this book, maybe she'll know some of my thoughts. I just pray she doesn't feel any guilt or any sadness about what she reads. I also hope my father does the same. I'm a survivor no matter what the odds are against me. Hold your head high, Mom and Dad, your son is going to be a Marine.

At least I can accomplish that right in my life.

So there I sit on this plane to a new beginning in life, a fresh start as some will say. All of my bad and destructive past behind me at last. Maybe finally I will do something my family can be proud of. Most of my family considered me a looser until the moment I told them I was joining up. I had returned back to school to finish my senior year. After a few short seasons of scallop fishing commercially, I knew there must be an easier road to travel other than breaking my back for someone else to become rich from my labors. Just working side by side with some other three-toothed grilled junkie fuck that might possibly stab your ass while you're sleeping because he's on some weird trip due to withdrawals was enough to know it sucked ass. Believe me, back in the mid-'80s, a lot of heroin and crack flowed within the groups of assholes I knew. When you're pulling in stacks of cash from your trips that these boats had and I was privileged to go out on, I would hit the docks running. Whores, crack, drinking, strip clubs, more whores, more crack, heroin to help you sleep because you have been running for five days straight with no sleep. Only to turn around and head back to sea for your next escape from the mess you made out of everyone within your path.

Oh yeah, I'm that guy. Show up with a stack of cash to a crack house and get everyone high. If everyone's smoking, then there can't be some pig narcotics officer sneaking among you to bust you. After destroying your mind and everyone's lives around, you up and go back to the boat. You charge up the money for your smokes through fish supply and pay when you get back. No big deal, let them take it right from your check when you get back each and every time. The only bad thing out of this is your guilty thought process when you come down from your high. Leaving that dock heading out of the harbor toward the sometimes-peaceful waters of the Atlantic was always better than facing anyone within your family to own up to your actions or drug issues. Swearing to God that in this trip, you wouldn't fuck up again and stay straight and clean, telling your lying-ass self that you'll use the money to do the right thing. So each and every time without fail you said this. If you're a junkie or a crackhead, you know what the hell I mean. For the rest of the world that don't know what I'm talking about, guess what, ass head? You know now.

This was about my future and mine alone. I needed to see a light at the end of a tunnel for myself. "Please, God, show me the way," I would pray many nights starving and cold on the streets or the ocean as a kid. I was locked into a very bad outlook on my life, and it had to change. As I mentioned before, I had returned to school because I knew I needed to fix this shit life of mine right. Now this returning to school was no picnic either. I had to be picked up every morning by the truant officer and then dropped off at work after school. I wasn't allowed to ride the bus no more.

I was lucky to be given a chance actually. All this came to pass when I was arrested mid-senior year in Marion for trying to sell fake cocaine to undercover officers. That was another moment of stupidity on my part, trusting someone to be a stand-up dude only to turn out to be a rat in the end. I ended up being sent to the old Plymouth House of Correction for a short stay waiting trial. I was let off of those charges because it wasn't real. Maybe it was because I never said a peep about it being phony stuff and the cops were sure they had the bust of their careers only to find out it was a couple of kids trying to make a quick buck. Whatever though, I still was a juvenile spending time in a rat, cockroach, stinky, and unsafe adult prison. Not a good time at all, believe me.

God be dammed if I wasn't raised right and wasn't the model citizen in my youth if all that hurt and pain of growing up was behind me. If the world of drugs, violence, and pure self-destruction were behind me, I would excel in this new life I had put into motion. Prior to the cop incident, nothing would help.

So there I am, on this plane, with a full heart and a wide eye wanting and yearning for the title Marine. What a coveted title to hold indeed. They are the elite of the armed forces, also known as the few the proud. Wouldn't it be great? I thought as the plane touched down in the darkness of night. From the plane we were led to a bus, which transferred us over to the island. We had sat in an empty hangar for a few hours waiting for other recruits to arrive on different flights to join us in our quest to become better men. To make our lives mean something, to get out of trouble, to get off the streets, because we were tired of all the bullshit in the civilian world, to blow shit up, or to simply kill someone. Whatever the case may be, we upped the ante and signed our life over to Uncle Sam and we were proud to do so.

Riding on that big greyhound bus was of soft whispers of hellos and "where you from," all was good until about an hour into our ride when all of a sudden the bus slowed to a screeching airbrakes stop. The doors swung open, and these two big-assed, pissed-off military policeman hopped on board. Oh, they were not kind at all.

"Shut the fuck up," that was our greeting.

"Welcome to Paris Island, SC, you lowlife pieces of shit."

Thank Christ I wasn't in the front row, I thought. I was in the middle of the bus against the window out of harm's reach. A few recruits were yanked up and ordered to say a few general orders. Those answers have better come quickly or they would feel that bastard's hands around his neck. Well, this one meathead, I forgot his name, stood up and pissed himself right there and began to cry. I was overcome with laughter and didn't realize I had snickered out loud. Wouldn't you freaking know it they both ran over and snatched me out of my seat and flung me into the isle, arms and legs flailing like a rag doll. I was screamed at for laughing at the top of their lungs, spit flying all over my cheeks, but I dared not move. Who knows what these gorillas will do. I still to this day don't remember what they said or were saying, but the rest of the bus snapped to attention while I was forced to do push-ups at their feet. They spoke or were it more like yelled out plenty of derogatory statements toward everyone else on the bus. Nope, I had my head down pushing up and down. These guys scared me awake that I am for damn sure. My sleepiness wore off quickly from the long plane flight. Now these weren't your garden-variety regular push-ups, neither these were Marine Corps push-ups.

"Down-one, up-two, down-three, up-four, down-I, up-love, down-Marine, up-Corps." That was considered one push-up.

What the hell did I get myself into? I wondered while watching the rubber floor mat rise and fall beneath me in the isle. After God knows how long or how many push-ups or repetitive screams of "one, two, three, four, I love the Marine Corps" style push-ups and after a nice-sized puddle of sweat that dripped from the tip of my nose the size of a small dinner plate formed beneath me, I was told to return to my seat. I could see now I was in for a long, hard training period because someone pissing himself would damn near be an everyday occurrence. Me being a toughly raised kid, I would surely laugh at each and every opportunity. Knowing full well I could be that kid next. By no means did I ever piss my pants. Well, at least not during recruit training anyways. There had been drunken nights in my past where I have awoken in my own urine and also my own vomit. But I still laugh about that also.

The bus was back on the move toward our next destination after them two psychotic military policemen exited laughing.

Where to next? I thought. Would it be better or worse; did them MPs call over to say we had cleared the gate and were on our way? Would they have dropped my name to someone further down the line that recruit Mello was a troublemaker? That's all I needed, right? Would they say we had a pissing boy on our bus and we deserved more of this hazing also known as training? What lay in wait for us? Our bus traveled for a few more minutes and then came to another stop. I peered out of the darkly tinted window to see about eight guys waiting wearing those funky Smokey the bear hats all dressed in camouflage and looking extremely annoyed and pissed off. At first I really wasn't sure where we were exactly because most of our ride from the airport to our destination was within the cover of darkness. I never really felt the temperature change much either. We were gathered in a huge airport hangar that was air-conditioned then we were herded onto a nice, comfortable bus. All my senses were off and I wasn't even sure what time it was. All I knew was I was about to be let off this bus to be subjected to these neatly dressed maniacs. What will they be like? Will they break me down as a man? Will I cry out for my mommy like I already heard from old Piss Pants? No freaking way. I'm here to better myself no matter what. This couldn't be half as bad as running the streets of New Bedford or that slow-assed, boring town I grew up in. Or could it?

RECEIVING

"Get the fuck off my bus," that was the famous greeting we heard when the bus doors opened while one of the eight instructors boarded.

"Grab your shit and get the fuck out. Hurry the fuck up," he screamed.

Everything went by in a flash. I grabbed the folders I was told to bring along from Boston, and I grabbed the Marine Corps handbook I was issued and got out quickly. This meant to push, punch, or pull your way off the bus. You get the fuck out, period. No way do I want to be the last man out, and neither do the guys behind me. We could tell that it wouldn't go over well at all if it was you. I made my way out without a hitch, I wasn't last and that was great. I was told by another instructor to stand on some yellow footprints painted into the tarmac. Once I was there, I was in the position of attention and all was fine. The other two buses of recruits offloaded with more of the same yelling are of "Get the fuck out of their buses." It seemed like everything was good and maybe the worst was over, so I thought and kind of hoped. Maybe they just need us organized and they needed to keep order while receiving about three hundred recruits. Just then I was yanked out of my spot and told to get up front facing everyone else. Once again I was singled out to do some damn push-ups, but I wasn't alone and it was comforting in some weird way, sort of motivating in a sense.

Once we knew it was time to man up and deliver our best, we gave it. I pushed for damn near twenty minutes straight, again chanting out the old "one, two, three, four, I love Marine Corps" bit, with my other two comrades in arms in unison. While we were pushing away, the instructors told everyone they had picked out three people and told them they were the lucky ones now. I guess that meant us because there were no others up front along with the three of us. I'm really glad they made it clear to me. *Oh shit,* I thought. *Does this mean they are favoring us and putting us in charge of our platoons and we wouldn't get so much of an ass reaming every time someone fucked up?* Now you know as well as I do that this is far from being a privilege. As of right now, all it means is I'm out front of everyone else like some kind of circus freak in a sideshow act doing push-ups for their amusement. Just because we happened to be carrying these folders in our hands, we were punished.

"Hurry! Hurry! Hurry! Step right up and come see the snot nosed, jackass punk kid who hated being told what to do his entire life. He's now doing push-ups for the black drill instructors," the man at the sideshow spoke into my head.

It was actually three white kids doing those push-ups, and I noticed that. Maybe they knew something about racism down here, and they were going to prove a point or something. It just doesn't fly in the Corps.

"We are all green," one of them yelled out in between our cadence of "one, two, fuck you, Marine Corps" style push-ups.

In my mind I was thinking if that's the case where's the black kid next to us. Oh, my mistake, he's over in formation watching and listening along as you beat us three white dumb fucks down with these fucking push-ups. Right about the moment I spoke my mind, some black recruit began to laugh. Like there was something funny about the way these drill instructors were handling their methods of race discrimination. Big fucking mistake there on his part, I thought to myself while pushing. I wish I could've thanked this kid out loud because we were told to stop.

You see, drill instructors are very unpredictable assholes on their own. But when given a reason or provoked, they will attack. Provoked they were when this dumb hood rat nigger busted out laughing. This kid got the snot slapped out of himself and took a few well-deserved hits from there rubber-handled sticks that are not mentioned or talked about being used as a training tool to John Q. public.

"You mother mo FO dirt, dumbass nigger. Don't you ever think we are your boys or your hommies? We are not your friends, you're not back on the block, and you better damn well know it, boy." They were screaming out loud while bashing him.

Under my watchful, curious eye, I watched this kid cry like a little schoolgirl and whimper back a soft "Sir, yes, sir." The drill instructors made him strip down to his underwear and repeat the phrase "Sir, I will not interrupt again, sir" over and over as loud as he could muster. Everything began with saying *sir* and ended in *sir*, whenever addressed by an instructor. They next took a garbage can and put it over this kid's head and body to muffle out some of the noise so this drill instructor could finish his speech on racism. I thought it was great how they just set us up for the whole deal without realizing they had a plan. His speech went on for a lot longer than need be in my mind, we got the point with their visual display that's for sure. What I got from his Southern drawl speech was coming at me faster than I could comprehend anyways. I understood about half, I think. Try flying down to South Carolina late one night and piss some black guy off, then you'll see what I was dealing with. At least half of half of everything this man said was mumbled and, quite frankly, unclear to say the least.

But we all knew for some reason when he was done spewing out the unrecognizable big mush-mouthed mess of words and said, "Do you maggots understand?"

We all replied in unison, "Sir, yes, sir."

What a fine fucking mess I was in now. *What if this guy trains me?* I thought. *Christ, if I am ever sent into combat, I'd be dead in less than a week. I might as well be deaf because I'm not going to understand or learn a thing. Should I just say forget the whole thing, or should I press on?* Softly to my inner self, two words came into my mind as if they were spoken aloud, "Don't quit!" It reminded me of some divine intervention crap you see on the television or read in some obscure book you happened to pick up. Who knows, maybe this was God speaking to me. Whatever it was, I stayed at attention and kept my mouth shut. That's when we were herded into the doors of this huge-ass building in front of us.

Upon entering the building, we were told to stay in single file all the way through. We were hurriedly forced to strip down to our underwear and forced to stand ass to nuts against the wall facing forward. I'm talking like sardines here. This was much closer than any straight guys liking to be in that close on another male, especially in this manner of dress. The sheer control over us was unmatched by anything I had ever been through up to this point. Was this some sort of sick psychological joke? Was this to show us that it doesn't matter who you are forced next to, he is your buddy? You would carry his limp dick and balls if you had to escape capture. Worse yet, you would lay down your own life to save his pitiful, useless carcass and he would for you without hesitation. Well, whatever it was, we were definitely not moving, and it was uncomfortable to say the least. I wasn't going to be the one to complain, I have already been given a target on my back in the form of squad leader from them drill instructors outside. I wasn't saying shit and also wasn't moving until told to do otherwise. If anything, I would suck it up and lead by example.

When we were told to move, we shuffled through a staging area with our laundry in our hands from off our bodies. We were told to empty out all of our belongings onto a long table set up in front of us. This included jewelry, watches, combs, money, identifications, wallets, and all of our clothes. It was to be inventoried and placed inside a brown paper bag. They also told us to throw in our sneakers also. There go my new Nike sneakers to my surprise. Why my new sneakers? I thought I would need them for running during training? What the fuck, I paid good money for them bastards before I left, knowing they were the top-of-the-line running shoe. Now my new kicks were inside a shitty brown bag with tape wrapped all around it with my name and social security number printed on it. I guess I won't need them or that other shit I had with me. Is there some kind of scam going on in the back room? Is there a sneaker thief going to sell our nice shit? That's when we were forced to move the hell on down the line. Only at this table we were handed some cheap new balance crap sneaker called Go Fasters in our size and told to move the fuck on. That was no big deal. I tied them in a quick bowknot and draped them over my right shoulder as instructed and moved along down the line. My next stop was for socks, green and white ones, two pairs each.

"Now move the fuck down," I heard coming from a distance over the noise made from the hustle and bustle.

We then were issued two sets of camouflaged pants and shirts. Two pairs of boots: black leather ones called combat boots and half leather with green canvas ones called jungle boots. We also received new underwear and were ordered to change out of the ones we were wearing. The old ones were to be thrown out, they were too nasty and ass cheese crusted to keep in this man's Marine Corps. We were issued so much shit it's a wonder to see how well organized they kept us moving. Well, we had no fucking choice really, but hey, this was some guy's dream job to forcefully march a bunch of scared green, unknowing of anything, almost-naked recruits down this assembly line. What bullshit did this guy do to end up here doing this? I thought to myself as I shuffled along.

On with the cattle drive! That's exactly what you felt like while marching balls to crack through the line. Like being led like lambs to a slaughter. This is definitely not my ideal, dream job so far. Obviously enough, nothing my dumbass recruiter had told me was true. No mention whatsoever of this cluster fuck. I mean for fuck's sake, he should have warned me of this kind of humiliation and harassment. But hey! Guess what? I signed on for this, and I'm not going to quit now. So along the line I go, Go Fasters over my right shoulder and two pairs of boots over me left. One set of fresh un-ass cheese-crusted tighty-whities on under my new camouflaged pants we were told to put on which are hopelessly loose as hell. Onward I march collecting up a few green and white T-shirts, a toothbrush, and a razor with shaving cream, some soap with a container, and a few other small items such as some toenail/fingernail clippers, foot powder, and a fingernail brush later to be called scrubbies. A bit farther down we are handed two boot brushes, some polish, and a rag. I wondered why the hell I would need this crap. I remembered seeing how neat the drill instructor's camouflaged uniforms looked and how mirror-shined their boots were and gave up on that dumbass thought. I figured maybe his boots came that way. By the looks of the boots I have and the issuing of these polishing items, they're clearly not issued freshly shined. Nope, that will take some elbow grease on my end. I was thinking way too much into stuff while trying to hold on to all of my stuff.

Right about the time, I'm almost overloaded with crap they have told me to carry. They spring a few more fucking things on you. Two locks, one standard combination dial lock and another combination dial lock that has a funny-looking wire that makes about an eighth-inch loop then it locks back into itself. Okay? Well, shit? I don't know what it's for, but I'll keep a hold of them the best I can. Right at that moment, a guy a few spots ahead of me dropped half his shit.

"Holy dog shit," blurted out of the instructor's mouth nearest to us, and he pounced on this kid.

Two other instructors joined in screaming at him and kicking him in the ass as he desperately tried to grasp at his things. This kid was in total panic mode and franticly grabbed at his stuff to no relief from the yelling and kicking to hurry the fuck up. I moved on by, not wanting to help him or even to be part of this poor son of a bitch's problem. Good thing I didn't drop any of my stuff, I thought, while slipping by. The next station to receive something else to add to my steadily growing heap was only ten feet away. I was relieved I was going to make it there unscathed. Thank you! Jesus! Carrying a lot of stuff in your arms is tough enough, but add in the pack of wolves waiting to kick your ass and the fact stuff is flung at you from ten or so feet away just adds to the stress you feel. I was thinking, fuck me, I couldn't handle much more in my arms at the time while heading to the next station. To my surprise and relief, we were issued a seabag and a small shaving bag with some flip-flops. We were told to put all of our smaller items into the shaving bag and to put the rest of everything into the seabag, including that shaving bag of sorts. They ordered us to put on some green socks and them shitty Go Fasters along with a green T-shirt and already having them loose-fitting camouflaged pants falling down my ass. So now I was all set. I was holding up my saggy drawers with one hand and carrying this overstuffed seabag over my shoulder with the other hand. On our next stop, we were issued another sack, only this one was a backpack of sorts. We were told to put our jungle boots in there and were given a poncho, a few tents stakes, a half of tent, and very thin foam so called bedroll. We stuffed all that crap inside of it and put it on our backs and carried the seabag in front in a sort of bear hug carrying style. Okay, I had all my shit except for my belt. Whoever came up with the idea of issuing recruits their belts last is an asshole, I thought. Maybe he was a genius, whichever the case, it sucked.

After all that grabbing shit and nervous shuffling through the gear distribution line, I made it to the end unharmed by the wild drill instructors. We were corralled up in a movie theater of sorts with stadium-style seating without the upper deck. Kind of wish I was back at home watching the Red Sox at Fenway instead of being bullied by these jack-offs. Once inside this theater of sorts, we were finally given our belts and a nice brass buckle in two separate pieces. They told us rather quickly how to assemble them and were told to put them on our shitbag pants. I got this thing together on the first try and slipped it around my waist in a flash. I was then ordered to carry all my shit and find an empty seat. We were told to place our backpack on the floor in front of our feet and then sit with that seabag in our arms and then place it on top of that backpack before sitting. They had a plan for everything, every small fucking detail, it was insane. I climbed to about the third row, placed that backpack down, and flopped down like a sack of old sundried white dog shit into that red-velvet-covered soft-cushioned chair. Looking around wasn't an option either because we were told to sit at attention, and there was to be no fucking talking and they meant it.

As time slowly crept by while waiting for the rest of the recruits to make it through the gauntlet of getting issued their gear, we were instructed to read our Marine Corps handbooks. The truth is personally I was too damn charged up on adrenaline and couldn't comprehend what I was reading. I read the whole damn thing from cover to cover three fucking times and retained absolutely nothing, I swear to God. Now whose bright ideas have been that? Let's scare the shit out of the trainees and expect him to retain some printed information in a handbook. The only thing you learned up to this point was to fear and respect them damn hornetlike drill instructors. I next got the feeling of total relaxation from the sudden stillness of sitting. We were in a safe spot again, and there were only two drill instructors watching over us at the time. Well, the fifty or sixty recruits I was told to sit with anyways. I had thoughts of home and wondered how things were going with me not being around. I had left my mother's house around 4:00 AM. My recruiter had so nicely dropped by and offered me a ride into Boston, or it was to make sure I didn't change my mind in going. Let's see, I got to Boston at around five thirty; I went through the Meps Station, and that took about three hours or so, making it about eight thirty. I was ordered to have a tattoo covered on my hand before I could leave so that took some time also. We hopped on the plane around nine, and that must have been a three-hour flight I think. Christ, who can remember anything under all that stress and also from being rushed through everything I have done today, also all that bitching and hollering along the way. Let's not forget the tormenting task of the old "one, two, fuck you, Marine Corps push-up" bullshit either. Okay, I have to think a bit harder on this. Off the plane at noontime or so, sat around in that hangar for four hours, and the bus ride was an hour or maybe two if you include the MP incident. Oh! Wait! What the fuck? The bus ride was under the cover of darkness, and it was nighttime when we got off that plane. Why couldn't I remember what time it really was?

"Company! Attention!"

Oh shit! Was I asleep when we arrived? Did I lose time? Was I just asleep? I thought. I snapped out of my seat into the position of attention. Fuck it, it would have to keep, it's hurting my head. Well, it looked like everyone was done going through the gauntlet of pain getting their gear issued to them. I must have nodded off. A real short, nicely dressed Marine with funny-looking birds on his shirt collars walked into the theater and went to the center of the stage in front of us.

He blurted out, "At ease, gentleman!"

What the hell does that mean? I wondered. Well, someone must know, right? That's when I heard one of the instructors say, "Stand like this, you useless pieces of amphibian shit!"

Oh, that's the way, I thought to myself. *Thanks for that information on the proper way to stand, asshole.* My mind began to filter out some cobwebs and began to get clear. You see, the position of attention is standing straight up, shoulders back, chest out, stomach sucked in, and hands at your sides with your thumbs along your trouser seams with your feet together. We learned that before we even left Boston. *Remember, dummy?* I asked myself. Christ almighty, this was going to be tough. The "at ease" position was the way this meathead drill instructor was standing right now. I needed to get a visual on this new move so I had to get a look. *Okay, check him out quickly with your eyes and don't turn your head,* I told myself. *He will turn into a raging idiot if he sees you swivel your neck in his direction. Okay, here goes.* I looked fast and tried not to move my head. Great! He didn't catch me looking over at him and didn't say anything to me. A few other recruits weren't so lucky and got caught moving their heads in his direction. They got a nice cuff upside the head for doing so. Not me, I thought, I was too clever to fall for that. Thank God for small miracles as sweat beads slid down the back of my neck. He was standing with his feet shoulder width apart with his hands behind his back. *That's easy*, I told myself. I got this licked now.

"Welcome to Marine Recruit Training Depot, Paris Island, South Carolina."

The neatly dressed man in his light tan uniform with his funny hat, kind of a baker's style hat, only green colored with another silver bird attached to the front, spoke very calmly.

To myself I was thinking, *Thank God, a sane person among the never-ending siege of ravenous drill instructors.* During this guy's speech, a colonel, because of them birds on his collar and funny hat, told us we would be sent into a receiving barracks. We were told we had to wait for more dumbass recruits to arrive to begin our evolution of training. So in the mean time before we were led to them barracks, we were going to be watching some instructional Marine Corps video clips along with some lectures. Oh and by the way, that funny little bird on his hat and collar definitely means he is the head hornet in this room right now. He reminded me of a life-sized stretch Armstrong, a childhood toy, only shorter with a more round-shaped head and a pair of beady-looking glasses on his nose. Must be one of them smart Marines and not one of these, no neck having pit bull—trained goombahs we had to deal with on the way in. He seemed a very well-mannered Southerner and quite respectful looking up on stage, yammering away, getting us to feel a bit more comfortable with our surroundings and allowing us to feel a little bit more in control. What he failed to mention to us was that we would be subject to two days of speeches and movie clips. I swear that was the longest, boring, sleep-deprived session I've ever encountered in my entire life.

As for these movie clips running for a few hours and short speeches in between clips, I couldn't tell if this was something we needed to be doing at all. For me, it was like we had already seen this shit before coming here with our recruiters. I had already seen movie clips on training and what was to be expected of us. Well, to tell you the truth, it was fine by me. We were sitting inside a nice, comfortable chair in an air-conditioned theater and not outside in that hot, muggy air beyond the confines of these walls. I could use the break. I had been hustled here and there with my body going full-out on all cylinders since we arrived on this insane island. It was a blessing in disguise to me. Just being to this point was an inner triumphant celebration. Several others just from the goings-on up till now had gotten removed. They were never to be seen again by me at all. I recollect seeing three guys cry out for their mommies; they couldn't take it no more and that they wanted to go home. Where did they go? I wondered. Ah, fuck them, bunch of wet-nosed crybabies. I love it all.

Having time to myself once again, I tried to figure out how I had gotten here and what time it was, but to my surprise, I couldn't have cared less. Looking around from my safe zone of a seat, I noticed half the place asleep with others fading in and out of sleep. I call it doing the chicken neck bob. It reminded me of the heroin junkies nodding out from the dope actually. Kind of looked funny actually. This one guy in front of me was trying so hard not to slip off into sleep he would keep slapping himself in the face to keep awake. Good thing for him because the hornets were watching, that's for sure. Well, at least that's what I thought, but no one was being yelled at for sleeping. How come? I didn't sleep at all, and every time I thought I might nod off, I thought of what time it might be by running through the number of hours that passed during each movement and task up till this point. That gave me a pounding headache, so I wasn't sleeping. Nope, not this recruit, I was determined to be the best, and if staying up through however many crummy, boring speeches they had to say, I'd be wide awake to hear them all. *Bring it on, I will take it all and ask for more*, I kept telling myself. Now don't get me wrong, I'm human. I might have nodded during some of it especially when they turned on the heat from time to time just to fuck with us more. Quite frankly, I believe I watched every subliminal movie clip they had sent to my brain. Someone somewhere thought this shit up and designed it to help in the performance of a well-trained, highly motivated individual such as myself, and I refused to miss out on any of it. I might not have been trained yet, but this was part of the process I assumed. I was there 100,000 percent and very eager to get on with the physical training already. I even found myself wondering when do I get my gun, when do I get some grenades, when can I blow something up, and when can I shoot and kill my enemy. Yes, I have heard about the Marine Corps brainwashing you to kill, but hey, who gives a rat's ass anyways. I was here to better my situation as a man and steering into a better future. I was also thinking I never want to return to the pain-in-the-ass failure I had become in my parent's eyes. Don't get me wrong, I had worked hard at every job or task assigned to me. I just couldn't release myself from the draw of cocaine addiction, which was destroying me. I also couldn't handle knowing that the world we live in could be so fucked up. School sucked and I was an ass hair away from being lost in society's cesspool gathering of civilian scum—yep, you guessed it, right in fucking prison. I had been there several times as a juvenile and vowed never to return. Being caged like an animal has to turn a man's mind to mush, I figured. So you bet your ass I wanted to join the fucking United States Marine Corps. I mean what's the worst thing that could happen, I could die. So freaking what? I was heading that way anyway I might as well do it as a hero rather than some crackhead punk in my family's eyes. Put in another movie, pass nuts and keep it coming. You got an open book here that needs this information to feel proud about something. *Goddamn, this feels good,* I thought to myself. During all this time of pondering my future, I realized I very well could make a career out of this. I could possibly get through this shit on sheer determination. Maybe I was still a bit geeked from all that coke I snorted the night before and being wide awake all the way up till that recruiter picked my ass up. I knew it wasn't the coke, but it did feel good knowing I was on my way to fix my life and become a Marine.

"Group, attention!"

I snapped up out of my seat filled with the promise of possibilities running through my head to the position of attention. Could I find my place in this world in the Marines? We are told to gather up all our stuff and head out the exit. Christ almighty, these bags sucked. They are stuffed to the gills and your muscles are sore from dragging them around earlier. Your muscles burn from the weight, and your shoulders get sore from the straps of the backpack digging into your flesh. They were fucking heavy, weighed a ton, why the fuck? *Oh well, let's get moving before you get them hornets on you again,* softly spoken to your inner self of course.

One by one we filed out of our respective rows just like cattle, once again with the "Hurry the fuck up!" spurting out of some pissed-off jackass drill instructor's mouth.

I found that the weight sort of balanced itself out while crushing into your shoulders when you began to take strides forward. It was awkward to put a seabag on your back and a backpack on your front hanging from the same shoulders at first, but you adapted to it quite easily. To my surprise, it was daylight outside, beyond the exit. How the hell long had we been here? Who held that answer were those drill instructors, and I wasn't going to inquire at all, so it really didn't matter much at this moment. I was more concerned with staying upright and trying not to be knocked over from the pushing and shoving coming from behind me. All was good, I was going to make it outside to some sunlight for what seemed to be forever inside this theater. I'd been on this island far too long to just wimp out like some of them other guys had done. With a lot of grunts and groans from getting used to the weight of all this shit on my shoulders and all the pushing and shoving, I reached the doorway. Once outside, the sun of this South Carolina shithole hits you like a red-hot piece of steel being cut by a blowtorch. Instant sweating occurs and also a choking feeling overcomes you because it's hard to breathe this muggy hot air. It literally burned your throat and fried nostril hairs if you happened to be brave enough to breathe through your nose.

"Holy fried frog lungs, batman!"

I couldn't breathe that deeply for quite a bit longer at the very least. *Slow and steady,* I told myself while sucking in very slowly like sipping through a straw. Just by doing that, it seemed to alleviate the hot, burning moist air from cooking the skin off of your tongue. All I could do was breathe shallow and look at the man's back ahead of me and just follow him. There was no time to look around or anything, you just kept moving no matter how much pain you felt from them heavy-ass bags or how bad you needed cool oxygen pumped into your seared throat and lungs.

"Move your asses! Left, right, left!" barked a drill instructor.

We marched on the best we could, not knowing what the fuck "left, right, and left" meant. Just then the guy in front of me stopped short and I damn near knocked him over. Luckily he held sure-footed and steadfast because he saved my ass from getting the hornet's nest in a tussle.

I whispered, "Thank you, brother." And he replied, "No problem."

"Where the fucks are we?" he asked.

I replied, "Somewhere in hell, somewhere inside hell."

Our journey outside was quite a long walk from one building to the next. I'd estimate about three football fields long, but with the heat and all this weight, it felt more like three miles. My whole body was soaked in sweat and them damn bags were definitely rubbing my shoulders raw. *Goddamn that recruiter, what an asshole,* I thought while on this march to probably pick up more shit. *Yep! You guessed right, Mr. Mello,* I told myself while entering the next building. We were handed a sleeping bag to go along with our bedrolls, tent stakes, and a half of tent. *Are you serious? Why in the hell would I want a half of tent? Well, that's not my problem to worry about just yet. Just shut the fuck up and move along in the process.* That was the safest thing to do, that's for sure. I had given myself sound advice because I'd seen several recruits doing jumping jacks with all this shit outside of this building when I exited, and it didn't look like much fun to me. In fact I believe one of them was crying. *Better them than me,* I told myself.

The next stage of our long march was to form up into our respected platoons from this big garbled mess of recruits assembled. The drill instructor began calling out our names, each and every one of us in order. They had formed one platoon before I was called. I was called about tenth on the list for Platoon 2082. I was told to form up next to the guy holding a stick called a guide-on, whatever that was. In total, I believe we had close to eighty-five recruits within my platoon before they called out for a different one. Once we were organized, we were formed up and put into the position of attention. This young light-skinned black sergeant gave us the once-over and instructed us to drop our shit and stand behind our gear.

"Attention, right face," he yelled out.

That took me a second to comprehend, and it wasn't very pretty, but I turned and faced left. Oops! Shit! I swung around quickly to the right.

"Forward, march," he bellowed.

That must mean to go forward, so I proceeded to walk forward.

"Left, right, left," he yelled.

There it was again, that damn "left, right, left" thing. *Ding, ding, ding, I win a prize.* My brain caught on to this finally. That's how you march, and that "left, right, left" thing refers to your feet. It's a verbal cadence to match your footfalls to and which foot should hit the ground next. Holy shit! They thought of everything, didn't they? I sighed in envy of myself for being so gifted with picking up on that little gem so quickly. It would prove to be useful in the future I'm sure.

"Left, right, left," he yelled again.

"Platoon, halt," he snapped out all of a sudden.

During this order, half of the platoon stopped and the other half smacked right into the guy in front of themselves. We had just done our first real marching, and it was horrible. That receiving drill instructor in charge of us was not pleased with our out-of-step display at all. He had stopped us within twenty-five feet, maybe fifteen or so paces, and then went ape shit on us.

"What in the heck do you call that garbled mess? You look like a bunch of monkeys fucking a football!" he asked quite loudly.

Oh yes, indeed, he wasn't pleased a bit, in fact that was the first time I'd ever seen a black man turn bright red in the face while screaming out his displeasure and rage on us.

"Drop your shit and get your nasty asses down and give me twenty-five," he screamed.

That meant we were to do push-ups. I heard a few grunts and whines coming from a few people, but most of us yelled out,

"Sir, yes, sir!" Then we dropped down to start pushing without hesitation, especially me. I had been doing push-ups for several mistakes I have made, and I was accustomed to it. That bastard drill instructor heard them whine bags complaining and made us do ten extras.

"On your feet, Recruits!" he spat out loudly.

We then stood back to attention.

"Recruit?" he asked looking in my direction.

In my mind I was thinking, *Oh shit, he's referring to me. What the fuck does he want with me? Oh come on please, anybody but me.*

"Yes, sir!" I replied.

"Your name, shit bird?" he asked.

"Recruit Mello, sir!" I replied back.

Then he looked away from me and spat out some nasty-ass brown stuff he had been chewing on and wiped his sauce-covered lips with the back of his hand. He then removed a white cotton hanky from his rear pocket and wiped his hands off.

"What is the first word that should come out of your filthy sewer when addressed, Recruit?" he said quite loudly while slowly, deliberately removing his Smokey hat.

Now I'm in it. What the Christ does this guy mean? My mind raced to find the answer to no avail.

"Anybody?" he asked, like he was offering me a gift.

There was several seconds of silence, then someone to the rear of me yelled out, "Sir!" He put his rag up to his forehead and wiped away some sweat and walked closer to me while tucking his rag back into his rear pocket from which it emerged. He's right on me now, and I dared not flinch. We were nose to nose, in fact he's so close to me I could smell his nasty breath from whatever he was chewing on. It was totally foul smelling, like total dog shit mixed with a hint of mint. *That must be Skoal,* I figured. I've tried it myself before, and it works very well when you're out of smokes and need some quick nicotine fixing although it's not very pleasing to the nostrils at all.

"I will ask one more freaking time, Recruit." He asked in a calm church mouse voice, "What the hell is your name?"

Now at this point I was just as scared as hell, I've never encountered such a soft approach by such a pissed-off instructor. It was kind of spooky.

"Sir, this recruit's name is Recruit Mello, sir!" I screamed at the top of my lungs, almost bursting a vocal cord for the effort.

I knew he would have to mess off with that kind of reply. Well, I was wrong. He pulled me out of formation by the bill of my cover, my hat, out to the front of the platoon.

"Recruit Mello here is going to demonstrate what we are trying to do here," he screamed.

So he instructed me to come to the position of attention. He then gave me the "old left face, forward march, and I'm off." A few "left, right, lefts" for about twenty or so paces and he had me stop with the platoon halt. Then he popped a goddamn gasket on all of us.

"Get on your nasty-ass faces and start pushing!" he yelled.

I was on my way down with the rest of the platoon, and he yelled out, "Not you, Recruit Mello. You're the only one who seems to understand this shit so far. As for the rest of you guys, you all look like a bunch of drunken hobos back on the block!"

I felt great that I was not doing more push-ups, but I felt bad for the rest of our platoon. But hey, fuck them, better them than me at this moment. After they completed several push-ups, we were back on our way marching with all of our stuff toward another small building, only this time most of us were in step. *Wow!* I thought to myself. *These guys are really good at this training stuff.* I would've never guessed we were going to be marching this good as a group in such a short amount of time. Not too shabby for a bunch of idiots without a clue.

Our next stop was to pick up some more gear, what a surprise. This time it was a funny-looking harness thing with a four-inch-wide belt. There was a young corporal there as indicated by his two chevrons on his collar showing us how to put the thing together. This corporal instructed us how it went on our bodies and where all the other parts went. We were issued two green plastic canteens with a metal canteen cup, which doubled as a stove in the field, and canteen poaches that attached to the belt. Pretty cool stuff, I thought, but I could already tell these suspender straps over my shoulders were going to irritate my skin from prolonged use. Next he showed us how to connect two magazine poaches which held the ammo for our M-16s, which I couldn't wait to see and to fire. He also explained how to connect a funny-looking shovel, called an e-tool, along with its case to this simply ingenious utility belt with suspenders. This corporal must have been very well trained on how to give instructions because we only had a few recruits who couldn't figure out how all these items we were issued were supposed to be arranged. For those lucky few, they got to do some jumping jacks behind the platoon while counting off the old "one, two, fuck you" stuff. After they reached twenty-five, the young pale-skinned corporal with the manicured fingers who looked more like a desk jockey than a killer to me took them aside and helped the poor, dumb bastards arrange it correctly.

After them fine new toys were gathered, we were marched back to the rest of our gear and instructed to pick all this shit up and carry in platoon formation toward a building that was three levels high with what looked like a school building made of red brick with plenty of them school-type windows running along the face of the building. There were two cement stairwell entrances on either side going up and down both sides to their respective floors. Once in front of the building, we were ordered to move our asses single file up to the second floor, and the "hurry the fuck step" was in order of course. My shoulders were straight, screaming as well as my legs on the way up them freaking stairs. A lot of weight to carry, that's for sure. I weighed about two hundred and ten pounds, plus all this gear, which was close to one hundred pounds or more. Add in the fact I had been sweating for three hours into my camouflage outfit and damn near about a half inch of sweat was in my shoes, that must have added ten more pounds at least. So we are talking three hundred and seventy-five pounds being lugged while marching across a half-mile steaming black top and then up two flights of stairs into this building. By the time we had gotten into the building, several guys had passed out from sheer exhaustion or the damn heat. It must have been about eighty-five degrees out and muggy to boot, making it difficult to breathe along the way. Not me though, I sucked it up and pushed the kid in front of me up the stairs and reached back a few times to drag the guy behind me also just to get there. A couple of guys were crying on this endeavor, but they made it just fine. As for those guys who didn't make it from quitting or passing out from the heat, they were removed via a medic truck off to God knows where. We never saw them again at all. Everything about the Marine Corps up until this point is how much can you take and push yourself. Are you a hacker? Or are you a damn slacker? Those guys were slackers and considered drops. Holy shit! We have drops already! What pussy boys! I thought while entering the doorway huffing and puffing with my eyes burning from sweat and my ass going raw from all the new wet cotton chafing my tender white cheeks.

Upon entering the doorway, I looked in to see where we would be sleeping. If you could picture a wide-open squad bay with about fifty bunk beds running down both sides perfectly spaced and aligned to one another with flimsy cotton mattresses about four inches thick, you may be close to what I was seeing. The floor was high gloss cement with two yellow lines painted about five feet outside the bunk beds running the length of the room. That made about a fifteen-foot center area in between the painted lines in the middle also running the length of the room. It was about one-hundred-fifty-foot-long and fifty-foot-wide room with bunks and wooden boxes at the front of them. If you were facing the bunk beds and looked down, there were two wooden boxes one on each side at the foot of them. The box on the left was for the guy who slept on the bottom bunk, and the one on the right was for the guy who slept on top. These boxes were called footlockers. When all was said and done, I was about in the middle. We were told to stand and wait by our bunks until everyone else was positioned next to their racks as well. It was then when we were allowed to drop our gear. That was the worst thing for me. There I am soaked to the bones with sweat, ass stinging, head thumping from the lack of water, and damn near ready to puke, just hating life. Several of my recruit comrades had thrown up all over the floor in front of where they were standing, and it was beginning to stink something awful within the squad bay. *Will someone open a fucking window please?* I was thinking as purple spots began to flutter in my vision while trying my best to stave off my own twisting and turning sour stomach from retching up whatever was in me also. That would amount to a few stale peanuts and a lousy coke that I had on the flight into this madhouse. When was that exactly? Two? Three days ago? I thought to myself once again. *Mess off with that, Mello. Focus, you're the man, you can take anything!* I told myself while precariously trying to stay in the position of attention. My toes were positioned right along the bunk side of the yellow line, which was the side of the squad bay I ended up on. I was looking forward straight at some other poor bastards on the other side trying to do the same thing I was. I was eye to eye with a five-foot-six—or seven-foot-tall Marine hopeful across the way and he was struggling. He had puke running down his chin and a huge puddle of vomit right in front of him. The other two guys on his right and left had tossed their cookies also. I snapped out of the sick feeling and even began to smile then busted out in laughter. I winked at this guy across the way from me, and he began cracking up also even with puke shooting out his mouth and nose. Right then others began to join in every time some other poor bastard lost his breakfast from three days prior. I think we all kind of bonded in our moment of pain. Several of us began screaming out hurrahs, and it was comforting in a way to deal with the foulness of it all.

I think damn near forty guys out of eighty threw up all over the floor and themselves. Truthfully we were in high spirits and cheering one another on to puke and getting a good laugh out of the whole thing when our receiving drill instructor finally came in. He walked in right through the center of the squad bay just barely missing some of the more projectile vomit close to the center of the room. Some guys had great distance on their retch, and it was impressive. He actually stepped over a few spots to avoid some sticky brown puke.

"Way to go, shit birds. Too bad it's the most disgusting display of undisciplined assholes I have ever seen. It also stinks like shit in here. You nasty motherfuckers!" he screamed while striding by me to the head of the squad bay.

"Group, at ease!" he yelled out, looking a bit pale and green at the gills from the smell.

I knew he was feeling a bit sick to his stomach, and it felt good to me. For that brief moment we had won a small victory on him, and we all knew it. Damn, it felt good even though it was short-lived.

"Drop your shit and prepare for formation outside, it's time for chow!" He stated with a huge-ass grin on his face. We weren't in such high spirits then, brother. The three guys across from me kind of groaned and turned a bit darker shade of green just at the mention of food. I was glad to hear we were going to eat, actually I was starving. Before we left for chow, we were ordered to go into the bathroom and fill one of our canteens with water, like fifteen of us at a time. When it was my turn, I had to watch out for my footing crossing the first twenty paces due to the amount of puke on the floor. The smell was awful, but what really was nasty was the stink coming from a big brown puddle I damn near fell into when I slid about four feet to the side in its slick texture. I was thinking why in the fuck at first, but then realized it was all part of their sick, twisted training. It was to weed out the squeamish and weak recruits from training. I realized I loved it all in some sick, demented way. Upon entering the bathroom, called the head, I noticed an office to my left where the instructor slept or at least from the quick glance I got while running by. There was a neatly made bunk inside with a desk, so I assumed it was his office anyways. Inside the head to my left were these long metal troughs attached to the wall, about thirty feet worth running to the far corner then ten feet along the back wall, then about thirty feet worth of trough running back to me on a half wall about five feet high. At first glance I had no fucking clue what they were, but then I realized they were for pissing. On the other side of the short wall were the sinks about twenty or so on the opposite side of the half wall. There were twenty more sinks along another half wall to the right of them. Beyond that, I noticed about forty toilets just over the sink I stopped at to fill my canteen. There were no dividing stalls between them either it wasn't like high school. I had mere seconds to quickly look around before that bastard drill instructor started hollering to get the hell out and back on line, so it was an at-a-first-glance kind of orientation to my surroundings. I wasn't too keen on shitting where everyone could see, hear, and also smell my goings-on, but hey, this is the Marine Corps. It could be worse. Like the time I went out fishing on a commercial fishing boat scalloping called the Barnacle Bill. We had to shit in a bucket and throw it over the side during our ten-day trips out to sea. So beggars aren't choosers when it comes to taking a dump, right? When it's time to drop deuce, it's time to drop deuce, I always thought, and these facilities were fine by me. I finished filling my canteen and headed back out on line. Once our group of fifteen made it back on line, we waited at ease till everyone else had their turn. They either slipped in the puke or made it safely back on line or they fell into the nasty puke and got laughed at by the rest of us. Even taking that fall didn't mean shit. They still had to get back on line with a full canteen.

Once everyone had his full canteen, we headed out in front of the building into formation. I noticed about ten recruits who had the misfortune of slipping and falling on their canteen fill, and they were soaked with that awful-looking green, brown, and yellow foulness. I felt bad, but fuck 'em, right? It wasn't me, and that was definitely a good thing. God knows I would feel pretty shitty and might have even tossed my own cookies if I went face-first into that smelly-ass vomit myself. We were marched along the road leading to the chow hall without any major problems except a few guys stinking from that puke on them. The instructor had passed out four vests to our crossing guards two up front and two in the rear. I also got one because I was in the front in the first squad leader's position. It was called a road vest that went over your head and fastened with Velcro straps around your waist. We were in full camouflage gear with our sleeves down and wearing them ugly sneakers called Go Fasters. The guy in the orange vests job was to stop traffic if any on our way or to stop any other platoon that was trying to cross our path along the way. We stopped for every other platoon that even remotely came near our goings-on. We were the green recruits fresh off the block, and we held no immediate rank among these other trainees. We could hardly stay in step, never mind thinking we could ever match up to any of them guys yet. Actually I think we even entered the chow hall last, very much so last. We were shit boot recruits, and it was to be known by all. It's not like I really didn't know that fact already, but we felt it as we watched platoon after platoon go into the entrance ahead of us. Some looked tired and dirty, but a few of them platoons toward the front looked very good marching in their boots all shined up and with their pants bloused just under the tops of their boot line. Oh yeah! That was an awesome feeling, I was sure of it. Just knowing that you're much further in training than the rest of us must be a good time. They had marched perfectly and even kept in step with a rumble sound from each step that echoed as one. As for us to their ears, we must've sounded like a herd of confused cattle scurrying toward our feeding grounds. Yep, we were shit in their eyes, and we probably smelled like it also. Being a Marine was definitely what I wanted to become looking at the difference between our platoon and the looks of theirs at that moment.

Once all the other platoons had entered the chow hall, it was our turn to get in there and fuel up on some much-needed sustenance in my eyes and from the way my stomach felt. Our instructor marched us to the entrance, which was about a ten-foot-wide ramp made of concrete kind of like a disabled person's ramp only wider. The whole platoon could fit into this entryway even while marching four wide. He had us stop just short of the doors leading in, and the guide was instructed to pass off our flagless guide on stick to the recruit in the rear of the fourth squad. I was told to hold the door open as we filed in squad at a time. What happened next was totally traumatizing to say the very least just to get chow. I heard all sorts of screaming and hollering going on inside from about five different drill instructors from different platoons. It must have been crazy in there, I thought, but I didn't look inside to see. Nope, I just opened the door which was called a hatch and stood very still at the position of attention as our first squad filed into the mess hall. I was poised statuesque holding the hatch open when the drill instructor came over to me and told me I was to be the last one in. I was to take the flagless guide on stick from the last man and place it in a metal holder just outside the chow hall and get in there. "Sir, yes, sir!" I replied. I did as instructed and entered the chow hall last. What a huge-ass building this was, I thought, when I entered and semi-looked around. There must've been about six hundred recruits in there sitting down to eat, and we were just getting into line.

To no surprise to me, we were once again ordered to stand ass to nuts on the far wall leading into the place and were shuffled two steps at a time every few seconds or so. I was definitely not looking anywhere else other than onto the guy's head two inches from my nose. Every drill instructor in the place was screaming and hollering about something or another, and I wanted no part of it at all. Once we moved in far enough to reach the actual chow line where the trays were, we were instructed to remove a tray and hold it right up against our chest, actually touching our chest, and it should be touching the guy in front of you on his back. Onward went the two-step shuffle until we reached the silverware we were told to take a fork, a knife, and a spoon, that was it. They were to be held in your left hand. Still being sure your tray was touching the guy in front of you and against your chest. *Man, these guys have it down to a science in here,* I was thinking as we shuffled forward. Next came a cup that went into our right hand as we held our trays out flat and we were allowed to separate just enough from the guy in front of us. You must try not to drop your tray or knock over the cup you just were handed that you were told to put on your tray right side up in the left upper corner of the thing. You then turned sideways to receive your food, you did the two-step sideways along this part of the line. It was designed to have each one of them sideways two steps to stop right in the exact spot where a server was flopping food on your tray.

What's on the menu today? I thought when it was my turn. I could only see what were on the menu by looking down with my eyes only because we were instructed to look straight ahead. To keep our head nods straight ahead and to not look down or even think about it were our instructor's exact words. Several of the recruits in my platoon happened to be caught committing such a heinous crime. They paid for it by getting a quick kick in the ass and a spilled tray from some of the other instructors in the place. It was their sole purpose to fuck with the fresh recruits that day, I'm sure of it. I reached my first stop. Corn, one. Two, a piece of thick Texas-style yellow bread. One, two, a ladle of milk-looking cream-colored sauce with gray chunks in it over my bread. One, two, slimy-looking macaroni with cheese. One, two, collard greens. One, two, some red gelatin. One, two, and a piece of chocolate cake. That was my first real meal in the Marine Corps, and I was happy to get it. Thank you, Uncle Sam. The guys flopping it into my tray called that milky white creamy stuff with the gray chucks in it over my toast "shit on a shingle." Next we got our drinks. Someone grabbed my cup from my tray and filled it with a yellow-looking liquid that looked like a light-colored urine and not so much of a lemonade color. Honest to God, it looked like piss. The big jug he had gotten it from was labeled bug juice. In a matter of about five to six minutes, we had all been served our glorious first meal in the Corps. Hurrah!

Everyone was waiting with his tray in hand at the position of attention when I arrived at the table. The tables were cheaply made wooden Formica-covered deals that were about one hundred feet long with red plastic bench seats on both sides. When I arrived, the instructor yelled out, "Trays down," so we placed our trays down swiftly but also cautiously as not to spill our cups of urine called bug juice. Next came, "Ready, seats!" We were then seated in the position of attention staring straight ahead without any indication of whether or not we could eat or not. I was ravenous at this point. I could've eaten the ass out of a dead rhinoceros. I had arrived three days earlier, I think, on only some stale peanuts and a lousy coke to hold me over till now. *What a way to train someone,* I thought. *They starve your ass for three days, force you to carry damn near your body weight all over the damn place, you damn near pass out several times, or you puke all over the freaking place, which some guys did both or all of these things. Weak bastards,* I said in my mind. *They totally empty you out by doing all that shit, and then they stop you just short of actually eating something for about five minutes longer. What fucking bastards these instructors are,* I thought.

"Ready, eat!" the instructor yelled out finally.

Once that command was given, I ate with a fury. I skipped the fork and ate everything with the spoon, it was easier and quicker. When I was through with all my tasteless food in my tray, I half-hesitantly sipped the urine-colored bug juice. It wasn't that bad actually, kind of lemon flavored, but I could taste a semi hint of vitamins mixed with a metallic taste you might get when you stick a penny in your mouth. Well, what doesn't kill you will definitely make you stronger, I figured. As we were sitting there for five minutes, I had noticed a bit of sediment build up at the bottom, so before I risked drinking it, I gave it a stir with my trusty spoon. Surprisingly the spoon didn't melt off like in the cartoons. So I gulped it down with like three swallows until there was nothing but an empty cup back in front of me. What the hell was in that? I wondered while burping up a foul bile-tasting regurgitation of the stuff. To my surprise, it wasn't as bad as I was initially thinking on the first few sips because I held it down just fine.

"Get the fuck up and outside now!" our instructor screamed.

The command was given, and without hesitation we snapped back to attention and marched in two columns out, stopping first to pass off our empty trays to other recruits in a dishwashing station before the exit. The dishwashing station was nothing more than an enclosed room with opening in the front of it that looked similar to an ice cream parlor. It looked very clean and organized inside, but it was certainly steam filled. It must be awful to work in there, I thought when I dropped of my tray. There was no time to hang around and have any chitchat with anyone because we were screamed at going in the place and going out. That must be the way it was going to be on this damn island. From day one all the way until graduation or until your ass no longer belongs to the Corps, I figured.

We marched back to our barracks, and we were forced to clean up that disgusting mess of green-, yellow-, and coffee-colored chunks left on the floor. The task of cleaning up was delegated to a few others. They were told to take charge of this situation and get it done, period. No fucking around or else. With that in mind, I was sent with a few recruits to get mops and buckets out of the cleaning closet and to get some hot water with soap. Our drill instructor showed us where this closet was prior to us taking over the cleanup. He also told us he was going to be in his office and not to bother him. Now this cleaning closet was just a single wall locker, but it held the necessary soap, bleach, and floor cleaning tools needed for this task. There were four buckets with ringers, four mops, a few squeegees, and a lot of toilet paper, some rags, and various other things. I told two other recruits to go outside the barracks and grab the two snow shovels in the stairwell and that trash can they were perched next to. Everyone else besides the puke cleanup crew and the bathroom cleaning crew was told to make up the beds we were to sleep on later this evening. We were told we had three hours to get this place in shipshape. Clean the head, clean the floor, and it better damn well be done or else, or else what? I thought in the passing out of job duties to thirty guys. First and foremost, we had to get this stinking puke mess the hell out of here. I grabbed one of the squeegees and demonstrated how we would clean that mess up.

"Okay, here we go, people," I said.

"Push all the puke, spit, and watery slop from that end of the squad bay toward the front in this area," I instructed while pushing the first pass of the floor.

"Next there was to be a few guys manning the shovels over in the front by the trash cans to scoop it up and put it in there. If the shovels don't work that well, use the dustpan and brush and pour it into the can. Once that was done, they were to pour it into the toilets and flush it," I told them.

Now you would think this wasn't going to be a difficult task, but you would be wrong in that idea. I came to realize this rather quickly while watching these recruits. The first idiot I gave shovel duty just couldn't hack it at all. He kept puking every time he tried to scoop some up, making a bigger mess. I forced him to go into the head and help out the other guys already polishing the sinks and cleaning the mirrors. The next kid I asked just refused to pick up any of it because he would puke also. I told him to do it anyways. Sure enough, he reached out with the shovel and started gagging. *What a pussy,* I thought and gave him a swift kick in the ass away from me. Finally after two more jackasses with weak stomachs were screened out and a bit more vomit piled up, I found my man. This guy was from New Orleans, a tall, skinny guy who was a bit hard to understand verbally, but he was very quick to take the initiative. He just did not care one bit. He got some puke on his hand and up his arms while scooping up some of that mess. Now, that was pure manhood in my eyes, and I didn't hesitate to help him out, so I grabbed the dustpan and brush and got dirty also. We both started barking out some things to get done to them other squeamish momma's boys until our deed was done. The mop boys came next and washed the whole floor after the nastiness was cleared.

Now for me being in charge, that wasn't very accurate. I just naturally fell into that spot because I wasn't shy to tell others to get shit done. The drill instructor came out of his office and made it clear to me I wasn't in charge by making this New Orleans kid and me do some pull-ups for thinking that we were. After that, we were told to help out in the bathroom and to take orders from another kid he delegated to be in charge. As for why our drill instructor snapped on us was beyond me. In my mind the kid he put in charge ran from the puke cleanup and hid out in the head like a pussy. So anyways we go into the head, and the kid he originally put in charge was this short young black kid. Figures right, our instructor was black, so why not give another black kid a chance, right? *Who cares?* I thought to myself while listening to this kid tell me to plunge out a shit-filled toilet. I looked into the stall, and it looked like maybe some guy from the Vietnam era must have took a dump in there forty years ago. I looked at this kid and was like, *Yah right! You do it. I just cleaned up the puke you ran away from.* Well, he started getting loud and posturing in front of three other black recruits, calling me a stupid white boy and a cracker and all sorts of other shit. So I being quick-tempered and a bit short when it comes to the racial bullshit, I called him a nigger in return. I think I said, "Fuck you, nigger. You clean it," or something like that. I stood my ground and waited a second or two to see what my options were. Do I fold up and take this display of four on one, or do I smash this kid anyways? Well, I didn't have much time to decide because this kid pushed me and took a swing at me. I quickly returned a fast left to his jaw and connected a nice jab. I snatched him by his neck and slammed him up against the wall, holding him off the ground so his feet were kicking and searching for the floor beneath. I was then grabbed from behind by one of his buddies and had to release my grasp of his neck, dropping him back to his feet while he choked for air. The three others tried to surround me, but I backed against the wall and kept them at bay with a few kicks and punches. I received a slap or something from the smaller kid because he scratched my chest with his nasty uncut long fingernails. I was bleeding from three distinct claw marks when four white guys from Down South entered the bathroom to break up this skirmish. It wasn't the cracker comment or the nigger comment that got us fighting, it was more of a fuck-you fight. We had heard this shit our whole lives while growing up, and it made no difference in either of our eyes. What came next was typical. Our drill instructor followed very quickly behind them, screaming, "What the hell happened!" Well, I just kept my mouth shut because it was over and really didn't care much about being a rat. My point was made to the guy who started it and him alone. He knew he caused the whole problem and got put into check. So sure enough, the four black guys went through what happened and blamed it all on me and the fact I started it all by calling this kid a nigger. Never mind all the white boy cracker stuff. So whatever I said in defense meant nothing at this point, so I stayed quite because that word is a definite no-no in the eyes of this guy. He told everyone to get back doing what they had been doing and stood behind me while I had to clean out this shit-filled toilet. I was pissed the fuck off, so I didn't even use the plunger. I just reached into the shit-filled toilet and unclogged it with my hands and flushed it about five times to clear it out. I looked back at the instructor like, "Fuck you too, buddy!" It really didn't matter to this guy much because he just ordered me into his office. When I got into his office, he came in and slammed the door shut behind him rather hard. I was standing at the position of attention waiting for the flurry of punches I knew this guy wanted to throw at me. He was a bit more in control than I figured because calmly he got in my face.

"So you like to call people nigger, huh? Get on your face and start doing some push-ups, boy!" he softly whispered in my ears.

I got down and began pushing up and down. While I was down there pushing up and down, he was stepping on my hands and grinding his feet on them. It hurt, but I didn't give him the satisfaction of crying out in pain. I just grunted and kept on pushing yelling out, "One, two, three, four, I, love, Marine, Corps" on each repetition of going up and down. He wasn't content with that because he next stood on top of my back with both feet and grinded his heels into my shoulders, screaming to keep pushing. He then went ahead and told me he should throw my ass right out of the Corps. It was all bullshit; he just wanted to fuck with me without others bearing witness to him actually doing this type of shit to me. I was used to that sort of shit anyway prior to even coming here, so it didn't mean much. He just wanted to be in charge, and I wasn't allowed to say shit about it; besides, who was I really going to tell? This is boot camp, and I wasn't going anywhere. He had all the control, and he knew it. He went on to tell me this story about how his great-grandfather was bought and sold in slavery several times and received countless whippings and beatings at the hands of his white owners. While listening to this whole story, he never once stepped off my back. Actually, he grinded harder into my shoulder blades with his shoes as I struggled to go up from the floor. Well, his point was taken, and yes, I did understand the power of the oh-so-taboo-word nigger. To tell you the truth, I grew up with more black friends than white. As a matter of fact, one of my best friends during Catholic school was a black kid. Sure, when we first met we fought damn near every day during recess, but that was because we were both competitive in sports. We also never backed down from each other. But we became friends just the same, and I knew most of his family and cousins from going over to his house to play on weekends. We were on the same basketball team in grade school and practiced a lot together. I was a bit pissed off on how this guy handled this matter, but he had to make his point. I was totally in the wrong for calling this kid a nigger and understood the wrath of this jackass on my back right now.

While he was on my back, my mind drifted to a time when I was in the fifth grade and my black friend and I got detention together. We had to stay after school for disrupting class or something. I can't be sure of what or why, but it wasn't easy to piss off the nuns of St. Francis. So anyways, we got picked up after school by his mom who had missed some work and drove out about an hour to pick us up. She was bullshit to say the least. We got into the car, and Keith, my buddy, hopped into the front and I slipped into the backseat behind him. Well, before you know it, his mom started wailing on him, slapping and punching like nobody's business. She was irate and full of rage cussing and screaming God knows what, but when I heard Keith whimper and scream for his mom to stop, I began to laugh. I had grown up under the belt also and always found it funny when it was someone else on the receiving end of a thrashing. What a mistake that was. I had underestimated the rage of a black woman indeed. His mom reeled around in her seat and off she went slapping the shit out of me also.

"You're not above getting a beating either, you little brat," she yelled.

I sure as hell wasn't any different than my buddy at all. We both got our asses smacked up equally that day. Now I could have spoken up and gotten myself out of all this before this guy stood on my back and humiliated me, but to tell you the truth, I enjoyed the pain. I wasn't going to waste my breath on something so controversial. Did this guy even know that where I grew up, white kids and black kids went to school together and actually played with one another and visited one another's families once in a while? Well, maybe not for him or the guy I just choked, maybe they grew up segregated Down South and took great joy in finally getting some control over what is said and done in their lives when it comes to white suppression. Didn't he know that when I was arrested trying to sell that fake cocaine, I was arrested with three other kids who just happened to be black? Didn't he know that for most of my life my friends all greeted one another with "Yo, what up, my nigger" especially to me? Why won't he just ask me those questions? Nope, he just kept making me try and do push-ups, screaming away at me. I totally agreed with their plight and sympathized with their struggle completely. That is exactly what this man didn't know about me, and I wasn't going to tell him any of it. I took this degrading display in stride and just thought about simpler times hanging out with my buddy Keith and his cousins playing basketball at Point Road Park in Marion. That is what got me through about a half hour's worth of this man standing on my back twisting his feet around occasionally to hear me groan in pain. So my thanks go out to my buddy Keith, his family, and the whole Point Road crew for being there in my mind when I needed something to get me through something this humiliating and painful.

So after the entire cleanup of the foul-smelling gunk on the floor, the nasty toilet incident, and the personal training in his office, he ordered us all to get on line. The whole place was cleaned up rather quickly actually, but he just moved on with no mention of the good job we did. There was no mention to the rest of the platoon of what went on in his office either or the fighting in the bathroom, so I left it alone. He just carried on with his job. We were then ordered to put all our stuff into our footlockers and to secure it with a lock. Once that task was complete, we were ordered into a school circle, which meant we had to sit down around a set of bunk beds in the center of the squad bay by two recruits he picked out of the crowd to do. Our receiving drill instructor gave us a quick lesson on how the bunks were to be made properly. He then ripped everything off the bunk and threw it to the floor and instructed one of them guys to recreate what he had just done. Now that was a hard thing to remember in exact detail when you have Magilla the Gorilla yelling at the poor guy for not doing it fast enough. It was rather amusing to watch while this poor guy with the dumb, frightened look on his face as he desperately tried to get it done. It was funny to me, but for this kid, it might have been pure terror to have a highly motivated individual screaming and kicking him in the ass while he fumbled at the sheets and blankets. When he finally was done, the drill instructor let him off the hook with doing a few push-ups for being such a fuck-up. He then selected another victim out of us to do the top bunk. This kid was a bit portly in stature with pudgy, fat red cheeks, and the rest of his skin was like the color of an adult seagull's underbelly. As a matter of fact, the kid reminded me of Porky Pig, especially when his named was called out to do the deed. He sort of rolled to his feet and waddled over to the bunk beds. Oh yeah! I forgot to mention this, we had our names written on a piece of masking tape right over our right pocket on our shirt. I can't remember his name at all, but it was pretty funny what came next. Porky Pig seemed to do a bit better at the assembly of his rack, but when came time for his dose of yelling and hollering, he turned red as a beet, and I watched as his bottom lip began to quiver then out came them tears. Once those tears started streaming down his rosy cheeks, that was it. The evil bugger drill instructor got a whole lot worse.

"Get your lousy, crying Porky Pig ass down on your face. You're a waste of your mother's egg. I want you to call home and ask Mommy to come wipe your ass. Why the fucks are you in my beloved Corps? When you do call home, tell your dad he should have jerked off and not wasted my freaking time with this Baby Huey bullshit!" he screamed at him.

This drill instructor was just yelling at him to hurry the fuck up, and he folded like a young three-year-old. Just like any three-year-old would actually. Have you ever been in a grocery store and witnessed some kid acting a fool and their moms caught him being stupid in public. A nice quick jerk on the arm and a good yell would send any small child reeling into a straight blubbering, with snot-flowing crying mess. That is just what we had here coming from this plump Porky Pig look-alike. *What a sissy*, I thought. As for the instruction on how to make a damn bed, we learned it rather quickly to say the least. After that fine display of humiliation and instruction was behind us, we were all ordered to make our racks. That simple task of making our racks turned into a melee, and surprisingly enough, we cluster fucked it all up according to this beast of a man hidden beneath that neatly pressed uniform. About thirty of us actually got it right the first time, but we had to do it again. I figured that would happen, but knowing it and doing it is two different things. It took us five tries as a platoon to get it right. It was absolute torture to some of us more adept recruits.

Once we were all passed on making our racks, we were ordered to get back on line. I was absolutely sick of making this thing; they looked great on the second try in my mind. Well, at least the four or five I could see around my immediate area. While at attention again, our drill instructor started laughing with this evil-looking smirk on his face. I knew he was up to something sinister. He was going to fuck with us more, I thought. What a dick. He paused in the middle of the squad bay from walking up and down looking over our racks and told us to fall out and hit the rack, go to sleep. "You all have a lot to do tomorrow, so sleep well. You're going to need your rest," he told us while heading to his office. He yelled for five recruits to follow him by name, they were to be fire watch. Fire watch was a rotation every hour or so of someone walking around the squad bay with a flashlight and wearing full gear. That was nothing more than a fucking nuisance in my mind. Someone always had to be on watch though no matter what your issue with it was. So off into my bed I went without a care about them unlucky pricks who had to keep watch all night in shifts. Holy shit! I've made it through another day in the Marine Corps. I thought as I lay in my bunk picturing what life may be like at home. Were my mom and dad even aware that I had left this morning? Do they know I'm in the Marines right now? I had left early in the morning without a good-bye or anything. Not even a good luck from my brothers. That was a bit depressing, but I couldn't remember if I told them my exact date of departure. Oh well, I hope everything is cool with them. I began to ponder on how long I've actually been on this island again, but I drifted off into sleep rather rapidly.

"Get the fuck up and out of them racks!" the drill instructor screamed, startling me awake. *Holy shit,* I thought. *How long did I sleep? What time is it?*

"Make your fucking racks, put your green shorts on, and put on a white T-shirt with your Go Fasters on! Hurry! Hurry! Hurry!" hollered the bastard instructor.

Jeepers guy don't pop a gasket, I thought to myself while rushing through putting my bed back in order and putting on my clothes. I got dressed and fixed my rack in less than two minutes, I swear to God. Don't they ever give someone a break from all this hurry-the-fuck-up stuff? It was my first real chance to get some sleep, and they probably only gave us a few hours. Looking outside through the squad bay windows, it was definitely dark out there. Shit! We got into our racks while it was dark outside. *This has got to be some sort of joke, right? They can't just keep doing this throughout training to me. I require eight hours of sleep, not just a mere two or three.*

"Get on line!" he screamed.

"Get in the head, brush your teeth, take a dump, piss, shave your nasty faces, and get the fuck back on line!" he ordered.

One row at a time we filed into the head to fulfill on our morning routine. We completed this task rather quickly actually. We effectively accomplished our shaving tasks, relieved our bladders, and a few other recruits pinched out a few turds. *Wham-bam,* thank you, ma'am. We were done and back on line in less than ten minutes if I was to estimate. From the time we were hollered awake until the time we finished our sanitary needs. It had all gone by in a flash, I shit you not. I've never experienced so many people not talking and accomplishing so much so fast with effective results. *My word, this place is going to be fun,* I thought while looking across at the guy adjacent to me on line. He was bleeding right under his lip pretty badly with blood running down his chin. I guess he wasn't used to shaving, or never learned how. Maybe he was just some animal who shaved in all different directions and butchered himself with the cheap disposable razor we were issued this morning. Just about the time his blood was going to drip from his chin to the floor, our drill instructor appeared with a hanky. He told him he couldn't be all bloody while going to breakfast, nor could he look that way while we went for another physical and then to the barbershop for a nice fresh haircut. Excellent, I thought. We were going to get that cool-looking high and tight. We were going to be jarheads. Now we are talking Marine Corps. I was excited as we fell out and formed up outside our barracks. Well, wouldn't you know if everyone was a bit spirited this morning? We got outside quickly without a bunch of screaming and hollering going on from this mean-ass cuss who emerged from the depths of Hades who was put in charge of us. Nope, today was going to be a good day after all. Even our breakfast in the chow hall went by pretty smoothly also.

I think the drill instructor knew we were excited about our haircuts and nothing else seemed to matter to us. We had looked like a bunch of longhaired hobos coming off that bus a few days ago, but today would be different. We were getting our first real haircuts as Marines, and we were already feeling a bit more like men. We no longer felt we would be pieces of shit fresh off the block like the way we started. A bunch of green, longhaired, shit birds standing on them yellow footprints were soon to be behind us. No longer the jackasses we were in life at all. So off we went heading down the middle of the street. There were a few other platoons marching in the same direction as our gaggled mess of fools. They looked like shit also, all out of step, long hair, and were bopping along like they're strutting down Main Street. You might think it was the Fourth of July and we all were in the damn ticker day parade or something like that, the way we marched trying to look cool. They must be heading to the same place as us, physicals and haircuts, I thought. As we were marching along, I wondered why in the hell do we need physicals anyways. Didn't I just have one in Boston before this whole nightmare began?

"Platoon, halt!" our instructor yelled out.

I guess we marched for about five minutes or so. I couldn't remember much of that march because my mind was filled with what's next. It was comforting to know that you could block off all the pain and suffering your body felt from all the exercise up till now. It was the fourth day, and my body ached when I got up. I could just daydream and follow along with the old "left, right, left" cadence coming from our receiving drill instructor and block it out. I was already programmed into this mean son of a bitch's voice, and I was able to drift off almost to the point of sleepwalking but functioning. Who knows, maybe I was asleep. Either way, this trick of the mind was definitely going to help me in the future. As we halted, I looked up, and sure enough, we were at a hospital and it looked a bit scary to say the least. There were recruits coming out of one of the side doors rubbing their ass and both of their arms. *Oh shit!* I thought. *We are going to get shots.* I hate needles. I won't pass out from seeing them, but it does make me get a bit of anxiety just thinking of that sharp stick of the thing and the piercing pain that follows. *Oh boy, that sucks.* I was standing in my platoon scared shitless, and I was sure there were others feeling the same anxiety as I was. Looking around at a few of my fellow recruit comrades in arms, I was right in my observation. There were a few guys already turning that familiar pale green tint looking a bit twitchy and ill. Right about the time when I was about to yell out, "Fuck this Marine Corps bullshit, I don't want no damn shots, I'm not a flea-bitten dog who requires vaccinations," my squad was told to march into the building. *I guess I'm going to wing it and man up,* I told myself. It's only a tetanus booster, a flu shot, or maybe it's just your run-of-the-mill physical with some doctor grabbing my sack and telling me to cough. Relax, man. I hope so because getting stuck by needles really does suck in my eyes. I don't need more than two shots, goddamn it.

I was right about both things. When we entered, right away we were told to strip down to bare ass and hold our clothes in front of ourselves. Yep! Along came a doctor cold finger. Only this was an industrial-style checkup. He walked right down a row of us grabbing sacks and asking us to cough out loud like we were cattle or something. Along came the stethoscope doctor checking our lungs and heartbeats. There was about fifteen of us in my group being examined all at once. We were ordered to the next station, and off we went down the line like good little cows wanting to fetch our nice blue ribbons in this county fair. I don't know who got the largest unit award, but I knew it wasn't me. My penis damn near disappeared just at the sight of this huge, fat black nurse wearing rubber gloves and holding some lube in her hands. We are ordered to bend over in a row and, you guessed it, spread them cheeks. Down the line she went jamming assholes one by one until she reached me. She didn't even change her gloves between each guy; she just added more lube to her fingers and in it went. No warning, no concern, no tenderness, no movie, and no reach around. Just slam, she's in there rooting around checking my prostate. Maybe she got some weird, sick pleasure out of inserting her fingers into several hundred dumbass recruits' asses all day long. Whatever her game was, it didn't matter. Either way, it was very uncomfortable to me and a bit humiliating to say the least. After I was done there, or should I say, she was done back there, I was handed a paper towel to clean up with then sent off to the next stop. What the fuck kind of freaky lab rat do they think I am? I was actually thinking I might get a piece of cheese and the exit of this horror house maze. Down the line I went with this funny goop that kind of still seeping out of my anus and feeling really uncomfortable. It was like having the leeks, or the beer shits after a long night of drinking with the boys back home. Our next stop wasn't as bad as the last one, by no means. This next examination was for our eyes. "Read the second line or the third line, look into the dumbass optic thing a majig, and keep moving, shit bird." That's exactly what this weird-looking bald guy wearing glasses and a white lab coat told me anyways. I was a bit shocked at first, but he started laughing, so he must have been joking. I started to laugh a bit with him, but I was greeted by my drill instructor right outside the door of this guy's station.

"What is so fucking funny, Recruit?" he asked rather loudly.

"Sir, this recruit does not know, sir," I replied, not wanting to reveal the bald guy's mock of him.

"Get your nasty ass down and give me twenty!" he yelled.

So down I dropped naked as the day I was born doing the old "one, two, fuck you, Marine Corps" push-ups with my pecker touching the cold tile floor as I went up and down. Real fucking nice, I thought. That bastard eye doctor set me up. Well, who cares anyways, it was funny and these push-ups were becoming commonplace in my mind. I just wish I had some underwear on. God knows how clean this floor was. My poor little guy down the nether regions must be in panic mode right now with all this cold and filth on the floor. After I finished doing my twenty push-ups, I was then told to put on my underwear. Typical assholes move on this instructor's part, but I'm sure he knew what was best. So

I pushed his twenty and shut the fuck up about it. I slipped back into my tighty-whities and entered my place in line against the wall. We were tucked in once again ass to nuts waiting for our next examination.

The next office or station was for a dental examination. I was rushed into the dentist's chair and given a quick once-over by the dentist. He barked out some weird names to this pretty assistant who took notes into a file. Now my teeth were really haggard from all the drug use as a kid. The whole tops of every tooth in my mouth was decayed and very rotten looking to say the least. I wasn't concerned with their appearance growing up because it wasn't common practice after our old man split on us to go to the dentist either. There just wasn't any money in my mom's coffer to do so. That whole exam was quick and simple, and onward I went to the next guy. I guess having bad teeth wasn't a concern when it came to being a Marine. This whole process was a total blur to me, and it was quite the processing plant if I've ever seen when in action. This next doctor checked over my whole body, reflexes, muscle girth—"Open wide and say ah!" He must have taken all of about thirty seconds to complete this exam, and onward I went. I was a bit confused and disoriented throughout this whole ordeal. It went by so quickly that you didn't concern yourself with any of the details or considered asking any questions. I remember seeing a few recruits being escorted out of the building and never seeing them again. This must have meant they flunked the physical for some reason or another. I was just glad everything checked out okay for me so far. I was healthy as an ox weighing two hundred and ten pounds, standing at five feet nine inches and pretty muscular when I entered this hellhole a few days ago. Now according to this scale I was being weighed in on, I only weighed two hundred and five pounds. I had lost five pounds already and our training hadn't even started yet. I hope I don't lose much more weight. *I'll be a skinny shrimp,* I thought. *How could I be losing weight?* I wondered as I shuffled down the side of the wall ass to nuts with our band of guys going through all these tests and exams. Maybe it was the lack of sleep and only eating once since I arrived a day or two ago. Maybe it was stress or the lack of water or maybe even the damn heat outside. I think I sweated at least a gallon out of me just from our march over and all the damn push-ups I was forced to do. That's got to be the reason why.

"Next!" someone called out.

I looked up and realized it was me being called. Oh shit! It's a blood draw. I sat down and held out my left arm. The nurse slipped a rubber band around my upper arm and pulled it taunt to restrict the blood flow to allow my veins to bulge and be more accessible to draw out what they needed. Well, in went the needle and it hurt and stung on the way in. She didn't allow the alcohol she swabbed on the evacuation point to dry. She filled several tubes, and I was sent on my way with a piece of gauze taped over my new wound in the crook of my elbow. Only God knows what the blood was needed for, but I really didn't care at the moment, my arm hurt at the time. Uncle Sam could do whatever he wanted with it and to me; I was now the property of the United States government and I knew it. Whatever it takes, never quit, that was my motto upon entering the Marine Corps, and I would do whatever they asked of me. Every time I felt a bit apprehensive about any of these tests, that's what I told myself.

At last, our group was done with everything except for one section of our exams. This was the beat-all scariest thing I'd ever seen in my stay on Paris Island. There were six doctors, three per side, with various injection devices waiting for me to walk between them. They were administering God knows what with them needles. They also had these air-pressured administering devices that looked like a water pistol with a long hose going to a tank of compressed air. There was a glass vile underneath the barrel of this makeshift gun hanging in front of its trigger filled with liquids. When it came my turn, I stepped forward. I was told not to move because these devices would cut you very badly if you flinch away. So I stood still, and they hit me from both sides at the same time into both of my upper arms close to the top of my shoulders. The two different pistol devices forced in a white and a yellow liquid. This stuff burned, and I stepped forward for two more of these injection pistol devices that made a funny *pssst* sound as more of this fluorescent-colored juice was forced into a lower section of my arm. This process was done very quickly and effectively with minimum amount of pain and no injury as they had warned if I flinched away. I was nervous for nothing, I thought as I stepped forward to the next two doctors. I was told to drop my underwear so they could inject their freaky juice also. This time it was with the real deal needles that looked a lot bigger than I'd ever seen before. They both injected my upper-ass muscles on opposite sides. This stuff hurt and burned from whatever juice they inject going into my dumbass. With everything shot into me, I was wondering what the hell they just gave us. Was I some sort of government experiment, or was this routine? Either way, it didn't matter to me at all, I was going to be a Marine. Whatever they'd do to me, I'd take it and ask for seconds. We were then ordered to get back into our clothes after our scary injections. I dressed quickly and watched as some of the others behind me got their shots. A few guys even passed out during the process. From the looks of the way they injected us with those air guns, it wasn't very sanitary at all. Once a guy was given a shot, they just reset and hit the next guy without cleaning out the gun or even worrying about transmitting whatever virus someone had to the next guy. Maybe it was because it wasn't a needle and it was a compressed air system. *Oh well,* I figured. *This is the Marine Corps, they must do this all the time, and who was I to question it all? It has to be safe, so why worry myself on such a stupid thing?*

After the group of recruits I was with was done with their gauntlet of needles, we were instructed to sit down outside of the hospital's entryway. I sat down feeling a bit queasy from the blood draw and that combination of injections I had been just given. While sitting there, I did not realize my butt was sore, and it wasn't from that nurse's finger in my rectum, nor was it from the injections. Nope, it was from sitting on this concrete sidewalk. If you have ever sat down on a concrete slab for more than five minutes, you would know what I was going through. After about forty-five minutes, my ass was absolutely numb. That is how long we sat there waiting until our entire platoon was done with their examinations. From the looks of our numbers, we had lost another five people from this endeavor. Holy Moses! *If this keeps up, no one will be left to train with,* I was thinking to myself.

"On your feet. Attention!" our drill instructor yelled out.

That was our cue to form up. We were moving out to our next destination: to get our haircuts. We marched down the road a ways until we reached the barbershop. Once there, I was excited about getting that coveted high and tight and to look more like I belonged in this man's Marine Corps. I was one of the first guys in, and to my surprise, I didn't receive a high and tight at all. I had gotten the lowest setting known to any barber on this planet who ever wielded a set of clippers. This guy shaved my head damn near bald in a matter of twenty seconds. My head was raw and stinging from the razor burn he just gave me instantly. I stood up and was handed a towel to wipe off my face and then told to go sit back outside. Once again we sat on some cold, hard-ass concrete. Oh man, my butt was really killing me this time. I sat for another half of an hour in the sizzling sun on my concrete sofa of a sidewalk with my head burning and eyes stinging from the glare coming off of the white concrete walkway. Why the hell did they shave my head so close? I thought. Then I realized something. Maybe it was to make sure no one had lice or it was to make everyone look the same. It didn't matter much to me. I was more concerned with getting the top of my head sunburned as I sat there thinking about why the heck did I pick the Marines and not the navy. Well, I guess I was connected to the navy anyways. The U.S. Marine Corps does fall under the department of the navy, doesn't it? I wondered that while shifting my weight from ass cheek to ass cheek whenever one side went numb, or I couldn't take the pain no more. My recruiter never gave me any warning about this bullshit. I was beginning to dislike that man every day, no wait, from minute to minute. I could feel the rawness of my cheeks already. Why the fuck would they sit us down on concrete and not that nice, cool grass only ten feet away? I couldn't wait much longer sitting here just baking in the sun with a raw ass much longer. I wish they would hurry up in there and get us on the move. As the last man came out, I jumped up without even being told to do so right to attention. I couldn't wait any longer, my ass was too raw from the dillydallying around with waiting on a command. Luckily everyone else took my cue and did the same. The drill instructor came out and was a bit shocked at our enthusiasm. He just nodded in appreciation. We were getting better at anticipating our every move or at least I was. Maybe I was cut out to be a Marine after all.

After what seemed to be an eternity, we were back on the move. We marched around a little ways to a big open field with a ten-by-ten-foot wooden white box in the center it almost looked like a stage of sorts to me. Our instructor halted us just shy of this funny-looking white box and had us spread out to double arm's length from one another as he climbed onto this stage. What the heck were we going to do? I wondered. He explained to us how and what we could expect from our real drill instructors during our physical training periods. We then did a lot of stretching exercises, jumping jacks, mountain climbers, toe touches, sit-ups, and some sun gods. Now I will explain those sun gods. They were done by standing with your arms outstretched from your sides, palms up, and you were to make about a twelve-inch circle by moving your arms. This was done to replicate raising the sun. Pretty simple training, I thought while we were going through the list of things we might do during training. The drill instructor gave us instructions from a list of exercises he had written on a crumpled piece of paper from within his pocket. I figured we were just brushing the surface of what was really going to happen when it was for real.

We had a lot of really weak individuals in our platoon, and it showed when we did our push-ups. There was even a bit of whining and some tears coming from some of them momma's boys. I felt like they should just quit. Why waste the Marine Corps's time with that pansy attitude? I was here to become as tough as nails fighting machine without any fear of death or my enemy. I really hated all this whiny shit, and it pissed me off something terrible. I could already tell with all these push-ups and other exercises, I'd become very strong and in shape when boot camp was completed. Our next stop was over to the pull-up bars. We had marched over in no particular formation to speak of. Once there, we had to do as many as we could use a technique called a kip. This kip was a way to generate momentum in your body upward using your legs. You sort of kick your feet slightly and worm wave yourself up with your chin going above the bar. There was a real trick to doing it properly without raising your knees above your waist in the process. I picked up on it rather quickly unlike some of these other fools. I think I did twenty-seven my first try using this kip style. There were a few others behind me with a higher count than me, but I was one of the first to go. I might have done more if I had a number to shoot for. The requirement was only twenty, so I was safe. My main worry came from having guys in our platoon that could barely do five pull-ups among us. That was definitely going to bite us in the ass a bit further on in training. You're only as strong as your weakest link according to this receiving drill instructor. I did believe exactly that. My biggest complaint about it was, and always has been, if they can't do five or ten pull-ups today, what happened to their physical requirements set by the recruiters and the station they left from? Weren't they supposed to weed out the weaker individuals beforehand? Maybe boot camp wouldn't be so difficult on these instructors and a bit less harsh on guys like me who have to carry around this dead weight. By having lesser-fit individuals in the Marine Corps, it has lost a bit of its luster to me at this moment. While watching a few others fail at this pull-up endeavor, I kind of hoped they would be dropped, but that was not to be. Nope, not today, maybe not the next day either, but just maybe when we meet the real drill instructors, it just happens. One can only hope. Oh yeah, there was a thing called an ASVAB test. Maybe these were the smart Marine hopefuls who did really well on their aptitude tests and weren't very physically fit to begin with. The process of boot camp would make them stronger—when there's a will, there's a way in the Corps. I suddenly realized it might not be about who's strongest, fastest, or the smartest at all. It was about how far were you willing to push yourself and then to help the less-fortunate individuals along. It was about teamwork. Like a lightning bolt from heaven hit me in the head, I realized we were here not only to train ourselves but to train as a fighting unit. I began to cheer on the next guy in line to do those pull-ups. This sort of motivation didn't go unnoticed either, soon others started rooting for one another and we actually started thinking a bit more as a group than individuals. It was that moment right there that would propel me into the future. I was no longer worried about my physical strength. I had what it took to make it through boot camp, and this receiving drill instructor saw that in me. I was here to train hard and to lead by example to the others. By my unselfish actions, I brought this group of gaggled recruits from bubbling fools to thinking and helping group of motivated, hard-charging devil dogs. Hurrah! I even believe some of them not so strong recruits actually managed one more pull-up than normal.

After our pull-up session ended, our receiving instructor put us back into formation and told us we were going to pick up our canteens from the squad bay and bring them along with us. We were going on a quick three-mile run. We marched over and retrieved one canteen and filled them in the head. Once we all filled our canteens and formed back up into formation outside. We marched back to the field where we did our pull-ups and sit-ups and all the other exercises. We were instructed to leave our canteens at our right foot and step to the right about fifteen paces. That was called sidestep march. Pretty easy to follow that command, I thought. We completed that without any real problems, thank God. We then were told to stretch out our legs with a few stretching exercises he explained while demonstrating it to us. Once stretched out, we got back into formation and were all set to do this three-mile run. Now you and I both know that a three-mile run isn't done very quickly at all. It's actually pretty damn far and should take a little while to complete. Not here in the Marine Corps, no, sir, it's done in less than eighteen minutes. At least that's what our physical requirement is set at to be a perfect score. We had to do the run in that specified amount of time, twenty pull-ups, and eighty sit-ups in two minutes to qualify as a three-hundred physical fitness test. Your PFT scores go into your record, and they base your next ranks on these performance records, so we had to give it our all. This wasn't test day, but our instructor told us this as we prepared to run these three miles this morning.

We started off marching; then the pace quickened into a jog. The drill instructor was flanking our left and stepped in with us as he sang out some cadence which we repeated loudly back to him. This continues the whole way, and his cadence was rather boring. It wasn't much more than left, right, left. He really didn't spew out cadence that was funny or interesting like you may see in the movies. Oh well, it kept my mind off of the pain and kept oxygen pumping into my lungs. When we completed the three-mile run, we were directed to the outdoor showers to cool off. We were also short about half of our platoon. The other recruits were still walking; half ass-running, they just fell out or passed out from heat exhaustion. I didn't really notice what was going on behind me because I was in the front of the platoon on this treacherous run. There were two rows in front of me with a recruit holding our guide stick, which supposed to have had our platoon flag on it, out front. We only had the stick, but at least we had something. The platoon flag was issued when we began training for real with our real drill instructors, and we finished this receiving process. As for our dropped runners, they were in a world of pain I could understand. Taking this into account, a few others and myself who had completed this god-awful run and kept up in this heat were dry heaving while cooling off under the cold mist of these outdoor showers. Now if I was dry heaving and almost passing out from this three-mile run, I felt sorry for the overweight, Fat Bodies as called by the instructor, who were still struggling to finish the run. After what seemed like an eternity, all of our fallouts and fall-behinds filtered in. We had gotten back into formation and marched back to our barracks.

Once back in our barracks, we were instructed to get into our fatigues. This process was done quickly and efficiently. I tore off my wet, sweat-drenched articles of clothing and put them into my mesh laundry bag hanging off of the back of my rack. I hustled to open my footlocker not really remembering the combination off hand so I had taped it to the back of my lock. Successfully opening it, I slipped on a fresh pair of tighty-whities, camouflaged pants, green socks, green T-shirt, long-sleeved camouflaged shirt, and my Go Fasters. On went my cover while rushing back to the yellow line painted on the floor. I put my belt on when I got there then snapped to attention. I was the first guy on line ready to go. I was determined to lead by example for the rest of these guys to follow my lead. Boot camp may be tough mentally and physically, but I definitely wasn't going to slack off or quit now. I was actually glad I was finally putting my useless ass into something meaningful, and I wanted to do it proudly. So that's how receiving pretty much went for the next several days. Wake up, shit, shave, and shower, eat, train, march, get yelled at, sleep a bit more, and get oriented to the basics. After a week or so of that, we got to begin the real training that was actually considered day one of the training evolution. These first seven days didn't count toward the ninety-one we were required to be actual Marines. What a load of shit this was. *Fucking lying-ass recruiter*, I thought during the whole thing.

MEETING THE DRILL INSTRUCTORS

After a week of orientation, receiving, being cheated out of seven days of training whichever you want to call it, we were all brought outside as a company, six platoons in all. We were told we were Foxtrot Company during our next evolution of training. We were told by several different people who spoke during this company meeting that we would be moving out of our barracks here in receiving to across the tarmac into a new barracks. I was totally excited about finally being done with all the physicals, dental exams, and just plain waiting around to finally begin. While in the receiving barracks, I had talked to a few other recruits, and some of them had been waiting for three weeks to be put into a platoon for training to start. *I'm so glad I showed up when I did,* I thought while listening to another high-ranking officer give his version of the motivational speech. I was already pumped up and ready for some action. I really didn't need all the hurrah stuff, but it was fun to shout it out loud for the whole base to hear our company. Look out, world Second Battalion Foxtrot Company was here and we were ready for anything. We met our company commander, our first sergeant, and a lot of other guys who just looked and sounded important. I was reeling in pain from once again sitting on concrete for longer than an hour of just endless and I'm-what's-his-nuts-and-I'm-your-base-commander shit. It really didn't sink in much at all for me at this time. Nothing and no one mattered. It just felt too damn good knowing we were just about to meet the three drill instructors for our platoon. Just imagine taking orders from just three people for thirteen weeks straight. Twenty-four hours a day and seven days a week. That was what lay ahead of me, and I was anxious and a bit nervous to say the least. I couldn't recall much of anything from them motivational speeches. All I did know was my ass was numb and I was about to give them three guys all the power over me they wanted and I would benefit greatly from their teachings in the process. Finally after a long-drawn-out almost-endless hour, we were instructed back into our squad bays. Once there, we were told to pack up all our stuff into our two bags and carry it once again from this squad bay to the next. Everything went smoothly because we had learned to carry all this shit once before. We had finally made it into a true training squad bay. It was no different from the first, except it came equipped with weights and pull-up bars at the front of the room next to the office and the head. I lay my shit down somewhere about six racks from the office on the left side of the squad bay. Once that task was completed, we all were instructed to sit down in the center of the squad bay and face forward toward the office and the back exit of the place. A captain entered our squad bay, and our receiving drill instructor was relieved from his job duties. He was thanked and told "great job" by this captain, and off he went out the exit. No good-bye, no "good luck," no "fuck you," and no anything. He just saluted this captain and bailed on us. The captain did a quick speech and began introducing our drill instructors.

In walked a short, stocky sergeant wearing glasses, looking rather calm and professional in his mannerisms. His movement was very crisp with a lot of precision. We were talking spit-polished shoes, perfect creases in his pants, super clean-looking pressed tan shirt with several ribbons and badges on his chest glinting from the lights above. He also had on one of them Smokey the bear hats tilted down so you really couldn't see his eyes. It was perched this way to give off the effect of being pissed off. He was a bit red in the face and looked irritated about something. All in all he looked like a very well-put-together Marine. It turned out that this guy was going to be our second, our number 2, drill instructor. From what I understood from what they were saying, he was the guy who would do most of our drilling and proper Marine Corps procedures and such. I wasn't sure what all that meant, but it was getting tiresome already with these introductions. Most of the guys around me felt the same way. I could tell this from the yawning and the dumb blank stare several of them had on their faces.

In my mind I was glad this guy was white. The only thing we had encountered so far were a lot of black Southern-drawl-speaking drill instructors that weren't very sociable. Not that it mattered in any way racially to me. I wasn't racist to begin with. I took people for who they were as individuals. It was just refreshing to know there were some white instructors, and maybe by some off-chance miracle, I would comprehend at least a few more words that this man had to say to me. There is a definite language barrier going on down here so far for me. I was getting a bit worried about missing a command or not understanding what someone was trying to tell me. Maybe this was all part of their plan. To keep you so damn disoriented and confused all the way up to this particular moment. Whatever the case may be, I was here and I had nowhere else I wanted to be. Sooner or later I might have picked up on the language, but I sure was glad the powers that be gave us an interpreter in my mind. This could save me a lot of pain in the upcoming future. I don't know about our entire platoon, not knowing what has been said or what has been going on for the past week. I'm sure half of our group, if not more of us, was completely in the dark. Even a few black guys from up New York's way I had talked to during receiving agreed with me. We kind of made a joke about it among us Northerners, not having a clue what in the hell they had been saying so far. Well, it turned out this guy was from Ohio, and to my great relief, he spoke in a language we could totally understand. This was actually one of the funnier thoughts I had while waiting for these guys to finish this introduction stuff and get on with training.

Our next drill instructor was introduced to us, and out of the office walked this super dark black sergeant. We are talking the pitch-dark, purple-gummed type you wouldn't notice in the shadows unless he smiled, which I highly doubt he was capable of doing from the looks of him. He strutted into position next to the other drill instructor and stood at attention in front of us all. Now this guy was straight out of hell, I was sure of it. He looked to weigh about 235 pounds and approximately stood a towering six feet three inches tall. Not only was this guy tall, but also he really did look awfully ripped through his almost-too-small shirt. Arms that looked big and ripped with huge hands hanging down by his side almost knowing inside yourself you definitely didn't want this motherfucker coming after you in a fight. *What the fuck do we have here? There must be a mistake! Hold the phone! Someone tell us this is some sort of joke? Christ!* This guy almost projected his discontent and hate for us by his sheer presence. He sure looked to me that he wasn't put here to teach us anything useful other than pain. Yes, sir, that's his job. He was to inflict as much pain and humiliation on us as humanly possible. The half smirk he held on his face and that look of a Doberman in his eyes gave it away. This spoke volumes of how much he loved his job. It turned out he was our number 3 drill instructor. He was going to teach us Marine Corps history and cover all of our knowledge requirements. Without fail, he would help with the training as well. I might be new to all this Marine Corps stuff, but being third in charge definitely meant you were the mean one.

As I sat in the front row waiting for our senior drill instructor to be introduced, I only half-looked at the other two. I didn't want to make eye contact with either of these guys, that was a definite no-no in the Marine Corps. Never eyeball an instructor. Shit! I learned that watching the famous movie released in 1987 called *Full Metal Jacket.* For some reason or another, I rather enjoyed the way that gunnery sergeant treated his platoon and thought it looked like fun. Kind of funny how a simple movie made to show the horrors of war slipped into my mind as something cool to experience. *Why the fuck would I be thinking about this shit especially at a time like this one? Maybe I'm just tired or simply bored to death with all this introduction stuff. Either way I'm here and it's all been cool.* It was much better than sitting home talking shit and causing the local authorities havoc. Like I said before, I was no angel as a juvenile. This place was where I was going to find myself and actually become a man. I hated my childhood just as many others in my platoon did also. At least that is what a few others confided in me when we first met. Most of us hated school, and several others thought just as I did. This was our last option. For me it was sort of prison or the Marines, and I chose to be here. I had no interest in college at all while growing up, and I always cursed the thought of not serving my country, as any true American should. Well, that's just my dumbass opinion anyways. I couldn't just fall into drug addiction anymore and wind up dead or in prison because of some mistake I had made. If there was one thing I considered wrong about my decision or myself up to this point, I would have to say not one thing. Everything I stood for as a kid—never say quit, protect the weaker guy no matter the odds, stand strong, and fight the good fight—will all come into play. This was a fight for my own survival. Many kids in high school hated me for this. I remember several incidents where two or three guys were going to jump someone after school for some bullshit or another. Well, whenever I got wind up with this sort of bullshit, I always showed up on the other poor bastard's side that was going to be grossly outnumbered and attacked. I used to show up and say shit on that idea. "If you're going to fight, I will fight also, only I'm on this kid's side." Mostly they gave up their plan and went on their way. Other times someone needed a smack to quell the situation. I was considered a guy who definitely didn't take shit and could certainly fight, or so they thought anyways. Maybe I just looked tough in their eyes because I never backed down and was willing to go toe to toe with uneven odds in their favor. I never struck first in any fight either. I liked to be hit and maybe a bit bloody before I really truly could enjoy an all-out knuckling. Call me crazy, but what's the point unless blood is leaking to lift my hands in anger. I had been schooled very well in battle prior to sitting on this floor in front of these drill instructors this day, and it meant nothing.

Just about when you were going to scream in agony from your ass being numb here, it came the final introduction. This was to be for our senior drill instructor. He was our new father, mother, leader, our worst fucking nightmare, and also our best friend for when things really suck—and yes, they do begin to suck. I might have thought I was tough, sort of brave, and confident I could handle anything. What happened in the next thirteen weeks was a total wake-up call. So in walked our top honcho. A white guy somewhere in his late thirties if I was to guess, kind of pudgy in comparison to the other two instructors, but nonetheless just as frightening. He looked a bit old in the face, sort of red also, but it could be from the heat. Maybe just maybe, he was feeling a bit embarrassed about being in front of us. Maybe he felt like one of them circus freaks who are on display for everyone to line up and ogle at. Not true at all. I think that was my weird sense of humor trying to make light of the actual tension building up inside of me. The anticipation was almost overwhelming. If ever there was a time when you could cut through air with a knife, now was the time. I could really feel something sinister coming. A few other recruits looked to be sensing the same thing because they were fidgeting around nervously. Just the look in their eyes gave it away to me. These guys were up to something, and we had no clue on what was about to unfold.

After our unit commander finished the introductions, he paused for a few moments and then told us good-luck. He also told us he would check in on us from time to time throughout training.

"Attention on deck!" our senior drill instructor announced.

With that we snapped up onto our feet into the position of attention. The drill instructors turned and saluted their commander who was a captain according to the rates and ranks book I was given several days ago. He had two silver bars on his collars and a similar set of bars on his funny green ice cream truck driver's hat. He saluted back and slowly made his exit. There was nothing but silence as he headed to the rear door called a hatch. You could've heard a mouse fart; it was that still in the room. This man opened the hatch door very gently and deliberately swung it all the way open to the opposite wall. Off this captain went down the stairs and out of sight. I watched as the door slowly made its way to the closed position. Well, that was my first real sign that pure doom was lurking. Call it sixth sense or call it intuition, but I was correct. That door's lock slammed home, and the door shut with an audible loud bang. The sound of the door reminded me of when I was arrested as a teenager on numerous occasions. The bars to your cell swing shut, abandoning all hope and regretting everything that has transpired to get you into such a horrible place. All your dreams have been shattered in that moment of time. Your stay inside that cell will give you lots of time to reflect on how fucked up you have become in life. I don't know why I was reflecting back on that moment in time at this juncture of making my life have meaning and to feel proud of myself about something other than the bad shit that has occurred. Maybe it was a reminder that all of that life was waiting just in the background of my mind. I had no choice but to make this Marine Corps shit work.

FIRST DAY OF HELL

All three of these drill instructors lost their rabid-ass minds at that very moment the door slammed close.

"Get the fuck in front of your bunks! Get the fuck on line! Hurry the fuck up!" they screamed.

We stammered around like chickens with their heads cut off. We were bumping one another and struggling to get to our respective spots. All the while these three ravenous dogs called drill instructors were spitting, screaming, and passing out a few kicks in the ass to several of us who were not moving fast enough. I watched a recruit get thrown about ten feet forward, tripping, stumbling, and then smashing into a set of bunk beds. He grimaced in pain and hit the floor. He then had one of them bastard drill instructors right in his face hollering inches from his ear that he was a pussy and not worth his fucking time to train. He might as well just fucking quit right the fuck now. It only took this drill instructor about twenty seconds to have this poor, dumb bastard crying and blubbering like a schoolgirl as he struggled to get to his feet. What must be going through this kid's mind? I wondered. Once that occurred, I knew eventually all of us would be broken down in the same fashion as to resemble this moment. I loved every second of this shit secretly inside, but I also had fear of what was to become of me. Would I cry for my mom and want to go home from a simple harassment? Hell no! That's my answer, I told myself. I had already gotten a menacing medieval black drill instructor pissed off at me and withstood his grinding shoes in my back without so much as one tear. Maybe a few grunts and groans from pain. I didn't wail out then, so why worry about it now? That's the type of person I was anyways, no pain no gain. I wanted their worst, and their worst was yet to be seen so far on this journey to become a man, a Marine. Would I find myself here and measure up to those who came before me? I could only hope my desire to change my life along with my sheer will could carry me through this.

Once we were all standing at the position of attention with our toes touching a yellow line painted on the floor, these instructors went to work. One by one they went down the line ranting, raving insults and racial remarks to anyone and everyone. Some guys took it, and some guys cried while tearing up being screamed at from three angles. A couple of guys were struck in the stomach with punches, and a few were slapped upside the head. Mostly it was pure hate coming from three very loud neatly dressed professional assholes. In my mind I wasn't thinking much of anything other than "Holy shit, these guys aren't screwing around down here in Paris Island." I better just shut the hell up and keep a low-key demeanor with these fellows. But the truth is, there was no ways to keep low-key and hide while hoping you're not picked on. Absolutely not! When it came my turn for their ranting and cussing at me, I was off somewhere else in my own mind trying to desperately answer their questions. I was trying not to flinch or shake. I stood there like a statue. I was a lifeless being without any feelings or emotions toward these drill instructors. Nope, I stood still while being bumped, slapped in the head, and punched in the stomach. These hits to the gut weren't very hard, but if you weren't expecting it, the wind would be knocked right out of you. I kept my stomach sucked in and tight just as they ordered me to. What came next wasn't necessary, but they must have had their reasons. Out comes spit from all three of them right into my face. At first instinct, you would want to punch someone's teeth down their throat for doing such a degrading thing. All of my inner self was screaming to lash out and smash one of their faces, if not all three of them. My chances were good to reach out a quick jab and smash one of them. As for hitting all three, my chances were very slim to none. They were fully prepared for that, I'm sure. *Dear Jesus, how do I handle this?* I prayed as they taunted me and provoked me into their will. They must know about my violent past. I was a hothead in their eyes, and they demanded respect, as did I even if it was a simple thing. They read my file, I figured. They were damn sure going to find a reason to make me snap so they could kick my ass then have me locked up in the brig for striking a higher-ranking individual. I wasn't falling for it at all. I stood there like a stone. I was a bit scared of what I might do and I was a bit nervous, but I didn't falter. Eventually after about two minutes of their taunts, they moved on. I had won a small victory within myself by using restraint. I had been punched, slapped, and even spit on by all three of them, but in my mind, I came out on top. I became a pride-swallowing better person in that moment. Maybe that "turn the other cheek" crap I had heard during Catholic school worked. Yeah right! I quickly recanted on that idea in my head. This place was designed to mess you the hell up in the head you were being broken mentally. Then you were being rebuilt in their image. No longer were you a person, an individual, not even a simple fucking human being at all. You were absolutely a number, nothing more, actually as of right now, you are less than the juice squirting from a dog's ass during a wet shitting session. If you're broken and happen to give up and quit, well then, these guys did their jobs today. No sweat off of their nuts, not one fucking drop's worth. I realized this simple fact very early on during my stay here and strived to overcome anything they had planned. Nothing was going to stop me in my quest for a meaningful existence in this world. Fuck them! I was determined. If I was to quit now, the life I left behind lay in wait and that wasn't an option at all.

So there we all stood on line simply in shock from our grand introduction. We had met our drill instructors under soft, innocent-toned voices. Then we got to meet the absolute polar opposites. It was quite brilliant. Their ability to lull us into calm compliance in the beginning was a miracle. Then when everything seems okay they fling a huge wrench into the gears and frighten the living hell out of everyone. There must be some Dr. Jekyll and Mr. Hyde requirements when applications are filled out for the job of drill instructor. These three gentlemen must have passed with flying colors in my eyes, and it was quite apparent who held control. My proof of that was reaffirmed as I stood at the position of attention with nasty spit running slowly down my face. It was a bit salty as it passed over my mouth. Yep, it's human nature to taste something as it passes over your lips. Sounds a bit gut-wrenching and foul almost to the point of gagging. In my mind I blocked it out to keep from spewing my breakfast all over the deck in front of me. I wasn't going to waste that sustenance for anything. I almost knew I needed all I would be allowed to consume from this point forward. Welcome to the Marine Corps. Hu-fucking-rrah!

Before I was even given the chance to think about what had just transpired, we were all ordered to retrieve our big green seabag. That which was filled with various articles issued to us prior to this new level of hysteria. Panic and confusion was the name of the game. I hurriedly ran behind my rack and snatched that bag and returned to my respective spot. In a flash, less than a millisecond, I was unscathed and back on that false sense of security place with my toes touching the painted yellow line holding that heavy-ass bag bear-hug style. There were a few unlucky recruits who were kicked, harassed, and tossed to the floor for not moving fast enough for them. This one poor bastard had his gear bag thrown at him from nearly ten feet away. He was desperately trying to recover his balance from a hard shove into the wall behind the racks when it struck him. I always faced forward and kept my eyeballs still. There was no point in looking around. I wasn't concerned with other recruits' problems or hardships, I could only take care of myself right now. It just so happened that it all took place within my field of vision. Well, this recruit who was struck with his seabag screamed and was instantly grabbed at the top of his head. He was then kicked and shoved back on line holding on to his bag bear-hug style by our number 3 instructor, the mean dark-skinned guy. As I was looking across at this kid, he's turning paler and paler in color before my eyes. His head was bleeding, and blood was running down his face with a steady flow off his chin like a leaking drippy faucet. It almost became a small stream from his head to his chin then to the floor below. Within about forty-five seconds or so, he collapses to the deck.

"What the fuck!" our senior drill instructor screamed when he noticed this crumpled bleeding pile of shit on the floor.

All three instructors ran to this kid's aid and instructed us to turn, facing away. It seemed like five minutes of frantic scrambling, cursing, and a quick dash to phone for help among the three of them. Our squad bay doors slammed open with two guys carrying a stretcher and a medical kit. They scooped this guy up and headed out the doors with him lying limp with a pressure bandage wrapped around his head. Yeah, I broke code and looked. Why not? The drill instructors were busy worrying about him and not concerned about me at the moment. I registered this complete assholic display of abuse and forgot it. We were told it was a simple training accident by these drill instructors and were told to forget it. We didn't need to know what happened, and we definitely didn't see shit. The truth was I did see what happened. That black son of a bitch threw the seabag at this kid and the padlock that we were told to attach to the carrying handle smashed into this kid's head causing his scalp to split open. Yes, it might have been tragic, and it was an accident like they said. In my eyes, it was a blatant disregard to safety. Well, who cares anyways? I'm sure the drill instructor didn't mean for the lock to split this recruit's wig open. So I let it go. Better him than me. Sooner or later we all may bleed. Who knows for sure? You are now government property, so why care if they spilled a little blood within the first hour of us being together. They needed complete control over us, and that tactic would definitely make its mark. Fear can be very powerful. I'm just glad to be here, and it was totally a typical dumbass response, right? That was the truth of it though. This was my chance to become a Marine, and seeing some poor bastard's head leaking in front of me wasn't going to change a thing in my mind. This was our first hour of training and he was our first casualty. There were plenty more to come, but at least I was still here and that's all that mattered. Self-preservation, brother. That is the key to surviving this. Speak no evil, hear no evil, and see no evil, my new motto. Shit! Who knows how far this place is willing to go to break your pathetic ass? I know for sure I could be next just as well as anyone else in this platoon. I was thinking of myself that is for damn sure at this stage of training. I'm sure other guys in my platoon would agree and felt the same way in this matter.

When the three drill instructors had seen that the two guys who rescued our bleeding passed-out comrade had left the building, it was back to business. They had seemed caring enough for this kid on the floor and showed absolute restraint while these medics were in their territory. They even explained how much of an unfortunate accident it was. Everything seemed on the up-and-up, so they exited without so much as an inquiry into the matter. Nope, even to these medics, we meant absolutely nothing. Christ almighty, we were truly in the hands of some sinister individuals and they're all in on it. So when the door shut behind these medics, our quite calm Dr. Jekylls turned right back into Mr. Hydes instantly. There was no pause whatsoever. A quick "shut the fuck up about it and start dumping out your shit in front of yourselves, you lousy pieces of amphibian shit!" This was how it was handled. Oh freaking well, they showed no remorse, and it seemed to me that they really didn't give two shits about it all. So why should we? I dumped out my seabag as instructed without hesitation. Out spilled a pile of assorted articles, camouflage pants, shirts, green T-shirts, green socks, underwear, that funny-looking lock with the wire connected to it, and a rag with various parts of an M-16 diagrammed on it. We are told to grab our other pack and empty its contents in front of us also. Tent stakes, two lengths of rope, a half of tent made of canvas, fingernail clippers, toenail clippers, shaving cream, soap, face cloth, towel, fingernail brush, boot brushes with polish, and a shine rag. I was talking every damn thing we were issued during receiving lay in front of me. Excluding what we all had on our nasty sweaty bodies.

With everything spilled out in front of us including a government-issued itchy green blanket with two bedsheets and a pillowcase, we were told to pay the fuck attention. They handed out an inventory sheet to all of us. We were then told to produce a writing device called an ink stick. I rummaged quickly through all my things and luckily I found the hidden treasure beneath my funky half-canvas tent near the bottom of the pile. A few others in my platoon weren't so lucky in this task. They couldn't produce this coveted ink stick quickly enough. Well, guess what? All of their things were flung behind their racks in a scattered mess by, you guessed it, our number 3 drill instructor. *Damn, this guy is an asshole*, I thought to myself. A few others couldn't produce an ink stick at all, and they got it even worse. That is when our number 2 drill instructor showed his teeth. These lucky few were grabbed by the back of their necks out of the crowd and led over to the pull-up bars and ordered to hang from them with their arms fully extended. He was screaming and hollering how much of a waste of human shit these guys were for not even caring to hold on to a bloody writing device. Our senior drill instructor didn't hesitate joining in the onslaught of hate either. He hollered for the rest of us to get down on our fucking faces and start doing push-ups. Those unlucky recruits who had their stuff scattered weren't off the hook either. They were ordered to drop right now also and forget about gathering their things. Nope, there was no favorites here, get the fuck down. Some of us got the joy of the old number 3 kicking them in the ribs and stepping on their hands, but not me on this moment. I pushed and yelled out the famous chant already known by all of us, "One, two, three, four, I, love, Marine, Corps" on each repetition. This went on for at least twenty minutes if I was to guess. I was really not quite sure, but my arms would no longer move up or down no matter how hard I struggled. My whole body was sweating, and another puddle was forming beneath my face from sweat dripping off my nose again. While I was struggling to push up from the floor, the guys on the pull-up bars were in a bad spot also. I heard a few of them crying out in pain and a couple had dropped from their perch atop them bars. As for them, they were ordered to run in place with their knees coming up waist high with each step. If they couldn't keep the pace set by our number 2, they were given a swift kick in the ass to keep up. I heard a few guys crying and sobbing from the pain of them kicks or the pain in their lungs and muscles screaming for mercy under such intense strain. Next thing you know, our senior drill instructor said to fall in. "Get the fuck back on line," were the words he screamed actually. "Position of attention, you lousy motherfuckers." At this time I was really feeling tired and even experienced a few purple spots within my vision. There was no end in sight to their madness either. We were ordered to file outside of our barracks and to follow our number 3 drill instructor down the stairs to side of the building. Now this was not done at some cheesy fire drill pace you may think of while in grade school. No way in hell. This was done at a flat-out sprint. This caused a lot of havoc on the stairs leading down. Several guys were trampled over, and a few just got forced to the sides without any hope of reentering our suicidal drive downward. I pushed, shoved, and even stepped on a few unlucky recruits who had happened to fall en route. No fucking way was I going to be the last man down, and neither were the rest of these jackasses around me. It was pure survival of the fittest at this point. Once all of us were out of the building, we were told to form up in this giant sandbox in front of some clotheslines. There were several tables there with sinks and water faucets attached to them. I figured we would do our laundry in this area. All three of these ravenous monsters called drill instructors screamed we better start moving our asses faster and paying the fuck attention when they spoke. Our senior drill instructor went on to introduce us to the pit. Yep, this giant sandbox we were standing in was called the pit. Have no mistake about it, this pit was exactly that. It sucked. The temperature outside was damn near ninety degrees with about 100 percent humidity.

I came outside sweating only to walk right into ovenlike heat outside. The air was thick and hard to breathe. I was in pain, my lungs were on fire from each inhale, my arms were weak, my vision was filled with little purple spots, and now I was a bit dizzy standing in this sandbox. The sprint down them two flights of stairs was what was making me spin and feel woozy. Well, it was more like a struggling, pushing, and a shoving match with other sweaty recruits actually. I was simply able to function on just pure adrenaline at this time, nothing more. I hadn't been with these crazy drill instructors more than two hours yet, and I was already spent. Now let me tell you something. This sandpit was no goddamn joke. We were ordered to do jumping jacks, run in place with high knees, push-ups, sit-ups, and drop-down stand-ups like you do in football practice. What really was the worst was being told to remove our camouflaged shirts and T-shirts. Then we were ordered to lie down on our stomachs and to roll to our right and then back to our lefts. In the process of this rolling, we had gotten completely covered in sand from ass to head and stomach to neck. It was all over me. Next came some leg raises while lying on our backs. We were then told to stay in a hold position at the bottom half of the exercise with our feet six inches off the ground. I hated every second of this exercise. It began to really burn your stomach muscles something fierce. We had to hold this position for like five minutes. A lot of us kept dropping our legs and got screamed at like we were absolute trash in their eyes.

We were then ordered to roll over and hold in the bottom
half of a push-up position six inches off the ground. While we
were in this holding pattern, all three of those evil bastard drill
instructors went row by row pushing our faces into the sand with
their feet, grinding our faces into the ground. When it was my
turn, I closed my eyes as tight as possible while good old number
3 pushed my head into the sand with his foot. He held me down
for like ten seconds and then let me come up for air. He then
asked me if I wanted to quit. I yelled out, "No, sir!" Down went my
head as I was yelling my response back to him. I had no time to
close my mouth before I entered the sand again. This sand filled
my mouth rather quickly under the forceful shoe atop my head.
I was released in about ten more seconds to come up for air, but
all I could do was spit out that shitty sand before I was down again
with taking in any air. My lungs were set ablaze from the total lack
of oxygen. I tried to turn my head under the pressure of this guy's
foot on my head to possibly sneak in a breath, but there was no
way I was moving. The more I struggled, the deeper I went and
the harder he pushed. This fucking guy was going a bit too far
in my mind, but oh well, I asked for this by coming to his island.
I was thinking, *Oh well, I'll just pass out from the lack of air, and he'll
just have to CPR my ass back into this world.* Just as I was about to
gasp in a lung full of sand and most certainly fade to black, he
released his weight and pressure on my head. I rapidly yank my
head up and spit out a lot of sand and gasp for air. The air came
in, but it was way too hot and filled with sand. I began coughing
and started to gag. The whole time I was having this coughing,
gagging episode, this black drill instructor was right above my
head screaming at me to fucking die. *Holy shit, Batman! I'm in a
pickle here,* I thought as I began to vomit out some sand and a bit
of breakfast into the hole from which my head came. The puking
lasted about five seconds, but it cleared my windpipe of this sand
and I began to breathe semi-okay without the choking or gagging.
This man above me had no concern whatsoever if I was okay or
not. I just heard "suck it the fuck up or quit, you fucking pussy"
from him. I just sucked up the Sahara freaking desert and just
puked it all out just too bloody well breathe shithead. Well, that
was my thought anyways as I screamed "no, sir" again when asked
if I wanted to quit again. Well, that just pissed him off I guess

because down I went again into this hole filled with puke, sand, and eggs. Only this time it was quick and just for effect, he knew I wasn't going to quit. He also knew I wasn't going anywhere. He just wanted to show me he was in control. What an asshole!

There was nothing I could do about it, so I stood up and tried to join in with the rest of our platoon who were ordered to do more jumping jacks. I stood up with that rotting mess covering my face while my vision was almost a complete purple view. Those spots I was seeing earlier had increased dramatically during that bullshit. I was upright but on unsteady legs, head swimming, reeling, and swaying as I regained my vision slightly. It took all of my strength just to stay upright without falling flat on my ass. While desperately holding on to consciousness, this pain-in-the-ass drill instructor was screaming right in my ear to start doing jumping jacks. I honestly was ready to pack it right in and tell this guy to go fuck himself. Just like before, something clicked back on and then came that inner voice, *Never quit.* So off I went hopping up and down with my arms and legs flailing. It wasn't pretty at first, but after a few repetitions, I fell right into a decent rhythm while sounding off in cadence with the rest of the platoon, "One, two, three, four, THREE! One, two, three, four, FOUR!" So onward up to twenty-five we went. It seems to be every damn exercise we have done is done on these freaking four counts. This definitely wasn't for the meek. You had to be tough or in shape to handle this pace. I was tough, but I guess I wasn't in shape because I was honestly struggling.

Once those jumping jacks were completed, they gave a little speech on how whenever we start screwing up, this is where we would end up. Now this place called the pit was going to be a punishment whenever someone screwed the pooch on anything. Well, at least it would be those individuals and not me because I planned on not being here again. We were then ordered to put our shirts back on. I grabbed my T-shirt and just threw it on as with that long-sleeved camouflaged blouse. No time to wipe off any of that sand either. They were quite clear on that fact when someone else made the mistake of trying to wipe off without being given permission to do so. In a flash, this guy was knocked very rapidly off his feet by one of the drill instructors that came out of nowhere. One quick snatch of this guy's arm and a quick slip of his legs and down he went. This must've scared the total shit out this guy because he cried out in a horrible death shriek. It sounded like he was being killed. At this moment I was dying to start laughing out loud, but I knew to keep it inside myself. This was definitely not the time for those shenanigans. I just stayed quiet and finished dressing. Meanwhile this guy was getting the treatment. All three of the drill instructors swarmed in and started kicking sand all over this guy while he was ordered to do sit-ups. They absolutely covered his useless ass. He'd be washing sand out of his ears for weeks. They made their point to him that's for sure.

They went on to explain how we were only allowed to speak when spoken too, jump when they say jump, we'll eat when they say we'll eat, and we'll shit when they say we'll shit. If you can't hold it, well then, you'll just have to shit in your goddamn pants. They didn't give two fucks, we were nothing to them and we better just know that fact right now. Absolutely everyone better understood this, or we'd be in this fucking pit until the sun would go down. "Now get the fuck back down on your faces and start doing some more push-ups." They better not ever catch anyone doing something they weren't ordered or told to do from this moment forward. We all dropped down and began to push; up and down we went for what felt like just plain old torture at this point. I was sure they would stop when we reached twenty or so, but on we pushed up to thirty. Well, mostly everyone including myself only properly pushed about fifteen. As for us, we were stuck in the up-or-down position and just yelled along that four counts chant "One, two, three, four, I, love, Marine, Corps." These son-of-a-bitch drill instructors went around kicking sand in our faces and either kicked you back in the down position or yanked you back in the up position by your belt. The whole time we pushed they were ranting and cussing and just being plain fucking nasty to everyone. Once we reached thirty reps, our senior drill instructor screamed for us to get back to attention. "Attention! Get up quickly, no hesitation, on your feet!" he screamed. Quickly we all sprang to our feet. Well, for me it took a bit of struggling and a lot of effort, but I managed it without any hitches, as did everyone else. It was like everyone knew this half hour of torture was over.

We were ordered to get back on line inside. Off we went sprinting the distance from the pit to the stairs. It was another stampede of sweaty, scared recruits with ravenous, doglike drill instructors barking in your ears to hurry the fuck up along with the occasional boot in the backside to keep you hustling. I don't know what the hell happened, but once we were all up the stairs and back on line, it wasn't fast enough or some shit, but we were ordered back down them fucking stairs and out into the pit once again. We had another scrambling mess of sweaty pieces of shit trampling over one another downward. It was always worse going down the stairs than coming up them. No one seemed to care who got stomped over or shoved. It was very dangerous, but it was also kind of fun. It reminded me of the mosh pits I had been in at a few concerts I used to go to with my younger brother. It was total and absolute chaos. That is the closest thing I can think of that could compare to our suicidal descents down the stairs. Once again we found ourselves doing up-downs and push-ups. No breaks and no sympathy at all, even if someone was crying or collapsing from exhaustion. Nope, they got screamed at or pulled off to the side if they couldn't get the hell up or keep up. We went up and down them shitty concrete stairs four times before their madness finally came to an end. Most of the platoon was or had already puked. About ten guys had quit or passed out. As for where they ended up, I have no clue, but we started with about eighty recruits this morning. When I finally had a chance to look around at our numbers, we were definitely short a few bodies. The weeding process was still in effect, and it wasn't even lunchtime yet. It was all a blur to me during their three-hour onslaught of pain.

We were finally back on line inside our squad bay when they allowed us to have a damn drink of water. They ordered us to grab our canteens and stand at attention with both canteens out at arm's length in front of our bodies. Now as thirsty as you may have been, these guys made us hold those damn canteens out for at least five minutes. They were masters at fucking with you. Once ordered to finally drink some, it wasn't a reward at all. We are not talking "have a few sips and feel better," nope, we were to place one down on the deck and start guzzling the other. They kept a close eye on this and made sure everyone finished every last drop before we moved on to the second canteen. Now this second quart of water was a bit more difficult for some guys. They just couldn't drink the amount we were being forced to consume. So here we go with drill instructors damn near drowning people, forcing them to finish it all. This tactic had gotten a few people scared and upset. A few of them begged for the instructor to stop and cried like babies about it. The drill instructors were not playing with these guys.

"No fucking way you lousy maggot piece of walrus shit! Drink it now or fucking die!" he screamed.

That was very true indeed. You could very well die from dehydration, and they made it very clear they weren't fucking around. They explained how if we didn't drink the amount specified, bad things could and will happen to us. They even guaranteed us that a thermometer would be jammed in our ass by a medic and IV fluids would be pumped into us. Hopefully if they caught us in time, we would survive this ordeal and live. If they didn't get there in time and slacked off on our water intake requirements, our brains would fry and most likely become a vegetable. So there would be no half-ass efforts when it came time for consuming fluids. Yes, they would use force to ensure this and they meant it.

So there I stood on my damn yellow line guzzling water, sweat running down my whole body, half-covered in sand, feeling a bit woozy from the heat and the pure adrenaline loss. Why the hell did I not just fall out like them other pussies beyond me? It began to feel like that was the key to freedom. Our drill instructors sure as hell wanted us to quit. They would get a wonderful joy out of it actually. They would be accomplishing their jobs in breaking you this early on in training, what bullshit! *I'll never give those mean-assed red-faced hornets the pleasure.* So that was what I was thinking to myself while chugging my second canteen of warm water feeling bloated and a bit pissed off at the way my ass felt. It was filled with sweat and chafing within the crack from the sand inside. Once our canteens were emptied down, our filthy fucking sewer holes we were ordered to refill them in the head. This was also done at the hurry-fuck-up step also. Actually not one damn thing we were told to do this far was at a calm pace. I was starting to catch on to this rat race, hurry up, shut up, do what they tell you, and scream out when asked a question. It's simple stuff to remember, but let me tell you something though. As soon as you think you know how things go and begin to fall into any sort of rhythm, a drill instructor will be there to foul that right up for you. You are no longer in control of anything, that's for damn sure. These drill instructors become your new mind, and there is no need to resist at all, trust me on this one simple fact if you're reading this and decide you are willing to brave boot camp. Your body, mind, and ass have now become the property of the U.S. Marine Corps and it is theirs to decide how it's going to develop. This whole process of being reprogrammed reminds me of the show *Star Trek: The Next Generation*. It's the episode when Capt. Picard and his happy group of assholes encounter the Borg. The Borg is our instructor, the collective whole is the Marine Corps, and we are to stop resisting and prepare to be assimilated. Most certainly you will get this feeling when you are a dumb as recruit trainee. Your mind will be melted and reprogrammed to fit their wants and needs. So my advice to you is this, shut the fuck up and suck it up, you devil dog shit bird, it's all good stuff. This whole shitty feeling is worth every penny spent to train your ass by John Q. Public. Who knows it may all save your ass sometime in the future, so pay attention, okay? This was my first day into this training, and trust me, brother, you need to be prepared before getting down here. I wasn't, and that was clearly present by the way I felt. I'm all heart though, and it helped get me through the remainder of this first day.

After all this went on, we continued on with inventorying our stuff. We were told to find whichever item our senior drill instructor called out from the list he had and we went item by item to be sure we had all the required gear. There was a demonstration on how everything was going to be stored neatly in our footlockers as well. Everything was to a certain guideline and had to be exactly right or they would spill your shit out on the floor and make you do pull-ups for not doing it right. This went on for at least another hour without getting done to their standards at all. My stuff was dumped three times, and I had done twenty pull-ups on each session to them bars. I was so freaking exhausted by the time they finally gave up on this footlocker episode I almost collapsed. Thank God we were ordered to form up outside for lunch because any more pull-up sessions might have broken my spirit.

Our first trip to the chow hall with our drill instructors was absolutely a waste of time. We were hollered at and harassed through the chow line as usual with food flying all over the place. Some of us were lucky to make it through with some mashed potatoes or something left on our trays. The drill instructors would wait for you to be served and smack the tray out of your hand and spill everything all over the floor. We had to scoop up what was on the floor and place a few morsels into our trays and go. We were ordered to sit down with the scraps in front of us that were not worth the effort in getting. Once all of us were sitting at attention and looking straight ahead, they told us to stand the fuck up and all we were allowed to do was drink that urine-colored juice and get the fuck outside again. We had gotten nothing to eat at all, so what was the point of this shit, I wondered. Like I said before, these guys were masters at fucking with people. It's all about discipline, they kept saying over and over. All I knew was I was tired and hungry and full of sand—that was all. I guess we'd be able to eat dinner, I thought and headed back outside after dropping off my nearly empty tray. This was total mistreatment in my mind, but they masked it by calling it training. I understood all the exercise, but I couldn't fathom not allowing us to eat anything. I definitely hated this shit so far, and with no food, it got worse.

I was glad I got that jungle juice though. It must be packed with all sorts of minerals, vitamins, steroids, and most likely some saltpeter thrown in to keep you from getting horny. It's okay to starve and to be violent, but what they won't tolerate is anyone getting a hard-on. Everyone here was eighteen or nineteen years old, and hormones are natural occurrences at this age. The government is prepared for this aspect of sexual desire, and they block it to keep you limp. They don't want a bunch of horny guys jerking off all over the place or, worse still, seeing their bunkmate's ass to be a good enough substitute to some real pussy. So there will be no ass fucking among the ranks or any gay stuff going on at all. Truthfully they didn't allow gays in the military. It's a good thing in one aspect of the scheme of things because they are weaker individuals when it comes to natural aggression according to this establishment. The bad thing is, they are being discriminated against in a country that is based on the Constitution, and it states all men are created equal. Not in the Marine Corps though, and it was totally ridiculous not to have them when it comes to being able to be effective in combat. Anyone can learn to fire a weapon. That's just my opinion though, and right now I'm not allowed to have one of those either. Actually if you think about it, the gay guy out of the group would be an asset actually, he could relieve a lot of pent-up stress occurring in the ranks. No offense to the gay people of the world at all, but this was a good moment to have one among us. With all this stress, a good late-night blowjob to one of these asshole drill instructors might help relieve them of some pent-up rage and then maybe they would lighten the fuck up on us. I personally don't give to shits what someone else's sexual orientation may be or what gets them off. I just hate the people who take without permission, meaning the rapists and the ones who diddle children. I say we should hang them child-molesting bastards up by their balls with meat hooks and let them suffer until death himself shows up and takes them to hell. That's also my opinion, but that comes from a person who was abused by an adult as a child. He happened to be my own brother, but I forgave him in my heart long ago. I wish he could forgive himself over this and end his own guilt. So my opinion is bias at best when it comes to the convictions and punishment of these predators. I guess I won't be picked for jury duty anytime soon on that matter. Crazy thoughts to have during boot camp, but you're not allowed doing much else other than have conversations with yourself because you're not allowed the simple pleasure of farting let alone making a verbal peep.

We were marched back across the steaming hot parade deck of asphalt and hustled back indoors. My stomach was empty, I was full of sweat mixed with sand, my head hurt from holding back inner rage toward these drill instructors, and I got to look forward to being greeted by the pit again when we arrived. I swear to you it doesn't matter to them, and there is no letup on the pace at which we need to be going for their liking. Everyone is screwing up left and right all around me. No matter the offence, we ended up in this sand a lot. This last mistake was someone daydreaming while marching and didn't halt when it was time to stop. The drill instructors love when people screw up and thrive on causing pain to individuals. So here we are again doing sit-ups and leg lifts again. What the hell was I thinking of when I signed on for this type of treatment was beyond my comprehension during my duration of pain. That is exactly what you felt, pain, every time. I can say one thing about my experience though, it was far better to be here in pain than to be in some crack house frying my brain on drugs. Actually it was that crap which made me end up choosing my path in life. I was failing at everything—relationships, school, friendships, and was most likely going to be in prison without a damn prayer. So I gladly did everything they screamed at me to do. That's the power someone loses when they are faced with a rotten past, your dignity. You are a puppet, and they are the puppet masters.

We finished up with our dose of punishment, i.e., training and fell back on line as instructed. Most likely to finish this mess they had made of our things and to get squared away, I thought. I was wrong again. They began cruising up and down the squad bay saying some more shit about us not being good enough for the Corps and we should quit. This approach was soft and on the subtle side this time. They engaged in a few conversations with a few recruits to find out where they were from and such. That was a guise to get them to think about their families back home and make them miss their loved ones enough to give up and quit. I think they got two or three guys to quit in this way, I can't be sure, but I was glad I wasn't asked a thing at that time because it was a brilliant tactic on their part to discourage you. I may have fallen for it a little bit, but I sure wasn't going to say, "Yes, I give up, I want to quit." They better come up with a better plan when dealing with me. Which I'm sure they were planning something for all of us. It was yet to be seen though. They worked their magic charms of good guy, bad guy for a few more hours, just inquiring on simple matters of concern. I knew it was a trick the moment they began changing it up on us. They started asking about people who had criminal records and such, and it was our obligation to step forward, so we could be discharged. We would be court-martialed if we didn't speak now because they were going to find out about it anyways. I knew it was to see what you would do under interrogations and how simpleminded you were and how easy you might crack. Some do and some don't. I wasn't revealing shit about anything in my past to these assholes at all. I had already been told before leaving Boston to shut the fuck up and everything would be okay. So that's what I did.

After they snagged their couple of quitters, we were told to straighten up our mess and it better be done correctly. The quitters were brought into the office with all their shit in their bags and were escorted out the back door never to be seen again. I sort of felt bad for those guys in a way, but the truth was they wanted out of this right now. They were in way over their head and knew it. I was still here and didn't care what was done to me by them. My future was more important to me. That was good enough for now it seems because they let me be. I had this strange feeling they had already read my file by the way I was looked at by the three of them. As fucked up as this situation was for me, I didn't falter because I couldn't. So onward our barrage of insults came and went throughout the evening until suppertime. I can tell you we were allowed to eat, but we were only allowed to eat certain foods. No cake, no pie, no cookies, no red gelatin, only some nasty spaghetti mixed in with mystery meat and our jungle juice urine once again. Upon returning to the barracks, they had us strip and line up single file ass to nuts and marched us into the head for our showers. When we got inside the head, we were not allowed to do a thing except stay along the wall and briskly walk through about fifteen showers. No time to wash anything off of yourself one bit, just a quick hurry the fuck up and get moving. I honestly was left still half-covered with sand and now I had soap mixed into it all. I returned on line, and they told us to get into our green shorts and to put on a white T-shirt. There was a bit of a problem getting into bed though. We had to do it a certain way. We had to stand by the side of our racks and be ordered to get into bed quickly at the position of attention while lying down. This went on over and over until he got sick of telling us to get in and out of bed at least twenty damn times. We were next ordered to sound off our Marine Corps history we should have known by now from our handbooks. It went by swiftly, and I sort of half-followed and verbalized answers after everyone else did. I didn't know much about what we were supposed to know I guess. There was sort of a mixed few who actually did, and the drill instructor didn't get pissed, he just had us say the answers along with him. We would learn by practice. He then ordered lights out, and off he went to his office with the other two instructors in tow. I was so tired I fell right asleep I had made it through the first day and it was all good.

FIRST SQUAD LEADER

I had survived my first day without much of a challenge other than being forced to push myself beyond pain. It was the second day when things went wrong for me right from the rip. We had gotten up at zero dark thirty as per usual. Being woken up this early was killing me. My whole body ached. My muscles were sore, and the drill instructors didn't care one bit. It was business as usual to them. We were startled awake by all three of them banging trash cans up and down the center of the squad bay. I wasn't yanked out of my rack, but a few others had been and were thrown to the ground for not moving when they said to. I was a lucky guy this morning. We were told to go use the head, piss, and shave, brush your teeth and get back on line. I was in the toilet for less than two minutes trying to pinch a morning turd when all of a sudden our black drill instructor rushed into the bathroom and started yanking people off the toilets screaming we didn't ask to shit so get the fuck out now. I was able to grab a few wads of ass wrap on the way out wiping while being pushed from behind. It was totally uncalled-for on his part, but hey, this was his problem not mine. I was busy trying to wipe off my ass. *Great way to start the morning off,* I thought to myself, not caring he was screaming at me to get my ass moving. I hurriedly wiped, dropped, and grabbed another bunch from the next toilet paper roll and did the same all the way out leaving a trail of soiled toilet paper behind me. *What an asshole,* I thought to myself. I was able to semi-properly clean myself off, but a few others weren't so lucky. It was those guys who had it rough throughout the day I'm sure. Just knowing you haven't wiped up properly will irritate you and you will begin to start burning and itching. They definitely had to suffer because we definitely were not allowed to move around once we were on line at attention. I was fine with being told to get the fuck out of the bathroom, but I wasn't fine with the manner in which he did this bullshit. Oh well, this was just another thing, they wanted to be in control of us and to fuck with you some more.

For my reward of trying to wipe my ass off, I was ordered to get up on the pull-up bars and start doing them until he said stop. I did probably like forty or so until he told me to get the fuck back on line.

I'm standing back on line sweating within less than an hour of being awoken. Not to fun at all; never mind the itchy ass thing that's beginning to happen which I knew was going to. Never mind the fact I wanted to punch that asshole right in the face. Never mind it all. I was going to snap. Once again, I put my emotions in check and focused on what we were being told to do. We were ordered to make our racks and then we were to put on our go fasters. I hurried to the back of my rack and grabbed a dirty sand-covered T-shirt that I had in my laundry bag. I gave it a good shake to remove the sand and used it to clean my shit-filled ass. I had gotten most of it with the paper, but I was yanked off the bowl in midpinch, so I was forced out without getting the proper push time or clean up method I was accustomed to. Fuck it, I thought and snuck my shorts down and reached in and cleaned off with my dirty shirt properly. I wasn't seen doing this at all, and even if I was, I didn't care at the time. I was not going outside smelling like shit, nor was I going to be itchy all damn day. You overcome and adapt just like they teach you, I figured. I threw my now-shit-striped shirt back into the laundry bag and continue on with making my rack. I grabbed my go fasters, sneakers, and get back on line with one of my canteens as instructed. Like I said before, I really felt bad for them other guys on this day because I know they were subject to the same stuff that occurred in the head. I just had the chance to clean up well, and they didn't. Who cares for them anyways, everything was good to go for me and that was the main thing—self-preservation, baby. I keep telling myself this because the madness of this day was going to be a whole lot worse than the first day. I was beginning to feel a bit nervous about what was to come, but I was also not going to ruin my inner strength over a bad experience during a morning drop and plop. I resisted the urge to punch this guy, and that was a good thing in my mind.

We were ordered outside the barracks and to get into formation. Our drill instructors followed us out screaming and hollering the whole way to hurry the hell up about it too. It was nothing new to witness a few kicks in the ass and a few recruits being tossed to the ground, in fact it became commonplace during our training. Once we were formed up, we were marched off into the darkness toward the chow hall for some breakfast. Once again we were ushered in and screamed at to get out only being able to drink that urine-colored bug juice and a few scraps of toast. All of the rest of the food on my tray was dumped into the trash. What a total waste of time. I was going to be starved, it seemed. *So suck it up, Mello.* That was my usual thought or the motivational whisper I would tell myself when dumb things occurred during each day of training and there would be plenty to come. I think only one-quarter of our platoon was actually able to eat just a bit more than me, because they would sneak it by stuffing it into their mouths when the instructors weren't looking. As for me, I had one right behind me or alongside of me at every moment, so I was unable to sneak anything. All of us definitely didn't get anything into our now-tired wasted bodies for nourishment this morning. So outside we were again within five minutes of entering the chow hall. It was just plain old torture to be led to the food trough, allowed to smell, taste a small sample, and then throw out everything that looked good on our trays. It was a total mind fuck on us to deal with. Being poor as a child, it was nothing new for me to have to skip a meal or to go hungry, so I wasn't fazed by this display of power and control.

Our platoon was hurriedly marched over to the physical training field, and we were put through the usual paces. There was a lot of yelling and screaming from them and a lot of sweating and some tears from us during this morning's exercise program. The sun wasn't even anywhere near coming up on the horizon yet, and we were covered in sweat, sand, and mud. I was certain of two things, my body was very tired and my head hurt from dehydration. The mornings were the worst for me anyways, even before coming here, I had dragged ass each and every day just to get ready for school. This sort of training was going to make me or break me. If pushing yourself to the extreme was what they wanted, well then, that's what they are going to get from me. Come hell or high water, I was going to make it.

After our physical training was completed, we were marched back to our barracks and we were allowed to do the walk-through-shower session once again, nothing but the best for us in this modern-day Marine Corps. Once I semi-rinsed off. I was back near my rack toweling off and tossing my dirty clothes into my laundry bag. This was the moment of all moments up to this point in training that was going to define my position in this platoon. I just didn't know it yet. I was getting dressed, and all of a sudden from behind me our third-in-charge drill instructor appeared screaming at me to move my ass and get back on line. I hurriedly threw on my clothes rather haphazardly and grabbed my boots and ran over to this line on our side of the squad bay. I felt a kick hit me in the right ass cheek as I bent over to put on my boots. I went flying forward but stopped myself from smashing my face on the floor with my hands. This drill instructor was way out of line, but I blew it off and just stayed sitting while completing this boot process. I took my time to be sure they were tied correctly and to piss this guy off a little more. I was defiant instantly after he kicked me, and he knew it. He was screaming right in my face to get the fuck up and hurry up over and over. My inner temperature was on full boil by this point, so when I got up I deliberately jumped up and bumped into this asshole on my way by to get on line. While standing at attention facing straight ahead, he began flipping out on me more. He was screaming that I assaulted him and all kinds of crap. I thought to myself, *You really don't know what an assault is, you dumb black bastard.* Here's a purple-blue-gummed black guy screaming at me for bumping him all the while he initiated all this with the kick in the ass on me. He for sure saw my discontent, and this is why he reached up and began to choke me. I instantly knocked his hands away from my throat. That was a big no-no on my part, but hey, fuck him, I wasn't going to let him choke me on top of that kick in the ass. I was fed up with this bullshit, and it was ending today. As he reached up yelling again, I blocked his advancing hands to my throat and sort of pushed him back. He recoiled and looked rather stunned as fear swept into his face. I was sure of the fear in his face and eyes because he stood at a distance and with a rather shaky voice told me to get into the head and I better hurry up about it.

Once inside the head, he was right behind me rather closely. I spun around at attention and stood alone with this pissed-off drill instructor coming at me rather aggressively. All of the other recruit trainees were in the squad bay at attention on their painted line. So this was it, I was out of everyone's vision and he was going to attack. My mind raced in that instant. *Do I comply and let this man pummel me, or do I resist his attack?* I had a mere few seconds to decide because he reached out and began his choking move on me once again, only this time he was a bit more aggressive, so I grabbed his leading arm and spun it into an odd angle and flipped his feet out from under him. It was in that moment I was sure I would be kicked out of the Marines and sent off to the brig. So what the hell, I might as well kick this prick, so I returned the kick in the ass upon him and stepped on his hat in the process. He was screaming at the top of his lungs, but I couldn't hear a word of his bullshit. I was consumed with rage. I definitely didn't hear the senior drill instructor, nor did I hear the number 2 instructor rushing in to this guy's aid. I was tackled to the ground and pinned down by them both. It was typical of someone to start shit with me and end up on the losing end, and that's why when I was down I received another kick from this black instructor. It was a cheap shot, but it was typical. The senior drill instructor jumped off me and slammed the other guy against the wall and pinned him there screaming at him to maintain discipline. He calmed down instantly as did I. The senior drill instructor told me to get into his office right now. I was released from the pinning force on top of me and allowed to get on my feet. I hurriedly speed-walked into his office with all three instructors in tow.

Once inside this office. I was instructed to stand at attention in front of his desk. What happened next was totally surreal. My senior drill instructor sat in his chair and leaned forward to speak to me. He started to scream at the top of his lungs about how he was going to get on the phone and call the military police and have me arrested. Right in that moment, the other two instructors began screaming and hollering while banging shit off the walls.

They were absolutely destroying this office right before my eyes. What happened next is something I have never spoken about to anyone until now. My senior drill instructor beckoned me to lean forward so he could whisper in my ear. He told me that if I ever disobey an order again or strike an instructor again, he would make sure that not only would I be arrested and kicked out of the Marine Corps but I would also leave this barracks on a gurney. I wasn't impressed with that threat, but I could see he probably wasn't kidding about me getting beat up just by the tone in his voice so I stayed silent and just listened. He told me to go back out of his office and not say a damn thing about what had just occurred in this office to any of the other recruits in our platoon. He stood up and pulled my shirt ripping a few buttons off and made me look like I was in a fight. He next told me I was the first squad leader from this moment forward. One of the other instructors opened the door, and the senior drill instructor whispered in my ear, "Not one fucking word about this." I was pushed out of the office rather hard and went flying out stumbling to stay upright without falling on my face. My footing was lost, and I fell forward onto my stomach just like a piece of trash being tossed to the curb.

I got back on my feet in a flash and hurried back to my spot on line a bit stunned from what just occurred. Once back at my rack, I switched shirts and took my position and stood at attention. I was sure they were just screwing with my head and were calling the military police to have me escorted out in chains, but this never happened. Our senior drill instructor emerged from the office alone after what seemed to be five minutes, but it was a whole lot longer in my mind. He walked slowly and deliberately toward the center of the squad bay before he said a word. The whole platoon was watching me with a sort of blank frightened stare when I had gotten back on line and fixed my clothes just a few moments ago. They had continued this dumb scared expression on their faces when he walked by them. I was a bit puzzled by this also, but from this moment forward, I knew it was a game. I had just pissed this whole group of instructors off, and they used this opportunity to strike fear into the rest of our platoon. It was all a sham, but it worked. These guys around me were rattled to the core. I was in on their twisted psychological mind fuck, and it felt kind of cool, actually it was funny and a bit weird at the same time.

The senior drill instructor stopped and began telling us how when we break the rules, we will pay the price just as I did. In my mind I hadn't been touched in that office nor was I beaten at all, but to them it looked as if I was. So with that known by the instructors and me alone, it felt great when he told them I was the new first squad leader. It was something I had earned by just being steadfast with my decision not to allow someone to grasp me by the neck. It was also given to me because they wanted to keep a close eye on me and to push me a whole lot harder than the rest of these guys. I was in for the worst they had to offer. It was explained to the platoon that whenever someone fucked up, I would be included within their disciplinary action. So guess what, I was chosen to be first squad leader because I was the asshole who fought back and this was my reward. You have to believe me when I say this definitely sucked knowing this, but it would make me stronger and I was actually proud to hold the title of first squad leader. The pain and suffering I was going to endure was a minor detail in my mind because I was above the rest of these shit birds. Regardless how I became the first squad leader, I was the go-to guy when someone had a problem or a complaint. I also was in charge of fire watch detail, so it was me who came up with the list every night. I had a position to fuck with people also, and I was going to enjoy my new job. No longer would I be told by anyone other than my drill instructors what to do. I was going to be the guy screaming out orders passed down from them through me to the platoon. I also had the authority to pass out blanket parties to those recruits who were fucking up badly during training. If you're thinking this hazing stuff within the military doesn't exist, I definitely have a bridge to sell you and a prime piece of swampland for sale also, it does exist. Some people are against this form of training tactic, but let me assure you it is a vital part necessary within our ranks to keep people in line and to develop into a fighting unit together as one. These blanket parties are kept secret and unknown from the higher commanders to-be and also the instructors themselves. It is an unwritten rule among enlisted personnel not to speak of any such actions taken against another to motivate them or to tighten them up. This shit must be learned in boot camp. If you ask, I will deny that conversation under oath before God himself who spoke this to me and who handed this power over to me. So bottom line, don't fucking ask me, just join the military and find out for yourself what goes on. Just be sure you're on the other side of this blanket party. Be the deliverer, not the receiver. I have been both, and I recommend the latter.

I can honestly say without any hesitation whatsoever this new position of authority was an absolute blessing to have. Within the next couple of hours, I had been forced to run up and down the squad bay at least twenty times. I had also been told to get on the pull-up bars on four different occasions from other people screwing up or taking their sweet ass time doing something. I was being broken down for all to see by these insane instructors. This also was done on purpose because unbeknown to these screw-ups, I was taking inventory on who was getting fire watch or some other shitty task passed down. There were a few who would be dealt with after lights-out in the future. This wasn't a task done by me or done by the instructors. I would pass a name to someone, and that person selected would have to carry it out or the following night their name would be chosen for the receiving party. I left no choice in their minds but to carry out what was being asked of them. How and what was done wasn't my issue at all, there was no real instructions or rules to follow other than make sure this asshole starts paying the fuck attention. For the most part, everyone understood if you fucked up, there was going to be a price to pay from the rest of your platoon, so you were no longer an individual, you affected us all. There were the occasional black-and-blue marks, but nothing really horrible. A few people were tied up and smacked around in the shower room or their head was shoved into a toilet while a few guys took turns giving them a kick in the ass. I wasn't concerned with the tactics or the details, just as long as no visible marks were left on someone's face, so that meant no blasting someone in the face with anything and this included fists. I wasn't going to tolerate any of that. Fear was to be used as a tool to make someone start hustling, not to hurt them in such a way that they no longer could continue training due to some unfortunate training accident. Well, guess what, cheese dick? That's what it's called when someone is injured during training; it's called a training accident. Never ever is an instructor blamed or at fault, nor was it because your platoon gave you a blanket party. You shut your fucking mouth and sucked it up just like everyone else did, including me. If any outsider came within this platoon asking questions, nothing was to be spoken about how we train or deal with screw-ups. All knew the fear of lights-out, especially those who screwed up during the prior day of training.

Like I said before, my new position was a blessing. I held power over this platoon on a low level, but at least I held a title and I was given some sort of structure basis to follow. I no longer was confused about what was going on from day to day because I became focused within my new job duties. No matter what went on from this day forward, I can tell my family they have a son, brother, uncle, or a cousin who became a first squad leader within the Marine Corps during boot camp. There have been many first squad leaders within the Marines, but ask any one of them and they will tell you they loved and hated their job equally, but it was a position of honor and everyone around you knew it. I mean everyone, even other platoons passing by, knew it wasn't the idiot holding the stick out front who held sway, it was the first squad leader. The front row of any platoon marching by was the first, second, third, and fourth squad leaders of said platoon behind them. The idiot with the stick was the guide, and ours was a definite meathead. The order of rank within these four individuals is obvious of its numerical order dumbass. Just being picked first squad leader was a huge fucking achievement on my part considering my past. I was feeling very proud this day, and nothing was going to take it away from me, ever.

DELUSIONS

I have decided to stop telling a story about each and every day in detail during this book and just put in certain sections, which were either funny or traumatic to others or me. So with that said, read on because struggling through this book is becoming painful and old to me. Looking back into one's past is a daunting task, almost overwhelming. I am sick of hen pecking out words on this keyboard. My mind works very quickly and my fingers never keep up. I should have narrated this dumbass story for people to hear it instead of reading it. Well, never mind this paragraph of total resistance. Today, for me, in reality, and not back in my fantasy past's brainwaves, I am about to begin another experimental HIV drug. I am a bit nervous about the side effects. The last regimen brought on lucid vivid dreams filled with nightmares and during-the-day hallucinations. Perhaps that's the key to time travel within my mind or anyone else's for that matter. You have to be whacked out on pills to regress into your past and unlock some weird door or open some spooky memory stuck in a microscopic misfire of your brain's natural rhythmic electrical impulse. Well, for me at this point in life, I would drink Drano just to kill a virus that was planted in my mind by the government. So yes, I do take their poison each day and night for a small chance it may work, and I don't wither away to a walking stick, all bones showing looking like a holocaust victim. That's just not the way I want to look or feel at all. I would definitely open the doors to the oven in Auschwitz myself and climb in fully willing to cook.

As you can see, the delusional thought flows out of me like a hot river of lava spewing out of a volcano killing the villagers beneath during an eruption. If my brain was the volcano and my good brain cells were the people in a village living beneath its summit, and my medicine became a toxic mixture of adrenaline, dopamine, and acid and it erupted and flowed, it would be this toxic shit mixture that would become the lava. My brain cells don't stand a chance now, do they? I have total split personalities also, that is why I am able to speak to you from outside this storyline. Oh yes, be aware the government can fry your brain with something simply added to your water supply. Possibly even cook your mind from some unseen satellite floating around the earth's atmosphere in space. One flick of a switch while you are in the open outside and presto, instant walking zombie drone. My advice to you is this, buy some aluminum foil and wrap your head with it to disrupt their gamma rays or particle beams directed at your melon. This will give you some protection from them reading your thoughts, and they also will lose track of you because their signal from that tracking device they call fillings inside your teeth will be temporarily disrupted. Trust me, I know it to be true, go get a piece of foil and put it into your mouth right now. Do you feel that weird, shocking feeling in your mouth? That's your proof something is going on. Do like I did, yank them bastards out if you can handle the pain! I pulled out at least five teeth including a molar or two within some freaky drugged-out state while freebasing crack for three weeks straight. This process was done just to stop my overwhelmed mind from snapping, which could cause a stroke or some shit. It was preventive maintenance I guess. But either way, some doctors may say it was the drugs, but I still believe it was the medicine that dropped me into a clinical depression with nightmares and daily hallucinations of snakes on the ground beneath my feet or ants crawling on me or better yet still flashes of some sadistic shit planted in my mind from some obscure television show I had viewed. The government controls it all. That also means you better go smash that television also, and while you're at it, smash your computer, rip that phone jack out of your wall, cut all power from the pole, and definitely smash that all-seeing eye on your cable box. It's a way for them to watch you and to listen to your words spoken aloud. Don't think for one second that the huge-ass satellite dishes pointed skyward are for listening and searching the heavens for alien life-forms, that's all bullshit. They are directed toward the outer space satellites, which in turn point straight down at you. Start tunneling under your house and hide from them deadly beams. It is definitely not the bullshit they feed us in the news about it or the stories we read about in the paper, trust me.

Oh shit I'm sorry it was only a delusional trip of mine. Hopefully you haven't preformed some backyard dentistry on yourself over this. I also hope you haven't smashed up your house while wearing a bandana made of aluminum foil wrapped around your head. Well actually, I kind of hope you are wreaking a little havoc, you boring lump of zombie shit. I want you to just feel for one nanosecond of what I felt during that time of my life. So suck it the fuck up and follow my instructions. I am the puppet master now. I hold the damn strings. Go smash all your shit. Sell everything you own for the almighty crack rock, and smoke up until you sizzle that fucking government-planted, brainwashed cell formation in your psyche. I dare you to live like a free person for just one moment of your pathetic life.

I need to ease up and calm down on you; I must remember the audience who reads this hasn't been gifted with the insight granted to me by the gods of Zercowa! Those are the tiny blue people who live just out of your vision. Every once in a while you will catch them when the wind blows. It happens fast, so be very still and just watch, they hide behind the leaves on the ground that are rustled during a stiff breeze. I have seen these little blue bastards. They sneak up on you and whisper in your ear to go smoke crack to kill the demons and voices in your head. I have been dealing with this since I was thirteen years old. Trust me, they are real and they are out there.

Or maybe it's the visions of killing people as if it were a sport that has me so mind twisted. It's shown over and over again on the fucking news, and within our televisions, it has become almost laughable like its entertainment. That sort of thought process in me drives the psychiatrists wild. They presume to think they can learn from someone like me who has firsthand knowledge of the crazy mind-melting details. It has become a game to me already watching them foam at the bit prescribing me heavy doses of God knows what sort of mad scientists brew called medicine just to see what will happen to me or what I will share with them. Fuck them idiots also. Round them happy hippie new wave sandal-wearing motherfuckers up and give them a healthy dose of electrical shock therapy for once in our pathetic lives. Have we not seen enough of their psychological mind trip within our media to scare us into the belief that we have enemies trying to kill us? They are the enemy. We will march naked, toothless, with foil wrapped around our heads across their fluorescent green lawns. We will snatch them from their homes under the cover of darkness. So grab a torch and a weapon and follow me, soldiers of Zercowa, we will smash down their doors and round them up. We will crush their skulls with makeshift weapons made from a stone tied to a stick. We will burn their bodies in a pile for all to see and witness. The fear shall be struck swiftly into the infidel's heart and break their will. That word infidel *comes from them whacked-out religious fanatics within the Muslim groups. You may have heard this before actually. Guess what, look back to when you heard it. It was most likely some damn television show or some other government-controlled newsletter. I rest my case on all the skeptics who say I'm nuts. As for the fanatics, well, grab that C-4 explosive belt and walk into a crowded market and scream "God is great" and pull the pin or push that button, you weak-minded sorry sack of shit. Do you see the virgins yet? All I see is entertainment on my television screen. Save your whining about how your prophet Mohammad is God's messenger. You're a pawn on a chessboard being sacrificed by a government who hates your very existence. Better yet, grab your balls and just rip them off and stuff them into your ears. The voices will stop in your mind. You are not a martyr; you are another fool programmed by the government to be exterminated. Call the Columbians direct for the pure shit when you get to that point in life, asshole. Fill your hookah with a giant monster mud-crack hit the size of a gumball, put that on top of some cigar ashes in the bowl and just toke up. Pass it around to your twisted Imam or spiritual advisor. Release your tortured soul and twisted fucking mind and come back to reality. Allah Akbar motherfucker!*

You know when I think about all my past life which you are reading at this moment, I can honestly say I would never dream of strapping a shitload of explosives to myself and blowing the snot out of a grocery store or some shit because they have the wrong-colored plastic bags in the produce isle. This statement just about sums up the whole religious war and Jihad bullshit going on within them radical Muslim groups within my opinion. It's all lies, and it means nothing, human life is a miracle granted by God, so cherish it fuck stains. I don't give a holy monkey turd which religion you follow, God says let there be love among his people in all faiths, also from the immortal words of your friend and mine, Rodney King, "Can't we all just get along?"

A fellow crack-smoking fool just like myself I must add. The only difference was he got paid for his ass whooping from the cops, I got to join the Marine Corps. Big difference between crackheads sometimes. He was a cracked-out, drunken, combative jackass just like I'm sure most people are when they indulge in the extra pleasures who got his ass cracked silly by them pigs on film. Shit, you know what? If I would've staged the whole thing and had a film crew with me when I was pummeled, well shit, home boy, I would be one rich bastard also. But you know what? I don't really care that much about money or crying wolf for money when it comes my turn to get beaten up. I have had my share of wins and losses, but who really counts when every day of my natural pathetic life is filled with, and only consists of, not grabbing that Lizzy Borden axe and burying it to the handle into the boss's chest, or maybe the wife's, or maybe even that asshole next-door neighbor's chest who let his scrounge dog into my yard to take a healthy dump and wiz on my precious lawn. How dare they believe I have lost my inner hatred toward them all? If you are keeping with me thus far, reader, I give you props because you're thinking the same thing I am. Fuck it, grab the gasoline from the garage, get some nails with a hammer, march to that prick's house, and nail all the doors and windows shut then dump gas under the front door and light it. Fuck them all, and that little dog too. Holy Christ! I got a headache! Ahhh!

If only I could harness the power of this brain juice that drives me to come up with this shit, I would certainly be a rich man. Does money bring happiness? You bet your sweet ass, it does. I would much rather do lines or as I call them rails of cocaine with a hundred-dollar bill rather than a lousy buck. So tell your damn friends to buy this shitty book, don't let them cheap bastards borrow yours. Tell them Uncle G needs the money, so help a poor white trash, tattoo-covered, disease-infected crack junkie and a veteran who has seen the light become rich before he dies. I can promise you one thing, when I burn in the furnace upon my death, you will be able to get high from the smoke.

I have definitely been in the spirit world these past few days and have crossed over several times in the past. Actually, you know what? I will save you the details for now and continue on with the story. My mind just melts and seamlessly weaves topics on top of one another without any real understanding of it on my end when I begin ranting. It becomes normal talk if I let it consume me. So I will stop. Doing that sort of stuff has landed me in the psych ward before. I will share some other weird shit as we go on. Hopefully you as the reader don't mind. Actually you are probably thinking this guy needs a damn straightjacket and a round room with cushioned walls, but believe me, I am quite sane. It's all of you who have been brainwashed to think everything is normal.

SWIM QUALIFICATIONS

This was a close-call week during training for a few others and me. So without any further brain-fart episodes, I give you over to the storyteller once again.

I shall tell you about the day we were formed up on an early morning in full gear with our rifles, boots, utility belts, and backpacks filled with just about fifty or so pounds of gear on our backs. This process of putting our gear into the backpacks was a crucial step if we were going to stay afloat within the next phase of training. This training week included the unlucky possibility of drowning. For me, I wasn't concerned with any of the water training at all. I grew up near the ocean and learned to swim at a very young age. I was four years old I think. I was taught at Silver Shell beach in Marion, Massachusetts. That is where I learned to blow bubbles into the saltwater and then was taught to float and eventually I was able to swim. Since then, water has never been an issue at all to me. A whole lot of others around me barely knew what the ocean looked like or even what it tasted like. They had only seen it in pictures. As for them, going swimming on a hot day was very unlikely.

A few guys told me the closest they came to swimming was a bath or playing in the street during a hot summer day when the fire department purged its water lines through the hydrants. I called that Tar Beach myself. Everyone who heard me say that laughed, so it was definitely true. I could only imagine the cesspool cities they came from on this planet. You grow up seeing nothing but concrete and tar within some housing projects within a nasty crime-infested slaughterhouse neighborhood that's barely safe to travel through during the day. More drugs, prostitutes, gangs, stabbings, gunshots, murders, drive-by's, stick-ups, cop bashings, dealers, stealers, liquor stores, killers, rapists, and all sorts of shit I could most likely continue listing until I passed out or ran out of space within my computer memory chip about how shady your living arrangements were. Surviving up till now was a bloody miracle all in itself. What a fucking cut across the guts with a dull knife that must've been like for you knowing you had to be cooled off during the ninety-degree weather with a fucking rusty water-spewing hydrant to cool off. Even with life being at that level of danger growing up in your barrio, hood, ghetto, or others call them neighborhoods and you survived and became very tough and considered yourself gangster, or even a roughneck, yet you never learned how to swim and became petrified by the mere thoughts of lakes, rivers, oceans, streams, pools, and quite possibly deep puddles. As a matter of fact, you most likely have had nightmares concerning the whole drowning scenario. I would be sure to sing out that reply very often after lights-out to shit birds in this platoon who tried acting like they were gangster ghetto fabulous tough. In my eyes, these guys were doomed, I thought to myself while lining my backpack with a big black trash bag. Our packs needed to be watertight inside or the clothes inside would become like rocks once they soaked through with water. I cinched it up as instructed and tossed it on my back as did everyone else. I also smiled as I relished in the thought of the gangster ghetto boys who most likely fucked up their backpacks and then they would sink.

We were then formed up outside and marched to a different part of the base for this evolution of training. I was expecting to be marched toward the ocean, but I was wrong in my first guess on where we would eventually be tossed into the water to semi-drown. Nope, this was going to be a controlled environment where they could keep a close eye on us. We headed the opposite direction of the ocean all together. We arrived to this huge outside swimming pool after several miles of marching with these heavy packs on our backs. After that uplifting sweaty march, going for a nice cool dip in the pool after struggling in the heat sounded just fine to me. Looking toward our destination, I had noticed there were platforms at different heights. There were recruits from another platoon who were jumping off of them into the water with all this gear on. We were ordered to stand at attention facing toward the pool and a swim instructor took over the talking from our drill instructor. I don't remember this guy's name, but he seemed like a highly motivated individual. He explained all sorts of shit, most of it was to scare you, but I knew this from prior experience. The past episode with becoming the first squad leader was a definite indication. I was beginning to see how fear was clearly used as a weapon within this training. But the truth is, it's about breaking your fear and crashing down any resistance or hesitation you may have inside you to complete the mission or order given to you. Knowing this will definitely help when it becomes your turn to drop off that ten-meter high platform, I figured.

After this swim instructor was finished, we were told to leave our gear stacked neatly in a platoon formation where we were standing. Everything was left at our feet. I was left wearing just my basic camouflage uniform and my jungle boots. The whole platoon was ordered to the edge of the far end of this Olympic-sized pool. We were away from the platforms on the opposite end. We were told to form up five across separated at double arm's length to jump into the water. It was very organized with a strict concern for safety. Each row was told to drop into the water in turn and swim to the other end of the pool. This task was very simple for me to complete once I was accustomed to swimming with these lead weights called boots on my feet. The swim instructors were in the pool or around the edge of it with a floatation device in hand at the ready if you were one of them unfortunate bastards who couldn't swim, and we had a lot of them. Several recruits were so petrified of water they began to shake and cry when it was their turn to just drop into the water from the edge. I watched this one kid cry and shake so much he even pissed himself. Our drill instructors were bullshit about people in our platoon making such a big damn deal out of getting into the water. These pricks just began walking back and forth behind the next five in line and pushed them in. There would be no more freezing up at all. Fuck you, get the fuck in the water, fucking drown you piece of shit. I watched this display from the other end of the pool, and it was comical to say the least. Several of them no-swimming fools dropped in and just began panicking right when they hit the water. Yelling and thrashing around like wild animals only to be thrown a red floatation device and yanked out of the water by a swim instructor. Luckily they were there to fetch them a line because some of these fools would've surely gone to the bottom.

One of our drill instructors was over by this guy with the rope just waiting for them to be pulled to safety. He would scream and holler for them to do jumping jacks, push-ups and to run in place for at least five minutes each nonstop. The pressure was on for people not to panic in the pool, but it made no difference. If I was to guess, the weeding process was full-on to find the poor bastards who couldn't swim or the ones who panicked right now. No fucking waiting at all they needed to know. I watched guys in my platoon who acted tough and tried being Billy Bad Asses during training up to this point fold into little schoolgirls. A few guys shocked me, but I sort of knew they were pussy made all along just by the way they talked and strutted around thinking they were roughnecks. Once again the playing field looks a little less appealing to a few of them, and it makes me laugh every time I see another person panic or just absolutely piss themselves. I knew they were pissing themselves because they hadn't been in the water yet and they were soaked halfway down to their knees on both legs. It was pretty foul if you think about it because it mixes right into the water once they take their panic piss-soaked plunge. This pool is most likely one-quarter filled with piss and I was swimming in it. That's just fucking great, I think to myself while watching this show unfold before my eyes. Good thing the chlorine in the pool was very high because it burned my eyes a little bit when I opened them underwater when it was my turn to jump in. Maybe that would kill off some of the bacteria before I'd swallow some. You and I both know if you're in a pool you're bound to get some in your mouth. Never mind the few extra gulps these guys were taking during their fits of sheer fright like thrash swimming. Thank Christ for the chlorine. In my mind that's exactly what I was thinking. That's for damn sure.

My joy of swimming was rapidly being removed from within my very soul after this display of humiliation was set before me. Once again I have thoughts of being a child growing up and remembering my older brothers half-drowning me in a pool.

They would call it toughening me up or just call it breaking my fear. Whichever the case, it wasn't uncommon to be held under by them until you panicked to go for the surface for that sweet, cool savior called oxygen just several feet above. They were crafty bastards though; upon releasing their grasp and while you broke for the surface, they would stop you just short. Your lungs are sure to be set ablaze from the burning, but you have to take air. In goes a few gulps, and they force you to the surface to choke and gag thinking you could have drowned. All the while it's all laughter and comments of how much of a pussy you were for panicking in the first place. I would have to thank them when I'd get back home for that lesson which helped me on day 1 of our swim qualification training. Funny how something traumatic in your youth can help you out in this situation and carry you through without any major problems. Maybe if some of these guys around me should've been raised at my house, then this sort of thing wouldn't have happened. So if you're someone who is thinking of joining the Marine Corps, take my advice go to learn how to swim and break your fear of drowning also. That is my only advice for you on this matter. Toughen the hell up and go down to Paris Island, and I am sure some sort of cloned instructors just like the ones we had will dish out the same crappy treatment upon you.

So with our initial plunge into the pool out of the way and all them nonswimming types shuffled off to a different section of the pool, we learned a new trick. We learned how to stay afloat by treading water wearing all your gear minus the backpack of course. These pricks would never allow you to just hang out on any kind of flotation device whatsoever. "Fuck you, Recruit! Get your ass in the pool and start fucking swimming or drowning, you lousy piece of shit." The famous words of our esteemed leaders always were at the ready for us to find encouragement to perform our task. Was it encouragement or their way of saying, "Get in the pool, we need to know how much you can handle"? To assess what we need to train you in, also for your ass to survive within that big blue sea. There are always a bunch of past scenarios to use as an example within these moments, and we got one from one of the safety instructors. He told us about being a rescue swimmer for an injured fellow Marine. Would we not want to try and save our friend who is badly wounded and is unable to swim for safety on his own power? The answer is, yes, sir, loudly and in unison with the rest of the guys in our platoon. So with that said, he explains how to properly move your arms and feet within the water to maximize lift and increase our buoyancy. My technique was very similar to what he was explaining to us. All I needed to add in was the cupping of my hand slightly while doing a modified breast stroke out in front of me pulling the water toward me and then downward. Automatically creating lift using this hand technique and then adding in the long stroking kicks with your legs as if you were trying to pace out a full yard really works well. The relaxing and staying calm part was entirely within the individual's hands at this time. As for me, I had absolutely no problem at all other than fatigue setting in during the ten-minute opportunity to be one of the first in the pool. You guessed it once again, I'm out front with a few other recruit squad leaders being the guinea pigs for others to learn by example. Water was never my phobia at all, so why not be first in line? I was definitely thinking about what this swim instructor said if you were wounded and couldn't swim on your own, you would need someone there to help you to safety. You bet your sweet ass, I was in that water putting on a performance so these block heads could get a clue and possibly save mine. Wouldn't that just be great, survive some horrible helicopter crash only to drown because you were unconscious and the meathead with you can't swim to save his own worthless hide, never mind yours. So there is a good reason for you to step forward and jump right into the pool and save yourself. I really didn't need a reason at all, but that one would do for me.

One of the basic steps was completed finally. It had taken us most of the morning to weed out all the nonswimmers from the swimmers from within our platoon and then getting them up to speed with the rest of us. As time went by during the day, mostly I was standing along the edge of the pool dripping wet. Good thing its hot outside, I thought to myself while watching people tread water or panic and cry for help then beg for the safety ring to be thrown to them. I was actually not too fond of them select few. I would much rather see a guy desperately panic with max effort and sink to the bottom than some whining little girl squealing for a ring. Believe me when I tell you this, there are very timid individuals within the Marine Corps during recruit training, it's very comical. Our next order of business was to be ordered back to where our packs were for some chow. There would be no chow hall visit from us today. It was brown bag lunch for us. This was fine with me 100 percent. Now all I have to do is go sit on my fat ass and eat, no marching around the damn base like usual. We actually got some decent stuff this afternoon, an apple and a ham sandwich. Not a bad meal in my mind. Maybe a few others complained, but I sure as hell didn't. Every single bit of that apple was eaten, including the whole core of it, seeds too. I wasn't wasting one morsel. I needed the little bit of nutrients they had inside them if I was going to survive this week's worth of aquatic adventures. I was happy for the break also even though it was very brief. We were back on our feet within minutes. I wolfed all of my food down in less than three minutes and was told to drink a canteen of water to wash it down. Everyone did the same. Regardless if a handful of some these guys were forced or not, we had to eat and drink it all. I wasn't surprised to see two recruits getting yelled at and also told to do push-ups during lunch either. I was just glad I wasn't the sorry select few ordered to eat the brown paper bag because they crumbled it up next to themselves. That wasn't supposed to be, we were told to eat, not crumble the bag. In fact we were told to fold the thing neatly to our sides after we consumed our meal. Yep! It stays very anal at all times during training so you better stay alert and not find yourself with three very irritated drill instructors on your ass. So I paid attention to the details, dumbasses. It was beyond me how some of these idiots even made it through grammar school never mind achieving a high school diploma or that less than popular equivalent, the GED. Now there's a piece of wasted paper if I've ever thought about. Shit paper gets more done these days. I already had the real deal high school diploma, maybe that's why I was in charge of these boneheads. I call them boneheads because I thought everything was cool because I was just about to hand my bag over to be collected when good old number 3 drill instructor reminded the senior drill instructor how if anyone fucks up I would get equal put upon me. So guess what? That brown bag went down rather dry, and the jumping jacks and push-ups were very tiresome. Once again I took mental note of these clowns to be dealt with after lights-out and rejoined our platoon at the water's edge for more training. I was thinking to myself why the hell I agreed to this shit anyways during the whole episode, but it was mostly anger during a time of complete fucking with me, by them pricks in charge, which carries me through it each and every time. So fuck you from me, which was all I could think while chewing and swallowing some disgusting brown bag which originally came into my possession from someone else's dirty ass-picking fingers. I would try not to think about that guy who had to pack them or maybe even the guy who drove them over here. That is just too much thinking about which one of these guys who touched it actually took the liberty to spit or piss on them prior to its arrival.

Back at the pool feeling totally pissed off, I listened to the swim instructor show us our next task within the water. Not wanting to miss anything important, I listened intently. He was going over how we will be tested on water survival. This would consist of several different aspects of our training throughout the week. Everything was a test, and you needed to qualify to move on to the next phase of training in boot camp. Water survival was just part of the deal if you were going to become a Marine. Nothing really that difficult for me though or you if you learn to tread water, swim a few hundred feet, jump off a tower into a pool, with and without gear. Sounds simple, doesn't it? Come on down and give it a try, city boys. I would love to see how well you handle all the stress from these asshole instructors hell-bent on watching you suffer.

As the swim instructor was going over all these details, I noticed that our drill instructors had vanished. They were no longer breathing down our necks or giving us that weird piercing stare from just off in the distance waiting to pounce on you. It was a relief to me in knowing this, so I began to relax a bit because everything this swim instructor was going over must have been important enough for us not to be harassed or disturbed while we were being programmed. Did I say *programmed*? What I meant was being instructed. Our basic swim qualifications were a vital part of our training if we were to survive in combat. I had watched some of the World War II documentaries about soldiers who never even made it to the beach during an invasion due to their lack of swimming capabilities. I for one didn't want this to happen to me at all and the powers that be learned from the past I guess. We were put here to learn without any interruptions whatsoever by our drill instructors from this moment until the end of the day. Most of it was different ways to stay afloat and to tread water. The swimming aspect with our packs would come tomorrow morning. We were dismissed and told to gather up within formation outside of the pool area next to our things and to await our drill instructors' return.

As I was standing at attention next to my gear, I could feel the tiredness creeping into my body from today's activities. The water training had zapped the strength right out of my body. Now within the heat of this direct sunlight, it only compounded the issue. I stood at attention sort of half-nodding off into sleep and trying to stay a hold of reality. My mind drifted several times into the beginning stages of realm sleep. I would be unaware of my surroundings for several minutes but conscious of my ever-slowing breaths and slowing heart rate. I would feel very warm and drift off to sleep even while standing at attention. Several times I caught myself and looked around sort of in a panic state. I was truly expecting upon opening my eyes that there would be a drill instructor positioned right in front of me just waiting to scream at me. Each time I nodded and snapped awake, it was the same vision just before opening my eyes. This was a never-ending nightmare. I decided to quickly step forward out of my rank and stretch my aching body. As soon as I began, sure enough a drill instructor appeared from thin air, he wasn't one of ours, and half-screamed at me and the platoon to do exactly what I had been doing. I guess I would slip by without getting my ass handed to me for not remaining in my place. Everyone began to stretch their arms and legs out together for a few minutes while we were waiting. It wasn't very long after that our drill instructors were back in force screaming and hollering at us to grab our shit and get back into a formation at the position of attention. I didn't know where they disappeared too and really didn't care because it was a break from their onslaught of anal behavior even if for only a few hours, and I definitely accepted their gift with gratitude. As for the rest of the jokers in my platoon, they also agreed with my assumptions 100 percent because they let out an audible whine of complaint when told to get the hell back at attention with all our gear in tow. Our drill instructors weren't deaf, and it would bite us in the ass once we were away from prying eyes. This was a mistake that would not be made again that I am certain of. We were marched pretty fast back to our barracks and told to get inside quickly; at the double quick was the command.

Once we arrived inside them barracks, our drill instructors were right back to their no-bullshit attitudes about every detail within every instruction. This was certainly a way to get them pissed off further because someone always screws the pooch and fucks something up during their scrutinizing nitpicking cycles called training. We didn't last long inside the barracks at all, nope, we were ordered back outside several times this afternoon to the almighty sandpit. This went on for at the very least eight times up and down them treacherous stairs followed by an ass kicking within the grips of the searing sun, sweat, and sand exercises. This was all a blur actually, I had gotten so used to hearing the drill instructors screaming at us that we fucked up it became just a background noise as I focused on the jumping, pushing, running, and complete exhaustion overcoming my whole body. These guys definitely do not slack off one minute for anybody. Their policy is, fuck you quit. After countless hours of nonstop hustling around and eating chow, it was bedtime again. I was handed a sheet of paper by my drill instructor which showed me the outline of what our swim requirements would be according to Marine Corps standards. I don't know why he only handed this to me, but I was told to read it tonight and give it back in the morning prior to lights-on. This is what it said,

Combat Water Survival/Qualification Standards and Test Procedures

The following qualification standards and test procedures are applicable and will be accomplished while wearing full combat gear unless otherwise stated. Full combat gear will consist of boots, utilities, helmet, flak jacket, H-harness, cartridge belt, two magazine to Marine Corps combat water survival training. All testing procedures pouches, two full canteens with covers, rubber rifle, and a standard 40-pound pack, with frame, which has been properly waterproofed. Gas mask, first-aid kit, magazines, floor mats, and sleeping bags will not be used during testing or training.

Combat Water Survival, Third Class (CWS3)

To qualify Marines as CWS3 involves teaching and testing. Emphasis is on personal survival under combat situations and while on maneuvers. Teaching occurs throughout instruction/evaluation.

Enter shallow water (minimum 1 m) with weapon and wearing full combat gear.

Walk 20 meters in shallow water (minimum 1 m waist deep) with weapon at port arms and wearing full combat gear.

Walk 40 meters in chest-deep water wearing full gear and weapon (weapon slung around neck) using a modified breaststroke arm movement and modified combat stroke leg movement (bicycle stroke).

Travel for 40 meters in deep water (over the head) with full gear and weapon.

Enter water from height of 5 feet using the modified abandon ship technique, into deep water with full gear and weapon (weapon inverted at sling arms), travel 10 meters, remove pack, and travel 15 meters with pack and weapon.

Jump from minimum height of 8 feet (maximum of 15 feet) using the abandon ship technique wearing utilities and boots only and travel 25 meters using either a beginner swimming stroke (on front or back) or demonstrating a basic knowledge of any survival stroke or combination thereof.

Combat Water Survival, Second Class (CWS2)

Develop skill level to be able to assist a wounded Marine to safety as in a river crossing. Marine must have completed CWS3.

Uniform will be full combat gear and contents of pack will be waterproofed.

With full combat gear minus pack, swim 50 meters in deep water, with weapon slung across back (muzzle down).

Wearing full combat gear, perform 25 meter collar-tow on passive "victim" similarly dressed, simultaneously towing two packs and two *weapons (secured to packs). Packs may be used for floatation devices for "victim."*

Combat Water Survival, First class (CWS1)

Demonstrate ability to rescue yourself, assist a victim/distressed swimmer to safety, and survive under adverse situations. Marine must have completed CWS2 qualifications. Steps will be executed in sequence wearing only the utility uniform. Uniform will be utilities only (no boots).

Survival strokes: Properly demonstrate the following:

25 meters breaststroke
25 meters sidestroke
25 meters elementary backstroke

Rescues: Dry land drill, water demonstration, and student practice time of all three rescues. Students must properly demonstrate each rescue for qualification, utilizing ease-in entry technique with victim 5 meters away. Victims are passive during carry or tow.
Front head hold escape, front surface approach, wrist tow for 25 meters.
Rear head hold escape, rear approach, double armpit tow, cross-chest carry for 25 meters.
Double wrist grip escape, swimming assist to the front.
Swim 250 meters using one or a combination of survival strokes.

Water Survival Qualified (WSQ)

Successful completion of CWS1 and the following procedures are prerequisites for WSQ.

Splash Recover Technique. Swim underwater 10 meters, on the surface 40 meters in simulated burning oil spill situation. Uniform will be utilities and boots.

Abandon ship technique, enter water from a height greater than 8 feet but less than 15 feet.

Without surfacing, swim 10 meters.
Using splash technique, go to surface.
Remain on surface, use modified breaststroke splashing technique, and swim 40 meters.
Enter water full combat gear from a minimum height of 8 feet (max 15 feet), using abandon ship technique (weapon inverted at sling arms).
Remove pack, assume a reconnaissance position utilizing the pack, traverse 25 meters simulating sighting in and engaging enemy on either flank.

Tread water or survival float in deep water with utilities and boots for 30 minutes without artificial floatation. Boots will be removed after 5 min. and retained. Five min. prior to completion of the 30 min. float, and without exiting from the water, replace the boots and swim 500 meters using one or a combination of survival strokes.
Trouser inflation/back floats for 1 min.

*The water safety qualifications you just read were quoted from Military.com. A fellow Marine posted it on a thread. They can be found in the Marine Corps training manual also. I say this because some jackass will accuse me of plagiarism or something along those lines if I don't make this notation.

I read these requirements after we were in our racks and the lights went out as instructed. As you can see, the Marine Corps is not fucking around when it comes to its swim qualifications. I already knew I could complete each and every task on the list even prior to seeing it. As I said before, I am a frog in the water. I wasn't sure if my drill instructor gave that to me to scare me or to just show me what was expected if I planned on furthering my career. All I knew was it wasn't a scare tactic to me at all. I felt as if he considered me gung ho, hard-charging, devil dog quality I guess. Either way, it's better to know. Maybe everyone else already knew this information and my crackhead dumbass was so oblivious he felt sympathetic tonight. Yeah right! He isn't that nice. As I would later discover, the very first requirement was all an individual needed to pass and become a Marine. Truth is for some it's a daunting task to achieve. For me I wanted the whole goddamn show. I rested my head into my pillow and tucked the paper underneath it after reading it and envisioning the whole swimming scenario as if I had already mastered each task that lay ahead of me.

I fell asleep quickly and didn't dream at all. I woke up to the sound of fire watch banging on the instructor's steel door three times yelling out ten minutes to lights-on, aye, aye, sir. He was to repeat this process every minute until he flicked on the switch for the lights. Consider this your chance to get up and get your rack made and to put on your damn uniform. Oh and by the way, new fish, try not to wear the wrong outfit, for this will cause you plenty of pain, trust me. Our snooze button was a recruit smashing a steel door called a hatch, but it certainly was effective. We had been warned prior to this week of swim training that we better start getting the fuck up when our fire watch began his countdown. I was most definitely up and in the head, each time taking a quick poop prior to the day's training. One thing I knew from experience was to never have to take a dump at the wrong time. I completed my morning tasks and was on line waiting with several others even before the fire watch reached three minutes to lights-on. I handed the swim qualifications sheet back to my drill instructor on my way by him prior to entering the head. He liked to poke his head out and scream at someone to hurry the hell up every so often, so I just got lucky to catch him. You move quickly when you know it's the difference between going to the chow hall or its visiting the sandpit prior to breakfast, so it was luck to hand this off without having to bang on his door to request permission to enter. Doing that dumb procedure could waste several precious minutes while getting ready. As always, several jackasses within our platoon couldn't seem to get their act together and we visited the sandpit each morning without fail. I also got to visit the pull-up bar until they were ready. I kept those idiots on fire watch every night actually. Maybe they would find a way to get motivated and actually enjoy a full night's rest, until then, fuck 'em.

This entire evolution of training is a test of inner strength for me, and it would prove to be pretty tiresome. I also knew I was getting stronger each and every time I visited the pull-up bar or the sandpit regardless of the pain and suffering I had to endure. So when the last day of swim qualification training was upon us,

I was pretty beat-up. I was able to complete each and every task up to combat water survival, first class (CWS1). I had completed this without an issue at all. I totally enjoyed watching others fail miserably at their attempts to jump off the fifteen-foot platform with full gear on. They would jump in and just sink to the bottom without any attempt to reach the surface, straight panic mode was all they could muster before an instructor dove down to retrieve them. A few times we were ordered to face away from the pool because someone had blacked out while underwater and needed to be revived, but truthfully it wasn't very serious at all. A couple of quick breaths in their mouth and a few pumps on their guts and they were right as rain after puking out the water from their lungs and coughing like crazy.

I was offered the next level of training Water Survival Qualified (WSQ) during the next day with a handful of others, plus we were there with several failures that needed to be retested on the basics just to stay in the Marine Corps. This was a onetime offer to be qualified during our boot camp which was awesome because I definitely had that in myself also. They had made it clear this wasn't going to be available anymore to recruits in boot camp training if we didn't accept. It was a total shock to hear that it was being removed from standard recruit training actually; I thought boot camp was supposed to evaluate an individual's capability. Perhaps the Marine Corps should allow recruits to test as far as they can complete regardless and not limit guys like me to just CWS1 level of training prior to entering the fleet. This would eliminate unnecessary bullshit within chosen MOSs, jobs, in the future. That's just my opinion anyways. I would never get another chance to be tested within a pool again during my stay here on the island, so I accepted. I passed this test with only one reprimand. This wasn't one of my requirements, but as I was mocking the injured soldier rescue as the victim, the idiot who was supposed to be saving me was pulling me along underwater instead of keeping my head above water. He damn near drowned me halfway across the pool because he was getting tired. I broke free of his headlock before he quit swimming because he was about to stop so he wouldn't fail or possibly drown me. The swim instructor gave him another chance to make it across seeing how this was his final stage to be completed. Before we began again, he pulled me aside and told me to just hold my fucking breath the whole way across if need be. If he fails, you fail regardless, got it numb, nuts, suck it the fuck up. I knew he meant it, and it was definitely true, if I was really injured, I would certainly drown without this idiot, so on this next attempt, I just completely relaxed and held my breath the whole way across. I was near pass-out stage when we reached the other side, but this guy passed and so did I. Water survival qualified (WSQ), baby! Hurrah!

THE GRIND

As the pace never let up during training whatsoever, my only real rest came from going to church on Sunday. That was one time we were not messed with by the drill instructors at all. I went because I was raised that way. I remember seeing plenty of other platoons within the huge place during various levels of training. It was comforting to know you weren't alone in the belief of God during training. I have always enjoyed the stories of the Bible, even though it is a book filled with violence, including the Koran if read the wrong way. Only during these visits to the church I closed my eyes and drifted off into sleep. It wasn't that I found the minister boring, it was because of exhaustion. The peaceful sleep of twenty or so minutes was welcoming. I never missed a service, actually, and I always dreamed about home.

On one occasion I dreamed about a time when I was younger somewhere around fourteen and my brother Jeff, seventeen at the time, had just gotten paid from his job. Someone snuck into his room and stole his check and cashed it without him knowing it. I just figured he would blame my other brother who was a heroin addict. We all stole from one another all the time, and if we got caught, we paid it back. Well, at least I did. I guess I was no better being a crack junky myself at the time, so why should I hurl stones at him for choosing heroin? It turned out after I had run to the city and got high and blew all his money, I was wrong thinking he might not catch me. He kicked in the bathroom door while I was sitting on the shitter and totally pummeled me. My brother outweighed me by close to fifty pounds and threw a heavy fist when angered. I was trapped in the corner taking hard punches to the face by him and lots of knees. My only defense was to grab the plunger and crank him in the ribcage with it. He backed up because I cranked him hard enough to snap the stick. I was left with the broken end in my hand, but he pursued again. I yelled for him to stop or I was going to stab him with the broken end. He retreated and I was super pissed because he had totally gone overboard with the assault. As I was trying to exit the bathroom, he smashed me several more times into the walls by my head. When my brothers and I fought as kids, we never stopped until someone was in the hospital, no doubt. Only this fight was caused by me, and I deserved the few punches, not a full-on ass kicking. I would've paid him back, but not after all this. I was pissed, so my rage turned into smashing his car with a rim and tire that I carried up into his tree fort and tossed it through his Fiat windshield beneath it.

I then went over to the side yard and laid a piece of plywood on the hood of his other Fiat and proceeded to try monster truck, the riding lawn mower, up on to it to smash it also. This was a mistake. I drove that lawn mower as fast as it would go straight at the plywood, and the lawn mower flipped over backward on top of me, pinning me to the ground. My brother Jeff being a bastard just like me in our youth seized the opportunity and ran outside the front door when he realized I was smashing his stuff and proceeded to kick me repeatedly while I was stuck pinned under the lawn mower. I eventually got free and found a bat lying in the yard from random baseball games or to hit rocks into the cornfield beside the house. I had gotten lucky to find it too because the kicks and punches kept coming. I grabbed that bat and said fuck off. He then told me I didn't have the balls. I cranked him in the arm with it, and he screamed like hell and ran back into the house. I remained outside until help arrived. No cops or ambulances were called. My older brothers arrived to keep us from killing each other. I had fought with this dude my whole life, so this battle was one that may seem violent to the normal reader but to us it was small potatoes. Actually us brothers would love and hate one another equally. I still had to pay him back. It just ended up costing me more money and a bloody face for stealing and getting high with his money. As to why I dreamed of my violent past in church during boot camp, I haven't a clue.

God must send these dreams to me because I need to remember them and learn from my mistakes. I also remembered how my oldest brother Dennis stood in as the head of household so to speak. He would keep us in check when we went nuts on each other. He was an absolute asshole but he made sure my mother was taken care of. He worked his ass off and was always my boss within roofing. I have learned plenty of things from him over the years. The one thing I'm proud of about him is that he has the sharpest mind out of all five of us and he is a constant role model to me. During boot camp my brother's voices and their spirits kept me focused regardless the pain.

Our next evolution of training included constant physical activity and was filled with marching. I was now learning to use the rifle along with my steps. Left shoulder, right shoulder, present, inspection, and order arms—we had to master it. This was always filled with constant yelling from a drill instructor and plenty of push-ups and trips to the pit. I know one thing for certain when it came to holding that rifle out in front of me for close to twenty minutes at a time, my arms burned very much from the strain. The marching caused me to get shin splints actually. This is very tiny fractures within your shinbones, and it hurts like hell, but it becomes tolerable. I also had hemorrhoids so bad I could barely shit without crying. This training also included the worst crotch rot and athlete's foot of my life. I had to seek medical attention for the crotch rot actually. The navy corpsman told me to keep my feet dry, put some cream on, powder my junk, and to be sure I put on clean clothes each and every day. Now if you were within this platoon with me, you and I both know our laundry was done once a week. How the hell am I supposed to wear clean clothes every day?

My solution was to lose precious hours of sleep at night to wash my things. So while everyone was sleeping and resting, I was up washing and drying my clothes from then on within training. I had gotten caught by one of the drill instructors doing this, and he tried to give me a hard time because it wasn't allowed. I literally told this guy to go fuck himself. I dropped my shorts and showed him a rash from knees to nuts. I reached down into my crotch and pulled a handful of cheese from where my crotch had been rotting away. He never said a word about it. He just said, "Don't ever be late in the morning when training begins, or I'll have your ass." It's sort of fucked up in a sense, but boot camp is no joke. When I had a problem, I fixed it, I overcame it and adapted to the problem. Overcome and adapt, baby. My crotch rot ceased to exist, and I began functioning on practically no sleep at all.

The chow hall duties were next; I was put in charge of all the other platoons who were there right along with us. This was a bit challenging because the other first squad leaders of these platoons were just as protective of their own platoons as was I. Yelling at someone else's guys turned into resentments, so whenever someone was fucking up, we would have to deal with it and not the drill instructors. Sometimes I would be yelling for someone to do something and they would try to blow me off because they didn't know me. This never worked out well for that individual. I simply called over their first squad leader and told them to handle it. The chow hall was a lot of work. The squad leaders in my platoon handle their own squads very well, and I didn't have to worry much about what they were up too at all. Most of the real bums of this platoon had been dropped, or they had quit. We worked long hours and got screamed at constantly. We were up long before the base even showed signs of movement, and it began to show. We were marching in formation one day and I was carrying the guide stick because our usual guy had gone to medical or something. I was asleep marching I guess because when I no longer heard the drill instructor saying "left, right, left," I turned to see no one behind me. He had given a command to turn, and I missed it. I was two and half football fields away. I ran back into formation, and it was laughter not screaming and hollering.

I remember being so exhausted from this chow hall duty and lack of sleep it nearly broke me when I shared a smoke with one of the mess crew corporals out on the loading dock, on the sneak. I looked toward the rear of this building just beyond a grove of trees, and I could see the ocean. There were fishing boats traveling several miles away heading out of the port. I knew I could swim the distance and also knew I could most likely get a job with them because I knew the trade. I decided against it and went into the furthest food storage area I could find, away from everyone. I fell asleep under a huge pile of dirty mess clothes within a bin. One of the guys in my platoon kept watch for me. He knew I had been running on all cylinders since day 1. I awoke refreshed after two hours, and the thought of running away left me. I helped him get in the bin and covered him up as well. I returned to the mess hall area and got yelled at by my drill instructor because nobody could find me. I simply said I was in the dry storage helping put away the morning shipment, sir. He never knew I took a quick nap, so why bother getting into trouble over it? I was told to remain out front and to delegate people to do things, not to go do them myself. I said, "Yes, sir," and that was how my chow hall week went. Standing around getting others to do shit, delegating others as if I had any authority over anyone. I sent a runner to wake up the kid sleeping after a few hours and began sending guys on shifts that definitely needed sleep. All done underneath all these blatant assholes' noses, but it was necessary to keep the morale.

I also snuck in a phone call out front of the mess hall also. I set up a few guys to keep watch for me and called home. I talked to my mom and asked her to send me some hemorrhoid suppositories because my ass was killing me. I told her when I was supposed to graduate and everything was fine. To send it to this address please; I gave her the address and said, "I love you, Mom." That was actually our conversation, nothing more. I didn't want to go to medical again; I had missed some vital training with that crotch rot day. I didn't want to feel weird again not knowing what I missed. I remember when the package arrived also. My senior drill instructor had the scribe pass out mail call usually, but on this occasion, he did it himself. My name was called, and he was sure there was contraband in it. So I had to open it in front of him and the platoon. He shook his head when I revealed ass medicine. Another guy wasn't so lucky on one occasion. Someone had sent him some Copenhagen in the mail, and he was ordered to eat it. He was one tough son of a bitch too. He swallowed it all down and turned a pale green for several hours remaining of the day while training without a word of misery. It was only when we were told to go to sleep when he tossed his cookies in the bathroom all night. I saw him blowing chunks, but he told me he wasn't going to give the bastard the satisfaction of seeing him quit or puke. I washed my clothes and wished him well and hit the rack.

This was also about the same time one of the fat bodies from the beginning of training had been put on diet meals. He was allowed a hardboiled egg, some toast, jungle juice, fruit, and never the main meal. I hadn't eaten much either, but when I was allowed at least, I could get a full meal. He had been on it for a very long time. I asked, "Why haven't you said anything to the drill instructor?" He was scared, and he was starving he told me. He didn't look very overweight to me at all. I really didn't know how to help this guy. I had no access to food in this place even working in it. The drill instructors watch your every move in here. I had to sleep on this. He was working in the mess hall setting up chairs and keeping things neat every day so far in the dining area. I had him switch with a guy in the serving area and told him, "Be careful, don't get caught sneaking food. I'll kick your ass myself if you bring anything back to the barracks also." He thanked me for the switch, and he got to sneak a few small mouthfuls of food without anyone knowing. It was only during that last day of our stay on mess hall duty though. He was forever grateful. I might have defied some of these rules put upon us during this training, but never once did I slack off, nor did the guys next to me.

The rifle range phase of training was very cool. I had long waited to finally fire my weapon. We had been training with it constantly within marching, and I certainly know this is a vital part of training. We were moved out of our original barracks, and we entered a new one closer to the range. This barracks had a pale green floor; it wasn't that cool one I got to see in the movie *Full Metal Jacket* at all. It didn't matter though I was still here dealing with a complete group of assholes down our throats each step of the way. We were given five-gallon water cans during these days. I had to run up and down that squad bay every afternoon without fail. I was then ordered to pick someone out and hand them off so the next guy could run back and forth. I was told if anyone dropped the cans or quit, I would have to carry them. I was certainly not nice at all during this moment, and it haunted me a little. I got behind all of them and gave them a few kicks in the ass to keep moving and yelled all sorts of shit. They went as long as they could, but eventually I had to carry them again. I passed them off plenty of times to different people, and this went on for several hours. Once again I found humor to break the tension when we were through. The drill instructor heard me call the Oriental kid Chopsticks and damn near wet his leg in laughter. It wasn't a derogatory thing. Everyone got a nickname from somebody during boot camp. We had been called much worse by them instructors. I don't remember if he remembered me at all, but I certainly remember him. He was a funny little bastard once you got to know him. I wonder if the nickname stuck throughout his career.

During all this hazing, a.k.a. training, we learned the inner workings of the M-16. This weapon is an instrument of death in my opinion.

This is my rifle. There are many like it, but this one is mine. My rifle is my best friend. It is my life. I must master it as I master my life. I must shoot straighter than any enemy who is trying to kill me. I will . . .

My rifle and I know what counts in this war is not the rounds we fire, neither the noise of our burst nor the smoke we make. We know that it is the hits that count. We will hit . . .

My rifle is human, even as I, because it is my life. Thus, I will learn it as a brother. I will learn its weakness, its strength, its parts, its accessories, its sights, and its barrel, even as I am clean and ready. We will become part of each other.

We will . . .

Before God I swear this creed. My rifle and I are the defenders of my country. We are masters of our enemy. We are the saviors of my life.

So be it, until victory is American's and there is no enemy, but peace.

I say these words over and over until they become so firmly engrained into my head that it becomes my only words. I focus on everything I'm told to learn. I become an unscrewed jar and allow them to pour this into my mind. I certainly do not want to fuck this up. A whole week of listening to a primary marksmanship instructor, lots of different breathing techniques, sitting, kneeling, standing, and the prone position, sight alignment, bone structure, body alignment, sight picture, sight alignment the whole damn thing plus more. We fired on the prequalification day, and I shot expert. When qualifications rolled around, it was raining the night before, and where I was firing from there was a huge puddle at each spot I came to within qualifying. I even had to piss so bad I just let it go right in my pants. I was already soaked to the gills, so whatever. The truth was there was no excuse for fucking it up, I damn near didn't qualify. I was bummed out. All that training and all that knowledge didn't matter. Oh well, I'd retest later on in the future. Goddamn it, fuck! I got the lowest badge within the three offered. The toilet bowl badge was on my chest now for graduation. It was depressing to me and a bit embarrassing. I was supposed to be shit hot.

As soon as that evolution of training ended, another began. I was sent into the field for the fun stuff. We were told to set up camp. This meant I would have to share a tent with someone. I only had one-half of the tent; I was put with the scribe. He was a pretty cool guy. Before we began, I told him to take a look around. I then pointed out to him we were in a lowland area, and if it rained, we would certainly be flooded. I then began digging in with my e-tool and piling the earth a bit higher off the ground to provide a nice platform for us. I put leaves down for the bedding. I had been trained well by the people of my youth within the forest. Our shelter was up, and then I piled dirt around all sides creating a trench to carry the water away. Our tent was done. We had taken the time to slow down and use our heads and it paid off. When it rained, we stayed dry as a bone. When the flood came, we remained dry. When the drill instructor wanted our tent, I told him, "Fuck you, buddy, you should know better," and went back to bed. The whole platoon was flooded within them trees, and we had to move into a Quonset hut in the middle of the night. We went as well. When I returned in the morning to our area, all our things had remained dry also.

When the evening came the next night, our drill instructor had us strip down to our underwear and stand at attention. We stood there and weren't allowed to move as the mosquitoes came. We were not allowed to move to build discipline in case we were ever within the combat theater and we had to remain still. Control of your mind must be strong to not swat them away as they were filling up on your blood and flying off sort of fluttering as they try to keep in flight all swollen to the max. The enemy will hear you and you will end up dead. That is a no-shit assessment from what I had seen and heard from the Vietnam War veterans prior to even being here. It was irritating but manageable, yet only another test of course. I was trained in hand-to-hand combat, boxing, pugilist sticks, repelling, land navigation, threw a few grenades, ran my ass off, and did a lot of sweating. The gas chamber was exactly like the back of that police paddy wagon, only I happened to have a gas mask this time. Being marched into them fire ants was fucked up, I watched as that prick drill instructor halted us right on top of them mounds only after we marched through them. Those things hurt like hell, but you suck it up. The iron man was decided in sit-ups instead of pull-ups, or I would've been crowned king for sure. I was able to do over a hundred of them, no problem using the kip. I remember looking straight into one of our drill instructor's eyes completely pissed about something. I pulled up and down till both my hands bled and the blood flowed down my forearms. It was an experience for sure. Like I always say, go try it out, I recommend it to everyone.

We returned from the field and were allowed to finally get our jarhead haircut and to blouse our boots. It was elating to see we had almost made it to the final day of boot camp. The count became fun as the days passed, getting closer to the actual graduation day, fifteen days, and a wake-up! And I'm a gone motherfucker. I also enjoyed the feeling as we marched into the chow hall respected by the new guys on the island.

Our pictures were taken, we marched our asses off for final drill inspection, the parade deck tarmac was broiling in the August weather, the battalion commanding officer's inspection was stressful, we were dressed in the green long-sleeved uniform with coat at the time. I had received an unexpected meritorious promotion from them; my senior drill instructor pulled me into his office and proudly said congratulations personally along with the other two instructors. I guess I deserved it for being hard charging from gate to finish line. I was the first squad leader graduating class of Platoon 2082 on the sixteenth of August 1991.

Our drill instructors showed us a lesson to remember while wearing our nice new uniforms too. Wouldn't you know it, down to the sandpit? Doing sand tricks until we were all close to passing out from exhaustion. My parents arrived to visit on family day along with my youngest brother. I was very proud to walk with them and introduce them to my other boot camp buddies. Graduation day came, fucking aye, motherfucker, I am a United States Marine! Hurrah!

I do not hold a grudge to any of my drill instructors at all. These men did their jobs exactly the way it was supposed to be done. I miss having them screaming over my shoulder telling me what to do next. I swear to you it's true. I'm mentally fucked in the head to think this, but I loved every goddamn moment of boot camp. It's the toughest thing by far on this planet so far I've ever experienced. All the other stuff beyond boot camp means nothing in life. Walking upright and proud took a lot of pain, sweat, blood, tears, and plenty of stress, but it's worth it. I recommend it to anyone. There isn't one damn course that compares. I don't care what your profession is; this will change your life forever. It has kept me alive plenty as I draw on the knowledge passed down from them. I love those guys, all of them. You trained me well, thank you. I still to this day see your faces with the utmost hate and love combined. My forever respect, sirs.

When I arrived home, I heard of a friend who had died leaving the bar Bananas late one night. It was horrible. I had wished I was home to stop that fool from drinking and driving. I miss him, but I remember him because he had a tattoo of the words Your Name on his ass. He got all the chicks in high school, and he was another loved member of our age group within our community lost to the perils of alcohol. It was depressing news of course, but I needed to celebrate. Shit, I just did the unheard-of, out of my immediate family.

I had gone out with one of my older brothers' hooting and hollering and carrying-on. I ran a stop sign unknowingly and was slammed T-bone style into the passenger side door. The car that hit me stopped instantly, but I continued into a mailbox, a street sign and flew it straight into a bridal shop window. I hit several manikins dressed in beautiful wedding gowns and finally came to rest half in the store and half out of the store. My brother had warrants, so he climbed over me and began running down the street before the cops came. I noticed the guy who hit the car I was driving, which happened to be a borrowed vehicle from a friend, heading toward me all pissed off, bleeding, and screaming holding a tire iron in his hands, yelling he was going to make me bleed also. I wasn't afraid of the guy with the tire iron; I had a few beers from the bar we just left. I didn't want the DUI, and hard habits are tough to break. Running from the law was so common to me I swear it was as if I was Luke Duke himself from Hazard County.

I didn't hesitate; I took off down the street to avoid getting cranked over the head by that piece of steel and to avoid the cops. I should've stayed at the scene of this accident, but sometimes it's better to get to fucking stepping. I managed to reach a phone several blocks away and called my friend to report his car stolen. He was pissed and certainly didn't. I had to report to the police station the next day because my plane ticket back to California was in my jacket in the backseat of this car. No ticket, no flight, unauthorized absence, loss of rank, the brig, integrity, and honor all ran into my head, so I showed up and faced the music so to speak. I was arrested, arraigned, sent to court. The judge gave me a further date. He knew I needed to report back to the military, but he never brought it up. So why should I? I just flew away. I would face this when I returned back home I guess. If I even return back home, without a doubt, I'll be within enemy territory within the next year. No sense in causing myself red tape before I embark on my quest to kill.

CAMP GEIGER, NORTH CAROLINA

My next evolution of training landed me within a thirty-day basic warrior training course. This whole training was the most fun I had during my training thus far. We were in the field throughout this training. I was at home once again as a first squad leader. I raised my hand when they asked who was a squad leader in boot camp. I didn't mind the job.

I don't want to give away any military training secrets, so I will just tell you about a day I got bored during training and needed some action so to speak. We had been bused around within old cattle trucks designed for cows in some previous lifetime of these vehicles. Now it carried us around to different training areas. I remember we were given a bag lunch during this ride, we were told to eat while standing then hold on to our paper bag and trash. I don't know why, but I just drank my milk and tossed it out the window without thinking. Like I said, I was bored. Sure enough the bus pulled into our destination and a corporal entered our cattle wagon bus with the milk carton in his hand. He yelled out asking, "Who the hell tossed this out the window?" I was shocked to see the whole bus turn and point at me. *Oh shit! I'm screwed*, I thought. This guy didn't say a word about it and exited the vehicle. We were told to hump over to our campsite and set up our tents. This was where we would be camped during this training within the field.

So here I am, fresh in the field already causing a problem for myself. I wasn't reprimanded until just about sundown for this littering incident. The corporal told me to just follow him. I knew I was in for something difficult, or an ass chewing for brain farting. He told me to look over by some obscure canvas building about three football fields away. I looked over, and he told me to look at the top of the wooden telephone pole. Sure enough, there lay the damn milk carton. I had to low-crawl all the way there and get it back. I dropped to my belly and began crawling. I picked up the pace to almost a full jog for the corporal to keep up to me. I had to go right through some uneven terrain within the forest and a creek but oh well. I caused this mess, so I went at it 100 percent. I reached the pole ahead of this corporal actually and just went right to the top before he arrived underneath me thirty feet below me. It was near dark, so I could barely see him. I told him, "Yes, I have it, it's a bit windy up here, and this pole is swaying actually." I asked him if I was to fall off, would I get in trouble or would he? He got super pissed with my asshole question, but really I was just breaking balls. He started yelling for me, "Get down from there, numb nuts, hurry up." I had to low-crawl to the company hooch back across the damn creek to face a company commander. When I was told to get off my stomach and get my ass inside, I entered the hooch gasping for breath, dizzy, and sweating like crazy. The commander just asked me one question, did I learn my lesson? I replied, "Yes, sir." "Good, now get the fuck back to your tent and go to sleep, we have a long day of training tomorrow. Smarten up, dismissed."

Another funny time had to do with putting people in check when they had been screwing up repeatedly. I wasn't involved with this little caper, but I found it to be rather funny. Our training time in the field was for several weeks, and there were porto-johns set up for our bathroom needs. The commanders that designed this idea weren't very bright I guess because there were about ten porto-johns for close to three hundred Marines. This definitely didn't turn out very well. I remember entering one and the refuse was overflowing and piling up above the seat. I refused to use the damn things after a while and just scurried out off site with my e-tool and just dug a damn hole.

It was about eight in the morning on this fine day of training when I was heading toward the usual nasty porto-johns to scurry into the trees to do my business. I reached my usual spot and started digging. I dropped deuce and as I was pulling my pants back up, I heard some commotion over in the direction of the porto-johns, and then heard a loud bang followed by somebody screaming but it was muffled. I quickly filled in my hole and covered up any evidence that the ground was disturbed with some fallen pine needles and circled back out from my cover within the trees. I would hate to get caught taking a dump where I wasn't supposed to be. I reached the area where the load bang came from and noticed one of the porto-johns was tipped over door side down. Someone had run up and pushed it over with someone in it. I was laughing the whole time listening to this kid screaming and yelling for help. Some platoon leaders arrived and began to laugh while telling a few of us to stand it back up so this kid could get out. I had to hold my breath the whole time, but we managed to get it standing upright to release this kid from the clutches of the blue lagoon of death. We stood back, and the door flew open and this shit-covered half-blue monster jumped out. He hadn't even had the time to pull his pants up. We laughed our asses off because he was saying, "Oh, that's bad, oh that's bad," and then puked. He actually laughed with us, but I'm sure he was pissed when the platoon leaders wouldn't let him shower off for a few hours because we didn't have any water available in this area. That poor guy went damn near half the day covered in foulness beyond belief. He wasn't in my platoon which was fine by me because he sat right in his platoon without anyone saying shit about it. I was glad it wasn't me. I guess that kid was a total shitbag and needed a bit of hazing to straighten him out.

I was a bit more of a tactician when it came to the moment of getting even with people who caused me problems during training. I got my chance during a forced march with all our gear on, with weapons. It was a ten-mile hump, which was a cake walk for me. I was so damn physically fit and had endurance for days during this moment and time of my Marine Corps experience. In fact while this hump was taking place, I was ordered to circle our platoon at a run. I never once bitched or complained about the impartial treatment toward me at all. I just followed orders to circle the platoon, and every time someone fell back, I was to motivate them back into the main platoon or collect their ID card. If they dropped on this hump, they would have to do it again. It was fun to watch people fall out especially knowing in my mind that this guy caused me to do extra push-ups or caused me to have to run farther, faster, and quite possibly this guy was one of them who pointed at me for throwing that milk carton out the window of that cattle wagon. I took pleasure in marching next to somebody and just talking them right out of making it to collect up their ID card. It was a cool game to play actually.

I got alongside a guy from my platoon from during boot camp and just knew he was a total shit bird beyond belief who didn't deserve my time. I asked if he was doing okay, because he looked a bit pale. He told me he was running out of energy. I told him he should drink some water. This kid was such a pussy, he asked me to get his water because he couldn't reach his canteen on his belt. I reached for it and undid the cap for him and everything. He tried to drink his water, but it was to warm for his liking so he spit it out. He began to cry and wail his legs hurt and his feet hurt; he was always crying during boot camp also. Our drill instructors went easy on him, kind of babied his ass in my opinion.

I told him, "Okay, never mind that one, here try mine." Now mine was colder, but it had some trace elements of Skoal chewing tobacco spit in it from yesterday. I had used it as a spittoon the night before while relaxing in my military-issued tent. I hadn't been able to smoke a cigarette since being home, so Skoal mixed with Copenhagen did the trick. It was rinsed out well enough for my liking and the water was cold; I gulped down half of it and just asked for his card as he sat down off the trail. I guess this kid's body didn't agree with it. He turned greener and greener before my eyes and began to puke. He dropped like a wet pile of monkey poop. I couldn't have planned that better, fuck him.

I had collected about twenty-three ID cards on this hump. My total distance traveled was possibly double the required distance than the rest of these guys, but I seemed to have made it. I certainly couldn't quit, or just say no to any of the dumb tasks I was ordered to do. I was a first squad leader, we can't fall out. It sort of discouraged me to know that all the guys who dropped during this hump didn't have to repeat it. What the hell was the entire ID collecting for then? I asked our platoon leader. He told me it was to fuck with me. He knew just a simple march meant nothing to me physically; he also needed a list of guys to perform cleanup duties when we returned back to the base, when we got out of the woods. I thanked him for being a total jackass actually. I laughed it off and so did a few other platoon leaders within earshot.

I remember we did some daytime training which involved a few foxholes predug as a defensive position. I ran to my foxhole predetermined by the powers that be and jumped right in. Ouch! Something stabbed my leg, felt like briars. I looked down and it's a medium-sized rattlesnake coiled up with its body preparing to strike again. If I reached for it, the damn thing would bite me again. So I decided to kill the bastard and take him with me. I removed the BFA safety device from my M-16 and shot its tiny head off with a blank. The BFA stopped a paper wad from exiting the barrel during mock assaults. I just knew this prior to killing this snake. I was always told to bring the snake with me in the Cub Scouts if I couldn't identify it. I already took one hit, I didn't need another. So anyways I carried the thing back to my company area, and a corporal yelled at me for killing the wildlife. I said, "Okay, great, it bit me." He didn't give two shits about me getting bit. He snatched the dead snake from my hand and said, "Follow me." We head straight to the company commander's office. I was thinking I might be in some sort of hot water now. He burst through the canvas flap and yelled out, "Snake bite victim coming in." I was checked over; I showed them the two holes which looked a bit like a minor cat scratch on one side but the other side definitely punctured my skin. They tossed me a suction device, and I let it suction out the fang hole. There was minimal juice inside, it was already in my bloodstream, it's been a few minutes already, like twenty-five minutes had elapsed already. A quick dressing and out the door I went. "Oh yeah, if you notice you can't breathe, come back." It looked like a false strike, a defensive strike. I got a little woozy that night, but I wasn't fined for killing the snake. I might even have felt tightness in my chest, but I remained calm about it. I slept pretty well once I calmed down.

While in the field, we learned camouflage techniques, squad movements, within a mocked combat environment. The camouflage part of it was very cool. I have always been good at sneaking around at night in my criminal youth days. So this was just adding to my already decent skills of my past. I also liked painting my face regardless if it was the military. Halloween was my favorite holiday actually. I loved to get dressed up and become someone else. It is the only time of year that you can put on a costume and just become whomever you desire; you can create an alter ego and just have fun. In the Marines, they wanted you to become the invisible man. It was fun. I remember in high school some friends of mine at the time wanted to dress up as the band Kiss one year. I forgot who I was actually, I think I was the guy with the star on his eye, Peter Chris, I think. Everyone wanted to be Gene Simmons of course, so we drew straws. I also remember leaving school on my street bike at the time doing 132 miles per hour up a hill within plain view of the local cops. I got a huge speeding ticket for that when I was finally stopped at the end of a dead-end street I tried to sneak down ahead of him. Wouldn't you know it, he thought I was completely insane when I took off my helmet and he was looking at Peter Chris. I mention this because back then it was a game to me to run from the police and I got caught and had to pay a fine. Within the Marine Corps, the game stops when you know it is your life you're going to lose in payment of your mistake if you don't pay attention to proper cover and concealment techniques. I listened very closely.

Like I said, this part of training was actually very fun. I completed this course without any problems at all. It was a piece of cake, on to California, baby. My new training awaited me. I was asked several times during training where I wanted to be stationed and I always said California. I had seen enough of the East Coast already; I want to see the west. I got exactly what I asked for when this training ended.

School's Battalion

Amphibious assault vehicle crewman school was one of the most exciting on my first day actually. The Paris Island—trained Marines arrived a week sooner than the West Coast "Hollywood" Marines did for the class. We got to pick out the beds we wanted first and also got to replant the school's front lawn. We painted some rocks, redid all the white paint on the surrounding area actually. We arrived to be the groundskeepers, I guess. Good thing it was only for a week. The other Marines arrived then we began our schooling. Once again I was the first squad leader during this evolution of training also. I must have asshole tattooed on my back or something. Only this time it was only a position to pass out fire watch and delegate cleanup to secure our weekend passes to go off base. Nothing in the Marines comes free, you have to earn privileges. One of the perks of this base was definitely the beach, big waves to learn how to surf on. The E-Club was an adventure also. All these things were available as long as we kept our shit together. We had a Burger King, a commissary, a gym, and kick-ass machines to learn how to operate. A rather peaceful existence actually until they let me loose, meaning, we have freedom during the evenings.

I wasn't really interested in anything other than drinking and paying very close attention to every small detail within this class. I passed this class in the top 10 actually. I didn't study very often either. Each and every classroom was a shut-the-fuck-up-and-pay-attention atmosphere. We got breaks every few hours to have a smoke, I bought a hacky sack to pass the time. We played as a platoon actually. If you dropped it, you were out. I would use this time to mentally go over each thing discussed in my head. I would register it and store it in my mind during our hacky sack showdowns. It was cool to make it to the final three or four people within a group hack. We got downright awesome as a platoon actually. Playing that game kept the blood flowing, and it kept me focused. What people fail to realize about that game is that a lot of kicks and knees are required to keep that leather bean bag in the air. Flexibility, speed, and eye coordination come into the game as well, making us more agile soldiers. They should make it mandatory in training just like we all chose to do.

When it came to the drinking after liberty was called, I certainly didn't pay attention to my alcohol consumption. That was certainly apparent to everyone around me. I just was very gifted when it came to mechanical things and identifying components. We had lots of book work and classroom hours. I went nuts I guess, or maybe it was boredom. All work and no play makes Jack a very drunken fool. It makes Gary create drinking games while at the E-Club. I went out every night I was allowed and always returned drunk as a monkey. I constantly messed with our fire watch guy also. I would come into the squad bay and just yell, "Fire watch! Get the fuck over here, what are doing? Are you just going to let a drunken bum all loud and belligerent access? Why aren't you at this door watching people as they come in? Someone could slip in here at anytime and wait for all of us to be asleep, then awake to cut all our fucking throats. Pull your head out of your ass." I did this to every single guy, no exceptions. One of the guys who lived up in Massachusetts used to tell me they would make bets on who might beat me in a late-night drunken, phony assault. Eventually we would end up wrestling, and I would submit him right quick and I would stagger back to my rack. I never once tried to hurt any of them; I was a gifted individual, drunken-monkey style. Eat that, Jackie Chan, love your flicks, dude. Sometimes we would have group wrestling matches; I never lost control and started punching anyone, nobody did. We had fun. When you're able to submit someone unarmed, you definitely can dispatch his life in combat. Well, that's what I told them, anyways. I just liked to keep people sharp and aware.

There was an ongoing game right as the club closed within my happy group of drinkers who followed in tow with me. I swear I had gotten drunk with each and every one within my platoon. So how this game worked was one guy lined up on the right side of the club in front of his side's six tables and another guy lined up on the opposite side of the club in front of his own six tables. As everyone exited the club, there was always full pitchers or half pitchers left behind. The object was to drink all six leftovers regardless the quantity and get out the club first. This was a classic game. Plenty of puke, pass-outs, fall-overs, fights, stumble bum drunks within this unit. It's all good. I was one of them. When it was my turn to go, I ended up in the front bushes of the E-Club, passed out in the shrubs. Yes, sir, that's me. I would make it back to the barracks late most of the time. Several hours late on occasion, I would always be locked out from the doors. Fire watch was usually trying to get me busted, because he wanted my job. I would always have someone leave my window or theirs unlocked and I would slip in. Another fire watch mistake, I would yell out, "Fire watch! What the fuck, son, don't you check these windows?" Oh yeah, the random guy on fire watch hated me. It was all fun and games to me.

Toward the end of my class, I began knowing the unit next door actually. I was headed that way on my graduation, so what the hell? I hung out a few weekends in a row down in Mexico with some of them. It was off-limits while being in school, but when you're invited by the guys within the permanent unit your about to enter, you fucking go. I had some fun times. Crossing the border was very cool. I remember stopping at the very first beer stand. They had ice-cold bottled Coronas with a lime for nineteen cents a piece. As a group, it was mandatory to consume a six-pack each before heading to the famous Revolution Street strip. They have some really great clubs, lots of college girls. Plenty of watered-down tequila mixed with lime juice; guzzling this piss while being spun around in a barber's chair was awesome. The trick to this game was having a high tolerance; I guzzled half this guy's bottle and was willing to drink the whole thing. He spun the hell out of me in this chair; I got up and had to walk a straight line to the other side of the club. If you make it, the booze is free. Great way to get a free drunk actually, go, give it a try. Don't forget to check out the strip clubs, the whorehouses, the sleazy motels, the country side. Eat the food, it's amazing. The tacos served from the pushcarts are the best. Explore, because it's a once-in-a-lifetime opportunity.

Being friendly with my next unit helped me out prior to graduation actually. I had returned back from the E-Club early with a good buzz with another guy in my platoon. We decided to play pool against two other guys from a different class living in our building actually. One of the guys was a civilian, the other a Marine's brother. Anyways, we bet money on the game and won. These two clowns had to pay up. No big deal. We collected and headed out, back to the club for more booze. These two guys got pissed, they mouthed off, and my friend pushed one of them inside as we were leaving. Next thing you know we were outside. I turned around to say, "It's cool, I'll take him next door, no need to have a problem." *Whack!* I was punched right in the mouth as I turned to say we were leaving. I grabbed this kid by the head, two hands, and slammed him to the ground. My right thumb sunk into his left eye by mistake on impact. He screamed bloody murder. I looked up and *whack!* His brother cranked me in the mouth. I released the kid beneath me and went to retaliate on that punch and I was tackled to the ground by guys in my platoon.

The scuffle ended, I headed into the bathroom to look at my lip because it was bleeding pretty well. I noticed a void right through the middle of my jaw, between my lower lip and chin, actually. My tooth cut through it from his fist. I filled my mouth with water and squirted a stream through the hole. It stung like hell, but it needed to be washed out. I went and lay down to sleep it off actually. No need to carry on. I was awoken by MPs and brought to the emergency room. Three stitches inside and three on the outside. No charges, totally self-defense. I would run into this pair the following afternoon in the dayroom, I was playing pool alone actually. They entered, and the Marine's brother was wearing an eye patch. He didn't lose his eye, so that was a good thing. I guess they wanted to kick my ass because they entered with ten other guys. I was alone, pool stick in hand, big fucking mistake for them actually, but I didn't have to do a thing. I looked in their direction and noticed them coming and just waited for one of them to lunge or swing at me. Nobody came within five feet of me actually. They stopped short and looked scared actually. I never raised the stick at all, but they stopped dead in their tracks looking at something else and not me. I turned around, and lo and behold, like eight guys from my next unit and two from my own were in the door way filing in to make things even. These guys got told off by a huge fucking guy from New York within my next unit to fucking let it go. "You guys got your wounds and Mello's got his." Like I said, they came in handy at the right time to save my bacon, no doubt. Saved me big-time actually, being alone against numbers warrants the pool stick smash off some people to lower the odds.

I have been attacked before by nine people, and that wasn't very pretty at all. This course of events was similar, but I had no help when I was a teenager. I was at a wedding with some high school friends in Fall River. Got drunk, danced with some guy's wife I guess. My friends left me behind actually, nice friends I had at the time. Anyways I began to walk home and turned a corner at the bottom of a hill and got punched right in the nose by some fat guy, my nose exploded with blood spraying out both my nostrils. I looked up and saw eight more guys behind him. I was getting jumped. I punched with all I had and knocked the fat guy out cold. I crossed the street and got into the middleof the road to create some distance between us. I faced them while retreating because I hadn't the strength or the legs to run, I was drunk. I heard someone closing on me from behind, and at the last second, I dropped to my knees and flipped this guy underneath me. I punched this guy repeatedly while being kicked and punched by his friends. I popped up and threw one of them on the ground to create a gap to cross the street and escape the barrage of kicks and punches. I ended up jumping into a car actually and shutting the door. There were three girls in the back seat screaming bloody murder for me to get the hell out. I took a few hits from them also. I said, "Just hold on, I'm being attacked, I need a breather." As I was saying this, one of the guys on the attack happened to be the owner of the car I hopped into. He opened the door with his key, just my luck.

He began to kick me in the face and ribs. I took like four kicks to the ribs and one to the head. On his third kick to my ribs, I told him, "One more time, buddy, and I'm fucking you up." He kicked, and I grabbed his foot flipping him on his ass. I jumped out the car rapidly and kicked him right in the head and dazed him. I placed his leg into the door and began smashing his door closed at least six times. I most likely broke his leg, if not he won't enjoy walking or chasing after me that's for sure. He was down, but more guys were coming. I managed to recross the street and get away temporarily. I was chased for several blocks but gave my pursuers the slip. I circled back behind them after grabbing a long-handled shovel from someone's yard and closed on them. Three of them were together talking shit about how when they catch me they were going to stab me to death. I crept silently behind them and got within striking distance. I yelled hey; the guy in the middle spun around quickly with knife in hand. I cranked him right upside his head. He dropped like a dead guy. His friend threw a bottle at me, and it hit me in the shoulder. I stepped into a full swing and connected with his elbow. He screamed and ran. The third guy just ran. I staggered in the opposite direction several blocks and passed out from blood loss and drunkenness.

I was awoken to someone kicking me, so I grabbed the foot and flipped the guy on the ground. As I got up, someone yelled, "It's the police, we are here to help you. We have been looking for you all night, we thought you were dead." I stopped, thanking God I wasn't still within this fight for my life. The police brought me to the station and allowed me to sleep it off in an open cell actually. No charges against me, they were actually congratulating me for a well done job of putting five out of the nine guys in the hospital. They were impressed, and they told me I got lucky. "The guys attacking you are a known group of violent offenders around here." I didn't care who they were; I was attacked from all directions and got out alive. That's all that mattered. The police gave me a ride halfway home actually the next morning. I was covered in blood and walked twenty miles home. It is very difficult to get a ride hitchhiking covered in blood. You would think somebody would stop and offer assistance at the very least, but this is Massachusetts, fuck you. Walk, scumbag.

I definitely remember the outcome, and the stitches I required after that scuffle also. I was surrounded by enemy within my own state, never mind this moment in the dayroom with another group of Marines. I was glad someone stopped a course of events within the dayroom actually. On the streets it was different; I was abandoned by so-called friends. They knew a fight was coming and left me unknowing of this attack. I don't consider them friends, but sometimes people get scared and flee. I have fled before, but on these occasions, I had nowhere to run to. I was prepared to fight for my life no matter what. I had gotten lucky I guess, or the friends I have made within my next unit and the platoon I was in cared enough to stand by my side to stop an uneven assault. That is how it goes in the Marines. We believe in protection of others. These guys are the friends I want in my life. They are my new family for the time being. Oh yeah, guess what? It turns out none of them wanting to attack me in the dayroom remained my enemy either.

I awoke to my corporal screaming at me to open my wall locker for inspection. I was out of it really. I was on pain meds and semidrunk. The emergency room released me only a few hours ago with a no duty slip for one day actually. I had it on my rack taped to the bed's frame actually. I was totally cranky and sore and not in my right state of mind when the corporal yanked me out of my rack. I hit the floor and bounced up quickly. I grabbed the paper from the ER and screamed, "Here read this, asshole." I tossed it at him and opened my wall locker and threw all my shit on the floor, yelling, "Here look, that's my clothes.: It was a total baby Huey temper tantrum; I crawled back into my rack and passed out.

That evening the corporal fired me as the squad leader, and it was up to another guy to secure for liberty on a cleanup day. I had pissed this guy off on the very first day our school started actually. He was having us do push-ups outside the barracks, and I asked him why he wasn't doing them with us. I thought, *Once boot camp was over, Corporal, you weren't allowed to ask us to do push-ups unless you yourself did them with us.* He hated me from the start. We had a major cleanup once a week on Friday to secure for the weekend. This poor guy got the job. I stayed silent during the cleanup and only did my area. This was something he had done mostly, so he got the same treatment. I was on no duty. So have at it. Delegate some jobs to people; work it out like I have each time without fail. A few guys approached me to ask me what to do because they knew we weren't going to pass inspection. I apologized and told them, "Nope, can't help you. Go ask the new first squad leader." Well, it turned out our gunnery sergeant showed up to do inspection on our barracks. We failed miserably, and he questioned me why. I just handed him my slip and told him, "I'm no longer the first squad leader, Gunny. I got fired this morning, actually." The gunny turned to the corporal and said, "Where do you get off? You hold no authority to fire my choice of squad leaders anyways. I do the hire and fire around here."

I guess he got the skinny on why I was such a bastard this morning. He turned to me and said, "You're still the first squad leader, get this place cleaned the fuck up. You got thirty minutes. If you guys want liberty, you will get it done." I snapped right into action, "Hey, go do this, and go do that, start doing this. Hey motherfucker! Why are you just sitting on your ass? Grab a rag, a mop, that buffing machine." People took direction from me easily because I spoke clearly and loudly. I don't take no for an answer—fuck you, get it done. I was hands-on also. They learned by watching me. I had some great helpers actually. I allowed a lot of slackers also. Some guys were just lazy dumbasses who just get in the way actually. Those guys you have to do the dusting. We wrapped it up and secured liberty. I was a drunken fool, but things got done around me. School's battalion was very interesting.

I totally enjoyed another day of training about safety. We were instructed by a class coach during our ramp hours to learn the inner workings of the amphibious assault vehicles. As the ramp closes on the back of your vehicles, do not reach in or stand near it. About a week later, the guy who gave us the safety class on proper procedure during the rear man's job duties as the ramp closed got hurt. We were gathered in formation waiting to leave for the day, and he yelled, "Oh shit, I forgot something." He reached into the tractor and tried to grab a bag. The ramp closed completely on his arm. He screamed bloody murder. I was shocked when the ramp was lowered once someone jumped up and alerted the driver to lower it. This guy's arm was completely flat within midforearm. I was surprised it wasn't severed. It turned out nothing was broken either when we arrived to work the next day. This man got lucky. Great example, I will certainly remember it.

Driving these vehicles was a total rush. They could float on water, and they had tracks to traverse on land. I held the class record on speed actually. I would allow the vehicle a dose of clean air from a bottle during water tracks setting while on land. This machine comes complete with its own air to keep the engine running while in the water. This was almost similar to a nitrous boost actually. I reached a good clip heading down a really steep hill actually. I caught some air off a huge mound of dirt also. This machine hauled ass with me behind the wheel. I got yelled at for driving like an animal, but it was all good. These machines need to be rung out prior to me being deployed. I wanted to know its capabilities. My threshold of fear is nil at home base, in combat I have to be sharp in knowledge on what this machine's limitations are. I would much rather destroy one now than in a firefight. I loved this shit.

After graduating from my class, I got to look forward to initiations within my next company, my permanent unit. No bones about it, they have a ritual for each and every one of us. I was already told they couldn't wait. I knew several of them already, and they had to show up in my defense already during that pool game incident, it was a no-way-out situation for me. Some of the other guys in my platoon avoided the whole initiation ceremony. They stayed off base till Monday. I had no fear, because these guys have to kick my ass, and then I would be accepted. I arrived, was shown my sleeping area and my wall locker. As soon as my stuff was inside, they pounced on me. I defended myself with punches as I was being kicked, punched, and tossed around. I was stripped and duct-taped and tossed into a truck outside of the barracks. I was held down by three guys, and they took me off base and dumped me in a McDonald's in the dark area of the parking lot. One of them tossed me a knife and said, "Adios. See you in a few hours." I was fucked.

I wasted no time grabbing the knife with my hands and began positioning it to cut myself free. This is a difficult task to complete when your hands are bound behind your back. It took a few minutes to work my way through at least ten layers of tape. I was free within five minutes once I had the knife in my hand. The next trial was to make it back to the base without being arrested because I was naked as the day I was born. It took me about an hour to make it back to the front gate of my base. When I walked toward the entrance, I was met by one of the MPs. He asked me what in the hell I was doing. I told him it was initiation night and I was trying to make it back. He shook his head in disgust and laughed at me, but he let me pass. He also told me not to be seen by anyone because if I got caught running around naked, there would be hell to pay. With that, I hurried into the shadows and made my way back to my barracks. As each car approached, I would ditch into the grass and lay down flat so I wouldn't be seen. This whole ordeal was definitely not fun. I arrived back to my barracks and was told to run around the building three times and then I would be allowed to enter. Upon completion, I wasn't messed with again. I was one of them. All I needed to do now was give them the list of graduates from my class who failed to report in during initiation night because they were chickens. I certainly wasted no time doing that. To hold a fear of initiations was not a good thing at all, what would happen in combat? A Marine suppresses his or her fears and does things anyways. These cowards need to be dealt with, what were they really afraid of? These guys are hard training, hard fighting, totally psychotic trained killers who were here to protect them in any situation. I certainly didn't mind the hazing.

If memory serves me correctly, we only stayed Stateside for a few weeks. We were slotted to go overseas. My memory sucks these days so I'll share you a story about going to the shooting range to learn our vehicles' weapons systems. I'm unsure if this happened during school or if this happened while in the fleet. Well it goes like this, see. We were firing all day at fake targets with a mountainside backdrop. Several fires had started in the process, but we were told it happens all the time and they would burn out because it was mostly sand with a few clumps of desert grass mixed in. We camped for the evening after the live fire exercise, and that was that. Upon waking, several people let out some death shrieks of fear. I hopped up out of my tent and wondered why someone was screaming. I swear to God as my witness there were thousands of brown tarantulas all within our area crawling around. The fire on the hillside drove them down toward us. I have never seen grown men become such little girls. "Eeeek! A spider, kill it." I laughed my ass off this day. I thought it was kind of cool. I picked a few up and let them crawl around on my hands and arms. I found one in my boot and luckily didn't put it on in a rush. The spiders were welcomed guests in my mind. I had never seen so many in one area or at all. One of my brothers had one when we were kids, and that sucker bit me as I was changing its water dish. It hurt like hell actually. I held no fear of them, and it was nice that nobody killed any of them. It was just funny to watch guys bugging out when they found them in odd places.

OVERSEAS DUTY

I was blessed to be accepted within my new unit, and the guys in my platoon were all decent fellow American Marines. I noticed that they were of all races and backgrounds also including several homosexuals. The Marine Corps is filled with different people who were standing beside me. I no longer held any bigotry at all in any way, shape, or form, but I really never had it to begin with. Unless you are willing to experience being in the Marine Corps serving in a foreign country and possibly heading to your demise, well then, you really don't have a leg to stand on with your racial slander in my opinion. I was willing to protect them as they would for me. We received the word we were deploying for overseas duty and were heading to Okinawa, Japan. I was thrilled to be going actually, this sort of travel would never happen again in my lifetime. The deployment was very quickly done.

We loaded onto a huge Federal Express plane. This plane was massive, there were like eight seats across the center, four seats on each side next to the windows on both sides. It held our whole battalion it seemed. I remember the flight took a very long time. We landed in Alaska for a refuel pit stop, and then it was thirteen hours straight to our destination. During this flight we were given permission to smoke them if we got them only in the rear of the plane though. I swear the whole unit stood up and headed into the rear of the plane. The pilot had to come onto the overhead speakers to tell us smoking would have to be done in shifts because the plane was now flying ass heavy and it wasn't safe. That was funny to comprehend; I just pictured the poor guy fighting to keep the nose of the plane down and then getting super pissed off about it. That flight sucked because it took forever, it was also very exciting to be headed to foreign soil. I would be the first of my brothers to say I had gone there, or they could say, "Yes, my brother Gary is in the Marine Corps stationed in Okinawa." It's not every day you run into a Marine, most of us are lost in battle, and I expected the same to occur for myself when the call to arms happened. Maybe they could be proud of me for defending freedom in the unfortunate event of my death. I was now expendable; I certainly felt it when we had to fill out the life insurance forms. I also remember not knowing who to give the money to. Why should anyone profit from my death?

This new duty station was absolutely amazing when we first arrived. It was quite tropical, and there was lots of wildlife all around, as for things to do on base, not very much else going on toward entertainment other than a bowling alley and a movie theater. I did enjoy the day several of us were getting together to go cave snorkeling though. I entered the water with a mask, flippers, and no gloves which was a mistake. The ocean floor came alive because it was all coral reefs. I got to see what a sea cucumber looked like and was able to hold one in my hand after I broke the fear of "I wonder if this thing bites" of course. Turned out all they seem to do is let out some long stringy-looking white fluid when you mess with them, wasn't very entertaining. The sea urchins were absolutely awesome and came in a variety of brilliant colors. We were told prior to heading out into the water to be careful of these things because most all of them had poison on the end of their sometimes foot-long spines. They would give you a nice sting and, yes, I found out the hard way when I reached out to a black one and I got poked. It doesn't shoot out spikes like a porcupine or anything, I just reached a bit too quickly and my range perception was off just a bit from my mask. There were all sorts of colorful fish hidden in crevices all around. I was told that scuba diving was the way to really experience this coral reef but on a different base not ours, figures. Camp Foster I think it was, because about a mile or so offshore was a sixty-foot drop-off just teaming with all sorts of sea creatures. Sadly, I never got to experience that while in country though.

We decided to snorkel out toward the massive rocky outcroppings possibly two miles away from the shore to reach the caves. I didn't mind the distance one bit. The depth never really got much deeper than ten feet the whole way. I got to see so many cool fish and even caught a glimpse of a small octopus hurriedly taking cover into a crack within the coral sea floor beneath the waves. I was in heaven. When we reached our destination, the guy leading the way had been here on a prior occasion while deployed last year. He was a great guide to have because this next part of swimming definitely took some knowledge of the way to go. All we had to do is grow a set and hold our breath and follow along. He told us there were three really cool caves we would encounter. The first one was a piece of cake. We dived down like ten feet and swam into a six-foot-wide dark hole which led us down about five more feet deep, then it went across twelve feet and you reentered the light from above and surfaced. It was a bit scary at first because it was dark in the beginning but quite amazing to see the exit. The light from above pierces the darkness like a knife and guides you up and out. The swim to the surface was the worst actually. You sort of forget that you swam down ten feet and then another five feet deeper into the hole. I managed it just fine, we all did. That was our warm-up swim, if we couldn't make that one or we panicked in any way, he suggested we don't attempt the next two because they were more difficult.

The second cave we entered was about the same distance from the surface to enter as was the first. The hole was a bit narrower at its entrance, but it tightened right up to damn near not passable. There was a constant low light within this cave because we only went into the coral reef about three feet down and began our swim just under the surface of it. There were holes leading upward which allowed light to penetrate, but they were too small to exit out of. Once we were committed to this swim, there would be no exit for at least seventy feet with twists and turns throughout our journey. Once again it was manageable and a bit claustrophobic at times, but we all came out just fine.

The third cave we were about to embark on was definitely a serious deal. We swam down the normal ten feet and entered the hole in the coral reef floor. We swam through a similar scenario as the second cave, but this time it angled downward bringing us to close to twenty five feet deep within the cave. Our exit wouldn't come for close to eighty feet more in distance, and it remained a cave the whole way. I remember the ascent to our destination because I smashed my head really hard on an outcropping as I was nearing the surface. I saw a huge white flash and damn near was knocked right out. I was the last man to enter the cave from the beginning of our start also. I didn't panic, but I certainly might not have made it if it were not for the guy who appeared from nowhere and shoved me to the surface for the next fifteen feet. I say saved because my orientation was really off once my noggin hit the ceiling of this cave, I might not have swam the remainder of the distance to the surface and drowned. I don't know who he was or if it was just luck on my end, but this man was wearing scuba gear and was able to be there at a critical moment in my cave diving experience. When I reached the surface, he gave me the thumbs-up and I returned it. I was okay, but my head was certainly in a bad way. I had a pretty good scrape along the top of my head which was bleeding and the egg forming underneath the skin grew rather quickly. I didn't drown because of this "angel" from out of nowhere; he was definitely not within our swimming expedition. The exit of this cave was actually within an enclosed pocket of red rock all around us with plenty of air to breathe, there was also a ten-foot hole at the very top allowing the sunshine to enter. It was the center of one of these massive outcropping of rocks we originally swam out toward. I was thrilled to have made it regardless the bump on the head. The reaching of this oasis was very long and painful to complete, but the journey to this spot was well worth it all. I wish I would've had a magic marker with me at the time, I would've tagged the wall with a familiar "Gary was here in 1991, bumped his head, should be dead, got fucking lucky, and reached the air and the sun."

As time dragged on while stationed on this Camp Schwab, I began to realize there wasn't much to do. It was becoming rather mundane and boring; alcohol filled the gap between the end of the workday and the morning formation. The booze was cheaper here than in California too. A bottle of Jack Daniels was like seven bucks, so you know whiskey was my poison during the downtime. Damn near our whole platoon eventually got fucking drunk because we were rushed through everything all day every day only to hurry up and wait. The waiting around ripped at your sanity, there was no women available on this base whatsoever other than the young cute bowling alley girl and the few Japanese relics MacArthur himself possibly may have shoved his sausage in within the barbershop back in his heyday. The bowling alley girl was banging like three guys as it was, and she definitely let you know she wasn't interested the day she greeted you too. Or you try to be slick and ask her out on a date. Nope, she was a cool piece of eye candy, not much else. She became the five knuckle shuffle fantasy of half this base, if not the whole entire thing. I know I snapped one out thinking of her back at my barracks, on more than one occasion, no need to lie about masturbation. It becomes a sport. I always had fresh magazines and some videos available, I was not shy. I rented them out after I was done with them. As long as I got them back undamaged, no sticky pages, it was all good. I also ordered a few penis pumps, fake pussies, and even a few blows-up dolls for married guys who couldn't purchase them on their own credit cards because their wives would find out or something. I just think they were just embarrassed to get those things at mail call.

I don't remember how long we did the zombie shuffle to work and then home prior to orders coming down the wire that we were heading to the Philippines because our military bases there were being turned over to the Filipino government. Mt. Pinatubo had just erupted as well. The place was getting a bit hostile I guess. We were sent over with speed and at all possible haste. Our amphibious assault vehicles were outfitted with their exterior armor, and we definitely had our weapons also within our turrets of these machines. The command never spoke of anything other than we were heading there to do some training. In my opinion it was an expeditionary force sent as a show of force and military presence to keep the hostiles in check and to make the transition as peaceful as possible. I remember getting to drive as we were loading up onto the USS *San Bernardino* (LST 1189) just outside the edge of the coral reef within our coastline of Camp Schwab. I also remember hearing it cost somewhere in the ballpark of ten thousand dollars to launch each individual vehicle into Japanese waters due to some government red tape. Our whole platoon left that early evening, so twelve tractors drove across the sand and entered the ocean. That is a lot of money if you add it up, the cost was steep to our government because of the damage those vehicles cause to the natural coral reef, for sure. Quite possibly it was very steep of a price because we dropped a few atomic bombs on them years ago and now we get the asshole tax in return.

The vehicle was running fine, and we were fourth in line to enter the back of this ship. What is cool about this LST ship is that it can flood its rear end with water and lower its ass in the water to help with launching and retrieving our amtracs. It also had a helicopter deck on the topside rear, and the front came equipped with a 112 feet bow ramp to unload tanks, artillery, and Hummers to shore also. All of which were already onboard waiting on us. The key to successfully entering the rear was to cross-steer while heading up the huge ramp, so we were told. I had never done this before at all, so I only went on my staff sergeant's advice. When we entered the water with coral reef beneath us, the waters were calm, but as the vehicle headed beyond its protection, the swells were pretty big. The first amtrac in line was able to enter the ship without a problem at all. The second vehicle wasn't as lucky; it slid back off the ramp and had to fall back to the rear. The third vehicle had done the same. I remember hearing some flash radio messages in my helmet about the seas being too rough for us to get into the ship and the lieutenant was thinking about calling it off till morning with the navy captain. The added weight of the armor was creating a problem as well. I was already on my throttle, and the staff sergeant just simply told me, "Do not fuck this up, Mello."

I approached very fast and had to time the rear ramp as it came completely out of the water and plunged back into the ocean. I swear the ramp missed the nose of our vehicle by sheer inches as it went down into the sea. I punched the throttle and the tracks began to grab on the ramp as the water jets roared us forward as well. It was a bit scary because the nose of your vehicle points straight up once you begin the climb. I never let off the throttle one bit and counter-steered to the right and back to the left one time each direction. No slipping at all. There was minimal room for error because the opening to the ship was about two feet on either side of a fully armored vehicle. If I misjudged the distance, we would have hit the side and certainly would've slid off the ramp possibly within a barrel roll at speed and full throttle. The vehicle was on a wheelie or it felt like one as we entered the rear of the ship at speed. The front end suddenly came down, and I mashed the brakes once it planed off within the safety of the ship. What a rush, I thought as we were ground guided by the navy personnel into final position after having me turn the vehicle around midway into the boat. This obviously is done for our rapid departure during launching. I even turned the wrong damn direction at first thinking the man giving me the hand signals with flashlights indicated to turn left instead of right. My staff sergeant came over the vehicles com system and said, "Great job, Mello." It took well into the dark of night for each vehicle to get onboard, and it took several hours to properly dog down our amtracs with four thick steel cables per along with safety chains. I was tired and covered in well deck grease, but we were heading to the Philippines, baby.

We were brought into our berthing area, sleeping quarters, and it was a very large area with rows of canvas beds going from floor to ceiling like six high-stacked evenly spaced from floor to ceiling. I chose one of the beds closer to the top of the stack. When I crawled upward to get into it, there wasn't much room left once I positioned myself lying down to the bottom of the guy above me. We were packed in like sardines. This was definitely a test of patience. Living so tightly packed in definitely began to wear on my nerves. The smell of other people's farting and vomit from seasickness during this trip was insane. We had traveled through a typhoon while heading to our destination. This boat was a total bad ass within the giant seas in my opinion. I had been out to sea plenty on much smaller boats while commercial fishing, and they got knocked around plenty in far less weather. Actually, before we went through the craziness of the typhoon, the visits to the chow hall while onboard sucked, there were far too many people in line from other platoons on ship. After the seas came alive and started rocking and rolling, it diminished to damn near three people within my platoon, and a lot of other Marines from other units didn't venture toward food either. I become very hungry at sea actually, maybe it's inbred from the fishing days. I ate like a king.

While we were in the rough weather, we were told not to go on deck at all. The waves were close to 100 feet high and the winds were really whipping over 160 miles an hour. If you were dumb enough to go topside during this, you would certainly wish you hadn't. I tried to tell some of the guys in my platoon who had thought they were going to die that if they got up and ate something, they would feel better. That wasn't happening. During the night, I had gotten up to go take a leak so I jumped down off my rack and I was standing in four inches of vomit and seawater within our sleeping area. It was disgusting. All night people were moaning and puking on themselves straight out of their racks without much effort to make it to the toilet. These guys were fresh fish to this kind of sea. I laughed at them at first because some of the guys who were in charge of our platoon were knocked out of commission and turning green before my very eyes. I thought back to my first trip out in the Atlantic with my older brother Kevin on the fishing vessel *The Settler* and just knew that whole crew would've laughed their asses off at this sorry bunch. I guess I can thank them for giving me sea legs and the knowledge to stave off illness if you happen to feel dizzy. You had to allow yourself to be loose. The trick back then was to finish all the gear work and stow all the food quickly, eat something, and go to sleep on the way out to the fishing grounds. Your body naturally adjusts its equilibrium to the ebb and flow of the waves while sleeping. The roughest seas I had been through prior to this were 25-40ft seas, but that vessel was less than a fifth of the length of the USS *San Bernardino* which was 522 feet. I never got sick then, and I sure as hell wasn't going to disgrace the mighty New Bedford fisherman of the past with crawling into my rack like a pussy crying and puking. No way, that would be sacrilegious.

I sloshed through the vomit and reached the head only after walking on the walls as the boat violently made its roll from starboard to port. I hate the fact we changed that term *port* from the old version *leeward*. I liked the old-school *leeward* myself. Reminds me of the book *Moby Dick* where Herman Melville wrote about the New Bedford whaling fleet. I could rehearse most of that book in my head from the movie adaptation starring Gregory Peck as Captain Ahab aboard the *Pequot*. I even did a pretty good impression of him while we were out at sea on our voyage to the Philippines. I always turn a bit toward madness within my own soul just remembering how the tale was told. The obsession drove him nuts to seek out and kill the white whale. I, on the other hand, drew power from it while heading to the toilet. I also know my own obsession was similar when I sought out the drugs as a child, nothing mattered more. I'm also here because I want my license to kill and not get arrested for it. I have massive rage. I could relate. I guess that would be a great learning tool if you're an addict, or if want to be killer, you could draw insights that may help stop your own madness. I just happen to like the tale because I'm from the New Bedford area; we all become a bit crazy at times. It's in our blood.

When I reached the head and turned to enter, there were several guys lying on the floor vomiting and some just blew out leaning over the sink waiting on their next vomiting session. As I was nearing the toilet, the ship must have really began pitching very hard because the toilet exploded a stream of water out off itself, and it hit the ceiling. Each time it pitched back to the port side that we were on, the toilet spewed. It was filled with brown excrement and foulness beyond belief. The seas had gotten bigger I would assume. I left that head and felt bad for them guys who couldn't move themselves to avoid the mess from sloshing over them. I continued down toward the well decks where our amtracs were stowed for this voyage and pissed right on the floor because it didn't mattered anymore. All the sewage was mixing into the seawater within the lowest decks anyways. I reached the hatch to the amtrac parking area and stepped into a very peaceful place. Nobody was screaming and crying they were going to die, the stench of vomit and shit was gone too.

I didn't stay long; I immediately went back to my rack and grabbed my gear. I stopped off at my lieutenant's bunk and told him I would volunteer being on fire watch and on mess duty if he would allow me to go sleep in my tractor. He rolled his head and puked on himself and told me, "Yes, no problem, leave me alone." I was glad he was green, actually. He made us try a morning run several days earlier on the upper deck in a bit too rough of seas. I was tripped by someone behind me losing his balance, and sure enough, I cut both my palms on the rough black sandpaper-gritted no-skid surface on the helicopter deck. I tried to tell him prior to the asinine attempt at running together that it was unsafe. Oh well, he's pretty much paying his due to the god Poseidon anyways. *He demands respect, dumbass. Keep puking.*

I laughed as I made my way back out of this area. Several guys in my unit asked where I was going and wanted to come with me, but I refused anyone who looked green or pale in any way, shape, or form. There were about six of us. It was a blessing to have company and to be out of that stink fest which lasted close to four days within violent weather. The ocean remained rough, but once people had gotten seasickness, it lasted for a week or more.

I entered my tractor and forgot about everyone else's problems within the puke-filled sleeping area. I totally created a reason to head toward the upper decks too. I reached the chow hall and asked one of the mess crew if I could volunteer, he accepted. I slept like a baby in my amtrac and ate with the navy personnel for the next several days. I never missed a meal. I mostly just hung around drinking coffee and shooting the shit with them. I helped peel some potatoes and laughed my balls off with the cooks. I even ventured topside and into the bridge with a chief petty officer from the night crew so I could check the view out during the storm. This guy was funny, and we got a lot of laughs together as we shared stories. I was blessed to be normal on this ocean within rough weather because of my brother bringing me out with him on a scallop boat. The lessons learned were harsh then, and it paid off for me now.

The view was absolutely magnificent. The waves were a wall of water heading toward us and this boat crashed through them like they weren't even there. Huge plumes of white spray washed upward as the sides cut into the seas as the bow of the ship submerged temporarily and then reappeared. The wind howled just outside the viewing bridge, and it was very dark. I was impressed by it all. I don't remember the crew's name or who were on watch this evening, but you are all forever etched in my memory. I thank you all for doing a kick-ass job navigating that old bitch safely through that storm. When I returned back to my amtrac, I heard a really loud snap and then a *boom, boom, smash.* A twenty-six-ton amtrac had snapped its dogging cables and was smashing into another until it broke free as well, and both were hitting off the inside of the ship on one side and another amtrac on the other. Use this as an indication on how rough them seas were. A full one-inch set of cables on the rear of them amtracs snapped and broke loose two amtracs, but the third vehicle held strong. Even the safety chain popped on them both. It remained only two vehicles toward the rear smashing around for several days with no way to stop them without being killed in the process. We also no longer walked between them during this storm. We remained on the tops of them at all times. I looked it up, and I believe it was the Super Typhoon Yuri at the time, I could be wrong though. If I did my addition and subtraction correctly, that is, of time and approximate location, I could be right. My memory has been damaged. It was a huge storm. Just knowing we were sent over there on the tail of this dragon kind of gives me the impression we were sent with haste. Something was happening for the powers that be, having had sent us through it, wouldn't you think?

We had arrived safely into Subic Bay and were going to be doing a live fire at the range and have a mock attack on Green Beach upon arrival. This was totally cool to experience. It was very late and everything was done as if it were a real assault. The Marine Force Recon guys headed off the ship first within them Zodiac boats, close to three hours before we took off. We splashed into the water just before dawn, and it was a bit lighter in the sky. These recon boys were definitely bad ass heading out in the darkness the way they did. It certainly took some coconuts to slip off the back of a perfectly good ship with a rubber raft. The rafts had motors on them, but I'm sure they did the last half mile or so with them paddles, or quite possibly swam into shore to avoid detection. I know they got dropped off pretty far off the beach. As we prepared to exit, we were briefed about our plans, and it was pretty much follow the leader out the ship. The ship sank its ass in the water just like loading us in, and it maintained a decent speed while plopping us out like turds in a long line across perhaps a half mile. We were then told we were heading to the beach in formation, so to pay the hell attention to our spacing. This was to simulate separation because it has been learned in the past it was definitely better not to be bunched up as incoming artillery was trying to blow the shit out of you.

I hopped into the driver's seat and awaited our turn to depart. We loaded up all our gear and ammo along with a mortar crew from the infantry along with us for the ride. This was a total rush,

I watched the tractor ahead of me damn near submerge fully
as it left the ramp and splashed into the water. It's impressive
because these vehicles weigh over sixty thousand pounds, and
they still pop right up and float. I was next; I held the brake
and was positive everything was a go on my end. I had shut the
plenum doors to keep the water out of the engine compartment
and from sinking us. The water propulsion was engaged as well as
the tracks, and the bilge pumps were turned on. The navy even
has a traffic light attached to the wall for us drivers to know red
means stop and green means go. I held the brake and roared
that engine to life several seconds before green as if I was in a
dragster at New England speedway. No messing around at all. The
light turned green and off we went all hatches shut, and I was
looking through a three-inch-high slot of glass that gives you a
decent-enough view. I never hesitated neither; my foot remained
on the floor. The tractor held the ramp with its tracks as long
as it could, and we were off that ship and plunged underwater
for several seconds. I switched the tracks off and held the gas on
while opening my hatch to see where I was heading. We didn't
have to remain buttoned up, this was a simulation, and I'm sure
in combat I would keep it closed to stay away from stray bullets.
Well maybe, that's in God's hands anyways. I didn't have to make
that decision right now, and it was awesome swimming into the
beach in my twenty-six-ton beast.

As we were cruising toward shore, several attack helicopters
flew in formation above our heads and headed toward the
mountain just beyond the palm trees and the beach. They fired
some rockets at the hillside, and huge bursts of fire appeared
and then the noise followed several seconds later. It was quite
the spectacle. As they flew back toward the sea, the pilots stayed
very low along the treetops and lifted a group of guys right out of
the jungle connected to a rope it seemed. There were five guys
attached if I remember correctly. This was a simulated recon
jungle extraction. The way it worked was very cool to watch in
person. Our vehicle arrived just short of the actual sand by a
hundred yards. The motor completely shut off, and we lost power.
I opened the plenum doors while within the ocean, which was
very dangerous but it had to be done. I screamed down to the
maintenance guy to get his ass up here with me. He crawled

through and popped up out the driver's hatch as I was lifting the engine compartment doors. He asked what was wrong, I told him the damn thing just died. We lost all power and if we couldn't get this thing running, we would definitely be sinking in a little while. The lieutenant was already talking to the staff sergeant about abandoning the thing. Before we'd lose this piece of equipment to a poor decision, let's fix it. He crawled down into the engine and noticed a few wires were screwed up. He had to splice them, and it would take a few minutes. I told him just to hold them together with his hands because water was already flooding us. He was scared but I jumped into the driver's seat and listened for him to say give it a try. I pushed the Start button, and the machine roared back to life. I heard him scream from the shock he took as it started also. The bilge pumps kicked on, and we were out of danger. I could've waited for a discussion about the whole thing, but I decided to get into action. That maintenance guy saved the taxpayers a serious amount of money if not some lives. He had got his reward already, two burnt fingers.

We proceeded to the sand and we drove inland toward the mountain. We followed a tight jungle trail for close to a mile. During this jungle expedition, I observed everything. I even noticed this double-decker Gilligan's Island bamboo and grass-built building. Inside on the second floor and hanging out the window waving and yelling at us were beautiful topless bronze-skinned Filipino women. There was close to twenty of them. It was a pleasant surprise. Hell yeah! I guess our sergeants and a few navy guys weren't lying, the women are very hot over here and they love American soldiers.

"Hey, Staff Sergeant, did you see that chick on the far left? I think she likes you. Please tell me we will definitely be returning this way," I yelled while driving by.

He replied back to me, "No worries, Mello, you haven't seen anything yet."

Being on that ship certainly gets lonely, and I could use a few cold brews and a nice woman to wash this grease off me and to rub me down. It was a short-lived experience, but it certainly had lasted the test of time in my mind. I felt bad for the guys who were stuck in the belly of our amtrac, they missed the warm greeting and them tatas.

We emerged from the jungle trails into an open valley pot marked by craters from explosions long ago in the past. I had to avoid some of the larger holes because we would certainly have got stuck or throw a track while driving through them. Throwing a track within deep sugar sand is very easy to manage. A few simple bad turns on a steep hill like the other side of these craters was exactly the place it would happen. The sand would build up as the tracks desperately dug in for traction, and the driver would countersteer naturally, thinking it would help the cause. Pop went the tracks right off the rear idler wheels and the rear sprocket drive because the sand was mightier than the steel. I wasn't looking forward to breaking track in this heat. It was better to steer around them. One of our vehicles happened to get swallowed up in front of our column actually. We laughed at them as we drove by. Another vehicle had positioned itself to tow them out of the hole after they reattached their track of course. I loved how we all knew these things already about our vehicles and their capabilities, yet guys just screw the pooch anyways. I was glad it was them in one sense, but sort of disgusted because they were part of our unit. "Let's go, people, pull your head out of your ass." If this was a real attack, we would be wasting valuable time and putting others at risk by bunching up on the beach. We would be sitting ducks for even a small mortar crew to have a field day plopping shells on us. I would certainly have chewed someone's ear off if I was in charge of this outfit, but guess what, this was our leader's tractor stuck in the hole. Shit happens!

We drove into the actual range and dropped off the guys within our tractor. They were setting up their mortars and firing downrange within minutes. These grunts don't fuck around. As for our unit, we took up a firing line off to the far right of this range well ahead of the infantry. It was a safety thing. Before we could begin to fire our ordinance downrange, our commander told us to be aware for incoming rounds would be flying overhead. The ship was going to fire her guns along with the artillery battery also. This was absolutely balls deep, bad ass. I could hear the blast of the guns far off in the distance, but as I looked up, I could actually see the damn rounds flying above. The damn things must be the size of a Volkswagen, I thought as it impacted the mountainside and exploded with a far bigger fireball than them cheap rockets from the helicopters. The noise reached us and it was an unforgettable eerie sound. It was a distinct series of hallow thuds, and it definitely caught you in the chest, but then it was followed by the noise of explosions. The ground shook slightly also because I felt it in my cushioned seat in my vehicle. We were close to a mile away or maybe even more, but it was scary to think about. I definitely wouldn't want to be on the receiving end of those guns. No fucking way.

During our live fire exercise, we each took turns within the turret firing the fifty calibers and the mark nineteen belt-fed grenade launcher. I thoroughly enjoyed cutting down a tree over a half mile away with the fifty and then dropping high explosive grenades from my awesome grenade machine gun. This thing could fire forty rounds in a minute. It was very cool to traverse the turret and let the rounds explode in a long succession of explosions. After our live fire exercise was completed, we loaded back into our vehicle and drove back toward the beach. We stopped in a huge clearing and created a half-moon with our vehicles and cleaned our weapons and established our fire watches for the evening. We were going to spend the night. As we were doing our jobs, the villagers began arriving carrying trinkets and hammocks and swords. The trinkets were all carved from brass and copper, the swords were made from the leaf springs of vehicles, and the hammocks were just simply hammocks. I noticed several of the children were missing arms or a hand and a few older ones had been missing legs. I inquired what had happened to them, but they kept saying, "You buy, you buy."

When darkness came, I snuck off from my unit and headed toward the double-decked grass hut. I got there in a short amount of time and saw several other soldiers already there also. I was looking for answers, not pussy; an old man stepped outside who spoke English and I asked what the deal was with the missing limbs. He told me, "The children go up into the mountain and retrieve the brass and copper. Sometimes they pick up unexploded shells and they go off. It's very bad place and we try to keep them away, but we are poor people. Sometimes hunger will drive them into the mountain regardless the danger. They sell the brass and copper for food, and if they get lucky and find a good unexploded shell, it is sold to the guerilla forces or the

Filipino army. Depending on who is closer or willing to pay more."
I thought of my younger years of stealing copper pipes to fuel
my own addictions and how I scraped and scratched just to feed
myself at times. This was definitely my ultimate test within life.

I completely lost interest that night within the killing of
another human being. How the hell do they expect me to kill
people who are poor and hungry? I grew up poor and hungry
when my parents divorced. I certainly questioned my soul. I
know I would defend myself if attacked or in the protection of
another, but I certainly don't want to kill someone because they
are desperate to feed themselves or their family. I would be going
against everything I had been taught as a child. I would never be
able to look into the eyes of my mother and be honest with her
also. If I was asked this night to leave the Marine Corps, I would've
packed my stuff and left. I was ashamed to be there after thinking
all the blowing up stuff was cool. I even began to think about the
arrogance of it all. I know I'm a soldier and I'm going to protect
my fellow American Marines if need be, but what the hell are we
doing cruising around blowing shit up on some obscure hillside
within a foreign country and then calling it training. We then in
turn pretend to think it is all okay. I had seen enough to know
I didn't need a weapon within this country regardless the civil
unrest. Our show of force was heard for miles around I'm sure. I
wasn't proud of myself on that day at all when I saw kids missing
limbs, that is the God's honest truth of it. I traded some batteries
out of my flashlight and even returned to my vehicle and gave the
kids who followed me a box of MREs in exchange for a hammock.
I slept in it that night with a very heavy heart along with a very
pretty Filipino girl that Papa-san had sent me late that night. I
gave him more than the usual for a hammock, I guess. I never
told anyone about how I felt about any of this until now. I didn't
even ask my commander if it was okay to give these people some
food. I just did it. Fuck it, it's the right thing to do.

After this night of realization, I became distant within my mind
but never once voiced my opinion, which was not what I was in the
Marine Corps to do. I was in it to follow orders and experience
everything. I was in a foreign country who was our ally during
the war against Japan long before I stepped on this piece of the
earth. I wish I had arrived with ships filled with food rather than

a ship filled with bombs and bullets. As we returned to the ship, I didn't even jump into the driver's seat. I sat in the rear of the vehicle and pulled watch on the rear hatch. I didn't mind this spot one bit. I was there to ensure no one panicked and reached for the rear hatch while in the ocean. If someone panicked, it was my job to beat them back to protect the machine and the men inside from sinking to the bottom. It was a less-thrilling spot to be sitting, but each job is vital to maintain the mission. I liked to talk trash to guys about sinking to scare them. That was my entertainment while within the rear hatch duties.

On the next practice attack on the beach, God must have been watching over me and us. I was in the driver's seat once again behind the gunnery sergeant's amtrac waiting for them to exit. We were the last of our platoon of vehicles left on the boat to join the fun in the ocean once again. Practice, practice, practice. That is how things get mastered within the military. Well wouldn't you know it, the kid driving the vehicle in front of me lined up on the wrong painted line on the well deck floor on his departure? I noticed it only after he roared full throttle toward and into the wall of the ship's rear. He then panicked I guess because he reversed really fast and bounced up the opposite side of the inner walls. He was out of control. Good thing the navy ground crew hurried to stop him from trying to actually leave the ship because he certainly had it heading back toward the exit.

It turned out he had ripped the whole front of the amtrac's left pontoon wide open. They would have surely sank and rapidly at that with this flotation area breeched. I remember us not having to exit this boat that day because of this bonehead's mistake. I guess it was our entire fault also because even the three guys behind him in my amtrac hadn't noticed the mistake prior to him taking off, including me. The two guys in his vehicle that had their heads poked out of their own hatches hadn't noticed either. One of those guys was our gunny. I was just glad no one was injured or killed. The only thing hurt today was this kid's pride. I also wouldn't be firing weapons at this mountainside again either, causing a child in the future a missing limb or possibly his life which was my inner prize. We formed up in formation later that evening when our entire platoon returned to the ship and this poor bastard got a brand-new medal to wear around his neck. It was a huge piece of aluminum from the mangled amtrac attached to a loop of two-inch chain. He was to wear it for the remainder of our time on ship including the chow hall, and he had to wear it to bed also. We laughed our asses off at this guy for actually trying to get another run at exiting even after smacking into the side. It was funny but also serious business. We were now most definitely going to be doing a more thorough prelaunch checklist no doubt about it.

My stay in the Philippines after all this was clouded in a haze of nonstop drinking. Once our training and simulated warfare was completed, we were loaded up and deposited into our new base just outside Olongapo City, at the Subic Bay naval station. We were housed in temporary plywood-framed canvas tents, and my new bed became a raised canvas rack. I don't remember the military terms for these items anymore. I just remember the first time I crossed the bridge from our base over into the city. The water beneath it was called Shit River. It was most definitely the foulest-smelling water system I've ever encountered. As we crossed this river I thought nothing of the why it stinks at the time. I would later discover that the whole surrounding area had makeshift troughs dug into the ground leading into the river. This was the sewer system for many of the houses, absolutely disgusting. We tossed coins into the water and watched kids dive into the murky waters and retrieve them. I guess this was a tradition. They certainly had a great time waiting on people on the riverbank awaiting our tossed-out money. I hadn't discovered the sewage problems when I first tossed my coins. I just had fun watching kids battle over them. It reminded me of when I was younger battling with my brothers over just about anything.

We were allowed to venture into the City for Liberty, but we would have to be back on base prior to the morning formation each day if I remember correctly, like I said it's clouded. I remember the exchange rate of my currency was one dollar to twenty-five of theirs. I never traveled very far at all within this place if I think about it. I headed right to one of the first clubs I saw. This place was by far a den of mischief, booze, women, and plenty of mojo. Mojo was a mixture of liquors and some local fruit juices. This stuff was cheap, and it did the trick. I swear to you I could leave the base, get fed, get drunk, get laid, have my clothes washed and pressed, and get a ride from a kid peddling a rickshaw cart back to base for less than five bucks if need be. This place was like heaven to me; I was young, dumb, and full of cum. I was a kid in the candy store; I didn't have to do a thing. The women were somewhere in the ratio of five to one man within the clubs, they ran up to us. Buy-me-drinkie girls were all over the place. I guess my hormones were on overdrive because without fail each and every night I did these things. If I think about it, everyone did this within the military that happened to get the privilege to experience this port. Well, at least the ones who aren't complete liars filled with sacks of shit. In no way whatsoever was I rude to any of these people either. This was their culture, I was a visitor, an American, a Marine and they loved us. I can't say I went to just this one club either because I went to different ones with different guys each night from within my platoon and plenty of other serviceman were out and about also.

I also remember the pushcart vendors selling food as if it was Fenway Park and I was outside the stadium buying a hot dog. The guy I went to sold different food items though. He served chicken feet charbroiled, chicken heads, roasted dog, lizards, and really delicious teriyaki-flavored slivers of monkey meat all served on bamboo sticks. It was just like being served beef teriyaki at any local Chinese restaurant only in smaller portions. I didn't notice it was monkey until someone pointed it out to me closer to the end of our stay. I staggered to this guy's cart without fail all the time prior to knowing. If I did know, I don't think it would've made a difference actually, I was drunk. My stay off base was restricted within two weeks actually. I had missed a morning formation by damn near ten minutes one day. I had drunk far too much and stayed with a young pretty Filipino girl at her house as usual and overslept as did she. I got scared when I awoke actually and rushed to the base to find my platoon already in formation. I wasn't alone either in the late arrival. A black corporal had done the same. Guess what, restricted duty for a full week. No liberty. What a drag.

During my week of no liberty, I became the guy riding shotgun and sometimes driving within a Hummer making trips to the bridge to pick up and drop off Marines throughout the evenings. I didn't mind this job. It was funny to watch guys all smashed from too much partying. I was jealous actually. I missed the women. I was taken off the no liberty with one night remaining before our ship was to set sail back to sea. I should've stayed on the base knowing full well I was going to get drunk. I went out anyways; I was saying my good-byes I guess. I had just gotten paid and felt generous. I paid for ten girls' bar fines to Momma-san and went wild with them all. We bounced from club to club. Sure enough I awoke late once again within the entanglement of naked women within a cheap hotel, and by the time I got to the dock, the USS *San Bernardino* was gone. I was screwed, I figured. Was it really a bad thing though? I loved this place. I could surely find something to do; there were Vietnam veterans already living here who own businesses here. They seemed to have survived. I certainly could. I was thinking this as more Marines and sailors began to show up late also. We began discussing what the punishment would be but decided we didn't have to worry much because there were higher-ranking individuals other than us among us. I think I even seen a few high-ranking officers late as well, among the fifty of us give or take. I wasn't worried when I saw that because these guys would take the worst ass-chewing for sure.

The ship sent out a smaller vessel to retrieve us a few hours later, and we returned to the ship. The navy shore patrol officer and I talked while on the way. He told me it was totally expected and wasn't uncommon for guys to miss the boat. He told me a lot of guys disappear within this country and go AWOL actually. He said that's when things become difficult for young Marines and young sailors. He also told me now was not the time to be going AWOL in this place. This whole base will be closed very soon. I was grateful for his words, and it was comforting while I was thinking I may spend some time in the brig or something. I already knew my lieutenant was going to be pissed off, along with my gunnery sergeant. It turned out they weren't pissed off at all either when several of us returned to our berthing area to check back in. They almost looked surprised we returned. It was an odd feeling but no harm, no foul.

I remained within my fire watch duties within my amtrac area the whole time. I wasn't bothered by my command because they knew where I was and periodically they would come down to check on us and make sure things were okay. Living on ship is very boring with not much to do. I would venture to the berthing area where my platoon was and play cards and shoot the shit when it wasn't my turn to watch over the vehicles or help out with the mess duties. I just sort of floated around the ship looking to stave off boredom.

Our next port of call was Hong Kong. This place was amazing. I remember pulling right into Hong Kong harbor and seeing an entire floating city beneath us filled with smaller boats along the docks. The city was huge on both sides of the harbor. When we were allowed to leave the boat, I was off and running once again. Only this time I really didn't pick up any women. I was amazed by the use of bamboo for staging. I come from a past of construction, so seeing how they used natural materials to reach the height to build buildings instead of the steel I was accustomed to was fascinating. I was thinking, *Holy shit, that looks dangerous, especially thirty floors high, sometimes higher.* It was cool watching the dance of Chinese construction workers going about their jobs at such incredible heights on bamboo. My family would be shocked also. I spent close to an hour just looking up in awe. The group of guys I was hanging out with at the time was from the maintenance platoon, they enjoyed it also. Like I said, I hung out with a lot of different folks. We ended up going to eat at McDonald's of all places. Typical Americans I guess. I think it was because all the food service places and restaurants displayed plenty of dead things in their shop windows. They didn't want to be adventurous. I on the other hand definitely made it a point to try a lot of different cuisine while in the country. Just not with these guys. I tried dogs, ducks, cockroaches, grasshoppers, lizards, sea clam, lots of sushi, snakes, all sorts of crazy stuff, and plenty of rice. I enjoyed them all. I cannot lie. The Chinese put out a good spread, and the streets were filled with great spots to eat. I also noticed the elderly people live to staggering ages, and they were upright and walking pretty damn good, Chinese got it going on within the world of longevity upon this earth.

We ran into some British Marines in a bar we happened to walk into and stayed the afternoon drinking Foster's of all beers with them. These guys were very hardcore as was our group when it came to the consumption of alcohol. They partied hard and trained hard just like us. It was a treat and a blessing to share a few brews with our long-past countrymen, I even broke their balls a bit about the American Revolution. Guess what? You bloody, wankers, I'm also from just south of Boston, New Bedford, area. No taxation without representation, take your tea and shove it. Long live the King, Manchester United, and all that jazz. We laughed and enjoyed one another's company within a sea of Oriental people. We parted with a hurrah, and back to the ship we went. I didn't need to linger long because Hong Kong is an expensive place. My money didn't go very far over here. I got like eight bucks for each of my dollars, but things were expensive. I wish I had more time and money to tell you the truth. The hospitality of these people was unmatched anywhere, but you need the chicken scratch, the money to experience it. I was on a budget.

We stayed at this port for like five days I believe. I rode the train which runs underneath the entire harbor to another part of the city on one occasion. This place was a marvel of engineering. I distinctly remember there was a curfew in the nighttime also. The Chinese Red Army marched the streets to enforce it also. It was under British rule militarily speaking at the time, but these guys ruled the streets at night. I know because I was wondering back toward the boat sort of lost and I was approached by a really pissed-off Chinese officer as they were marching down a main drag. This guy totally flipped yelling for me to get back inside where I had come from. I tried to explain to him I was a Marine off the naval ship USS *San Bernardino* docked in the harbor just down the way. He wasn't hearing a word of it. I was escorted to a hotel and told to stay the night, no exceptions. I wasn't going to argue. The Chinese definitely don't play games with their law enforcement. Go act stupid over there, and find out on your own. I just had the sixth sense to know not to cause a problem. I think it's awesome actually. The crime rate definitely gets lowered I'm sure. If you kill someone over here, you definitely are killed shortly after, their rules, their show. I didn't want to find out the punishment for disobedience or disrespecting this officer or this group of army soldiers. I just simply obeyed. It was my fault for not heading to the boat sooner. My cost for this fuck up: $240, American, for a stay in a shabby hotel for four hours, but it was worth it. They looked pretty cool marching in their dull green uniforms, with a distinct red star on their hats, I was impressed.

The tour of the Orient continued on to mainland Japan next. We headed to Mt. Fuji actually. This was the last stop of our Hollywood cruise as they call it in the military when you don't head into combat while on a float. How true, this really wasn't in my lifetime on this planet. I certainly didn't do much, but I was available and within harm's way while serving onboard. Anything can happen, and the call can come at anytime. I was proud to be on this expeditionary task force. We would later cruise back to Okinawa after our stay in Mt. Fuji of course. But this was the end of any new ports of call for our grand vacation tour while I served aboard an awesome ship with a huge laundry list of service within her lifetime at sea. You should take the time to look this old girl up online if you have the time. It certainly kept me safe within some wild weather. She was beyond her years and held together with more coats of paint scraped off and repainted than the thickness of her steel, but she was definitely a strong seaworthy ship. She was launched in 1970 and even served in Vietnam, partook in Desert Storm, and just returned from the Philippines during a natural disaster crisis. This vessel was decommissioned from service in 1995. As much as I disliked being away from loved ones, she rocked me to sleep every night I was in her arms, just like my mom did when I was a baby.

The arrival to Mt. Fuji was actually a welcomed relief. The mighty mountain lay just behind our barracks, but I would not see her till morning. We arrived at night, and it was awesome to bump into a different platoon from our own company already staying there. I guess the guys who skipped out on initiations had been dealt with also because they all cried to me about getting bum rushed in the middle of the night one by one while sleeping. It wasn't a bad thing at all, I told them. "You should never hold fear within your own unit. It makes others weary if you are scared of them. It leaves a question in our minds if you will stand beside us in the off chance the enemy actually attacks." I secretly relished in the stories of mayhem, and we all got to share our trip to the Philippines and how wild it was over there. According to these guys, Tokyo was the next happening place to go and check out because they loved it. Tonight was strictly on base only. So in my head I figured it was a good time to have us a get-together outside. A few guys went and bought several bottles of vodka, some ice, and I went and purchased a bunch of fresh fruits and some juices. Before we left for the on base commissary, I had someone really clean out an aluminum trash can. He had this thing spotless when we arrived. It was time for Mello's own silver surfer party punch. That's what we called it anyways. I mixed it all together within the can, and we all got pretty lit-up in celebration of being together. We had a few laughs wrestling one another and most certainly talked a lot of smack about how guys screwed the pooch during our operations, but we all came home uninjured. It was a great time in my memory.

The next day when I woke up for formation the mountain was snow covered at the top, and it looked like a giant volcano just waiting to explode. I felt an immense sense of sleeping energy within it filling me with power and joy. This was a once-in-a-lifetime experience to see for the very first time in person. I stood in silence as I gazed over the barracks and took several relaxing deep breaths and felt at peace. Anything more said would ruin the moment in my head and in yours. We were released from duty and given a three-day pass of liberty. Yep, you guessed it, Tokyo, here we come. We took the bullet train to get there. I remember being able to buy Mickey's big-mouth beer right out of a vending machine in the station. Our trip to the biggest city in Japan was on.

Another fine place in my mind to be, the women were very pretty and most certainly loved us also. Japanese girls definitely know how to get down in them clubs. I had sex with a girl right on the dance floor. She lifted her skirt and just slipped up onto my lap as we did the roadhouse grind right there. I looked up to see my buddies laughing and pointing behind me. I was shocked to see us on a jumbo screen damn near twenty feet across and ten feet high, just bumping and grinding for all to see. We completed our little rendezvous and parted company as one of her friends dragged me out the club by my hand. She damn near ripped my clothes off outside and lay down her fur coat right on a gravel road for me to lay on as she rode me to her own bliss. I was a piece of meat to some very hungry, horny Japanese girls, and it was fine by me. I even got the chance to meet a sumo champion at the time across the street at the Hard Rock Café; he was related to one of the guys in my unit. He was his cousin. This man was Hawaiian and very, very large. He traveled like royalty within this country. They even used a man lift to get him into the second floor of the club. I was greatly honored to meet this guy, and as he shook my hand, it disappeared into his like a child's hand being held by his dad. He was called Takamiyama Daigoro in Japan, birth given name is Jesse Kuhaulua. If you want to check him out also; he was the first non-Asian sumo champ ever. I'm unsure if he remembers me at all, but it was awesome meeting him.

I was later picked up by a very attractive businesswoman who drove a Jaguar of all vehicles within this country as we were leaving the club. I never traveled alone when I was going to spend the night in a new environment, so sure enough, she allowed my friend and his date to come along. This girl must have had some serious money because she paid for all of us to stay in an expensive hotel. We had our own separate apartments actually.

I remember heading into the bathroom within this place she paid for but couldn't find a toilet or a urinal. I was standing confused as this super-hot girl came into the bathroom behind me and just squatted and pissed right in the middle of the floor. I was like "what in the hell are you doing?" in my mind, but she then turned a valve on, near the wall, and water washed the entire floor and everything went down a drain hole in the corner of the bathroom. The floor was pitched. I certainly stepped out of that bathroom rather quickly knowing full well people drop deuce also on that floor. Nope, I put on my sneakers first, prior to entering again. With that said, I had completed the trifector. Three girls in one night within the biggest party place on earth in my mind. The gods must favor me, I thought at the time. The next day was filled with visiting a few tourist spots of interest and then heading back to base. My visit to Tokyo was unforgettable.

Our visits to the exotic places were over, and we headed back to Okinawa by ship and removed all our gear and drove our amtracs back to boring ass Camp Schwab. It took us three days to complete that journey from Mt. Fuji to Okinawa, and it was nice to be back in my barracks so I could take a comfortable shower and wash off some of this grease. Several days had passed by before my next problem arose to hurt my actual Marine Corps record. Everything I had done in the past came with minor punishments. A few late arrivals warrant to be just given extra duty or restriction to base. I lost rank in this issue, and it pissed me off. The way this all came to pass was a night of hanging in the bowling alley with several guys having a harmless few beers. One of the idiots in my platoon had gotten drunk and was really giving the girl at the bowling alley a hard time about being a whore and all sorts of rude statements. I noticed he was drunk when she came over to our table and asked us to take him home. He was acting stupid and rude. I certainly took offense to it as did a few other guys once we watched his actions and listened to him talk for a while. One of the other guys noticed he was still covered in the grease from being on the boat also on his legs. The guy hadn't showered in a few days, we assumed, because this wasn't just being dirty from hanging around on the ramp. He was damn near black with grime from his knees down and had a few blobs of grease on him also.

When we got outside the bowling alley, we all decided to toss dollar bills at him and tell him to buy some damn soap from the commissary and clean up his act. Once we did that, he took offense to me only for doing it. He charged at me several times, but he was drunk so I simply sidestepped out of his way and tossed him to the ground each time. He stopped his crazy, violent bursts and began to cry and scream at us for making him look stupid. He was embarrassed for being a shit bird. I told him to go home, wash up, and just sleep it off. We left him there crying in his own filth and drunken stupor. He screamed and hollered we were assholes and all sorts of stuff. I didn't need to keep arguing or allow him to have violent outbursts toward me again. I would certainly have to punch him out I figured, so I walked away. I went home and went to bed without ever laying a strike on this kid. I was awoken by military police and arrested for assault. This piece of trash, drunken, bum called the MPs were on me. I was arrested and given a quick questioning on what happened, I even had a few witnesses on my side that told it exactly how it went down to our captain. He was in the wrong, not me. I should've gone to the bowling alley and grabbed the girl whom he was acting like an absolute jackass to, but I wasn't allowed. Nope, this Quentin Tarantino look-alike motherfucker outranked me by a month. The captain believed his cry baby ass and not us. I was given office hours, loss of pay, and busted down to private from lance corporal. I have to believe this captain still might have been sore about having to deliver my money personally when we landed in the Philippines. I guess he had to go out of his way to make sure I received my paycheck. Truthfully, I might have been better off without that money. I also didn't care much about that money either. I had never set up my direct deposit with a bank, prior to leaving the States. He held a grudge. This captain was an asshole within my command, no doubt.

I would have to go and clean the company office every night for the next two weeks. I was restricted to the base once again. This time I was totally not at fault. Several days later this same jackass I had tried to straighten out within his drunken rages, we all have them, but the unsanitary bathing practices wasn't cool, nor was being a dick toward that girl. He started a fight with another guy. This time he bit a huge bleeding bite mark into the guy's chest he was tangled with as they were rolling around in the barracks hallway. Wouldn't you know it, he's drunk again. As one of my sergeants was running toward them to break it up along with several other guys, I reached out and yanked him into my room. I told this sergeant, "You see what I mean about this guy? He's out of control. I lost rank because of this asshole just a few days ago. You definitely have to help me out with this bullshit and get that bad mark on my record removed." He told me there was nothing he could do. I even protested to my staff sergeant about it as well. "Nope, nothing we can do. The captain already sent the paperwork in, you're fucked." I was definitely steamed to the max. This guy got me busted down to private because the captain took sympathy on him for being a crying pussy within his office, nothing more. Oh, and guess what? They never did a thing about him biting this other kid neither.

I think it was somewhere around the twelfth day of restriction and of cleaning this company office that me and another guy who had just recently lost rank and pay decided to leave a present for the captain. We cleaned the whole office spotless, and just before leaving and calling it a night, this guy hopped up on his desk and pinched out a perfect eight inches of fresh, steamy, log-style shit, and it landed center within the green desk protector. He cleaned up with the paper towels I handed him to wipe himself, he tossed the paper into the trash bag he's carrying, I shut the lights out, and he closed his door. We left the door unlocked as we exited the building and went to bed. The next morning arrived and not a word was said to us at all. The whole day went by actually until we went to clean the office once again. The captain just simply asked us, "Hey, did you guys remember to lock the door last night when you were finished?" We played dumb and said, "We believe so, sir. Why, was it unlocked? Maybe we forgot, sir. I hope nothing's missing." He knew it was us, but couldn't prove it, or if he did cause a stink, everyone would hear about it above the rank of him. He knew he made a mistake in his judgment call on cutting our pay, smearing our records, and just being a total asshole about it all. He left the office and headed out the door, and even before the door closed behind his ass, we were on the floor laughing our asses off. I know one thing, this captain wasn't a prize to us. But he certainly got left a nice freshly pinched surprise from us. Fuck him.

How this next bit of training came along, I have no idea. I was selected along with a bunch of others within our platoon and company to go on a jungle warfare training course in the Northern Training Area of Okinawa. This training was absolutely intense at Camp Gonzales. We remained in the jungles of Okinawa for several weeks learning survival techniques within guerilla warfare. Prior to heading there, I had gone out to a local off-the-beaten-path bar after being allowed to leave the base once again. I met a few Japanese locals who spoke English within this bar at the time, and we shared stories. I listened to them tell me about their grandfathers and grandmothers and how they had lived through the battle of Okinawa long ago. They had gone north into the exact place I was heading to go train. I had actually apologized for what had been done as if I had anything to do with it. They just simply thanked me for my words, and we continued our pleasant conversation. We just simply swapped tales, and it was very cool to take the time to listen and learn. I then was handed a rather large glass jar with yellowish liquid in it which contained a snake at the bottom. I was told this stuff was medicinal, and it would bring me long life and protect me if I happened to be bitten by one in the field. I drank several shots with them, and we parted company with a firm handshake and a new friendship. I thanked them for their hospitality and the fine medicine.

I remember while we were in this jungle training area, the biggest concern we all had was the lack of toilet paper at the time. The training was very interesting to say the least. Survival in the jungle takes grit and lots of knowledge to master. Our instructors were definitely very talented at pumping us up and teaching vital skills. This one instructor was leading a group of us down a bamboo grove of trees through a very narrow trail on one occasion. He had told the small group to stop in our tracks and count to five. He then told us to be aware because he is now our enemy. It was a simulation of what not to do while pursuing the enemy hastily within this environment. We counted to five and began the pursuit to catch up with the instructor. He was gone from our vision within a flash. Within fifty yards of winding trail, he had set up at least five different trip wires connected to flash bangs. I was shocked when one of the guys tripped the very first one. The loud bang scared the shit out of all of us. If this had been real, we all would be dead or would certainly have gotten wounded. That instructor definitely impacted my mind. We were shown all sorts of booby traps designed to kill or to just simply incapacitate foot soldiers.

The night navigation course was very cool also. I walked through moonlit trails, rivers, swamplands, and climbed cliffs and stayed silent. The guy in front of me was walking slowly and creeping along exactly the same as me. I looked to see a massive yellow-spotted black spider at least the size of my palm if not bigger right on his shoulder. I tapped him in the back on the opposite side of the spider and said, "Hey man, something's on your shoulder." He turned and yelled as loud and as high-pitched as any schoolyard group of girls could. I nearly pissed myself laughing along with a few others behind me. We got reprimanded for breaking silence, but it was too funny to pass up. Along this same trail I had seen banana fruit bats for the first time in my life. These bats are damn near the size of any small household dog. If I was to compare a dog to it, I would say a full-grown miniature German badger hound, a dachshund for the uneducated. Just imagine that dog exactly and then add very large wings. These things were scary looking but harmless. They dined on fruits not humans. It was an awesome sight to see in the canopy above our heads. There were damn near sixty of them just chilling upside down from the limbs of trees.

I also got to encounter a very large brown snake crossing our trail during the early morning right in front of me. I wasn't fast enough as I reached to grab his ass to take a closer look. It slithered off into some dense bushes. I knew it would've been a mistake to try and catch a snake in combat also. The Vietnamese used to yank a snake across a trail with a wire attached, and if you were curios in nature like most people were, sure enough—*bah-boom*—you're one dead idiot. I was in training, and I loved the wildlife encounters. I could've done without the mosquitoes, which were very large in numbers at night. The training ended with a very long four-mile jungle-endurance obstacle course. I can only tell you it was very difficult to complete, but our team of twelve guys hauled ass through it. I was blessed to even get the chance at this sort of training. This was one of the premier training facilities within my Marine Corps career thus far, in my opinion.

Once again it was back to boring Camp Schwab for more of the zombie shuffle back and forth to the ramp to sit on our tractors and hold our peckers. I certainly liked the field much better. Things dragged and time stood still doing meaningless maintenance duties on these vehicles all day every day. It drove people to madness, especially me. My body liked to be moving and doing something physically challenging, not sitting around waiting. This was the worst kind of torture, hurries up and waits, not a good time. I also think this was the time someone was stabbed down by the phone booth during a fight between a black guy and a white guy from the infantry units who lived down the hill on this piece of rock also. They had a fight over the phone I guess. Some guys loved to talk all night to their wives or girlfriends back home. This was right around the time the Rodney King verdict came in and the riots happened in Los Angeles. I remember our commanders on the base saying they wanted to separate all the black guys from the white guys. What bullshit. Not one black guy from my platoon went anywhere or did the white guys. Those incidents had nothing to do with one another, and besides, I hold no beef about what goes on out of my control. We are Marines, why the hell would the higher-ups get all scared. I think I even laughed at the notion just as loudly as some of my black brothers, while talking shit together later that evening. I swear the command is fucked up at times, nothing like making a tense few days worse. I had no opinion anyways; the cops did that shit to me too. It's just the way the cards are dealt in life. In my mind it's just people overstepping authority and forcing their will on another. I'm biased about police, so don't ask me.

Our next destination was delivered finally and not soon enough. Our platoon headed to Kadena Air Base within Okinawa. We were sent to repaint the amtracs returning back from Desert Storm. They were sandblasted, re-greased, put through system checks, and then painted back into the green camouflaged color once again. We became the workforce and put in some very hard long days of completing this huge undertaking. There was plenty of dust, dirt, grime, and sweat within this new assignment, but it was better than Camp Schwab. The red-light district was very nearby this air base, and it was fun to go visit on our days off from hard labor. The massage girls were great, and the happy endings were off the charts.

I was returning home with a corporal one night from there, and we had been drunk and carrying on talking trash and roughhousing as usual. We lived in the same room together during the forced labor experience at Kadena. I can't say it was forced labor, but it was damn near close to it. Well, we had hit each other off the walls and pretty much proceeded to knock the crap out of each other. I can't say we were fighting; we were just blowing off steam. I awoke to a fresh black eye in the morning, and he woke up with a few broken ribs. I guess I connected a knee pretty hard on him not realizing my own strength. It was an accident; we both hit hard and threw kicks and knees at each other all the time. He on the other hand got on top of my bunk as I was falling asleep and mounted me and punched me to darkness. We woke up both in pain and asked what happened by our command. He said he fell down the stairs, and I said I caught him. Now that's how it was supposed to be handled within the ranks. No need to cause ourselves problems with loss of pay or restrictive duty. We got carried away and got dinged up by each other, so what. We laughed as we headed out the next night for more of the same. We remained friends also. He was a hot shit and a solid Marine.

Other times of recreation included a really cool volleyball tournament among some other units. Two on two beach volleyball was great exercise. I also tried my hand at some basketball a few times again in my life, but that turned into a sprained ankle and a week of crutches. I preferred the red-light district the most. Some guys from the maintenance platoon and I enjoyed a wild time at a place called the Stage. I swear if it wasn't for the military handing us an off-limits list when we arrived on Okinawa. I don't think most of us would've known about these places. This just shows how things can't be controlled in full. It was most likely said to be off-limits because some politician or maybe some other foreign diplomat owned the place in my way of understanding things. It was great advertisement in my mind and a lot of other guys' views throughout the ranks. Well, this place was a trip. We paid $25 at the door each and walked into this arena-style building. The seats were arranged just like the Coliseum in Rome around a huge red circular spinning stage. I wasted no time getting a front row seat along with my fellow boys in uniform. This place was loaded with military personnel, so much for being off-limits. The way this place worked was if you rolled a fuzzy set of dice and the girl on stage who was stripping at the time would have sex with you. The whole scary thing about this was everyone was watching. We threw caution to the wind, and each one of our group ended up there regardless. This was the Marines; we know we are asked to die for our country, why not get laid in the mean time?

Our service time had come to an end overseas, and our unit was packing up to head back Stateside. I personally would miss these moments of wild times within my youth. I hoped to return again sometime in my future. Within the last few days of being on Camp Schwab, a mother-daughter team arrived to try and accuse a couple of us of rape. We had partied together all night, and they certainly enjoyed our company. I remember watching a friend of mine heading behind our barracks with the daughter. The mother stayed in the cab with us. The mother began giving my buddy a blowjob, and I exited the cab to tell the other guy to hurry up for it was almost time for formation. As I turned the corner, this girl pulled down my pants and started after it. As we were enjoying the fun of him working the behind and me the front, her mother ran around the corner screaming at us. I was unsure why the big fuss, this girl was definitely thirty years old and the mom was close to fifty. Yes, my buddy in the cab was an older women fanatic, some people like that fantasy. We ended up going into the barracks after quieting this lady down a bit and telling her no way to the absolute blatant setup to pay them thousands of dollars or they were going to cry rape—fuck you, lady! It turned out the next morning the military police were with them and they were going up and down the ranks picking out different guys and not us. How clueless were these two sneaky broads. Those guys they fingered even were arrested.

My buddies and I couldn't allow these other fellows to take the rap. After the formation, we gathered in the dayroom together to discuss what we should do. We decided as a group to tell their gunnery sergeant the whole scenario. After telling him what the deal was, I went and told my own. My gunnery sergeant got pissed I hadn't come to him first about it. Honestly, did it really matter? He wanted to be the one who got the glory I guess as he ran to tell command. I had later found that out. At this time, it didn't matter. We were in a bit of a pickle; these women cried rape to the authorities. I thought we were fucked. We had to be interviewed one by one by naval investigative services and the local authorities about the whole deal. It turned out these women had been trying to pull this same thing on three other bases according to the local Japanese police. I was shocked to know we had almost let three innocent guys take the fall for us. I'm glad we stepped forward honestly because these women were arrested for trying to scam American serviceman. They had actually ripped a few guys off prior to getting greedy with us and their gig was up. I was certainly relieved once all that was sorted out.

You know what? Come on out of my storyline for a second and ponder this. What if this same exact thing happened to them young serviceman who were publicly caned in Japan many years later? Maybe someone else was too much of a pussy to step forward. I guess sometimes it is better to be honest about all your bullshit. I have to admit this was one of them times for us. I was proud to say on this day our honesty actually kept three innocent guys from a whole shit heap of trouble and most likely the loss of their own wives back home. It was scary when those words were used to scare someone into the fear of rape. Those women picked the wrong guy with me, I never take without asking, especially pussy. I'm a sex-fiend addict, with many fetishes, and I am a porn star in my own head, but what I'll never be accused of is being a rapist. I'm glad those bitches got busted. Prostitution is one of the oldest professions in the world. I have even been purchased from time to time myself. "You're pathetic for trying that scam of bait and switch. I hope you rot in prison for a while eating nothing but fish heads and rice, you're pathetic." But then again it was a good try.

So that was it. My tour ended overseas.

GETTING SICK

This day started out rather strange for me to say the very least. I had just returned from Tijuana, Mexico, where I celebrated my upcoming twenty-first birthday. A few guys in my platoon suggested a weekend visit to "party central" was in order. We actually decided this on our return flight back Stateside. I want you to picture being stuck on a base without knowing anyone in all directions other than your fellow Marines and sailors. We weren't in any hostile areas, but the truth is, anytime you leave American soil within uniform, you are in harm's way. Everyone I knew was sick of that miserable place; any longer than three months within a foreign country sucks ass. We were stuck in Camp Schwab, Okinawa. Pigeons are more entertaining to watch than what this place had to offer.

So guess what, we went off to the land of cheap booze, cheap flaming hot burritos, and salsa-flavored women when we returned to our home base in California. I had sampled all but one of my examples while I was in the friendly area of Revolution Street. What I didn't do was stop in to the red-light district on this occasion and purchase a good time with a hot Mexican prostitute. So when I returned back to my barracks Sunday evening around ten a bit tipsy from my excess with the libations, I fell right asleep once I entered my rack. I didn't even do my usual ritual of staying up till past midnight to wish myself a happy birthday as the clock turned from eleven fifty-nine to twelve o'clock. No cake, no candles, no one to celebrate with.

I awoke at like three in the morning with massive stomach cramps and feeling very hot. I was sweating and shivering at the same time. I knew something wasn't right at all. I grabbed my thermometer out of my shaving bag and popped it in my mouth. While I was sitting upright counting within my head the 180 seconds for an accurate temperature, my stomach did a backflip, and I could feel the liquid slosh downward. I jumped up squeezing my ass cheeks the best I could manage and shuffled all tight assed like a china man walking toward the bathroom. I had brown liquid running down my legs and dripping onto the floor leaving small brown puddles along my path. I was extremely nauseous all the while with the head spins from the fever or from the drinking. Whichever the case was, I began to gag. I had to grab the wastebasket along the way to the toilet seat and begin to wretch into it as I sat down spraying diarrhea out of my ass. I was spewing from both ends for quite some time. I had stopped puking once my stomach was void of everything including the yellowish bile. It was my ass that just kept flowing like a faucet every several minutes with massive cramps preceding each flood. The cold sweats were in effect the whole time. I sat on that toilet for at least an hour just spewing watery diarrhea. I looked around at my mess after most of the cramps subsided and the mud sauce eased up to a manageable rate. There was a whole flood of my shit leading out the bathroom all the way to my rack. I quickly removed the sweat-soaked sheets off my bunk and used them to wipe up my mess. Luckily my roommates were asleep because this would have been a perfect humiliating funny story to tell everyone in the morning during formation.

I hurriedly wiped everything up and hopped into the shower after finally reading my temperature. I was sizzling, 106 degrees it said. I knew I was entirely running on minutes too cool my core body temperature and not to go into convulsions. I was within the brain malfunction range for sure. I ran the shower as cold as it would come out of the faucet and stepped into the shower. I aimed the showerhead directly on my head to rapidly cool off my brain inside its bone casing. This produced a serious headache, but cooling off my brain was imperative. I let it run over my head until it was unbearable. I then began to rinse my body off. My legs began to buckle on me after quickly rinsing the swampy poop off of myself. I reached out for the wall for support, but I couldn't hold on at all, my head was spinning too much and the shower felt like the Tea Cup ride at the amusement park. Only I was being shocked by cold water on this ride and my brain cut off my leg functions I guess. I landed facedown inside the shower stall and curled into the fetal position rather quickly and let the water cascade over me. I was shivering, and the cold water was very painful but it was necessary. I lay on the shower floor for as long as I could bear. My whole body was beginning to convulse instead of just shivering from the cold. I was finally able to crawl out of the shower after a good long torture session of twenty minutes or so under the icy rain produced from the showerhead. I reached up from the floor and grabbed a towel off the hook above me and just lay it over me like a makeshift blanket. I was wet and shivering really badly the whole time. Even reaching up to shut off the shower was an impossible task at this moment, so I left it running. My thermometer was within reach, so I reached for it on the sink and popped it back into my mouth. This time it read 101.6. I felt a little better knowing my inner core temperature had dropped from its scary death-is-eminent feeling to an okay-everything-is-fine-you're-just-running-a-fever feeling. I remained on the bathroom floor for ten more minutes just lying curled up under my towel and decided to crawl back under the icy water again for a few minutes then tried to stand. I managed to get to my feet inside the shower grasping the sides of the wall and holding on to the hot and cold mixing lever. Eventually I was able to reach the showerhead and balance myself upright. I didn't stay very long inside the cold water this go round, but I'm sure it helped. I was able to shut off the water this time and exit upright without the crawling on my belly like some wounded animal anyways.

My head was pounding like crazy. Each heartbeat thumped and echoed within my head with a thunderous fury. It reminded me of the Mashpee Wampanoag Indian powwow drums I heard as a kid within the Cub Scouts at a reenactment ceremony. I began to stomp my feet around the bathroom shifting my weight from side to side on each foot listening to the beating drum within my own head. I could hear the whole tribe singing when I focused on my imagination and let the soothing sounds caress me. I channeled my mind into a peaceful rhythmic dance actually. This was strange how I drew my strength back imagining the spirits of an Indian tribe filling me with their power. This kept me from falling over and got my blood flowing enough to stop shaking. I gathered up my nasty sheets and shit-covered shorts and socks I had on and wrapped them into a nice neat ball with all of the mess invisible to anyone who may see me as I made my way out my barracks room down the long concrete walkway toward the laundry room. This was also in case my roommates had awoken because they heard the shower running for a long time and the toilet flushing repeatedly and had gotten curious or pissed off because I woke them up. Sleep is a necessity in the Marine Corps, and when it is interrupted, we get cranky. I knew this but I couldn't avoid any of what had just happened to me. I tried to stay as quite as possible while I was within my own hurt locker. I wasn't all loud and crying and whining during this onslaught, so hopefully they remained asleep. If they were sleeping, I wasn't going to wake them up over some weirdo having the shit's attack. They wouldn't know until I told them the story about it. Besides, it's most likely some bad burritos making me feel like this. So why concern myself or them about the details? They would get a bigger laugh when I told them on the ramp at work during a break anyways, so tonight wasn't the time.

I slipped out of the bathroom and put on a pair of clean underwear, some shorts, a shirt, and some flip-flops. I also grabbed my laundry soap and bleach along with my soiled articles and headed outside. My head was still throbbing and my stomach was still in knots the whole way to the laundry room. I made quick work of loading the machine and adding several pours of soap and bleach and set the dial to Hot Water/Regular Load settings and pressed Start. My mess would remain a secret if I wanted it to at this point. That was my intention anyway at this juncture. No need to spread it around that I had shit myself to anyone. In my mind no one knew, and that's how it would stay until several days passed, then I would share the laugh with others about it. For right now I was still quite ill feeling and tired. I waited by the laundry room sort of dazed and weak feeling for the entire wash cycle to complete then tossed my stuff into the drier. I needed to get some rest, so I headed back to my room and lay down again after setting my alarm for 5:30 AM. This would give me a half hour to get dressed and retrieve my sheets and other laundry prior to our 6:00 AM mandatory formation in the morning. It was already 4:45 AM, so a forty-five-minute power nap might help out just a little to make it through the day. I crawled into my rack and pulled my green blanket over me and just lay there the whole forty-five minutes making trips to the bathroom at least fifteen times during them precious forty-five minutes just shitting water out of my ass. I just couldn't stop it from flowing out of me, but I could control it from spraying on the floor or in my pants at this point. I could hold it for ten minutes tops, I think, and it was going to have to be enough if I was going to make morning formation. My roommates were up now, and they knew I was sick and it was rather tricky to sneak in and out of our shared bathroom without causing too much of a problem. They were cool though because we had lived together for over six months in Okinawa together and it wasn't uncommon to take a dump while the other guy was showering. It becomes normal when three guys wait till the last minute to get out of the rack and get ready for the day that lies ahead of them.

They laughed their asses off actually because I was in and out so frequently and each time I ran to the hopper without any warnings. I explained the night that I just had to them, and they laughed and sympathized for a brief moment between their fits of extreme laughter, at least I hoped they sympathized. I wasn't concerned about them laughing because everything becomes funny when you're stuck in some faraway place away from your country and the people you love back home. Before I took off for my adventure in Mexico, we were ending our work week and preparing for our weekend liberty in our room. It was then that we were talking smack to one another about our ordeal in Camp Schwab. We had laughed about one of them trying to jump out the third-floor window of our room in the barracks in Okinawa to go home. I remember this clearly as if it were yesterday. All of a sudden from across the room this guy had a full sprint heading toward our open sliding window and was in the air heading out. I was close by in a chair, and at the last possible second, I grabbed him by the legs as he was exiting. We had been drinking that night, and I guess it triggered some sort of missing-home mechanism in his head. Next thing you know he was thinking, *Fuck it, I'm diving to the ground to get out of here.* Good thing I grabbed his legs, and my other roommate helped me within seconds or I would have dropped his ass. We pulled him in the window, and he sat on the floor just sobbing about missing his wife and family back home. If we could laugh about those experiences together two days ago, you bet your ass we laughed about me squirting like a goose after a trip to Mexico. We sort of collectively agreed it was something I ate or it could be a bad case of Montezuma's revenge from the water in that shit hole country. So it was funny to us. I felt like a total mess, but laughter always helps in bad times and situations being dealt to you in life as a soldier.

I managed to ask one of them to help me with retrieving my sheets from the drier. It was a small request, and they hooked me right up. In fact they made my bed for me as I was once again on the toilet for another session of the ass squirts. When I came out of the bathroom, they just told me it was time for formation. I was very grateful for their help and told them thanks. We had been together through difficult stuff before, and one thing we all did was look out for one another. Lending a much-needed hand was very common when someone was sick or just too exhausted to move. All I needed to do was put on some socks and my boots and head out the door. I did this without too much trouble and grabbed my camouflaged shirt and rushed to the parking lot where we held formation. I found my spot within our platoon and stood at attention. I wasn't late, but I definitely was one of the last guys there, which was uncommon for me. I had noticed the look of disgust from my gunnery sergeant on my way by him as I found my place. I didn't concern myself with his dumb looks while I was standing there at all. I was more concerned with staying upright on my feet. My head was throbbing again, and I was dizzy. It was also in the back of my head that I could not only just collapse, but I could also have a shit attack at any moment. This possibility was alive and real. My whole body felt as if it could shut off at any moment and I would end up on the ground covered in my own shit. Just that thought of total humiliation in front of the entire company would demolish any self-respect I had earned.

Our formation was brief and to the point. Go get chow, do a "police call," which means to straighten up our rooms and the buildings surrounding area, all trash picked up from the parking lots, common areas, and be back in formation for 8:00

AM. When we were dismissed, I headed straight back to my room and went into the toilet and threw up from being so dizzy outside. I almost couldn't make it the entire distance I needed to travel upon entering my room. As I opened the barracks steel door, my stomach turned and I dry heaved then wretched into my mouth. I held it in my mouth for the remaining twenty feet so I wouldn't have a mess to clean up. Once I projectile-vomited into the toilet and repeatedly dry heaved several times to squeeze out every last drop from my stomach. I brushed my teeth to change the flavor from vomit to spearmint. I was a completely wasted individual at this moment, but I knew I needed to lie down longer. My roommates were back in the room when I emerged from the bathroom again looking very green in the gills. I didn't speak or say anything as I shuffled like a zombie toward my bed. Once I was lying down, I asked if they would bring me back some juice and some crackers from the chow hall. Maybe that would settle my stomach. I remembered hearing mumbling in the distance within my hearing like it came from fifty feet away, and then it was black. I had passed right out.

I awoke to my roommates shaking me and telling me we had five minutes to get to formation for our march down to the ramp where our amphibious assault vehicles await our attention. They brought me a couple of orange juices and about twenty-five saltine crackers back from the chow hall. I quickly drank the orange juices while changing into my one-piece ramp suit and munched on the crackers the best I could without throwing them up. I was able to eat about half of them before my stomach began to disagree with the consumption of these salty squares. Once again the crackers became a nasty pile of mush on its way outward from my sour stomach. I hurriedly ran to the bathroom and wretched them out along with the burning bile and orange juice mixture within my guts. My roommates were concerned just a bit and voiced their argument about me going to work today. I wasn't feeling well, but I knew it had to be something from Mexico that was causing me the problems and it would pass by lunchtime. I told them not to worry that I would be fined. It wasn't uncommon for me to wake up sick from a hangover at all and still make it to work, so they weren't too consumed with my plight at all after hearing me tell them I was okay. I used to go on the morning runs we had sometimes half-loaded on booze from the night before. Never once falling out or being concerned if I threw up during them. We headed outside and into formation with the rest of our platoon just like every other day like nothing was wrong. This was just another day at the office for us. Day in and day out we did this formation every morning during the five-day week, and it wasn't very difficult. I just happened to be progressively getting sicker and sicker.

I don't remember much of this week other than sleeping every chance I got and not being able to eat. Finally on Friday my roommates demanded I go to sick call or they would drag me there by my ankles. I put in for sick call with my staff sergeant early Friday morning before formation and he said, "By all means, go right ahead." He was actually going to tell me I needed to go. He had been noticing I wasn't looking too well, and he also noticed me just lying under the amphibious assault vehicle I was assigned to work on every chance I got instead of working. As a matter of fact, he also pointed out I wasn't acting like my normal ball-breaking self this past week, so I should go and get looked at. I explained the why I needed to go to this man, but he waved his hand and told me not to bother explaining. My actions alone were enough for him to warrant my visit to the docs. I was relieved that someone actually noticed my issues other than my roommates actually.

When I checked into sick call, I explained to the navy corpsman what had been going on and all of my symptoms up until today. Nothing had changed at all. Each night I would wake up freezing within a soaked mattress from sweat, and I continued to run a very high fever. The only thing I could do was crawl to the shower and cool myself off before returning to my bed. This had been going on far too long, and I needed something to stop my illness. I told him I hadn't eaten anything for four days because I kept vomiting everything out. I also told him about the diarrhea that never ends. He wasn't too shocked to hear all of this because I told him I had gotten ill right after a trip to Mexico. In fact he stated I most likely have stomach flu or a bacterial infection in me from that country. I was sort of relieved by what he told me and gladly took the antibiotics he prescribed me. He also put me on no duty for a week which was a surprise. The "no duty" note was very rare to come by within the Marine Corps, usually it's a suck-it-up, kick-in-the-ass, get-back-to-work diagnoses. This time was different I guess. Maybe I looked worse for wear in this young corpsman's eyes, and he gave me some sympathy. So with my "no duty" note in hand, I went back to my room, I drank several gulps of water to wash down my antibiotic pills and lay down. I was asleep within a few seconds of my head hitting the pillow. My whole body was exhausted from moving around. Each day was exactly the same. As soon as I knew I could lie down, I was asleep within minutes. If it wasn't for the shits, the spins, the fever, or the puking, I would swear I was becoming a narcoleptic.

Sleep was short-lived because at lunchtime my roommates came storming into the room asking way too many questions and quite honestly deliberately giving me a hard time and a headache. I answered the best I could because I owed them some sort of explanation. I had ruined their sleep plenty from my long bouts with the diarrhea episodes all night long. So I went over what the corpsman said with them and drifted back off to sleep without hesitation. I re-awoke when my roommates returned back to our room at the end of the workday because they asked if I needed some food or something to drink. I told them something to drink would be fine, but I was unsure on the food thing just yet. Time just vanished from my conscious mind I guess because next thing I knew it was morning again and I was covered in shit and vomit and sweat once again. My roommates were gone during the weekend just like I would've been also except I'm sick. I managed to get out of my bed and enter the shower to wash off this disgusting mess I've got all over me and put on a fresh set of clothing in order to wash my nasty clothes and sheets once again. I returned back to my room and swallowed another antibiotic with some Gatorade left for me on my bedside table by someone. I have to think it was from my roommates, but who knew for sure I would be out of it when they came home from work and left for the weekend. Once again I'm left to fend for myself and to suffer this madness alone.

Within my sleep I would have horrible night terrors, like I was slowly cooking in the hot sun on some makeshift raft in the middle of some ocean with only the sun and the moon to

keep me company as I slowly lost my mind. The thirst was so
unbearable I become a statistic and hallucinated after a prolonged
dehydration period and jumped into the shark-infested waters
thinking they were my friends beckoning me to the Gloryland.
At least there I might be allowed a cool glass of fresh purified
water. Once again, it's a suicidal nightmare plaguing my dreams.
I'm unable to stop myself as I watched almost as if I had seen it
before. I was experiencing my dream in a living room watching
myself on a television. I screamed at this asshole which was also
me through the screen that I was making a grave misjudgment.
No matter how loud or how much I pound the television, my
other self-image entered the water. I was now in the water
heading downward holding my breath as I descended within
the surprisingly clear water as I opened my eyes to look around.
Within my mind I decided to watch my own demise, my eyes
burned from the salt. I looked upward to look at my raft from
underneath the surface. It was a prison in my mind, so this had
to be done. Forever sinking slowly as I expend all of my air from
my lungs, watching the bubbles float to the surface above me.
I began to feel extremely cooler as I take several gulps of the
nice refreshing water around thirty feet down. The thirty feet
was preplanned while trapped on that fucking raft. I feel better
in knowing I would die cooled off anyways. A huge, great white
cruised beneath me in long-drawn-out circles. I caught glimpses of
him as he entered my field of vision. He rapidly closed his distance
toward the surface like a rocket being fired out of a missile silo.
I watched from the couch again with a panoramic screen which
showed me some scale as the view zoomed out. The twelve-foot
raft was less than a quarter size of the shark. I remember from
the movie *Jaws*, the character Captain Quinn said you measure
the fish from the dorsal fin to the tail. Seeing how it's a dream,
it's definitely one of those twenty-five-footers he was debating with
Mr. Hooper about when it appeared for them to see it firsthand.
I screamed at the screen to swim for the surface dumbass. Now
I was back in the water desperately swimming to the surface as
fast as I could. I know if I looked down I would be wasting time.
I got to the surface with time to grab the raft and hurl myself up
inside the boat. The crazy shark hit the bottom of the raft fully
mouth-opened and bit through the thing like butter. Luckily he

hit on the opposite side of the raft out of reach of my torso or he would have definitely got me on his first attempt at lunch. The raft leaked out quickly, and I found myself within the water floating like a fly in a fish tank with the number 1 predatory fish in the ocean on my ass. The shark surfaced just like in the movies, and I could actually hear the jingle in my head. The fin was fully out of the water, its dorsal fin rapidly flapping side to side closing fast. I remained very still and watched in absolute horror as it opened its mouth showing me six-inch meat cutters called teeth. I definitely saw its eyes rolled back white as it bit into the lower half of my body awakening me from my nightmare.

I awoke to my sweat-covered sheets within my rack looking at the window covered by the curtain our fine government allowed us to have. There was just enough of a crack to allow a band of sunlight to cross my head. It must've been morning. I slept with my feet facing the sun last time I was awoken looking around for a drink or cleaning up a mess. For some reason, I decided if my feet faced east, I might arise into heaven on my own two feet if I didn't wake up. I actually prayed to God, Jesus, Allah, Yahweh, and I even through in a few calls to the four winds during these times. I was definitely on my way out of this world. I had to grasp on to someone's hand. Speaking of hands and feet, I think to myself as my eyes adjusted from the blinding fire globe I sought out within my vision. For no reason at all, it's comforting to know it's still there, but I had to blind myself each and every time just to be sure it's still lit. I rapidly looked at my lower half to make sure I was in reality and not ripped in half by that sinister shark. My heart was pounding, and I was breathing heavily. I realized I was alive within my conscious mind and began to slowly shake off the eerie feeling from my nightmares or flashback from a well-crafted movie made in Martha's Vineyard area. Thoughts of home rushed into my mind, and I started feeling alive inside also. I wasn't covered in shit or vomit this time, and it was a blessing. I was drenched in cold sweat, and I actually could smell the fear within my sheets, it was sort of having a bitter-sweet raspberry smell with a pinch of copper within its aroma. I could feel the kinetic energy produced by the adrenaline blast hanging within the room's air.

My body was still intact as I focused my eyes downward. My wonderful legs were still attached. I swung them off the bed and stood up on shaky legs. I barely remained on two feet as the dizziness hit me like a ton of bricks. The blood rushed to my head rapidly or rushed out of my head too quickly, whichever the case I staggered like a drunk to the bathroom for some water. My mouth felt like the Sahara desert mixed with salt. I got to the sink in the bathroom and rushed to take a few gulps. I didn't even wait till it got cool from running. I tried to gulp down mouthfuls, only to find out it hurt like hell trying to swallow it down. I felt as if I was swallowing broken glass and razorblades. I only managed the one painful gulp and curled to my knees from the pain. After a few minutes of holding my breath and transferring my mind to some far-off land, panic struck within me to stand and turn on the light to look into my mouth in the mirror. I reached out for the switch and flicked it on.

What I saw was a holocaust victim staring back at me from the other side. I was skin and bones within my face. I could see my entire skull under the stretched-too-tight skin. I opened my mouth in horror looking into my mouth. It was completely white on my tongue including some green toward the back of it and the sides. My inside wall of my cheeks had big white patches almost completely covering all of its area. My dangling punching bag in the back of my throat was barely visible, but it too had been swollen and covered greenish white along with my tonsils. I reached for my toothbrush and began to scrape some of it away from the sides of my mouth, but it caused my skin to begin bleeding. I abandoned the inner wall and focused on my tongue. I scraped it mostly all off with the bristles of my toothbrush causing nearly half my tongue to be bleeding and the other areas became bright red with the purplish blood slowly wanting to burst out of the paper-thin layer of skin holding back the completely-fucked-my-whole-tongue-is-bleeding-now feeling. I stuck with the pain rinsing softly with warm water until I cleaned 95 percent of my whole mouth of this white-and-green mushroom-smelling shit growing inside of my mouth. I had dry heaved a few times from scraping at my tonsils, but it had to be done also. I finished up with a bit of mouthwash diluted in water to rinse, it burned like hell partially diluted. I was glad I eased into the full pain gradually. After three or four easy rinses, I gave a good thirty-second burn-your-fucking-tonsils-with-a-red-hot-poker rinse. The water running in the sink had a difficult time going down the drain in the beginning of my ordeal washing away the blood and gunk I was expelling.

I took off my shirt and saw all of my ribs exposed. I turned around and looked over my shoulder to see my back and my neck. I noticed the elevens made from my neck tendons, which was a very bad thing. I remember when I was a kid one of the old-timers explaining to me that when your neck shows the elevens, your time was up. My arms looked deflated along with my legs. I could definitely see I was losing weight rapidly. Only several weeks had passed by at this moment in time, so I knew something was definitely wrong other than some bacterial infection. I wasn't quite sure what it was, but this was the worst in my life so far when it comes to being dangerously ill. My mouth burned and throbbed during my staggering trip back to my rack. I was alone, no one to ask for help or to encourage me to seek out a doctor. The whole barracks was empty, and I would have to suffer until Monday. Hopefully the antibiotics were causing a bad reaction in me and it would subside by then. I drifted back off into the nightmare-infested realm of sleep. My head and stomach were definitely in no shape to move. I began tasting blood as I drifted. I stayed in the darkness of sleep all the way until Monday morning. I was unsure of how much time or how many days had gone by at this juncture. I lost time. I was awoken several times as my roommates came and went. I remembered awaking alone in our three-man room reading a note saying that they had moved to a new room because they were nervous it could be contagious. Who could blame them? Not me at all, I would get visitors at least once a day to see if I needed anything. They would only come to the door and we would talk through the window. Mostly food and water was left outside my room's door. I had become a leper to my friends and fellow soldiers. Neither my sergeants nor any of the higher commands ever stopped in to check on me at all for at least two weeks after I stopped showing up for work to just lie under a vehicle on the ramp. I think one of my fellow Marines made them aware of my condition after witnessing his friend dying before his very eyes.

I awoke to my lieutenant shaking me awake telling me to get the fuck up and get outside in formation. I tried to say I was very sick, but he cut me off prior to me speaking telling me he would put me up on charges of dereliction of duty. I handed him my "no duty" slip from the corpsman, he read it or just glanced over it and then he crumpled it up and just dropped it. I guess he was just an asshole, I thought as I dragged myself out of my rack to my feet. I stood before this man a shell of what I was in size. He gave me a direct order to clam the fuck up when I again tried to speak. I noticed my voice was gone, and all I could manage was a whisper. He listened to me tell him my throat was raw as fuck and I was dizzy. He turned away and exited the room without comment. Was this motivation, hard knock style? If it was, it worked. I was pissed off enough to muster the strength to get dressed and wander out my room bouncing off the doorjamb as I half-trotted toward formation. My canteen was in hand filled with undrinkable water due to my last episode two days ago with it. I didn't want to risk them razorblades again if I dared drink it. I carried it for show on this occasion because everyone else had one. I found myself outside on a run, but this was a battalion run. No wonder my lieutenant was in such a pissed-off mood. He wanted to impress his boss and have all present and accounted for him, what a suck pump. Who gives a shit what he was thinking or doing? I was up outside under pure discontent, and it was working so far. Maybe a morning run was just what I needed to recover from my own personal hell. Our battalion runs were very motivating actually. Once we began to run, I was struggling. My legs were sticks with very low meat content and girth. They worked but just barely. I maintained the pace set and sucked up all the pain, like a good Marine should. I was able to make the mile and a half route toward the beach actually. There was usually a good mile of sand running each time during a battalion run. Then there was usually a mile or so of the return back to our original spot during the runs of the past. The battalion commander was a definite running fanatic. I was also at the time, but my body wasn't cooperating with me. My mind and will power were there 110 percent, but my body failed underneath me. My legs buckled within a half mile of the soft sand, and I was down. Blackness overtook me instantly, but I did hear someone yell from the distance, man down, as I fell.

My vision returned to me after about a minute or so. I was looking directly at the ocean with my head cocked in an odd angle only seeing out of one eye because the other one was still buried within the sand. My lieutenant came into my singular view along with three other people, but I focused on him and only remember him being there within my mind. For some odd reason, to this day, I still can't put a face to the others who rushed to my aide. They are but a distant ghost image within my mind. I remember being lifted to my feet and held upright as they dosed me in water from their canteens to cool me off and to rinse the sand from my face and other eye. As I regained my legs slightly, I was lifted by someone and carried back off the beach and onto the pavement. I was told to rest and make my way back to the medic's station. The others who helped me off the beach had left to rejoin the others who were running ahead of them in the distance. I was held upright by my lieutenant when I finally regained my strength to walk. He walked me about halfway back to the barracks where the medic station was and asked me several times if I was going to make it. I told him I was fine. I explained to him how my chest was killing me on just my left side. I most likely knocked the wind out of myself as I hit the ground. He shouldn't worry himself because it's his entire fault anyways. I was supposed to be on no duty. I also told him I was going along good on the beach till the blackness overtook me. He reluctantly ran off to join the rest also after I told him everything would have been better if I remained in bed. He finally agreed I was a shambles also. I could see fear in his eyes as he looked at me before deciding to leave me to my own power. I was pissed at him for forcing me on the damn run, but I forgave him in my mind because he was genuinely concerned once I hit the ground turning blue before his very eyes. Perhaps the fear I saw in his eyes was compassion or maybe he was in shock, I would like to think it was compassion, but time proved me wrong.

I made my way back to the barracks under my own power. Upon arriving, I had to lie down in the grass to catch my breath and to vomit. I moaned in pain from the sudden sharp pains shooting through my left side as the vomiting began. There would be no relief from the pain until whatever was inside my stomach stopped forcing its way up and out of my mouth. I sort of go blind and deaf during these vomiting episodes, but it was only temporary during each straining wretch. My vision returned and so did the pain between each gasp for air, so I was not alarmed. I have wretched many a times in the past to know it's not going to kill me if I face the ground. My pain subsided a bit more, and the gagging dry heaves slowed to less than twice a minute. *I am fine*, I told myself and got back on my feet. The distance was very short, and I stumbled over to the door with the white and red cross painted on it. Going on instinct knowing if I'd get in there, I'd be okay.

I entered quickly and said, "Help me please," as I headed for the cheap couch they had with a blanket on it within the office. I flopped down sitting upright as them two corpsman came to my aid. They rushed to take my vitals and temperature asking me exactly what happened. They told me it's just fatigue and that the antibiotic wasn't working. They proceeded to tell me I needed a penicillin shot and to not be alarmed, I should be fine after they gave me an IV of fluids also. They put the IV in as I lay back on the couch and relaxed a bit. After thirty minutes of fluids, I felt a bit better actually. Before my departure, they stuck me in the arm with the penicillin shot and off I went to my room. Back to my prison, my display case, once again subject to people not wanting to be near me, glass separating us so not to infect the rest of our platoon. It was fine with me at the moment because I needed to lie back in my bed. It wasn't long before my former roommates and a few others came knocking to check on me. I guess they had abandoned all thoughts of fear because they entered the room to my surprise. I had been resting in my shorts and T-shirt the whole time. I hadn't the strength to shower and change. It was then within that visit when they noticed big red blotches forming on my neck, arms, and legs. I removed my shirt to see bigger patches covering 60 percent of my torso. This was definitely a bad sign.

My former roommates hoisted me up and allowed me to hold their shoulders as we hurriedly walked back to the medic station. I remembered someone yelling, "Call the fucking ambulance, you numb nuts, he's having an allergic reaction to the penicillin." From the tone of my friend's voices, they weren't allowing the brush off anymore. I needed proper medical care, and these two fucking idiot corpsman better produce. It wasn't long at all before an ambulance arrived to whisk me to the base hospital, quiet honestly they possibly saved my life. I had never been allergic to this medicine in my life prior to this occasion. In my mind I knew I had mere hours to live possibly minutes without proper medical facilities. My weight had dropped to a sickly 136 pounds within a month, and I was unable to eat let alone drink anything for the last week. The progression of white cheese and green fungus growth within my mouth had damn near closed my air pipe altogether, and now this reaction made it very difficult for me to breathe also. I was given an oxygen mask to wear during the ride. An IV is rammed into my arm and fluids were being pumped into me at a quick rate. The medics inside the ambulance checked my pulse and blood pressure every minute within our twenty-minute ride. I was told to relax and just breathe slowly the whole time. These guys were very good at keeping people aware and calm during a moment of sheer terror within your own mind. I focused on their voices and remained still as not to lose focus on my breathing in the pure oxygen through a partially closed windpipe and semicollapsed left lung.

Upon arrival into this base medical center, these medics had gathered all the information needed to breeze me right into an examination room and left for someone else to come find. A doctor or some other white-gowned fool carrying a clipboard asked me questions as they moved me from the rolling gurney to a hospital bed. He hung the clipboard on my rack and walked out of the room. I looked to my right and noticed I was in a pretty big place. There were seven other injured or sick service members in their beds also. This must be triage. A nice staging area to assess which person's life is more life-threatening a case to be seen next. I was very bad off indeed, they wasted no time drawing blood and giving me a sedative to help me relax some more. I was in pain, but I really wasn't all freaking out. I guess they felt it necessary to give me something to make me feel good. What they should've done was take the stuff themselves. A throat culture was taken as well, along with x-rays. This wasn't sufficient I guess. I was left on an IV for the remainder of the night, and every hour on the hour a nurse came in to draw blood. It was already later in the day, so I would be spending the night for observation and testing. I was given shots in the ass of some other stuff during these visits but didn't care what it was. Just as long as they gave me some answers in the next few days what the hell was wrong with me. Plus it helped to know I was in a hospital now and not within my barracks unable to move or better still scream for help. I would be watched over by these guardian angels. This continued throughout the night regardless of what I thought or felt. The pain wasn't the issue, nor was I upset at her for doing her job. It was quite bothersome though to get pricked by a needle every hour.

I was to be taken into an examination room this morning to do a more extensive search for an answer. I had survived another night battling severe fevers, chills, and vivid nightmares from the fever. They were going to stuff an endoscopic tube into my throat and take a few samples of my esophagus because they could see growth on the x-rays I guess. The blood showed acute mononucleosis, and the throat culture wouldn't be back for another day. That's what I was told anyways. They wanted a more accurate account of what was really going on. A biopsy from within would reveal more. As I listened to the doctor's assessment and course of treatment and diagnoses, something really weird began to unfold before my eyes. It was during this briefing when several people entered my room rapidly and escorted each and everyone out, including the other patients. What happened next was straight out of the x-files. Two men entered my room wearing them full yellow-hooded biohazard outfits on equipped with their own oxygen supply. Everyone had exited quickly, even the poor bastard with the cast on from a broken leg straight across from me. They had only taken blood from me all night and looked at x-rays thus far, but something had them spooked. It was close to 8:00 AM if my calculations and counting of the nurse's never-ending prick of her vampire needle attached to a tube during my restless half-sleep was correct. I tried to get their attention several times as they methodically went about securing plastic from floor to ceiling sealing all possible leakage with duct tape. Yet as they went about their task, they never paid me no mind at all. They had encased the whole room; I was now within a plastic bubble. A very cold feeling came over me like death himself reached into my soul and squeezed my heart. I knew this wasn't normal, and I was most likely very contagious. I got that realization quite clearly looking at a four-foot biohazard sticker adhered to the outside of my new plastic wall. I wasn't sure about anything when it came to contracting mono; I just remembered hearing young adults and teens get it from kissing. That's about the extent of my knowledge on it. Never knew you had to be wrapped in a contained area. Nope, I was sure I had some sort of black plague or something. I was just fresh from overseas, who knows. I lay there scared to death in the not-knowing-for-an-hour waiting on someone to come and talk to me. No one came for an additional thirty minutes on top of the maddening hour that ticked by. Nothing good at all enters your mind during this whole time, believe that. No "Oh, sorry, false alarm, we made a mistake." It's the entire worst-scenario possible. I can't tell you how many diseases I knew of at the time, possibilities I considered were gonorrhea, syphilis, typhoid, malaria, mono, the black plague, and the southeastern swine flu or some shit. A few more test and I'd get a shot and feel better when they were done, let's get on with it already.

My original doctor entered with his colleague, wearing the same biohazard gear as the plastic hangars had done earlier. I tried and talked to see what's going on, but they stayed silent the whole time. I'm unsure why they gave me the cold shoulder and became all business, but I went along with it out of sheer fear. I was removed from my bed and placed into a plastic-covered dome-shaped gurney to keep me contained as they wheeled me down the hall to another room. Once inside, they had me lie on my back as they pulled the plastic covering up and out of the way atop my gurney. I noticed this room's walls were covered also as we entered, so it didn't surprise me. They never once explained the procedure during this examination to me. I guess the little I knew the better. I remember being given a sedative of some sort because my whole face went flush and my entire body relaxed. I was slowly drifting off into sleep rapidly. Before I succumbed to the sedative they had given me, they inserted the long black snake-looking camera. It was at least the width of a garden hose if not bigger, but I swallowed as best I could while they shoved it down my throat. It hurt very intensely for a few seconds, but then I was within the safety of blackness. I don't know how long I was out, but I awoke with this thing still inside my throat and within a full-on panic-stricken desperate attempt to breathe while choking. I was yelled at to remain calm as my doctor's colleague rushed to hold my hands down as I reached to pull out my obstruction, this big camera lead. So down my weak hands went within this man's grip pinned to the bed. I choked and gagged for nearly two minutes before they finally pulled this monstrous probe from my windpipe. I heard them say, "Wow! This guy has a high tolerance to drugs, he shouldn't have woken up so quickly." Perhaps I did, but in my head I was thinking, *Why didn't you give me extra sedative to keep me under longer? Isn't that what you're trained to do to avoid things like this from happening?* I only could imagine asking these questions. I never verbalized anything because my throat was very raw and I could taste blood and smell it within the air. I wanted to sleep without pain if possible very soon. In fact I wanted to not wake up again into that kind of horror.

I was wheeled back to my original bubble-wrapped room and overheard the doctor tell the head nurse to administer morphine for pain until further notice. "Keep this kid comfortable until the results get back from the lab on Monday." I wasn't sure, but it might have been Friday when this doctor gave his course of treatment to her. So once in my room she entered all biohazard geared up and started giving me a nice shot of morphine to help with the pain each three hours. The first shot put me out. I went right out without warning. It came into my IV and my arm went warm, and then as I was watching, the television got closer to me within my vision and I went out cold. I awoke to the prick of a needle for a blood sample and my temperature was taken along with the relief called morphine. This process went on all of Friday and half of Saturday. I wasn't any better and the pain was unbelievable within my throat and inside my esophagus. It felt like steak knives were buried in my chest actually. I was relieved of this pain every three hours without fail, and it would keep me for two of them hours anyways. The rest of the hour was pure pain. The weekend shift was coming in to relieve the weekday nurses on Saturday afternoon to work until Monday I guessed because when I was due to have a blood draw, a new face appeared when I leaned over to see who was coming. I had been stuck damn near fifty times for blood up till now, my throat was completely fucked, and it took all I had to get through these long-interval remaining hours thus far. She entered and just drew blood and retreated out the room like nothing was wrong. I was a bit shocked and pissed at her deliberate avoidance of me asking her about my pain medicine. She couldn't have cared less. I immediately began to hit the Call button to no avail. Nobody came. I was left to suffer on my own within this. No sympathy granted.

I suffered the full three hours with the hope someone would come to my room if I just kept pressing the Call button over and over. I was insistent to press it five times each ten minutes that passed. Oddly enough as each ten minutes passed, no one came. I was super pissed off and cranky from the pain, never mind the blatant disregard. I was no longer a person, nor was I a patient with any rights at all. I began pressing the button as if I was mocking a Morse code message for almost a full thirty minutes. When my three hours were up, without fail, she entered again and did the same thing as the last time: avoided my pain medicine inquiry and just drew blood under silence and exited. Nothing prepares you for this treatment, I don't care who you are in this world. I was lost within my own suffering again, only this time I managed to close my eyes and slip off into a semi-conscious dream state to block my pain. I thought of my childhood and my mother; she would always take care of me when I was sick, hurt, or just injured. In that moment I wanted to see her again or to simply have her by my side. I pictured her sitting beside me holding my hand and we joked about the time I was four years old in the garage with my new Mickey Mouse swirly straw. I was in there with my older brothers who were semi-watching me. I don't know why I did this and couldn't tell you any other reason other than I was thirsty and I wanted to use my cool new straw. I undid the cap to the push lawn mower's fuel tank and began slurping up the gasoline watching as it passed through the many curves of Mickey Mouse's face and ears before I swallowed it. I drank about a pint of the stuff before my brothers saw me and grabbed me away. I remember my mom in a panic calling poison control on what to do. They told her not to allow me to throw up and to have me drink milk. If I was to puke, the fumes would cause brain damage on their exit. I can tell you one thing, my mom kept me out of harm's way then and was with me this moment to keep me out of pain.

I was snapped awake again by the prick of a needle for blood and once again no pain medicine. I was able to tolerate this no more. Nine hours had passed before I took matters into my own hands for some common courtesy to be shown me. I slept for about twenty minutes within this last three-hour stretch between blood draws. While I was awaiting her return, I removed the hose to my piss bag hanging from my bedside and let it run onto the floor creating a puddle of dark piss. I also took a poop into the bedpan and kept it at the ready for anyone who entered my room. I removed my IV and yanked out my catheter from my penis. This caused me to bleed, but whatever, when you're being mistreated, drastic things need be done. As she entered my room, I flung the hose from my catheter at her and demanded to see her superior, I would not allow another drop of my blood to leave my arm. I wanted answers on why I was not getting pain meds. She screamed and ran out the room scared to death. I guess this tactic worked because two other people entered, and I even had the chance to chuck my urine bag at them saying for them to send me a higher rank than some shit bird petty officer. Within an hour I was greeted by a captain within the navy ranks. I explained my situation to the man and the lack of care I was being provided. He tried to give me the routine reason, "Oh, we have to wean you off of the morphine so you don't become addicted" bullshit. I totally told this guy off. I replied to him, "Yes, weaning me off of a pain med is fine, but I'm in fucking pain, I just had pieces of flesh yanked from my esophagus Friday morning, sir. My doctor told the nurse I was to be on pain medicine until he returned Monday. Why the stoppage? I think you think I'm some sort of laughingstock fucking idiot. I know my rights, asshole. Believe me on this one thing, sir, if I survive and you didn't relieve me of my suffering to the best of your ability, I will certainly fuck you up. Now go get me some fucking pain medicine." I screamed. "I don't give two shits that you're a captain, I'm a fucking human being. I'm a Marine. I'm scared. You haven't told me anything and nobody will talk to me." I was screaming during this desperate plea to this man's inner soul and it penetrated. He said for me to hold on he would see what he could do. I was sure he would just shut the door and tell me to go fuck myself, but he didn't.

He returned with my chart and told me I wasn't scheduled to receive morphine. I was confused really. No matter the fact my doctor specifically told the head nurse on Friday to keep me comfortable until he returned. He told me, "Well, it's not marked in the chart for the weekend staff, so I can't just give you a narcotic." I was all set with telling, asking, or even pleading my case with this dumbass and their fucking weekend nurses. I grabbed my bedpan and threw it at him across the room. He never really came into my room at all, come to think of it. He remained outside the plastic barrier and poked his head through the door to try and talk to me. Good thing because he definitely didn't want that brown mess all over him. I was not bothered with again until early Sunday morning. I was greeted by an admiral as I looked toward the door; he stood inside the room by the door but outside the bubble of plastic. I was sure he was going to give me a hard fucking time about being combative, and I was right. He threatened to have me cuffed to the bed and sedated. I replied back, "Well, fucking sedate me then, asshole. That's all I want, it's what my doctor told me and your dumbass staff, pain relief. What part of that don't you fucking understand?" I went through my whole ordeal about being mistreated and ignored the whole time like I was a piece of shit. "Now here you are threatening to cuff me to a bed. Go right ahead, you fucking asshole." He was shocked in my manner of speaking to a higher-ranking officer, and he stated the familiar, "Don't you know your speaking to a superior officer?" I told him, "I am less than a human fucking being within this place according to the procedures around here. So don't think you're off the hook either, buddy. If I make it out of this bed and I see you again, I'm kicking the living shit out of you for days. We will then see how you like not getting treatment for your illness or pain. I don't know what's wrong with me, nobody talks to me, you removed everyone from my room. I'm quarantined, being treated like I have the plague, I'm a leper in your eyes and your staffs. You come in every three hours and take blood now, but it was once an hour for the first night and half of Saturday, on top of the torturous biopsy procedure that I awoke into. I suffered for a month just to get in here. This is total mistreatment of your fellowman. I can't take this pain anymore and nobody cares." I began to sob in tears, a shell of a man, desperate, alone, and lost within fear. I rolled over in my bed and gave this man my middle finger upright and proudly displayed as I curled into my own misery. He didn't say a word to me at all, he just exited my room.

I had fallen asleep during this fit of rage soon after the confrontation; it drained me emotionally and physically. I was within another crazy, wild fever-induced nightmare once again, but this time it wasn't just in my dreams, it had become reality also. I was totally a mess. A sharp poke of another needle entered my ass this time since my IV had been yanked out. I turned to look to see who it was, but I only caught the back of them as they were exiting. I wasn't sure who it was, but it was definitely morphine, I could taste it. It was a heavy dosage, more than they were previously giving me, but it was fine by me. I was released from the shooting pains in my chest and my mouth wasn't hurting as much either. All that yelling had made my throat raw and was bleeding from the effort, so it was good to not feel that pain also. As I began to slip into drug mania, I remember everything relaxing and me throwing up onto myself. I was out until Monday morning. I awoke to puke-covered sheets and a definite bowel movement within my sheets, I was shivering from the chills brought on by the piss-wet sheets, and my head was throbbing like crazy. I opened my eyes to see an old woman standing beside my bed with a tray of medicine, all liquid form, and a bag of fluorescent yellow liquid along with a new IV bag. She wasn't wearing any biohazard gear and was totally unafraid. She looked into my eyes and saw me within the mess I've made of myself and my sheets. I said, "Hello, why the no gear?" She went on to explain to me while placing the tray on the bedside table, how she was sixty-three years old and she couldn't continue on with the way I had been treated thus far. She had heard what I said to the admiral and didn't care if she died tomorrow from whatever I had. This woman wasn't kidding either when she spoke those words to me. We continued our conversation during my bed changing and my washing off within the room's shower with her assistance. I was totally accepting of this woman as she was with me. I was seeing my grandmother within her, totally relaxed and was just open to love. This woman was an angel sent to me by God I'm sure of it. She told me she had a long enough life to risk showing me some decency if I happen to be actually dying. I was dying, but she held faith for my recovery within her just being in the room with me.

I was back together as a human being in no time at all. I had asked her name back then and most likely used it plenty of times while telling my story, but for the life of me, it slips my mind today, so I will call her Grace. Grace went on to tell me about her life, and I listened with an open heart. It was funny to me how the hard-nosed approach just sent me off the handle when the admiral and his minions tried to reason with me. I had become a complete asshole toward them regardless if they were trying to help me even though they hadn't enough information to do so. I was put off by that cold shoulder biohazard gear and the disregard to me. Yet I'm gentle as a lamb around Grace. Her bedside manner was absolutely perfect. Let this be a learning experience to any and all nurse wannabes of the world. Treat your patients as if they were your own children or grandchildren. I viewed Grace as an angel sent from heaven; she kept me connected to all I had learned of caring, compassion, love, and kindness that I had learned as a child within the Catholic school I went to. I also learned these things among my grandmothers and the whole elderly clan that I knew in life.

After I was back in my bed cleaned up with fresh sheets and a new shaved face, I felt more like a man. I told Grace how I had acted was wrong but it had to be done. She told me not to apologize at all to her or anyone else for that matter. "You were quite correct to put us all in check when it comes to human dignity." I said I was sorry anyways, but only to her. I made her laugh with that one; I felt so much better, thanks to her. It wasn't any better looking from the outside, but inside of me was pure again and a flickering of hope slipped back into my dark cold heart. I had gone through close to thirty days of misery only to be subject to God knows how many more days in this hellhole called a hospital. She was on the verge of tears while confessing to me that she had seen too many young boys die over the years and she always reached out her loving hand to all of them. Yet on this occasion, she was terrified at first because I looked really bad and the doctors told them, "Stay clear, we don't know what he's got. He's considered a biohazard, treat him as such, keep the specimen contained and don't allow whatever he has to pass into you." I assured her that it was okay to be scared because I was also. My doctor appeared in the safe area outside the plastic room and told me the tests came back from the biopsy. I was told I had a severe case of thrush and viral esophageal candidiasis. It's so severe that we need to use the strongest antibiotic we have. He explained to me it was used for treating herpes, but he was sure it would make an impact. Truth was, he didn't fucking know what to do and I could tell in his voice.

I watched as Grace reinserted my catheter and placed the piss bag back onto the lowest bedside railing. She went about her business with a sweet, peaceful gaze and reached out her hand to me with a few cups of liquid. I was told to swish it around in my mouth and then swallow it. This was to reduce the fungal growth in my mouth and my throat. She proceeded to insert a fresh IV into my hand again. It stung a little, but it's bearable. I felt no pain as she let the simple saline solution run into my arm, it's actually kind of cool as it entered my bloodstream. I looked at her hooking up this fluorescent yellow liquid onto the holder next to my saline drip. I asked her what the stuff was called, and she had a difficult time knowing its pronunciation. Acyclovir was the name, pure form, or close to pure as they could use without killing me I guessed. She looked calm until I watched her hand sort of shaky inserting it into the IV receptacle on my line. That line was clear liquid flowing into my veins until she cut off the flow above where she stuck in the new stuff. The yellow liquid slowly followed the course of the IV line and dropped out of my sight beneath the bed and worked its way up into view again, then went into a quick loop on my arm and began to flow into my veins. It burned right away, up my hand, my arm, and into my chest; my heart was on fire as it beat the stuff into the rest of my limbs. I swear to you it was totally freaky how I felt this shit flow throughout my circulatory system. It was very hot the whole time, and my arm ached to high heaven. It became overwhelming; my vein burst in my hand halfway through the bag. This shit was super toxic I guess. My hand swelled instantly and turned a weird purplish black color around where the IV was inserted. I said ouch several times before Grace knew something bad had happened. She remained with me, but was busy straightening things up to notice that my vein had burst. She immediately stopped the flow of the medicine and removed the IV from my hand. Blood and yellowish liquid flowed back out the needle hole prior to her covering it with gauze. I had a good-sized lump of liquid and blood under the skin that forced its way out. She cleaned it up really nice and gently wrapped my hand in a makeshift ace bandage out of some funky mesh gauze.

I was thinking what the fuck could I do to get out of this, but there was nowhere to go, and there was nowhere to hide. I needed this medicine to get better, or quite possibly kill me in the process; my option was to try, so I shook it off when she positioned a new IV into my other hand. The same procedure as the last time was followed. She flushed my vein with the saline solution and introduced the burning yellow medicine. It burned like hell exactly the same. My left hand already was ruined, and this hand was killing me within several minutes and once again the vein burst. I was only able to get three-quarters of this pint of fluorescent yellow fire water, and already two veins were smoked. She didn't hesitate, nor did I protest as she reconnected everything into an artery in the crook of my right elbow after we had a quick conversation. My veins were too thin in my hands, so we both agreed we needed a thicker venial barrier for this stuff. It was corrosive like battery acid, but it too could flow with a proper delivery site. I totally came up with that idea and suggested it before proceeding but included her in on what could be the problem. I was going to die within days if this stuff didn't get into my system as soon as possible. I knew she was scared as was I, but in desperate times you need to be thinking rationally. I wasn't in any position to stop the course of events that just occurred, but I could participate in a solution to the problem at hand. In went the third IV into my elbow to finish off the remainder of this poison called acyclovir.

I was in complete relief in knowing I didn't have the plague, or some sort of flesh-eating disease, I was even told I didn't have HIV/AIDS according to the Elisa screening that they had done. I wasn't out of the woods yet, but at least I could be cured and would survive. This was about nine in the morning when I got all this news. I asked if I could call home and let my family know where I was and I'm okay. This wasn't because I wanted to speak to my parents at all. I wanted to get into communication with an outside doctor who happened to be my first cousin. I needed to hear from him what this possibly could be because quite frankly I didn't believe anything they had been saying up to this point. I could still tell they were confused and always had semi-shaky voices when I asked them questions. It was as if they were completely blind in a room filled with sharp objects trying to reach the other side without impaling themselves. Their fear and confusion were very apparent to me. I needed to take matters into my own hands. They agreed I could use the pay phone in the hallway. I was escorted by Grace, who actually half-carried my wilted, sickly body into the hallway and propped me against the phone. I held myself upright on my IV pole while she retrieved me a chair. I had no money, so this call home was collect, after dialing I waited for someone to pick up. I was scared nobody would pick up the line after it rang several times. My heart was racing with fear because I needed to get my cousin's number. I was relieved to the point of tears when I heard my sweet mother's voice say hello. I had tears running down my cheeks during our whole conversation but never spoke in a shaky voice. I wanted to cry and wail to her everything that was going on, but I held it together in order to not have her go into a panic. I explained to her what the doctors were saying I had and how sick I was. I also explained to her I wanted a second opinion and needed my cousin's number. I kept my answers short after getting the phone number because I didn't write it down and didn't want to forget it. I told my mom I loved her and to expect a call when I find out more. She was very loving within letting me go because my time to talk with her wasn't now, I needed answers. I wanted to ask her to come and sit with me because of my mistreatment and to comfort me within my fear, but I closed our conversation with "I miss you mom and I love you." I hung up and began to sob because I was happy, scared, relieved, and just overwhelmed by all these events. I wanted it to be over, so without any real concern with whether or not my cousin would appreciate a collect call or not, I dialed it anyways. He picked up within two rings. The familiar operator asked him if would he accept charges from a Mr. Gary Mello, he said yes right away.

He was excited to hear from me, and we talked just like old times with a lot of cursing, laughing, and carrying on. After that was complete, he asked me directly, "Hey what's going on?" "Nothing much, just sitting in a hospital in California," I replied. "I need you to look up some information for me and tell me what the hell is going on." I went through a list of symptoms with him and everything I had felt over the course of this month. I also told him that these doctors were baffled. I went on to tell him how they stuck me in quarantine and everything. "I just want to know your opinion and to call me back after you look this up." He told me to sit tight and let him look it up, but also gave me the holy shit reply during each shocking experience during my explanation of my symptoms and events till now. I gave him the number to the pay phone and said, "I will wait to hear back from you." He replied, "Okay, I'll get on this right now, talk to you when I figure out a few possible causes." He hung up on his end, and I said a little prayer to God asking him to help my cousin find the answer. I looked around and saw Grace wiping tears from her cheeks. She hurriedly came over after trying to turn away so I wouldn't see her crying. It was okay, I told her. "I'm in good hands now. My cousin is a very intelligent human being. He will figure this out for me, no worries." She offered to escort me back to my room, but I told her I would rather wait for the phone to ring if she didn't mind. I didn't have to ask permission, but for some reason with Grace I wanted to be a gentleman. She shook her head. "No problem, in fact I will wait with you if that's okay." So there we sat waiting together for some sort of news, information, answers, or any glimpse of hope in finding out the truth of them other doctor's diagnosis. Grace had agreed that something else was going on also, or she was convinced by me that a second opinion wouldn't hurt.

Time takes on a whole new meaning while waiting. It dragged on very slowly. *This must be how it feels to be waiting on the news of a loved one to come out of surgery,* I thought to myself. I had never experienced anything quite as dreadful before in my life. Absolutely everyone on the planet didn't exist anymore at all. I was focused on the floor in front of me. I stared downward with my head hung low, not wanting to look at anyone including Grace. She never spoke to me during this time of desperation. I was considering all sorts of different diagnoses because I was certainly not in a trusting mood at all after the way I was treated. I could picture my cousin breaking out his medical journal and reading each and every symptom and then seeing the cause of each one individually and then as a whole. My mind worked just fine, but my body wasn't very agreeable. The phone rang a bit quicker than I expected according to my imagination's time line. I was afraid to answer at first, and it startled me out of my dreamlike state.

It rang four times until I was able to reach for it and say hello. My cousin told me the news just like this. I quote him, "Cancel Christmas in Portugal!" Somehow I knew exactly what he meant. I didn't need to ask at all what that meant. I replied back to him very quickly, "I'm HIV positive, aren't I?" He was hesitant to reply, but after a few moments, he began to tell me why he thought so. I could hear the dread in his voice as if he was certainly saying good-bye to me within his research and conclusion. I thanked him for being straight with me as always and asked how long he thought I might have. This wasn't something he could answer directly, but he did say it's all up to me and how long I could hold on, for there is no cure. Within that statement alone I knew he meant not very long at all. He was my cousin, and I trusted the words he told me, so I knew it was up to me to just stay alive. We ended our conversation with me telling him it was okay to share with his side of the family with my news. He told me I should wait to hear the results of the Western blot test before I take his word as gospel, but it certainly did point to HIV. I told him I was grateful for his help and ended with "I love you in case I don't see you again. Send my love to your mom and the rest of the family." He said he loved me and to stay positive.

I hung up the phone relieved in knowing what was wrong with me. I really didn't know what HIV was at all. I never really seen or heard of such a thing. I was certainly not scared yet. I looked at Grace who was in a full sobbing cry and just reached out my right hand to her. She grasped it and held on tightly and said she was sorry. I told her, "Everything is just fine. What is this HIV shit anyways?" She laughed and straightened up in her seat and wiped her eyes off and told me everything she knew about this virus. So far she had learned by watching what had been on the television about this new gay plague, gay cancer, or gay fever and now it's called AIDS. I told her I had HIV not AIDS. She then told me that AIDS was the end result of HIV. She told me that was all she knew really. I was curious in nature anyways, so I had her tell me what HIV stood for and what AIDS stood for knowing they were just abbreviated doctor terms. HIV was human immunodeficiency virus and AIDS was acquired immunodeficiency syndrome. This was all very Greek to me at the time, but being a stubborn, well-aware individual, I wanted to immerse myself in knowing everything I could about what was going to potentially kill me. I would be a fool not to if I was going to survive this whole mess.

Just knowing what I had didn't mean a thing at the moment actually. I was unable to function on my own, and my health was still in dire straits. It had been damn near three weeks since I was able to eat any solid food and close to two weeks since any substantial amount of liquids have been swallowed. I was constantly in a state of exhaustion, and my muscles had nearly disappeared entirely. It was very difficult just to stand upright let alone walk. If Grace wasn't with me, I would've never made it to the phone. I had a long road to recovery ahead of me, but if I wanted to see my family again, that's exactly what I was going to do. Come hell or high water, I was going to get out of this crazy hospital. My whole sense of self-worth and dignity had been stripped from me, and I was treated less than human. I totally understood and felt the whole racism dilemma in this world during my stay here so far. I might not have been forced to work for no pay or had my family sold off into slavery before my eyes, but I surely felt the relationship of being considered less than dirt itself and nobody would step up to help me other than Grace at the moment. I was actually very pissed off about it all.

Grace escorted me back to my room after I called my mom and dad to tell them about what my cousin had told me. Our conversations were brief because neither one of them grasped the whole HIV concept very much because they were uneducated as was I. They both told me to just know that they love me and to keep fighting. I was relieved in a way because I could've stayed silent about this illness with them, but I just knew it was better they were involved. I was their son and they were my parents, I told them not to make them worry but to ask them to be involved in my recovery. I needed their love and support within this hell and told them I loved them and would be in touch if anything changed. I would later learn this was exactly what someone needs to do when they get infected to this disease. Staying all secretive causes way too much stress, and stress is a definite killer within the progression of this disease. I just thought back to when I was a child and scraped my knee or something and remembering the first words out of my mouth were either "Mommy, help" or "Daddy, help me." They needed to be included, bottom line. I told them I didn't need them to visit me in this horrible visual state at all, so they should just stay at home. They need not have such a horrible visual memory of me in case I don't make it. My mother protested at first, but I convinced her in her tears of worry that I would find a way to survive.

As I lay back in my hospital bed, I was left deflated and tired, so I slipped off into sleep. I slept until about four in the afternoon awoken by my doctor. He looked a bit weird, sort of nervous actually. He searched his mind kind of stuttering at first and then told me they had made a mistake earlier about the HIV/AIDS diagnoses. I told him, "Yes, I already know, so save your breath." I wasn't mad with him; it was more a frustration response. He sort of looked at me puzzled and just exited the room with his head down. I knew he felt bad about the whole situation, and he should feel that way. I was treated like shit since coming into this place, and I was pleased on the inside when I watched him tuck his tail and exit like a moping dog.

I was no longer visited by my doctor during the next few weeks at all actually. I would only get visits from the nurse who wanted blood and the daily visits with Grace who brought me medicine every several hours. So it went this way each and every day, veins would give out from the toxic fluorescent IV, I would awake covered in shit, most of the time I was puking or felt like I was going to at any minute, my whole body was aching from not moving much, muscle atrophy was in full effect, and to top it off, I was running a fever the whole damn time. This course of treatment was absolutely brutal beyond belief. I would see crazy shit in my dreams, and definitely each day when the sun came out, I would pray for death to come and take me. I had lost my will to live totally. It was right around this time when I received two packages in the mail from my parents. I would have to say if it wasn't for these items, I would have given up and joined my dead ancestors who were beckoning me to join them and release myself from this horror. Each and every night I was visited by these spirits within my dreams, or was it all real? I wasn't sure, but I stopped myself just short each time from leaving my natural life here on earth. Something always drew me back, either it was Grace waking me with screams of "Gary, Gary, Gary, wake up, baby, come back to us," or it was the angel of death telling me it wasn't time yet no matter how much I begged to stay. This was surely a terrible nightmare, so you think as you're reading this, but believe me, I was on the threshold of crossing over several times and that is a no-shit assessment. I guess my quest to kill became a reality. I have killed myself.

I had no longer feared death at all, in fact I welcomed it. I was giving up. I had enough suffering; my peace lay within the eternal dirt nap. I had even asked Grace and the nurse to give me extra morphine so I could escape this horrible pain and suffering. I had even cried to the point of sobbing as I begged them to release me. I promised them I would not hold them responsible for my death. I went as far as to scribble out a suicide note for them and even signed it as tears dripped from my eyes onto the paper. They wouldn't accept my pleas at all. Nothing I could do but suffer and hope God granted me peace. I even renounced God and called on Satan to help me but to no avail. No one heard my cries, prayers, or anything. I awoke to Grace shaking me awake along with her screams. I knew she had roused me from the depths of the cold sleep several times prior to this one because her voice reached me faintly from a far-off distance almost a whisper. She had told me it took her darn near ten minutes one time to get me to return. There was no resuscitation order given anymore, so it was Grace who kept me in this world. This woman believed in me. So when she handed me my packages from my parents, she did it with a huge smile on her face. She lit up the room actually upon seeing me focus on her and what she had in her hands. I smiled but I couldn't reach out to grab them, I hadn't the strength.

Grace opened my packages for me and was like, "Oh my, this is odd." I asked her what was so odd. She told me my parents sent me the same poem. I was kind of shocked to hear this and told Grace why. She was thinking my parents might be somewhat of in communication with each other, but I assured her she would be wrong to think so. My parents never spoke to each other at all really since I was very young. All I really remember is them beating me and not actually being anything more than hateful, stubborn jackasses to each other. They had come to my graduation from boot camp because my mother always gave my old man a ripping for not being there for his younger children during our childhoods. She was a bitter woman in that respect, but she got that stubborn bastard to do the right thing once in a while. So she's a powerful woman in my life who loves me enough to suffer talking to a cheating husband to get him to show up. I told her they certainly didn't talk about what each other was sending to me if they spoke at all. I had spoken to them separately, and as always my mom heard that I spoke to my father or she told me to call him. I usually tell her no. But this time was a definite, I needed his help also. I told Grace all this and assured her it wasn't planned. This was a for-real message from the heavens. They lived in different houses and different towns actually, so it wasn't like they would cross paths anytime soon. I asked Grace to read the poem aloud. Pay attention, reader, within these words I found the power of life and it saved me. I actually have this poem tacked on my wall on both sides of my headboard to my bed at home to remind me each day as I awake and as I go to sleep at night the power of God and his angels of mercy.

> *Don't Quit*
> *When things go wrong as they sometimes will,*
> *When the road you're trudging seems all uphill.*
> *When the funds are low and the debts are high,*
> *And when you want to smile, but you have to sigh,*
> *When care is pressing you down a bit,*
> *Rest if you must but don't you quit.*
> *Life is strange with its twist and turns,*
> *As every one of us sometimes learns,*
> *And many a failure turns about,*
> *When he might have won had he stuck it out.*
> *Don't give up though the pace seems slow,*
> *You may succeed with another blow.*
> *Success is failure turned inside out,*
> *The silver tint of the clouds of doubt,*
> *And you can never tell how close you are,*
> *It may be near when it seems so far.*
> *So stick to the fight when you're hardest hit,*
> *It's when things seem worst,*
> *That you must not quit.*
>
> *—Unknown Author*

While Grace read these words, my heart was alive and my tears wept from my eyes. I was in that moment at peace with myself and I thought of my youth. It wasn't the bad things I remembered at all about my parents; it was all the love they showed me growing up. I no longer saw them as bad parents at all, they were my source of power, and it was their love for me that came at me with such a rush it was totally enlightening and forever eternal. I next began to speak to Grace about how much fun it was doing all the cool stuff we got to do. I spoke of going to my dad's on the weekend and how he paid for us to go to camp while he was at work during the day in the summertime. He lived on a lake, and we got to learn how to water-ski off his boat. I remembered learning how to steer a vehicle while driving to Disneyland to see Mickey Mouse and his happy little crew, sitting atop my father's lap at the age of four. I used to ride on his shoulders in order to see above the crowd as the parade went by. He was a good man in my eyes at this moment, and I forgave him for splitting with my mother while I was very young. I started to realize he never left at all. He just wasn't in the same house anymore. It was me who chose to hate on him, I was all wrong. My father loved me, as did my mother. I had told Grace of the times my mother would sit with me and rub my head when I was sick to keep me comfortable. She took us snow skiing each year even though she couldn't afford it. She made sure we had food, shelter, and clothes on our back. This woman worked three jobs to keep me in a private Catholic school along with supporting my four brothers. My parents are divine creatures, and I miss them. "I want to hug them both and say I love them again, Grace. I need to get out of this bed very soon, Grace." It was then that I told Grace I was hungry and could she bring me something to eat. I hadn't eaten anything in two months, but today was a good day to try. My mouth was close to being normal again, and my throat was pretty much a mess, but I was sure I could tolerate swallowing something while in the morphine haze during pain treatment sessions. I began to eat small amounts that evening actually right after my nighttime pain injection. It hurt going down, but it was bearable. I had vomited each and every time I attempted this for four days three times a day until I was finally able to hold down some food. I was on the roughest road to recovery ever in my life, but my determination outweighed any downfalls.

After three weeks of hell on this poison IV drip, my body took a turn for the better actually. I forced myself to eat for a week to make this happen. It was entirely up to me to get well. *I fucking got to get out of here*, I kept saying over and over in my head. I told Grace of the good times and the awesome brothers I had each and every time we spoke. It was the memory of my family and my sheer will to see them which carried me to my feet. I remember it clearly to this day, walking with my IV pole which looked thicker than my arms and legs with Grace in tow each and every day down the hall, into the elevator, and outside into the fresh air. I would let the sun shine on me, warming my skin and thinking this was God's love. He would embrace me each day and warm my soul and to remind me he still cares for me and my family awaits my return.

As time went on, several more weeks I was up and about more often and could go a little farther on my walks outside before needing to rest. I would push myself to the point of collapse each day with diarrhea dripping down my leg and puking several times on my journeys, but this didn't matter to me one bit. I wanted my health back, and that was that. My total time in this hospital I couldn't tell you for sure unless I looked it up in my medical records. Let's just guess, I would say approximately two months to be well enough to go on leave to see my family. I believe it was within my last few days that I had completed a four-foot-by-two-foot color by numbers wilderness scene which had loads of trees and a small log cabin along with deer, squirrels, bears, and several other woodland animals tucked in the scene. I colored it with magic markers Grace had brought in to my room prior to getting my poems from my parents. Grace had watched me color it as detailed as possible. I did it as a New England fall foliage setting, and it came out absolutely beautiful. I took the time to add shadows and shading according to the position of the fading sunlight I created from the west of my imagination of the scene. I had told her it was for my mom. She encouraged my coloring every day actually. As a matter of fact, I had to stop my trancelike peace of mind one day because I had some unexpected guests who wished to visit with me. I was irritated because I had to stop what I was doing, but guess what, in walked a strikingly sexy as hell blond woman with out-of-this-world legs, would you believe it? Fucking Sharon Stone the actress took time out of her day on a public relations tour to sit with me. I was thrilled. I remembered her from several of my favorite movies, and we sat and discussed them. I told her I was thankful she came and would it be okay if she would send a picture of us together to my mom since her photographer was snapping away with his camera as we talked. She said, "Sure, no problem, just write down your mom's address and it shall be done." I wrote out my mom's address very clearly and handed it to Sharon personally. She left my room after giving me a kiss on the cheek. Totally sweet! I'm sure nobody would believe this, but I had proof she was there in my room when a cool picture of us together arrived to my mom's house. Sharon wasn't on this tour alone actually. James Brown, the godfather of soul himself, strolled in wearing a typical skintight leather get-up with some patent leather boots with them pointy toes. His hair was all wild, and he had a huge smile on his face as he greeted me. I was overwhelmed with laughter as I said hello to this man. "My god, you're James Brown, holy shit! You're the man!" I got a good laugh with him when I imitated Eddie Murphy's stand-up routine about him. "James Brown of all fucking people," I said. "What an honor to meet you, sir." He was very polite and gave me a firm handshake prior to exiting my room telling me to get on up, just like the song. It was priceless, and I'd never forget them for visiting me till the day I die. I'm sad to say that their public relations photographer never sent along a copy of those pictures. I would've loved to have them especially since James Brown had passed away in reality while I was writing this book. "Rest in peace, my friend, I will see you when my days are through here on earth. We will dance and laugh together in heaven. I look forward to it; you're one of my angels along with Sharon Stone. Maybe, Sharon, if you read this book or one of your friends reads this book, perhaps you could do some research and locate these pictures for me. I would love for my mom to see them and to keep as a memory tacked on my wall along with my poems from my parents. I must admit, Sharon, I was very bitter over the years about this and wish to end my suffering of holding bad thoughts about you in my heart. I forgive you within this book and in my soul. If you happen to take me up on locating these pictures, you did a public relations tour visit to Camp Pendleton's military hospital in August of 1992. I would forever be grateful."

On my last day of staying in this hospital, I watched as Grace helped me pack up some of my belongings before being discharged. I was up on my own two feet and able to walk very slowly and deliberately, but I was upright. I motioned for Grace to come closer to me and gave her a huge hug and told her, "Thank you very much. I love you, and please know I will never forget what you did for me." I reached for my picture and handed it to her and said, "This is to remember the life you saved and the lifelong friend you have even if we never see each other again in actual life." I had signed my name to the piece of art I had colored and wrote a quick thank-you to her on it. She cried and gave me a great big kiss and held me very close as we both had tears running down our cheeks. She had saved my life, and this was her reward however small, but it was from my heart. I wonder if Grace still has my painting or one of her relatives, if so, the same goes for you. You hold a piece of ultimate power within your hands, and it should be cherished not sold. I thank you for sending me an angel during my time of death and life renewed.

SAN DIEGO MEDICAL CENTER

I arrived to this hospital within several hours' drive south within a medical van. It was sent to retrieve me from this facility. Upon arrival I was told to check into the seventh floor. I wasn't walking very well, so the navy corpsman at the entrance provided me a wheelchair to put my wilted body into its comfortable seat and gave me a welcomed push. I thanked him for the assistance and handed the nurse at the first desk I arrived at my paperwork. She was very polite and showed me to my sleeping area. I was placed in a room with three beds. I noticed the other two bunks were taken because there was some gear and clothes on them. I was given the bunk closest to the door which was fine by me because the bathroom was straight across the hallway. I wouldn't have to go very far, and that was a plus. I had arrived late afternoon, so I was given new hospital wear: the long pants, some flip-flops, a few hospital shirts, and a few fresh sets of underwear, along with some toiletries. I felt as if I was checking into a hotel actually. I wasn't given much information other than I needed to take a look at the schedule which was within a folder they handed me. The schedule was for group meetings during the day and meeting with the staff. I was allowed to sleep the remainder of the evening if need be, but I needed to be ready to go at seven in the morning for orientation. I briefly got an overview of what went on here by looking at the schedule and an inserted pamphlet on the topics of each session. This was a course designed to empower, educate, test, and teach you how and what was killing you. How they are defending against it ending your life and to be properly informed about the research and knowledge of HIV thus far. The proper hygiene, nutrition, avoiding simple colds, and the course of treatment within the medicine available at the time to combat the replication of this virus within your bloodstream was brief. It was short and sweet, and it would cover most of each day minus the odd doctor visit, pharmacist appointments, and psychiatric visits also. This was all mandatory by the U.S. government I was told at the time because I was still in active duty status. I was cool with that anyways, it's better to know what's up about this HIV stuff. Maybe we can find a cure, I hoped as I laid the pamphlet down on the bedside table, took a shower, changed my hospital gear, and lay down for a much-needed nap.

I awoke the next morning to the voices of my new roommates. I opened my eyes to see two guys sitting on the same bunk waiting to say hello. I told them who I was. They introduced themselves and then I asked the time. It was six thirty in the morning, and I had thirty minutes to get to orientation class. I thanked them and slowly got out of bed and shook their hands on my way to the bathroom. I felt very good this morning actually, I was sick, but I wasn't dead yet, in my mind I needed to be given something to hold hope. If being educated was all that was available, I wanted to know exactly what they knew. I washed my face and brushed my teeth and straightened up my bed and followed the two navy guys to a conference room equipped with a couch, a television, a microwave, and several other recliner chairs and some classroom chairs within a circle for group therapy sessions. I was introduced to five other people who had also contracted HIV somewhere in the world. I believe four of them were semi-brand-new patients and the other three had already been in the program for a little while. I myself was the fresh fish within this place. I was told to follow a nurse all day who would give me the dime tour while they conducted a group meeting. I wasn't allowed into the discussion until some paperwork, blood work, and some other good stuff got completed today.

No entrance into this club without the proper pass I guess. I wouldn't want to ruin my tour of the place, so off we went to draw the much-needed precious blood, mine, all for testing. My tour ended with a cookie and a juice; massive blood loss causes lightheadedness from the drop in sugar, so they say. Old wives' tale if you ask me. It was like offering a dog a treat for being a good little boy. The doctor always gave me a lollipop as a kid. I think he is in cahoots with the dentist. No clue, huh? These people are yet but the first day consisted of a lot of rest. Minimal effort required to stick out your arm and let them drain your motor oil. Problems arrive when you need the blood and none is available. I would hope they kept some aside for me, just in case my brain popped from all the stress.

I was given a clear view of the place and who everyone was at the time, but my memory faded on names. It's designed that way. I never remember names. Lately in life everything becomes cloudy especially this day.

I went to group the next day and met the other patients.

I wasn't really sure why this happened or if it is entirely true, but I was told we needed to discuss our sexual behaviors. I so did not want to reveal I had sex with far too many people unprotected. But the simple fact is I was an out-of-control, wet-behind-the-ears, promiscuous young boy. I knew nothing of proper protection or the use of condoms back then. All I knew was this wasn't a disease which could be cleared up by a shot in the ass with a needle. This was for real. I could sense the dread and depression within our group. The unknown was frightening. They gave us a brief overview and a diagram of this virus with a few slides and a couple of fliers. The only medicine at the time was AZT, and I think DDI was available at the time to possibly save us from death. It was untested within long-term effects, or if it would actually kill you, but you had to try.

Our group had ended somewhere around 5:00 PM. After which, it was a waiting game. I arrived fully prepared to learn, listen, and just figure it all out. These group meetings helped each day as I struggled to remain calm. Stress will kill you within this disease, and they wanted us to be at ease. I remained at ease even knowing that each night I would be on the entire seventh floor of this hospital all alone. There was nobody within this building actually after the workday ended. I had nowhere else I could go. My entire family lived in Massachusetts, and the family I knew in the Marine Corps was gone. They had been deployed to Somalia when I was in the prior hospital. I really had no friends available to tell you the truth while I lay down to close my eyes each night. I grew to depend on someone telling me what to do each and every day and night. I was under orders to stay, so that's what I did. Each day was the same for me: I would wake up, shower, shave, get into a fresh set of hospital gear, and head down the elevator to walk to the McDonald's within this huge facility to get breakfast and lunch. It was the night which became bizarre over the course of six months.

I was totally isolated. I was alone. It was time to just relax and dwell on stuff. I had followed along just fine during each meeting with the doctors and even began taking AZT like I was recommended to do so after some more testing of course. I was sent to a lab down the road, a research facility actually. In this place I was given an MRI of my entire body including my brain. I freely signed a waiver to let them remove fluid from my spine, and I even allowed them access to my lymph nodes which were swollen as hell due to the virus. They didn't remove them or even take a sample, they wanted permission for after I was dead to remove a lymph node and to take a piece of my brain. I signed every paper they put in front of my face. Yes! Use me, damn it, just keep me from dying for a little longer. I was not ready for death just yet. I'm freshly twenty-one years old.

I willingly got onto the table into the fetal position and awaited this long needles business. When they stuck the needle into my spine, I instantly felt as if a rusty nail had entered my back. The needle popped through cartilage and must have nicked a nerve on its way in. My testicles instantly were set ablaze. Someone was lighting a brand-new Zippo in my crotch actually. I began to say hey, and some burly-looking nurse held me still by putting her weight on me. I couldn't move; she was much bigger than my weak body could push off at the time. I had to suffer regardless if I was screaming, "Let me up, you medieval crazy motherfuckers." I always holler out obscenities when something hurts me. All I could do was scream. I dared not move because they screamed not to move or I could paralyze myself or cause major damage to much-needed nerves coming out of my spinal cord. They had positioned the needle well beyond the end of my actual spinal cord, somewhere like two or three lumber sections lower to access the fluid running through my brain and spinal column. Only this needle was beyond pain, it caused an instant headache beyond comprehension actually. I was told to slowly slide over to an awaiting rolling hospital gurney and wheeled into a waiting area when the procedure was finished. I was told to lay completely flat on my back for the next six hours. This was to ease the pain.

Fat chance in hell! I remained motionless for six hours only to discover the pain hadn't left when I was told to get to my feet and sit in a wheelchair. I damn near fell unconscious from the piercing screwdriver buried within my skull sort of pain. The escort and the nurse grabbed me before hitting the floor saving me from smashing my head off the wheelchair footrests. I was headed straight for them. Great catch! Thank you!

I awoke safely tucked into my bed back at my room on the seventh floor. I had survived. I looked around, but no one was around. A bottle of pills lay on my nightstand with instructions on the proper doses to take every six hours. The note said I would be briefed tomorrow morning on how this was to be done. I dared not move at all because my head was still a bit cloudy and it was still within a dull sort of pain. I didn't risk moving a single muscle to try and stand. I just rolled back over on to my back from my side and went back to sleep.

I believe my actual AZT therapy began within the first couple of weeks after arriving within this hospital, but I'm not sure anymore. I know it began after we all were told what our T-cell counts were and our viral loads. For those of you who are uneducated or are on the moon, this was your immune system. T-4 cells are your first line of defense against the virus. If this number was low, it meant your immune system was being attacked. The viral load numbers are actually how much virus was in your blood. They had to keep track of these from this moment forward for the rest of my life. I was to be given no live virus vaccines at all. I had been given a pneumonia vaccine shot which would last ten years and my last ever flu virus shot this day actually. I don't recall the logistics. Throughout my remainder of days on this planet, I will be subject to blood tests every two weeks they told me.

My mind flashed to when I was a teenager. I remember trying LSD for the first time. This person was a friend who gave this to me. He told me I would trip balls and not to take it because from this moment forward life would be a trip.

I remembered getting scared by the weird visions I was getting from this drug. I was within the forest among classmates from high school when I began to see little blue people hiding beneath leaves and chasing me. I then watched as one of my friends approached me wearing a fluorescent windbreaker. He looked like an alien within my vision, so I politely asked him to go away. He was confused and a bit angry, but I explained what he looked like and we laughed. I tried to smoke some pot to calm me down, but it didn't help. I was bugging. The orange blossom mescaline was next, that made everything go all scary. I needed to go home. I hopped on my street bike and gassed it doing close to eighty through some side streets and winding country roads to get to my house. I had to stop once because the road had become like a pool of boiling tar before my eyes. Each bubble formed and popped in the road several feet to my right and left. My bike began to sink into the boiling tar while I was riding it actually. No way was I in a condition to ride. I pulled over into a hay field and just lay down flat on my back looking upward at the sky. I watched as crazy animals formed in the clouds, and every time the wind blew, I was on an ocean of long grass. I don't remember how long I remained on the grass, but I do remember getting home and hurrying back into my bedroom to hide. I would never be able to explain this wild mess to my mom, hell no! She would freak the hell out, and I would definitely get my ass kicked by someone in my family. I made it to my room and got into my bed and just stared at the wall. All of a sudden the wall became a portal and I could see into my older brother's room. He had elephant wallpaper at the time; I watched as they began to march forward in a formation, just like the old times during some Saharan desert battle. I closed my eyes tighter than normal because I was totally tripping. As my eyes were closed, I envisioned a burst of colors within my mind during each heartbeat. Then entered the needles within my mind, I was being poked repeatedly over and over again. I couldn't escape this nightmare, so I curled into the fetal position and hid myself under the blanket in tears.

I can remember this clearly as if it was a vision. When you read this, I never knew my vision as a teenager on copious amounts of hallucinogenic drugs I would see my own future actually. I was chased by the police as a youth plenty, being chased was common. I always ran from the police since they were the cowboys and we were the Indians. It was just a game to me. They were definitely the blue people. But here I am in this place now being poked constantly by needles and now for the rest of my life, all the time. I'm unsure if this was a true vision the Indians refer to, but it certainly was in my mind at this moment. Ah, what the hell do I know about such things?

All I know is I was told to go buy a watch and start taking six pills every six hours. This medicine was designed to slow the replication of the virus. This wasn't a cure, but it has been tested on other patients with promising results. They didn't mention any side effects other than diarrhea, vomiting, and the possible headache, nothing new in my world actually, so I swallowed six pills each six hours every day. As time passed while on this medicine, the sickness consumed me. All those side effects hit me within about an hour of taking the medicine. I remained sick and lost more weight during this regiment of pills which would never end. Every six hours—*beep, beep, beep*—and take them pills, back on the clock. *Ticktock, ticktock. Beep, beep, beep.* Take them pills, should've wrapped my cock!

There is one side effect which is rarely mentioned while taking this medicine. I began to see shadow figures in my peripheral vision. I would cross the hallway at night to use the bathroom, and I would always see someone duck into another room. They were dressed in black and I could never catch them in my direct vision, always out of the corners of my eyes. This became scary actually at first, but I knew it was the medicine that was causing it, so I tried to block it out. It became really difficult after the second month of being on this medicine when I awoke one night and crossed the same hallway and saw the same darkly dressed image down the hall once again. I was sick of this shit actually, I yelled out, "Who the fuck is here?" I then proceeded down the hall opening each and every room to catch whoever was messing with my head. I searched every square inch leading out to the elevator flicking lights on and off as I peered into each room, never leaving the hallway because I didn't want to allow the bastard to sneak by me. I was totally fucking crazy after my attempt at catching a figment of my imagination. I slumped back to my room scratching my head within a state of confusion. I tried to calm myself down a bit by taking a few long deep breaths through my nose. I felt weary and borderline paranoid, but I was fine. Right then the damn copy machine down the hall I had just come from turned on and a flash of light floated across the ceiling toward me. I turned my head rapidly in the direction of the noise and saw a shadow figure disappearing into a room to escape the light. I rushed down the hall into the room and nobody was there. I yanked the fucking cord out of the wall leading to the copier and said, "Whoever you are, go the fuck away!"

I headed back to my room and got into my bed and turned the lights out. Sure enough after fifteen minutes of watching my dimly lit doorway, a figure rushed past, sort of a dark mist like tall man. I gasped and tried not to show fear, but it's definitely got me spooked. In about ten seconds from then, the copier was back on lighting the hallway once again. I didn't sleep that night at all. As time passed I kept seeing this dark figure haunting the hall within my peripheral field of view and just considered him a ghost, or quite possibly the Grim Reaper coming for my soul. I couldn't do much about it at the time; I was really a mess on these medicines. I was definitely a test subject during this six-month endeavor.

I began to become very depressed and very suicidal within this isolation within this hospital at night. I remember asking the two guys who were a gay couple in my room if they wouldn't mind me coming with them when they left the next evening to go out for a few drinks. I asked why they never slept here anymore. I was told they just stayed here till they got reassigned to a new duty station, it was temporary, and not too often. Only on the weekdays, maybe once a week, I would have their company along with another guy. They told me it was a gay club and I might not like it. I didn't give two shits about all that. I just wanted a break from my nightmare in isolation. They promised they would consider it at another time; tonight they were going to a birthday get-together. I was left alone to suffer death alone within these halls. I never told a soul about this madness until now. I kept it a secret. I also never asked them to take me anywhere again.

Just like I kept the fact I was bisexual away from everyone except the few people that knew. Meaning the odd transsexuals I ran into during my travels overseas. It freaked me out to reach down and find a penis where a vagina was supposed to be after getting a blowjob. I was oddly turned on by this whole new experience. I certainly didn't have any anal sex or oral reciprocation, so why mention this to anyone? "Don't ask, don't tell" is the policy. Was I gay for liking a half-man, half-woman? Christ almighty, Captain Kirk from *Star Trek* screwed all the aliens. I liked the green bitch, whole scenario myself. It was a one-time encounter that was a common occurrence in foreign countries. Prostitution is legal. Large families in the Orient send off their kids to make money from servicing people. They will go as far as having sex changes to keep the money flowing. The eldest son remains male but possibly the younger child isn't so lucky. They are forced to be a girl visually and sometimes anatomically correct. You would have to be a surgeon to know or just look for the scar. Well, I was told that, but this chick was hot as hell. She was perfect in every way: very pretty face, long hair, nice tits, great legs, superhot figure, and an awesome-looking, sexy high-heeled outfit on. Yep, I was fooled. Once I found out she had a huge dong, I jumped up, saying, "What the hell," and then just relaxed and let her finish the job. No harm, no foul.

Nope, that stays with me; I don't know how to explain that anyways to anyone. I have told this tale since this hospital to people I just chose not to say a word about it while in the military. They frown on gays in the military. I didn't consider myself gay, nor do I live it. It was a wild time overseas, sort of a Vegas tale—what happens in Vegas stays in Vegas, but it makes for good entertainment.

While staying in this horror house of a hospital, I began to explore where and when I contracted HIV. I had to think back to right before we disembarked to head overseas, that was my last known time of not having it. I had sex with damn near a woman a day within the Philippines for a few weeks. In Okinawa, the red-light district was right down the road, so yep, I was frequenting those joints quite often. Was it Tokyo, or was it that transsexual? Was it the uncooked monkey meat on a stick? I couldn't tell you. It was beyond me to figure it out. I just knew I didn't have it when I left home to join the Marines, but when I returned from overseas, I certainly did. How does one really

know anyway when they are promiscuous and extremely drunk
in their youth? I asked. I wasn't using drugs during my military
days at all, so nope! I'm not an intravenous drug user, I was just
unlucky. It was more like a curse to me because a phantom was
roaming within my vision at night.

Was I possibly given this virus on purpose because I was such
a sex-fiend addict with multiple partners? That's the beauty of
it, I would never know for sure. Perhaps I was profiled correctly
during my stay in the government's control. Was someone else
involved? Is that why I got the visit from the celebrities? Did they
pay for me to be a test subject because a lot of their friends had
died or were dying? If I remember correctly, the government
did this to black soldiers during the syphilis pandemic during
the old days, only these guys never got any medicine at all; they
were observed throughout the course of the illness until their
demise. They needed solid-minded, well-trained personnel to
have as test subjects for medicines they would be creating. Medical
experiments have been going on within the military since the
beginning of time. The Germans during the Nazi era conducted
massive amounts of experiments on humans to advance science.
If you think about it, a lot of them criminals at the time were
protected by our government and the church in order to get their
research. The atomic bomb was created due to a German-given
asylum in the United States. How could I think anything but
them planting this virus in me? My mind raced through all sorts
of scenarios each and every night.

I remember one of the guys in my group was married with
children back at home. How was he going to tell his family he
caught a deadly, incurable disease? I had no answer. Nobody in
our group knew what to say, and neither did he. I was told this
man jumped from the building when I was away at one of my
lab visits. I didn't see this, but from the look of the group's faces
and the atmosphere, he must have. I see his face but no name.
Poor bastard. In fact we lost two people during my stay, or so I
was told. I never saw them again in our meetings, and we didn't
discuss their decisions to plummet to their deaths. They had
become statistics within this all-fearing disease.

After hearing this, my mind went into overload. I flashed into
a boot camp incident that stuck out like a sore thumb. A recruit

trainee after one of our live fire exercises during training handed me an M-16 round late one night during a long hard day. I had already been stressed to the max all day only to end up telling this kid to get that fucking round out of my site. Go put that in your pocket and bring it back to the range in the morning, drop it near one of the ammo crates if you have to. I don't want it. He did exactly that. He had fucked up, and he was nervous the drill instructors would kick his ass for it. I believed they would, so I gave him a simple solution without all the hoopla. Why I flashback to this moment is because that could've been my first test if I was actually suicidal or not. It's all conspiracy in this place on this fucking medicine. Somehow, some way, I have to get out of this madness.

I slept very little this night going over different ways to take my life. I could hang myself, but decided against that idea when I remembered waking late one night during boot camp and some bonehead was in the shower room trying to hang himself with his own belt. I got to him just prior to him passing out actually. I hoisted him up and untied the belt from his neck. He looked freaked out because I saved him from taking his own life that night. It spooked me enough not to try. I remember this same guy covered his whole naked body with shaving cream and scribed a big S on his chest like Superman wearing a gas mask late one night during recruit training and began screaming, running up and down the squad bay. He was whacked out, total section 8, dropped from training.

I thought of burning myself to death and thought about the time I tried to pour gas into a fire as a kid with a Styrofoam cup, only to discover gas eats through the bottom of the cup on my attempt and set both my hands on fire. I remember the pain of that burn that lasted fifteen seconds, second-degree burns. Fire sucks! I also got a few healthy kicks in the ass and a good belt beating for acting stupid with fire from my dad then a big bowl of ice water to soak my hands in. No hospital trip needed back then. Fire isn't the way to go. That's not an option.

As a matter of fact, I have watched every single *Faces of Death* movie ever made when I was younger, so I rapidly recalled the entire length of each episode. You remember the first one, don't you? The one where they put a monkey into a cage in the center of the table with only its head above the wooden top. These jackasses start clubbing the poor thing to death, and then they eat the brains to feel closer to God or some shit. Yeah, that whole series, plenty of options to embark on.

I came up with having a guillotine setup with me lying under the huge angled blade above my neck attached to a rope which passed through a candle. When the candle burned down enough, the rope would burn through, and that was that. I wouldn't feel it because I would be passed out prior from a nice big healthy shot of sodium pentothal, the shit they used as anesthetic during a surgery to knock you out. It's also a truth serum used to interrogate, be aware.

I wanted a shotgun between my legs with my big toe on the trigger aimed directly up and in my throat to blast away my entire spinal connection to my brain.

After a sleepless three days of conspiracy and suicidal nightmares and daily thought processes, I decided to find out what was up. I grabbed a wooden chair, the dinner table high-top style with four legs and put it out onto a ledge just outside my window which was seven stories high and two feet wide without a railing to stop me from falling or dropping headfirst. I am unafraid of heights due to my childhood of climbing trees, being a roofer by trade, the family business prior, to coming here, so no big deal. I hopped right out on my ledge in my chair and lit a cigarette. I was going to confront death or life right fucking now. I leaned out with an arm against the wall holding myself at the balance point of one leg of this wooden spindled chair. I looked up at the heavens and asked God to send me a message or this was it. I thought of nothing for several moments and was certainly beginning to sway to the fall side, life wasn't worth living. I didn't want to face the world or anyone knowing I got this disease while being a naughty little boy according to the way I was raised. All sex was bad, and naughty, you're going to burn in hell for all that fornicating. I could actually hear some God-crazed Southern preacher spewing that shit out his mouth in my head. My mind was blank, I began to let go.

"Hey, man!"

I grasped the wall and turned to see a young black orderly standing in my room wearing this blue hospital outfit. I hadn't let go, and this guy was asking to come out onto my ledge. I said, "Sure, come on out here." He asked me what I was doing, so I told him confronting my life and having a smoke. He grabbed a chair and placed it outside the window facing mine, several feet away. He politely asked me for a cigarette, and I handed him the pack beside my foot along with my lighter. He lit two and passed me back a lit smoke and my pack along with my lighter. We smoked together on that ledge for the next five minutes talking about where I was from and where he was from. I began to think about how cool it would be to see my family again. He never asked me once to come back inside with him or asked if I was planning to fall to my death. Shit! He didn't even say anything other than "Have a good day, and I'll see you later." He got up and placed his chair back into the room and walked out of my room. I was shocked, and kind of insulted actually, he never told me not to jump or to come inside; he just left me to my own business. It was in that moment I realized I could do this. I looked up to the sky and thanked God for sending me another messenger, another angel. I never saw this man again at all within this building or the surrounding areas of the hospital during the remainder of my stay. But he definitely kept me in this world. Imagine that!

I remained in this hospital for a total of six months, five and a half months of nightmares, and a wild black phantom plaguing my vision. Like I said before, I would guess he was the angel of death, the Grim Reaper, coming for my soul. I gained my strength back after deciding to take half of what they were prescribing me because I knew I was being poisoned. I didn't believe any of this, I am in complete denial. They didn't worry much about me at all staying alone on this hospital ward within a crazy nightmare, so why should I allow them to possibly kill me with massive amounts of this medicine which was stripping the meat off my face, legs, and arms? I had lost weight that I had gained back within the other hospital, and it was all due to this medicine. They kept saying to take it no matter what. I just couldn't allow them to force me this shit any longer. I slowly pushed myself at night when no one was around other than my shadowy friend to do push-ups, and I would walk each day all over the hospital grounds to stay away from these crazy scientists and their magic medicine. I firmly believe it was the best advice I would ever give myself. I was allowed to go home on leave once I looked healthy again. I was told to get my affairs in order because at best guess they told me I had about three years to live, maybe less. I had called home to announce my coming home on a convalescent leave granted by the military due to my condition. I would be allowed ten days, but I would be returning to the Marine Corps Recruit Depot in San Diego and placed in Casual Company. I was also given an accommodation by the navy for participating in this program. They said it was a selfless act of humanity. Okay, fuck it. I will include their words exactly.

The Commanding Officer takes great pleasure in presenting to

Gary J. Mello
A Letter of Commendation
In Recognition of Services as set forth herein

For Outstanding performance of duty while participating in ongoing medical research at the Naval Medical Center and the University of California Medical Research Group, San Diego, California, from 01 September 1992 to 28 February 1993.

Freely volunteering for a demanding research project, you demonstrated a high level of personal commitment, selflessly offering your time, as well as your physical and emotional resources. The importance of your participation was recognized by civilian and military professionals involved in this study and your actions can only be characterized as unselfish and in the service of humankind. Your benevolent commitment and voluntary participation reflected great credit upon yourself and were in keeping with the highest traditions of the United States Naval Service.

It gives me great pleasure to commend you for your contributions to Navy Medicine and to wish you continued success in all of your future endeavors.

Rear Admiral, Medical Corps
United States Navy

My family was cool with me coming home at first, but then I heard from one of my own brothers he didn't want me around his kids. He and his wife said it point-blank. I was crushed. I told them, "Fine, I am your brother and your children's uncle, but if you don't want me around them, fine. They will never know me at all. Don't even tell them I exist if you want." I also told them they need to do a little research on how this disease is spread before making such a harsh decision. I slammed the phone down after yelling, "Go fuck yourselves."

About fifteen minutes later, my phone rang and it was my brother. He said he was sorry. They asked me some questions on what I had learned about transmission of this deadly virus and became willing to listen. They were scared, but they were my family and I needed them. I was welcomed home by all of them even if they were uneducated and scared. We as a family hadn't a clue, and the news stations didn't have much information other than to watch out, be careful. Then some asshole came up with the idea it could be airborne within a sneeze, in our saliva, no kissing, casual contact was forever questioned, and the mosquitoes may carry it from person to person. No sharing of eating utensils, drinking cups, dishes, bathrooms. I was Frankenstein, and the villagers wanted me to burn. I was a witch to be hung without proof of her wrong doings other than the opinion of the masses. I certainly felt uneasy around them and anyone else who happened to know I was infected with AIDS. I was treated like I was a leper with them in the beginning; I ate from my own plate, drank from my own cup, and showered in the same bathroom. Each time my mother would follow cleaning the bathroom with bleach each and every day. My ten days of leave wasn't very enjoyable at all.

Prior to heading back into the military, I found one of my high school girlfriends I had dated before joining the Corps and showed her the hospital paperwork. I told her all my dealings with the prostitutes in foreign countries, the whole mess. She told me not to worry about that stuff at all, she loved me anyways. We reconnected and we were planning to be married when she flew down after I was retrained within a new job several months later. I had found my life partner, and it gave me hope. I certainly didn't expect a yes at all when I asked her hand, but she did say yes. I could be loved unconditionally I guess.

CASUAL COMPANY

I flew back to San Diego and reported back to the hospital. They refilled my medicines, and I was sent back to my original barracks on this day to gather my belongings after being discharged from the hospital. They had told me at the hospital I could no longer stay in my unit. I was no longer combat effective. When I arrived to my barracks on Camp Del Mar, the place looked abandoned. The majority of my unit had been sent to Somalia while I was in the hospital. I was completely abandoned, no friends, not even a soul in which I recognized. I entered the company office, and the only semi-familiar face was a first sergeant. I had seen him before but wasn't directly connected to him so to speak. I handed him my orders, and he just led me to my room which had been locked and untouched by anyone until my arrival on this day. He led me there and waited outside as I tossed my stuff into my seabag. All my things were taken in one swoop, good thing we travel light as Marines. All my field gear had already been returned prior to my collapse. Returning back from overseas duty is quick and dirty. Not much gear comes back at all, just personal shit and your uniforms.

As I left my original spot of my almost demise, I could sense a silence in this room while in it, and it felt weird to close the door and walk away. I was saying good-bye to all the people I knew for the seven or eight months I was in this unit with and overseas with them. Some of the others I had known since North Carolina. It was a sad moment for me.

I was brought to my new temporary duty station in San Diego, the actual recruit training base. Once again I was left in

236

a barracks alone and cast out in shame. I had to report to this gunnery sergeant the next day for him to assign me a job duty while awaiting my next permanent duty station. The powers that be didn't know what to do with me actually. They just kept me isolated and tried to give me some bullshit job standing at a doorway checking people into a chow hall for enlisted personnel and officers. I left that crap position within five minutes. I returned back to my barracks and just fell asleep until the next day. I told that gunnery sergeant he needed to find me something else to do because that was not a job at all. They didn't need me sitting there at all; it was all set up to have me doing absolutely nothing because I was a leper to them. I was ordered to have light duty and to take fucking pills and suffer, that was it.

After two days of just hanging around on my own, doing nothing and talking to nobody, I was ordered to report to a staff sergeant in the maintenance shed.

When I arrived, the staff sergeant introduced me to another lance corporal who would show me my job duties. We went and met with a platoon of trainees who were doing their maintenance week during recruit training. We loaded some of them up into a pickup truck and drove them outside the gate along some obscure road to weed whack and to pick up trash. I was left with these recruits to make sure the job was done properly. Each day was the same for a full month waiting on a new job within the Marine Corps.

During this time I was so freaking bored, depressed, and lonely I had to find something to do other than this dumb shit. So each day when these recruits finished the grass cutting for the day, I would reward them with smokes, dip, candy, soda, and several other cool things, like craps and cards, plus a little music to make them feel comfortable before their asshole drill instructor showed up to get them. I always told them to bring a few bucks each day because this shit wasn't free. I never overcharged them and always was sure to tell them to keep this stuff in house, no bringing it back to the barracks. I guess someone didn't listen because sure enough we had the whole rat brigade show up within a few weeks to shut down our operation. It turned out the staff sergeant didn't keep his job as maintenance supervisor because he never came to work to see what was going on, and the other lance corporal was skimming money from these kids by charging them double and sometimes triple the price for simple extras. I wasn't even named by these recruits whatsoever; I guess honesty helps when you're dealing with scared recruits. I wasn't supposed to be doing the contraband thing with them during recruit training, but hey, I wasn't going to be one of those assholes who eats, drinks, and smokes in front of starving, tired, and wishing they had a smoke recruits. I was just honest about my dealings with them. The other lance corporal got brought up on charges. I squeaked by out of all that mess, thank God. I was reassigned to Camp Pendleton actually, close to where my original unit was from, which was kind of cool.

I arrived there early and was brought to my barracks, once again all alone in a squad bay. I had no friends here in the Marine Corps it seemed. While staying in this barracks, I was graciously awoken by the sounds of sirens one night and followed them to a barracks to see what all the noise was. It turned out one of the coaches from this shooting range had hung himself in one of the empty barracks, sort of like my accommodations. Unlike him, I lived in my barracks, he just happened to wander into an empty one to end his life. Nice fucking first few days, welcome to the range I guess. I would later find out it was because a recruit shot himself during a live fire exercise. He couldn't live with the guilt or something.

I remember this black coaching school instructor who made me do a junk on the bunk inspection within a day or so of that. He wanted to make sure I had all my gear and to size me up. In fact the whole class I was going to be retrained with arrived dressed in their green uniform for formation. I was the only guy who had to have his shit all out on his bunk a certain way and displayed very neatly and all shiny. These guys to my right and left lived off base, so they didn't need to be inspected I guess. Besides they were all sergeants or above in rank, I was nobody. During this inspection, the coaching school instructor tried to make me feel good because he knew my status as a new AIDS person within the ranks and said to keep my head up. "You look good in this uniform, stand up straight, boy, and stand proud. You're all right, you're squared away. I don't care what people say about you, you're one tough motherfucker in my book. Sorry for the rough road to get here, but welcome to the Marine Corps Recruit Depot rifle range coaching course."

I was retrained within a marksmanship instruction course to become a coach to hopeful recruits during their boot camp experience. I thoroughly enjoyed this school actually. I was the lowest-ranking individual in the place but rank meant nothing during testing. I learned everything there was to know about this weapon and its proper firing. No scopes, just plain sights. If you can fire this weapon effectively downrange at distances of five hundred meters, you are qualified. Now all we needed to learn was how to teach someone else and have them understand it. Sounds very easy, but it would prove difficult once we completed our own pass-or-fail course. We were given a lot of book knowledge, but all of our testing was done live, in front of your classmates. It was pass or fail, with a lot of laughter mixed in. I guess they found me funny during my explanation of proper sight alignment. I passed the verbal stuff with aces and moved on to the pistol qualification range. I was tested and only became a sharpshooter, but I was happy with that. I was focused on the M-16 firing actually. I had fucked up my expert badge during boot camp myself, so this was my chance to be an expert. I would hate to be a coach teaching others with a toilet bowl—looking badge on my chest. I suffered from too many distractions, I guess, and pure exhaustion back then. That wouldn't be the case this time. I became a machine during this training. When test day came for the coaching class on this weapon, I wouldn't be denied.

We arrived on the range bright and early, 5:00 AM. The sun hadn't even awoken from the horizon yet. I was in the zone, I grabbed my weapon from the armory and my rounds needed. Not much bullshitting or breaking balls, our class was focused, I just offered a good morning and a good luck. I headed to the two-hundred-meter line, shot my rounds perfectly in the black of the target which was round, about the size of a basketball. The size of the average head, easy picking, once you're applying the skills learned. On to the three-hundred-meter line, same results, perfectly done. Now the five-hundred-meter line went perfectly, well, at least up until my very last round to get a perfect score. I aimed in on the wrong target accidently, got cocky and fired. Oops! My target didn't go down, I got a missed flag, and the target to my right went down instead. I looked over at the staff sergeant who was firing to my right and whispered to him, "Hey, that was me." I tried to cover it up by saying, "Hey, it's a gift, just shoot at my target." I guaranteed he would get five points, and it didn't matter to my score because I reached expert already. I was hoping he would take the gift, but he immediately raised his hand and called out the misfire on his target. I was humbled by this man's honesty. He was struggling all day with several bad scores and might possibly not qualify. In the face of requalifying again in the afternoon, he stood with integrity. My first true experience with a level of honesty I hadn't witnessed in a long time. Great lesson to be taught to me also, I learned no matter my assistance here on a range, this man had to perform on his own however it turned out. I'm sure he would've spent the next whole fucking day shooting till he got it right. We had all week to dial everything in, but from forces unknown to me, I screwed the pooch. I guess I'm not going to be a sniper, I didn't even know the qualifications, but a solid 245 points out of 250 wasn't too shabby, I even hit the black on the wrong target because sure enough up came his target to prove I hadn't lied either. It mattered not, I was pissed I didn't go full pull on the range, but it just went to show even in training, people miss. I was glad I missed actually; I didn't want the hype. Fuck! It felt good! Well done, sir!

"What the fuck got into your head asshole? Great fucking shooting, Lance Corporal. But hey, guess what? You missed! And you got the best score with that miss. You suck!"

I thanked the range warrant officer for his kind words. In my head I was thinking what if that was real; some poor prick standing next to my target if I was a sniper would've gotten wasted. But guess what? If they had me shoot all the targets from my field of vision, they all would fall within the kill range of five hundred meters to zero meter with an M-16. That's just a warning to enemy troops, we train to kill, one shot one kill. I just lost my train of thought after firing forty-nine rounds. Not acceptable to me. I could do better if we test again, though.

I was blessed with the lessons learned that day about honesty. I received my expert badge during our graduation and was told which range we were to report to the following Monday morning. The staff sergeant qualified as a marksman, which carried the toilet bowl within its square. It's a bull's eye, but we call it the shit badge. I was glad he made it; he earned that badge and was proud to wear it, fucking aye right! You are one honest motherfucking Marine. Hurrah!

When I was teaching my recruits, I would share that story with them whenever they brain-farted on me and hadn't a clue how to fire it correctly on target. I would gladly greet them at the five-hundred-meter line and prove to them their weapon worked just fine. I had to do this on their very first day if they were missing the target entirely. I would let them totally screw the pooch all day. I would shoot from the standing position, not the prone position which was far easier. The waggle of your front site post is less and your platform is much more stable in the prone position. At five hundred meters, you must be focused because while standing, heartbeat, wind, stance, and every other damn thing occurring can make you miss. I would make bets on making it a head shot with the other coaches just to break balls further to dumbasses who don't pay the fuck attention to their primary marksmanship instructor for the week prior to reaching me. Sometimes it was a simple elevation miscalculation, but mostly people lose focus. I did this each Monday, Tuesday, Wednesday, twice a day. Five out of six times I hit the simulated head area, the sixth shot ended up in the neck or chest. This always stopped a recruit from missing from then on.

I had a perfect record while working at this range. I even passed the damn PT test I was given. I certainly showed up for runs also and never fell out. I even stayed late for other coaches' recruits who didn't prequalify on the prequalifier on Thursday. Having to teach the real boneheads during the refire in the afternoons of Thursday never bothered me. It definitely helped the flunk ratio, and it gave us a chance to allow them to shoot in the morning in the odd case they messed it up on Friday's test day. We could have them requalify in the afternoon during the switch between the morning shooters and the target changers who fired in the second phase of the day. If they failed the morning, they got the toilet bowl badge regardless their score. They had to qualify and reshoot or fail out of their platoon and would be recycled. Not meaning we helped them, nope, no shaving points, no adding points, this was on them. I just gave them a quick briefing on what they learned from someone else, they usually ended up with me, and I wasn't having failures. They qualified experts with me, but because they fucked it up in the morning, they got that shit badge, just the same. No sympathy, fuck you! It was integrity, honor, and definitely a required task to complete recruit training. Not too fucking wise to allow some dumb kid to leave our range without something. He better know how to shoot effectively.

Teaching recruits how to fire the M-16-A2 effectively was a really cool job, and I was blessed to be doing it.

DISCHARGED

During this time of coaching I was married and moved off base to be with my wife. I also got to see some of my old friends that had returned back from Somalia. I won't lie, a few of them didn't return. Some returned with bullet wounds and shrapnel wounds. When I asked what happened, they just told me, "I wish you were there, maybe this wouldn't have happened to me." I didn't want that guilt, but it was true. I was back in the States sick and not there to protect my brothers. I made it a point to go places with my friends or to invite them to my home at least twice a month. I had missed the brotherhood we had together overseas. One of them was hit in the head with a piece of fragmentation and a huge piece of his skull was a divot from where the bone was removed; he had a scar from his eyebrow all the way back to the opposite side of his head below his ear. He would have head shakes from this, and it was sort of uncontrollable at times. He never wanted to leave his barracks when I would show up to pick those guys up just to hang out after work. They were maimed, I was diseased, but we remained friends. I don't talk to them now in reality because we lost contact over the years. I hope they read my story and remember me.

I was also told that one of the guys we were pretty close to flipped out one night after I was sent to the first hospital with the plastic-covered room. He had asked about me, my condition, and where I was several times to command, but they wouldn't tell him. I guess stress causes people to snap when you're placed in an environment of assholes, our command. He smashed a bunch of computers one night drunk in the company office and was arrested and sent to the brig. He might not have done it all for me, but I'm sure my situation didn't help matters. I went to visit him several times and brought him some stuff he may need while locked up and waiting to be dishonorably discharged. He would go home in one piece though. We actually shared a couple of large women together prior to me getting deathly ill. I say large because they were both above three hundred pounds each. They were named Hot Dog and Beans. No shit. They were a couple of wild girls, nothing better than the love from some big girls. I'm not into large women per say, but the opportunity was available at the time and we had a ton of fun. I spread her huge butt cheeks and fell into that Venus flytrap for a long time. I definitely was stuck, her butt enveloped around my hips and I became dental floss to her huge crack. When I came up for air and her butt released me, I was a complete mess. I had a poop streak running from bellybutton to my neck. I earned another stripe this moment in time, but it wasn't one on my shoulder. It didn't matter; it was the experience and the challenge that mattered most to me.

I was taking seriously way too many meds during this whole ordeal, and my mind sort of brain-farted when I went to visit another guy I knew who was being let out of the Marine Corps for drug use. I also knew he was the guy I pissed on during school's battalion. I had come home drunk one night and thought I was in the bathroom. I must have been sleepwalking or in a blackout. I was awoken in the morning with him screaming at me that I had pissed all over him. I didn't believe him at first, but as I looked down toward his bunk, I could see the huge puddle under his mattress. I swore to him it wasn't on purpose. I honestly thought I was in the bathroom. I even explained to him the distance from my rack to his rack is the exact distance from the bathroom door to the urinal. He was pissed, but I couldn't remember a thing. I washed all his blankets and sheets and switched out his mattress. He was cool with that. As a matter of fact, he was also the same guy who always left my window open or rigged the back door for me to get back into the barracks when I would stagger in late. Why would I do that on purpose?

For some reason we started hanging out watching hockey games together and our wives became sort of friends because we lived within the same apartment complex. I would feel like absolute dog shit from my medicine every single day. I had no real appetite at all, and this guy smoked pot. So what the hell, what's a few puffs going to do, right? Or maybe it was the brownies? Or maybe it was secondhand smoke? It took away my nausea, that's all I knew. Whichever the case the very next day after this night, I showed up to work, and surprise, you got a piss test. Total fucking conspiracy, I always knew he was a rat motherfucker and wanted revenge. He must have reported me because he was jealous of me being a better Marine than him all these years. I was a first squad leader and in charge of our platoon during school's battalion.

He had it in his head he was supposed to be an officer because he had college. I know it's jealousy because I also scored better on our testing during the amphibious assault school. As a matter of fact, he still to this day can't accept that a street guy like me could be picked over his pompous ass. Fuck him and his sneaky bullshit. "I'm glad I pissed on you one night, drunk as a stinking monkey. I also shouldn't have covered for your ass when you went AWOL over Thanksgiving weekend to go home to see your wife. I should've let you lose your marriage during them days of hardship when she wanted to bail on you if you didn't go home. I still think you ate the turkey sandwich on the plane ride instead of bringing it to me for covering your fire watch duties personally. You weren't supposed to leave the base much less the entire State."

I went to piss in the cuplike ordered to by the military police when I hit the range. I just knew for a fact these assholes were just waiting for the smallest infraction to use against me to push me out of the Marine Corps. Several weeks went by before I was arrested and sent to San Diego.

I wasn't going down so easy; I requested a special court-martial. I don't believe any of this bullshit. They were all over me like a cheap suit threatening me with a dishonorable discharge, no benefits, jail time, and the whole fucking nine. Never once was I actually asked if I smoked pot or if I had a drug problem or a drinking problem, or do I need counseling? I guess I wasn't going to get any of that. They found their answer to the AIDS guy. Throw him the fuck out like a piece of trash.

I totally knew they were completely trying to get rid of me as quickly as possible when my request for a court-martial was being referred to an administrative discharge board instead of a court-martial. This was something they pulled on me because they had the right to do so with my case according to the uniformed code of military justice. I didn't know what the hell to do. My lawyer was a brand-new boot lieutenant who didn't come up with too many solutions to these charges I faced. He also didn't say to me all you have to do is ask for drug treatment therapy and I would be able to stay in the Marines.

Once again I called home and asked my mom who my congressman was because I had always heard if you're being mistreated at all in the Marines Corps to call your fucking congressman. Mine happened to be Barney Frank at the time. I asked my mom, "Isn't he the gay representative in our state?" She said yes. Well, that's a plus; he would be sympathetic to the whole AIDS thing also. She got his number out of the phone book, and I dialed it. I don't know what the hell happened once I explained to this man what was happening and how things have been laid out on me like I'm some sort of piece of trash not worth a thing even after all these tests, isolation tactics, and complete mistreatment once I was diagnosed. He told me to stand firm and he would make some calls.

It turned out during this separation boards hearing that the prosecuting side of my case couldn't produce any evidence or come up with any theory whether or not secondhand smoke would affect an AIDS patient differently while on meds. Meaning it was possible. I had one character witness, my staff sergeant from amtracs showed up on my side, due to the hearing being in San Diego, and not Camp Pendleton, and they conducted this during working hours. My gunnery sergeant from amtracs refused to show up because I didn't tell him first about the whole mother-daughter deal in Okinawa. He was such a pompous suck pump worried about his own image, advancement, and security. How about you admit the fact you're a ball sucker, buddy. None of my other rifle range higher command showed up at all. Nope, they planned this very well.

It also was revealed someone had tampered with my urine sample after I deposited my urine. I had sealed it with red tape and signed the bottle in three specific areas. The seal was broken when it arrived at the lab. Right then, in that moment, there should've been a release of my charges due to tampered evidence collection, but not for me. Nope, I was getting pushed out any way possible. I should've had the reasonable doubt locked and be sent back to my new job as a marksmanship coach. I should've at the very least been retested for drugs in my system again. They told me they would discharge me under honorable conditions if I would just leave this all alone and disappear. I would maintain my veteran's benefits, and that would be that. I was fucked. I took their deal because they were definitely going to pull something else out of their ass next time and I would lose my benefits all together. How would I possibly survive this disease without proper medical care without being privy to the veterans' department hospitals? If I got anything less than an honorable discharge. I would certainly not survive for very long. My back was definitely smashed into the corner. So that was it. I was discharged from the United States Marine Corps. Total discrimination in my opinion.

If you're one of those colonels on my discharge board, within this book lies your fucking biggest mistake. I was a solid Marine who was mistreated, abandoned, beaten, broken, brainwashed, stuck with massive amounts of needles, given crazy medicine over the course of ten months, and then you discharge me on bum charges that could've been easily expunged regardless of guilt or innocence. Real nice government operation we got here. I didn't appreciate the reenlistment code of RE-4 either. That definitely stops me from ever getting back into the Marine Corps or any other branch of the service. The truth was I am now hip to the fact your whole objective was that you wanted me to kill another human. You wanted to simply drop me off within an area that our own government's action has caused someone else to become an enemy, not me personally. This has happened throughout American history. That addition of drug use on my record was never proven either. I don't deny my usage, nor do I deny I enjoyed lots of liquor, women, and the odd transsexual too, but we weren't in the court of law now, were we? Thanks for the ride into dangerous waters and them foreign countries without so much as a warning to be aware that these places were the disease capitals of the world at that time. Perhaps it was us who were the disease arriving with weapons instead of food.

I did notice that Iraqi amtrac was made in the United States. I hopped into it and started it because I leaned way under the driver's dash and read the placard attached to the hull when nobody could figure out how it started on a base long before 9-11 happened. This was this entire government's fault from long ago. Not the people of our nation, our government's leaders. I guess when you poke a hornets' nest, it sends attackers.

You know what, it doesn't matter anymore either. I look back and love the joyous moments within my Marine Corps career anyways. I was crushed beyond belief, and it was very painful to be forced out.

I have returned my uniforms all save one, my dress blues, in which awaits my death within my mother's possession for me to be dressed with honor, draped with an American flag, and then burned along with my diseased body. Really glad you guys set me up because you were afraid of the Marine with AIDS.

Veterans Affairs

Entering the system wasn't very hard at all actually; I arrived to San Diego Medical Center and told them I was being discharged. It felt like they already knew this entirely prior to me showing up and all I had to do was sign some papers, give more blood, and the check is in the mail. "Now get lost until two weeks from now, you'll have to return so we can check your counts again." That's how it went for me. I was considered a service-connected disabled veteran because I contracted AIDS while serving in the military. Simple as that. No bullshit about I'm crazy, no PTSD disorder, just an unlucky individual at the time who had bad luck. I am a casualty of war actually, Desert Storm was starting as I joined, and Somalia was also going on toward the end of my term of service. I signed up fully prepared to end up in combat somewhere. They needed troops however they could get them. I would like to say I served proudly. I certainly exited when they asked or forced me to. I also was a great test subject for them to have. I followed orders, especially doctor's orders to kill a disease we all knew very little about. God kept me safe from the madness of killing people by giving me AIDS instead. This burden I can bear, can you bear your own when Judgment Day arrives?

I applied for a job at a horse racing track in Del Mar for a cooking position. I had learned to cook from an older cousin when I was a kid. I started at the bottom in his restaurant back when I was fourteen years old. I washed dishes first, then became a prep cook, then learned the fry-o-lator, on to sauté, then finally up to head line cook running the broiler. I was even the Sunday morning breakfast cook. I worked for my cousin for about four years actually, sometimes ninety hours a week. I knew my way around a kitchen. I have to thank him for taking the time to teach me what he had learned in Johnson and Wales College. My cousin was a chef, and he passed his knowledge to me. I loved that job, but drug use was always my downfall as a teenager. I broke into the place while it was closed one night to steal money and beer. I had the damn key to the door, but I still broke in through a window. I cut myself on the broken glass, and it was only a matter of time before I was caught. I couldn't live with the guilt and the betrayal of my cousin's trust in me. As a matter of fact, I can't stop apologizing to his wife every time I see her because it hurts me to remember the tears he had in his eyes when he found out it was me. I was scared to death actually; my cousin was a good man and still is, but back then he was very large. If you're reading this, cousin, just know I stay away because I feel like a total jackass still to this day and it has been over twenty years. I'm sorry for our close friendship and bond that we lost because of me and my selfishness.

So anyways, I got hired on as an assistant chef, which was about third in line down from the head chef. I worked at this job for three weeks total. I was used to train people what they were supposed to be doing and then let go. It turned out the three Mexicans I was teaching were working for less than me combined. So once I trained them, I was fired. Not happy about that sneaky shit, but oh well. I hope they paid attention when I came upon the three of them butchering a big mahimahi fish trying to filet it. Luckily I knew how to filet the thing, or you would've lost lots of money over time.

I applied to another restaurant at a private airport working for a Greek guy helping with breakfast and lunch. This job was kind of cool actually. I happened to meet a celebrity while working there actually. Brad Pitt of all people came in and sat next to me one day. I said hello and said I liked a few movies he was in. That was all. Nothing more than idle chitchat, and off he went back to his life and I went back to cooking. This job came to an end when the owner got pissed at me for cooking better than him I guess; customers enjoyed my cooking over his. He was all pissed yelling at me for something stupid one morning, and he had a kitchen knife in his hand threatening to stab me. I took off my apron and wrapped my arm with it and grabbed a sauté pan. He charged and I blocked his knife with my wrapped arm and cranked him in the knee with the pan. He dropped to the ground and started screaming, "You're fired, and you're fired." I just walked out front and told his wife what had happened and I was done at this place. I took my last paycheck that day and left.

I tried to make due in California by going to work selling children's books door to door at my next job. I would wake up at 4:00 AM and drive two hours away to the warehouse to load my books into my truck and drop them off as sample books from Monday to mid-Wednesday afternoon to as many office buildings along the road I used that particular week. I would pick my books up from mid-Wednesday to Friday night. I had the highest sales count within this book sales division for the whole time I was there. I was getting worn-out from all the traveling and lack of energy caused by AIDS medicine. I was averaging about three hundred bucks a week, but it wasn't enough to maintain the apartment we had just recently moved to. My options were limited. I could move back to Massachusetts, or I could move to Florida, that was my father's suggestion. I had been granted 30 percent disability from the Veterans Affairs office at that time so that was like two hundred bucks a month, which would help out with lot rent in a nice mobile home park where my father set us up to move into.

My younger brother had come to visit us during our time in California while I was freshly discharged. The three of us went to Tijuana actually. I remember it was fun until I got completely drunk and caused an argument with my wife and him. I swore I saw them playing touchy-feely under the table. I became delusional I guess in front of them and stormed off into the crowd of people on the streets. I pushed and smashed people out of my way all the way back to the border. It was a wonder I wasn't arrested or attacked along the way. I remember hopping into my truck and my wife and brother jumped into the bed because I was going to leave without them. I drove home doing ninety the whole way and pulled into a gas station. My brother was drunk and so was my wife. My brother was puking the whole way back. I got the gas and drove home without a word spoken until I woke up to my wife at the foot of the bed crying and my brother scared shitless thinking I was going to kill him. I apologized for acting like a wild man and tried to convince my brother it was safe to stay until he flew home. My first real sign I was out of my mind. My brother agreed, and we actually put that night behind us as a group. He stayed the week, and I even let him win a few tennis matches against me. It was cool seeing my brother again.

The bills fell behind, and the truck payment wasn't getting paid. I assessed our bills and realized the payment for our wedding rings was definitely killing us. I convinced my wife that we should return them and just end the payment. She agreed. A month later, we got semi matching tattoos. That was our ring. We were faced with going homeless in a month's time. I certainly didn't want to move home to Massachusetts and become a burden on my mother or any of my brothers. I remembered the last time I visited quite well and felt alienated from them. It was best I move to Florida with my new wife and stay away. I will love them from afar. I definitely wouldn't want to have them freaking out every time I got a cough or if I needed to go see a doctor. These things are very hard for me to swallow; they don't need the stress. So off we went driving from California to Florida. It took three days total of driving. I got to see the bottom half of our country along Highway 10. Texas is a very large state to drive across. I even got to see Biloxi, Mississippi, where her brother lived. Baton Rouge, Louisiana, was nice also. It was a pleasant ride.

The honeymoon didn't last long with my wife actually when we arrived. I began working at a Circle K on the night shift from 11:00 PM to 7:00 AM, then I would rest for a few hours and show up for work at a pizza joint from 10:00 AM to 4:00 PM. There wasn't much time for me and my new wife to spend time together at all. I was trying to make ends meet for us any way possible. I didn't want her to work if she didn't want to. I could carry the load, no problem, baby. I took this on full force with all the best intentions regardless of my fatigue. I wanted to be her man and to provide for her. During this time, we got along just fine until I began to get cranky and controlling. I also didn't want to risk having children, but she wanted them. I just couldn't see myself having a child born with my disease. This was not an option. I never really allowed the conversation to happen actually. I just kept it in the back of my mind.

I also remember meeting a lot of correctional officers and police while working at the Circle K during my shift. They had discussed with me about possibly going down to the Naples Correctional Facility and applying for a job there because I had prior service. Since I had marksmanship training, I could easily be a rifle tower guard. They certainly needed the help. I thought on this for several weeks actually and almost committed to getting into my car and taking the drive. I had to say no to this based on my own stay within prison walls as a youth. I definitely didn't want to shoot anyone trying to get the hell out of that horror house. I'm sorry but no.

I had gotten a taste of dirt bike riding with a childhood friend. We had worked together at the same restaurant, my cousin's joint. He was a great rider actually, and it was fun to meet him on the weekends to go turn some laps. I purchased an older CR-125 and learned to ride it. I watched and learned from him and all his friends within the dirt bike riding community in Port Charlotte area. I had crashed plenty and even hurt my damn right knee very badly. But that is a common injury. He could do a nasty knack-knack before the damn thing became popular actually. What I loved most about all of them is the fact they allowed me to be their friends and kept me interested within their lives also. Not once was I told, "You're an AIDS carrier, get away." It was very fun times. The trips to the different practice areas were amazing. I didn't have a care in the world when I was on them two wheels. I have lost communication with that entire group, but you are definitely alive and real in my mind. Your family is amazing and so are your friends.

I remember the time we all swung out on that rope swing together at a cookout. I was stuck upside down hung up by my shorts and couldn't get free. I smashed into the ground and damn near drowned on the second swing outward. I was released only when my shorts tore completely off leaving just the waistband. All naked as a jaybird, embarrassed because I just fucked myself up in front of everyone. That was a great day in my memory, wouldn't change a thing. You guys are all awesome!

There were nights where I would wake up drenched in sweat, gasping for air. I would grind my teeth a lot. In fact I even slept with a knife and sometimes a pistol under my pillow. I was completely in psycho mode brought on by recurring nightmares. I would always be falling toward the ground and hit, it was on the bounce after I looked into the store fronts window and saw my tangled body within a reflection, then I would wake up. Other nights I wouldn't sleep at all because I was spraying diarrhea all night from my medicine. I remember my wife tried to wake me up during a nightmare, and I immediately grabbed her and flung her under me with my knife against her throat. I would snap out of it once I looked to see who was trying to kill me. If she was asked I'm sure she would tell you, I was a complete fucking mess. I would drink to pass out because the nightmares wouldn't arrive as often. She was completely understanding and loving about it, but I'm sure over time it must have dawned on her I wasn't normal.

I had gotten tired from all the work and no rest and discussed the possibility of her going to work so I could slow down a bit. She agreed to it and began working at a really nice outside bistro within a shopping complex. I would drop her off and pick her up. It was pretty smooth for a while until a night of chaos. I say chaos because that's what it turned into.

I was home half-sleeping in our room and my wife was in the living room talking on the phone. She was unaware I was home because my schedule changed at work because I cut back my hours at the pizza joint. I was in and out of sleep, but it felt good to be lying down resting. I heard my wife telling her girlfriend all about some guy she was starting to date at her work and how good the sex was. I was shocked, pissed, and completely out of my mind. I hopped up, snatched the phone from her, and just began wrapping the phone cord around her neck. I hung her over my shoulder and was completely going to kill her. My mind raced very quickly on where and when I would dispose of her body. I then heard a voice screaming on the phone. The women she was talking to heard the whole thing. I didn't care. This bitch betrayed me, fuck her. I then thought of them prison bars closing behind me as a youth and knew in my head if I continued, I would be there for a very long time. I released the chord from my hands, and she dropped to the floor choking and gagging. I immediately came to her aide and made sure she was okay. She was clueless about what had just happened actually. She must have blocked it out. I got possessed with rage, but I also knew it wasn't worth my own life. Besides I loved her. We had met so innocently as kids, she was riding her black horse down my road. I think we were sixteen; we went for a lot of trail rides together, kissing and just loving each other. We had had plenty of great sex then, and we still did as young adults. I had left for the Marine Corps. When I returned she was living with another guy, but still came to California with me. My wife loves me too.

It didn't take long for the police to arrive at our house because the chick on the phone called them. My wife greeted them at the door and told them everything was fine, which it was. I had gone delusional, or I had caught her in the act of the ultimate betrayal, adultery. The cops left, and we went to my job together at Circle K. We discussed our marriage and how we were just too young to be together, she wanted a break. I would want a break myself, so who could blame her? I agreed to the separation. Her friend was going to pick her up the next day.

I watched my wife load some things into her friend's car, and she left me. I was alone again. I was absolutely fucked now. The only person on this planet who was on my side in life was just pushed so far away I would never get her back. I couldn't forgive her, nor could I ever be sure she actually loved me at all. I may have been used by her just to get out of our town and try something new. All I wanted to do was cry, which I did. I grabbed my keys and just drove. I remember leaving Fort Myers and ending up in Orlando by nightfall. I had cried the whole time. I wailed because I was a Catholic, and this marriage was supposed to be for life. I wailed because I had scared my wife, I wailed because I was alone, I wailed to feel better. I wailed because my parents split when I was a kid and I didn't want that. I wanted to be married. How could've I possibly fucked this up? I wailed because I needed to. I wailed because I hated myself for being alive. I wailed for fucking up my Marine Corps career.

My wife stayed away for a week; I tried to talk with her but she was gone. I lost her. I told her I would forgive her only if she understood I would never forget the pain. I remember her bringing the police back to my house to get her stuff. That was exactly what she got to, her stuff. She arrived in my life with two trash bags of clothes and left with the same. She screamed and hollered wanting all the things I had purchased her over the previous two years, but those were gone too. Good thing she didn't check the trash can because she would've found a stack of ashes damn near the top of the can.

I fell into the absolute worst depression of my entire life. I drank nonstop day and night. Kentucky Tavern and Uncle Jim Bean were my poison during these times. I would average a handle per day. Handle meaning the big bottle. I remember changing jobs during these days. I worked at an Applebee's for the remainder of my stay within Florida.

By the time our divorce day came, I was a complete stumbling drunk. I didn't care about any of it. I only came to my wife's aide once during our divorce. The guy she was dating had gotten rough with her and had left bruises up and down her arms where he had grabbed them and squeezed very hard tossing her around. She came to my house to explain it all in tears actually. I couldn't do anything other than comfort her as a friend. She had wanted to leave him and come back to me or some shit along the lines. I didn't want anything to do with it. But the truth was, I did confront this guy late one night when he was leaving his work. I called his name, and when he saw it was me, he stood in shock. I punched him once and he was out cold. I waited for him to awake so he could see me again. I pointed at the money bag and told him I wasn't here for his money. "You're not being robbed, you're being put into check. If you ever lay your hands on my ex-wife again, I'm coming back with a bat." I helped him up, straightened out his clothes, and handed him his money satchel filled for a night deposit. He walked out of my sight with his head hung low.

The next morning my wife called me freaking out because the guy is scared to death. I just told her, "Don't worry about a thank-you, it's on the house. I'm still your friend, perhaps he won't hit you again."

On the day of our divorce the judge really screamed the hate toward me. He was disgusted with us both probably. I gave him an attitude anyways. I didn't want to be divorced, but I went along with it. I even told the prick if we were in Massachusetts, she might be dead. He asked why. I replied, because Florida has the death penalty, Massachusetts doesn't. I was just being a wise ass. I wasn't angry at my wife at all for wanting to leave me. I was a drunken loser, failed Marine, shitty-job-having bum. She deserved the right to have kids and raise a family, who the hell was I to stand in her way? I then stated, "Let her have it all, because I won't need it. I am a man. I will get it all back again." I certainly am not someone who would stop her from taking everything, fuck it, and let her have it. My wife said no, she didn't want a thing. The judge banged his gavel. Bibbity, boppity, boo, we are divorced.

We left that courtroom and met outside on opposite sides of the street. I looked to see her just standing looking lost. I asked if she had a ride home. She said no. I offered her a ride, and she agreed. This led to us toasting our divorce with champagne and fresh strawberries, and a fun filled evening of absolute mind-blowing sex. We were young; we didn't need to be married. She went her way, I went mine. We tried to date for a while, but it didn't work out to well.

I was starting to use drugs again, crack to be specific. I had called my mom to ask permission to come home. She said yes. I was all set to leave and escape my drug demons by changing locations. My ex-wife called me having massive stomach pains and needed a ride to the doctor's. I brought her there and everything was fine. Once again she had tested for HIV, and she was fine. Each and every time she was tested actually. I told her I was leaving soon. She didn't say a word. It was over.

I sold all my stuff as a package deal exactly what I had paid for the car, mobile home, and the furniture. Not much money at all, enough to purchase a newer piece of shit car, a Pontiac Grand Prix, completely faded from sun damage and bounced. I left Florida as a complete drunken, crack-addicted, newly divorced, AIDS-carrying loser.

RETURNING HOME

I returned home with all my things. I say all my things because I left everything except clothing and my television. Anything that didn't fit in my car I gave away to the neighborhood. I arrived at my mother's house a complete shambles. No need to make a fuss, no party, no nothing. In fact I drove home on a revoked driver's license actually. It was revoked due to my running of the stop sign all those years ago. I guess once I hit the East Coast, the computer system caught up to me. I avoided the town cops as I entered my hometown because they were certainly waiting for me at my exit. No kidding, I drove by one of them going the speed limit and watched as he recognized my face and he spun his vehicle around. I had a pretty good lead on him, so I gassed it and pulled farther away through winding roads. I made it a point to quickly turn into somebody's driveway out of his sight as he drove by. I walked into this man's breezeway and knocked on his inside door and asked to use his phone. I called home to ask one of my brothers to come and get me and my car, but no one answered the phone. I waited for a few minutes, and the police car went by the opposite way in search of me and my car. I hopped into my car and pulled out after I checked to be sure he was gone. I hurriedly made quick work of this check and buried the pedal to the floor the rest of the way home. You have no clue the harassment the local police did constantly to me and my brothers when we were kids and still to this day. That prick would've loved to snatch me driving without a license and compounded my whole life further into oblivion.

I pulled into the driveway of my mom's house safely and noticed a mobile home trailer in her side yard. It turned out her house had nearly burned down. I don't really know the details of this fire, but my younger brother got out safely and we lost one of her dogs to smoke inhalation. The house was a total mess. Smoke damage was throughout and fire damage was within several rooms. We were lucky to have a house actually. The cellar had flooded to four feet deep with water because the power was out for too long. All her things were totally trashed. She tried to salvage some stuff, and it was stored in the garage.

We remained in that trailer for a long time actually. I helped with my grandmother in the morning, cooked her breakfast, and helped her to the shower, made sure she had her medicine for diabetes. I did this when others weren't around. Eventually a neighborhood girl came to be with her in the afternoon. I also went to the courthouse in full default of the place for damn near four years. I walked in and surrendered. I was put on probation for several years and was ordered to pay restitution and had to report to a probation officer. I reported at night actually because I had gotten my old job back roofing, for a cut in pay. I'm not sure how that all worked in the boss's mind, it wasn't like I forgot how. He was just a cheap bastard. That lasted for quite a while, longer than need be actually. I should have called the authorities because he wasn't allowed to cut my pay by law because I was serving in the military when I left this job. Oh well, life sucks sometimes, it was better I was working.

I also got introduced to an amazing Cape Verdean woman. It was my brother's wife at the time that happened to see a personal ad of a twenty-nine-year-old girl with a son who happened to be single, living with HIV also. She was six years my senior, but age is just a number. I called and we talked and everything went fine actually. As a matter of fact, when I went to meet her, she was very pretty. I didn't know what Cape Verdean was at all or what she looked like. The girl answering the door wasn't her. She had gotten nervous and had her friend answer for her. I wasn't shocked or the least bit concerned when the real girl turned in the corner from the living room and she was dark skinned. She was black. But not too dark, sort of soft mocha color. She was way better looking than the girl who answered the door, actually. I liked her from rip. We had a great time that night actually and made love till we passed out. I got to meet her son, he was awesome. Just turning four years old. He was a white boy actually. His dad was white, and it happened that way. I had a new girlfriend who came with a bonus, a really cool son. We dated for quite a while actually.

I remember looking at one of her pictures on the wall of her family. I noticed a guy wearing a police uniform, and instantly I knew he was the cop who had punched me in the face back when I was a kid prior to joining the Marines. I told her the whole story, and she was concerned. I remember the first night I met him for the second time actually. Do you believe the luck? I begin dating his younger sister, talk about karma. We went to his home for a New Year's Eve party actually. I walked in, and it was like the music stopped in the place. I was a white boy in a sea of black people and his fellow boys in blue, but not only that, I was someone they recognized but couldn't place me yet. I walked past everyone with my new girl in tow and reached out my hand to her brother to introduce myself. He looked at me, and it all registered in his mind as he reached for my hand. We shook and I told him, "Let's leave the past in the past. I was young and you were a rookie. It won't happen again that way at all. I am back from the Marine Corps living with AIDS, and now I am going to be dating your sister." He was shocked by my manner of approach, but the only logical step was to accept. I had apologized for my actions as did he. His sister liked me regardless the hate and discontent we held for each other. I am sure it would've gotten ugly if I didn't offer forgiveness first. I hadn't forgotten a thing, time rolls on everyone. I was prepared to smash his teeth down his throat just on principle alone. But I considered a different approach. Truth is, we became sort of friendly over the years actually, so it was a good start on that night to make peace. I even enjoyed when we all got together for cookouts and birthday parties. I got the privilege of knowing his children. His wife was very nice also. My discontent toward this man and the police changed. I hadn't forgotten any of it, but in my heart I had to offer friendship.

The relationship with his sister lasted for as long as it had to, close to three and a half years I think. I have no complaints at all. She was a great mom to her son and an even more tolerable girlfriend to me. We did a lot of drinking together, which was our downfall. Other than that, we have plenty of awesome memories together. Those are ours. Good or bad memories, they remain ours. I miss her. I also am proud of her son for being in college. We have kept in semi-communication with each other, several times, over the last fifteen years; we still catch up and care about each other. It was something I ruined, but I exited a decent man. We remain friends. So call me sometime, girl. I also lived right inside the ghetto, so to speak. United Front Homes are all considered state housing. I had no fear within this community at all. In fact I got to meet plenty of really nice people among the so-called gangs of New Bedford. I met Spanish, Portuguese, Cape Verdean, Caucasians, Africans, Puerto Ricans, Jewish, Orientals—all the different backgrounds. I hold no cause in any of them.

I would help each and every repairman that would come to fix my mom's house, just to learn something new. I actually ended up doing a lot of work for my mom, which was fine. I was her son, and she needed the help. It took several months to get her home livable. Just prior to moving back into the house, my grandmother slipped on some ice and broke both her kneecaps. I had asked one of my brothers to be sure he was home to help her walk to the van for daycare. I was going to the veterans' department for my usual blood tests and refill of my medicines, I wasn't available. The van driver lost his grip and down she went. I blamed myself actually. If I didn't have this fucking disease, I would have been there. Although accidents sometimes just fucking happen to good people outside of anyone's control. But that happened on my watch, it hurt.

Things went downhill fast for my grandmother, which sucked. She passed away not very long after them sequence of events unfolded like a nightmare. I was watching in shock as I witnessed my own mother's absolute best friend on this planet passed on and then left this lifetime. It made me very sad. I was sadder still for my younger brother and his son who was born three days afterward. I felt the pain of not being able to share his little boy with his grandmother. I blamed one of my other brothers knowing full well it was just her time. I apologized. Hopefully when you read this, you yourself will find peace. I lost an amazing woman and gained an awesome little nephew all in the same week. On the night of my grandmother's death when I fell asleep that night, I dreamed of her sitting across from me at a table. We spoke about many things, but I insisted she tell me where she was, but she told me to not to worry, she was with friends. "Take care of yourself, my Gary." I was actually visited by someone beyond the grave in a dream the exact same evening she passed away. It was spooky. I woke up and told my mother what had happened actually. I told her she had said good-bye, "I will watch over you from heaven." She was with Jesus. My mom thought that was very nice actually. I remember going to stay with her many of times as a teenager. I would always bum a smoke from her secret stash of Carlton's. I would only be allowed to have a cigarette if I went outside and stayed out of sight. Her sister, my aunt, lived next door; she told me if my aunt caught me, that was it, no more sneaking cigarettes. We came to an understanding. If I didn't mention the sweets she had stashed to my mom, it was okay. My grandmother was a diabetic, but she loved her Suzie Q's once in a while.

My grandmother lived with us when we were babies actually. She called us the little baskets. When we caused a ruckus, she never swore. I always found that odd. I completely miss her.

On the last evening of my grandmother's wake was when my brother's little boy's appearance took place. We all rushed to the hospital to see this little man while still wearing our funeral clothes. I arrived first actually, and they ushered me right in because it was time. I witnessed the crowning and half of his little head poking out before my younger brother arrived to take over. Within five minutes of me exiting the birthing room, we were introduced to a brand-new baby boy. I was very proud on this day and very sad at the same time. I thanked God for allowing us a sense of joy during a rough week for all of us. Rest in peace, Gram, I love you.

Welcome to the world, little man. Guess what? You're within a family who loves you unconditionally; grow up strong in your mind, become whoever you want to become. Your path in life is ahead of you. I'm your guide, partner, friend, uncle, your father's best friend, and the cool part is, you know me, because I was you so long ago. Trust in knowing I will help when asked upon.

I believe it was around this time I was given a succession of experimental medicines due to availability. The powers that be came up with several possible helper medicines called protease inhibitors. What a nightmare. They each failed over time with defeating the virus, and they caused lots of side effects in the process. I remember some of the names of these medicines because of the side effects I experienced on them personally. I could look into my medical records and surely name each and every one of them if asked to do so, in the event I may possibly have a lawsuit against these companies for failing to produce a cure, and only peddling deformities, illness, and death. I'm not sure I want to bad-mouth them pharmaceutical companies or not, at least they are trying something. Try testing that poison on you yourself for a while, good luck with the vertigo, the shits, the headaches, the fat displacement, the growth of a mass on your testicle, the wasting, the fatigue, the night terrors, the hallucinations, and the lack of control do to the fear of death. No matter the bad side effects, your psychologically mind twisted to the point of, I'll take anything. Even knowing you're HIV negative while on these medicines will cause you suicidal and homicidal thoughts. I swear to you, it's all true. Oh yeah, be careful not to drink or do drugs also. Depression will happen prior, which may lead you down the wrong path. But also be aware of liver failure, anemia, heart failure, neuropathy, and all sorts of really nasty stuff. I loved when they told me if I get an unexplained rash, I had to stop taking a certain medicine called nevirapine or I would die on the next dose. You could imagine how it felt when I got poison ivy while taking this medicine. It rapidly covered my entire body since I have a weakened immune system. I ended up in the hospital for a few days actually. I stopped that medicine, petrified my heart would explode or something. Good thing it was only poison ivy and not the unexplained rash. After that scare, I was back on the medicine once again.

I watched doctors and pharmacists document current side effects from me on particular medicines and then, only after I reported my problems, did they end up on the label. I also remember D4T, a nasty medicine that caused my nipples to bleed. I started to grow massive golf ball-sized swollen glands behind them actually. I came back and was flipping out thinking the doctors were playing a joke on me. I guess I had a right to get angry. I didn't expect to grow tits like a woman; I was too young for that. It's natural to grow man boobs later in life, not now. The doctors surely got excited with this new piece of information for the side effects department. My nipples were bleeding, my chest was swollen like I'm premenstrual, and to top it all off, I went on display for no less than ten other interested parties. All doctors, nurses, radiology people, pharmaceutical personnel, and the works. Why not call in the maintenance guy while we are at it? At the time, I shared all the problems without fail. I just hope they documented each and every word. My thoughts were on someone in the future. They need not experience the horrors I had to endure.

A whole new language was created actually. As new medicine was being developed, I would get the chance to be a test subject. The protease inhibitors were combined with nucleoside reverse transcriptase inhibitors and the non-nucleoside reverse transcriptase inhibitors. I know it actually sounds all Greek to me to. Believe it or not, this is what the new language became. I was given combination therapy beyond belief. There were times when thirty pills a day were normal. The HIV wasn't eliminated; it was slowed down within its replication and new infection of your natural immune system the T-cells. All of them pills taken had a potential to kill you, never mind the disease itself. I remember taking Crixivan, it caused me to become very nauseous almost instantly once my body digested the pills. It also became a flood of water out my ass every five to ten minutes for several hours. I would vomit almost all the time also. This medicine was a total horror. I had to plan my days around taking this medicine. I couldn't leave my house most of the time because it kept me in the bathroom damn near three hours every time it was taken. I watched my stomach become extremely bloated during this year's course of absolute misery. I would get motion sickness to the point of immobility. My equilibrium was all out of whack. It became unsafe for me to be in the sunlight for prolonged amounts of time. I remained on the job roofing because one of my brothers was the foreman. He allowed me to just go lay down when I would have to run for empty glue cans to vomit in or to shit in. Half of my day was wasted being horribly ill, and it wasn't fair to subject my coworkers to my visual death. I ended up retiring due to my health turning for the worst and complications with medicines. I remember trying to get through a workday with the absolute worst diarrhea that lasted well over a year. I was given massive amounts of pills for plenty of years. I could list them all actually, but I'll wait for my day in court I guess. They each have their own set of problems and side effects, feel free to look them up online sometime.

Here is a list of the ones I have taken: lopinavir, ritonavir (liquid and pill form), saquinavir mesylate, fosprenavir calcium, nelfinavir mesylate, lamivudine, zidovudine, abacavir sulfate, emtricitabine, tenofovir disoproxil fumarate, didanosine, stavudine, efavirenz, nevirapine, indinavir sulfate, and bactrum. The bactrum is used to ward off pneumonia when your T-cells are low. Most of these medicines are within combination therapy within one or two pills now. I was given them separately back in the day. Trust me when I say it absolutely sucked. I remember being on efavirenz quite clearly. This medicine caused wild vivid dreams and during-the-day hallucinations. I remember waking up from a nightmare that was so real I had to run down the stairs to wake up my oldest brother in the middle of the night. I shook him and was sweating like crazy from fear. I told him like three times I killed a woman. "I swear to you I killed her, man. I burned her remains in the woodstove, man." I was in full-on panic mode not knowing what was going on. He told me to go back to sleep because it was a nightmare. He told me I was asleep on the couch upstairs all night. I didn't believe him at first but then realized it had to be a nightmare because I was in my mom's house. In the nightmare I was in a dank boiler room area, sort of like the Freddie Krueger scenario, but I clearly remember chopping her up and burning her in our woodstove. I lost all concept of reality completely. I couldn't determine if I was dreaming or awake anymore. I also never went into the far end of the basement to check and see if it was real. I was completely spooked by it. I just stayed away because it was evil. I think *The Amityville Horror*, the movie, played a big part in this delusion. I was definitely seeing weird stuff and hearing odd voices within medicinal side effects.

I had wild wet dreams also while on this medicine. Here I am, pushing thirty years old and I'm waking up covered in my own spunk like I was fourteen again. This medicine was a bugout beyond proportions. I was so freaked out by this stuff I offered a friend to just try one dose to tell me if I'm nuts or not. They tripped their ass off all day and swore to me they would never try anything I gave them again. I gave them one pill, I took three per dose. I took this medicine every day for several years until I was told it wasn't working anymore. If I remember correctly during the course of this medicine combined with tenofovir, all food I consumed tasted like burnt cedar ashes, all the time. I forced myself to eat actually. I certainly had to be very tough during these years. I would be hungry all the way up until the food was put down in front of me each and every time. I would begin to gag actually from the first bite till the last. Sometimes I would hold it all down, and other times I would vomit it all back on to the plate. This is the way life went for me during the nineties.

I was well into a new relationship with another woman when my right testicle began to hurt like hell. The woman I was dating was very nice. She looked like the girl in the movie *Braveheart* that Mel Gibson married in secret actually. We had been engaged and were living together in an apartment within New Bedford, Massachusetts. She had three children that would visit every weekend that were amazing. Before we had the issue with my testicle and before we moved in together, I will tell you how we met. My next-door neighbor of my childhood home was getting married, and I went along to be a part of it. I had gotten massively drunk and went home with this new woman. I awoke to us wrapped in each other's arms, naked. I left that morning scared to death I may have just given her HIV. I confessed to her later that night on the phone about my status actually. She got super pissed and hung the phone up on me screaming about her children and their futures. About five minutes later, she called back and asked me to come back to her house. She wanted to talk about all this. I was scared to death she might be waiting with a gun or a knife or something when I arrived. We ended up staying up talking all through the night. I explained it all to her. She no longer blamed me for what happened between us because it takes two to tango and we were both drunk as skunks. I knew it would be my entire fault if she got sick, so I was scared right along with her. We got her tested right away, and she was negative. During the three-month waiting period of her next test, we fell in love. She remained negative our whole time together over three years actually.

I had brought her over to my mom's house quite often with her children also. There was one day in particular I remember clearly. I had been telling my mother very often that her house was filled with demons and spirits for quite some time. She tried to make them all go away by having a priest come over and bless the whole house after the fire and before we moved back in. I told her the priest never blessed the basement though, it was still filled with water when he did that blessing. They were trapped in the cellar. My girlfriend and my mother thought I was nuts, so I escorted them down into the basement. All the doors were closed including the windows when we got into the middle of the open space. Right when they were about to take off and exit back up the stairs, an icy cold breeze hits us from nowhere. Neither one of them said a word; they just looked as if they were both in shock. I knew for sure they felt it also, so I said, "See, I told you so." My mom tried to say it was a window left open and brushed it off. I knew it was the evil spirit coming from the woodstove area. I wasn't able to go anywhere near that woodstove because in my head it was all real. I still remember an eerie feeling when I was a kid also; maybe it wasn't just the dead woman in the woodstove haunting me. I had always felt as if something was watching, me and each time I would run up the stairs in absolute fear as a child that they were going to grab me and kill me. Maybe it was because my father's parents told us that the boogeyman lived in their basement to keep us kids away from the homemade wine in their cellar. Whatever caused this in my head, it never left me and it was certainly enhanced by them medications.

Oh, and just in case you would like to try this out sometime, my girlfriend lived fairly close to a cemetery, so I got it into my head I would try and scare her oldest daughter with a ghost tale. I had her convinced you could see the dead spirits roaming around at night but only on All Hallows' Eve. She thought I was full of it until I proved it to her. We had just returned from going trick-or-treating, I was dressed as the Grim Reaper as usual to scare the kids in the neighborhood because I'm just a big old kid myself. The younger kids went to bed, and I told my girlfriend the plan. She just told me to be careful and said, "Don't freak her out to much." I laughed and off we went down the road and into the cemetery. We walked in and continued for a while until we came upon a really dark area within the headstones. I told her, "Okay, this is how we used to do it as kids. You have to duck down behind a stone and wait for a few minutes being absolutely still and quite." As we waited I told her, "Okay, when my watch hits midnight, that's when we can catch them. Now jump up and look around quickly, you will catch a few roaming spirits trying to hide from us." Sure enough my watch hit midnight and we jumped up. Nothing happened for a few seconds, and I heard her begin to say I was full of shit. Right then a figure emerged from the darkness. I said, "Look, there's one, now hush, and don't scare it." I watched in shock myself as a creepy-looking guy wearing old-school black-rimmed glasses emerged from the pitch-blackness in front of us and walked past us and disappeared into the night without so much as a hello. He looked normal in every respect, might even have been a live person just passing by. What were the odds of that happening? I don't know. We both got spooked, I didn't have a problem laughing about it when we got home because my girlfriend's daughter was bugging out. I was just happy he didn't kill us both, he reminded me of Jeffrey Dahmer actually. Talk about a freak. Yep, I scared myself also.

I remember all the fun times we had together more than the bad times. As for my right testicle, that was a bad time. I'll never forget that. I went to the doctors to find out why the thing was so painful. It had a mass on it actually on the far right edge of my egg-shaped testicle. The doctor recommended that I have an ultrasound to see what was going on. It turned out to be bad news all around. I was told I may have cancer. The worst was yet to come. The doctor didn't want to risk taking a biopsy with a needle in fear of spreading the cancer cells due to my HIV/AIDS status. The cancer would spread like a wildfire in a dry field with a suppressed immune system. So guess what? "We recommend removal." "Wait a minute, hold the fuck on, Doc. I'm quite fond of my testicle. I don't want to lose it. You're not even positive I have cancer in my nuts, and you want me to allow you to snip one off just to check. These are a set. Here look." I juggled them in my hand for him to see and told him I would get a second opinion. My second opinion was exactly the same as the first actually. I was going to be half the man I used to be. That was a song actually, around this time. How ironic.

I arrived for surgery a few weeks later fully willing to get this testicle out of my body because if it was cancerous, I would surely die within a year. I didn't want that at all. As the doctor was preparing to begin surgery and the anesthetic was taking hold of me, I gestured for him to come closer so he could hear me better. I said, "Hey, Doc, how about you snip off both of them testes and I go racing style." He looked at me sort of dumbfounded and asked me why I would want that. I told him, "Less drag, my friend, much better for sport fucking." He dropped his instruments and began to howl in laughter. As I slipped into blackness, I was smiling because this was a very intense moment for all of us. I lightened the mood, and I'm sure it helped with the doctor's performance in surgery. I awoke from surgery a bit shocked actually, not because I was one nut short. It was removed through a small incision made just above my pubic hairline. I was expecting the ball bag to be cut open and stitched shut. This wasn't the case. The doctor explained how when before we were born within our mother's womb everyone has female parts. My testes were actually way up inside my pelvis just like ovaries are in women. Once the male chromosomes become present, they drop through a naturally created chute and become testes. The procedure to remove implements this chute from long ago. I guess I learn something new every damn day.

I remember it took weeks to heal, and it took much longer to learn how to sit down without absolutely crushing the good one underneath my ass. I swear to you it was very difficult. All I could think about was I hope my penis still gets hard the whole time. I was told to wait at least six weeks before any sex at all. I made it to week number 5 before I masturbated to make sure it still worked. My girlfriend at the time helped me out actually. I was able to get fully erect, which was a positive thing. The negative happened upon ejaculation. There was no semen at all. I shot wads of blood, and it scared the living hell out of me and was very painful. I quickly got on the phone and discussed it with a doctor. He told me it was quite normal during the healing process to bleed. I told him exactly what happened, and he told me I should've waited another week before attempting ejaculation. I was told not to worry, just watch for hemorrhaging and constant flow of blood. If that occurs, come into the hospital. Also, slow your sexual drive down for a couple more weeks. Talk about a scary scenario to have to live through. I liked to tell people losing my nut was from a dirt bike accident, but the truth is it was caused by all that medicine. I am a white lab rat within a laboratory that grew a mass within my body that had to be removed. It wasn't cancer at all. I'm grateful of that simple fact, but I'm not happy about only having one of my boys left. I had asked if they could put in a prosthetic, but the veterans' department doesn't do cosmetic surgery. I thoroughly enjoyed playing golf a few weeks later breaking my second-opinion doctor's balls about his expert advice. I told him, "next time I have a problem, I'll keep it to myself, going on your knowledge costs me too much." We laughed our asses off on the first tee together. I never hold a grudge, especially on my own cousin; he is one of my role models in life. I just like to ease the situation into laughter, much better medicine to swallow in life.

After healing up from this latest cruelty by the gods, I convinced my girlfriend on how happy I was while riding a dirt bike in Florida years ago. She suggested I get back into it actually. I couldn't afford this machine at all, so I asked my oldest brother if he would help me buy one. He bought the thing outright and allowed me to make small payments back to him over the course of a few years. My brothers are really and truly my support and biggest idols on this planet. I began riding with my younger brother who purchased a new bike also. We practiced together many of times in a sandpit within our hometown. He had gotten permission from the owner. I remember we brought shovels with us and started creating whoop sections and a few jumps. I can say for sure at this moment within dirt bike riding I was a better rider. As the years went on, he became absolutely awesome and left me in the dust, but at this time I could pass him at will. We had extreme amounts of fun together and several of our friends who owned motorcycles would come hang out and rip it up with us also. This sport definitely makes you stronger and healthier. It also kept me out of trouble. I remember meeting several expert and amateur riders within the Rochester area and began going to different areas to learn from them also. I freely shared with them my HIV/AIDS status because we always rode together in areas where medical attention wouldn't arrive very soon in case of an accident. It never bothered them at all; I was given a few "thank you for sharing something so personal" from them. I guess it allowed them to be comfortable. Most everyone knew my health status because in small towns the gossip runs quickly. Most people just don't know how to ask me, so sharing it freely with them eliminated the awkward moments.

Things fell apart rapidly within two days. My whole safety within my new loving relationship was built out of glass which shattered to a million little pieces. My trust for another woman in my life ended. We had been engaged actually; I had bought her a ring and she had said yes only a year earlier. In my opinion, I thought she loved me. I was wrong. She failed to return home one evening, and I became very worried. When I called her, she wouldn't answer the phone. I called several of her friends, but they just covered for her. I called a taxi to go by her work to see if our car had died and she was stranded. When I arrived, the car was sitting in the parking lot. I knew she was up to something no-good. I returned home and just waited all night worried till the morning. I waited for some answers; I waited in the hopes she hadn't been hurt or assaulted. I was close to calling the police to report foul play but decided I was jumping the gun. I had to be at a doctor's appointment on this day, so my waiting had to end. I began walking toward the bus station, and while en route sure enough, she was driving up toward home. I crossed into the road, and she stopped. I got into the car and asked where she had been. She was afraid to tell me because I might get angry. I told her, "I'm already angry so go ahead and spill it." It turned out she spent the night with another guy. From that moment on, my relationship was never the same with her. At best I remained semi-civil. I had been betrayed again by a woman I had allowed into my heart. She tried to blame it on me flirting with her sister and she suspected me of sleeping with her. I didn't like that excuse at all. I threw her out of our apartment that day. But we stayed dating, which was a mistake on both our parts. We eventually grew to hate each other.

I flung myself into dirt bike riding as much as possible. I tried to go riding every day if possible. My friends at that time all had jobs, which allowed them a few days a week to go riding, so it worked out well. I was sad and lonely, but my motorcycle gave me joy. I remained disconnected and alone for a few weeks, maybe even a month, until I got into a dumb accident. I had gone riding one day with two friends at the sandpits behind the New Bedford dump. It was a cool spot to ride; there was even a semi-track to follow. Sure enough, we unloaded the bikes and took off together, and within less than thirty seconds, I saw a flash of blue. His bike and him smashed into the left side of me and my bike. We had both been looking toward another direction and weren't paying attention to each other's whereabouts. It was a simple accident, but I like to break his balls saying it was his entire fault. I came to a stop after flipping off my bike and ending up on the ground several feet away from him. I asked if he was okay, he said yes. We both began to laugh. I felt wetness within my left palm and looked to see my ring finger bent at a wrong angle just at the first knuckle. When we crashed together, my clutch lever damn near sheered my finger completely off. I took off my glove and asked my friend to look at it. I turned away because I was starting to go into shock from the ordeal. When I turned back to ask him what he thought, he was green looking and pale. I knew I needed to go to the emergency room, no duct tape fixing available this time. I asked our other friend to load up my bike for me, and all he could do was jump around laughing saying, "Oh man, your fingers fucked up." I said, "Yes, I know, dumbass. Oh man, I got to take a dump, where's the napkins. I get the poops each and every time I go into shock without fail when I'm hurt." He loaded my bike only after taking it for a joy ride around the sandpit for a few minutes. Nice guy, huh? Oh well, I was glad someone got to ride more than thirty seconds today.

I arrived at St. Luke's Hospital close to nightfall by the time we got loaded and traveled across the city. The guy I was first seen by told me he wouldn't be able to do anything for me other than clean out the wound and dress it. I would have to travel to Rhode Island to see a specialist. There wasn't one available at this facility tonight. I agreed to him cleansing the wound. He took out a huge needle and injected pain medicine into the wound itself and on both sides of my ring finger in the web. Talk about painful, ouch wasn't the word. He flushed it out and gave me a quick couple of stitches and sent me on my way. I called my semi-girlfriend and told her what had happened and asked her to pick me up please and take me to the hospital in Rhode Island. The bitch told me no. She was busy. Nice girlfriend I chose at the time. Anyways my brother and my mom arrived and drove me over to the next hospital. I arrived and was kept comfortable till morning after the specialist reopened the stitches to have a look. He gave me an x-ray also. He discovered that when the other doctor flushed out my wound, he accidently washed a big piece of cartilage out as well. The specialist told me he couldn't put it back correctly, it would have to be fused. I awoke from surgery with two pins poking out of my finger. I had one pin running the length of my finger inside the very tip to the palm, and the other pin was inside the center of my fingernail into the bone on an angle. I was given some Vicodins for pain and told to get lost for four weeks for a follow-up.

I returned home and ate Vicodins as if they were Tic Tacs because they did nothing for the pain. I pretty much danced around my kitchen table for like three days trying to ward off the pain by circling and cussing. This was by far the worst pain ever. I guess when you sever a finger damn near off and it begins to heal, the nerve endings go ballistic on you. I finally rested and awoke to an empty, cold house alone. I looked in the extra bedrooms where I had bought bunk beds for her children and was deeply saddened by them being gone. I opened my refrigerator and realized it was empty. I was in no shape to go anywhere, so I called my ex-girlfriend, the Cape Verdean girl, and asked her if she wouldn't mind going shopping for me. She was a solid friend to me; she went to the store and even cooked me dinner. It was very sweet of her, and it was cool seeing her son again and talking with him between video games in my living room. Typical kid I guess, it's all video games and no time for conversation at them ages. I thanked her for being my true friend and passed out asleep while she rubbed my head.

As time passed, my fingers healing the damn thing turned entirely black like it was dead. I arrived to the doctor's on my scheduled appointment and simply asked the man if everything was okay. I asked if we needed to put a leech on the end of my finger because blood wasn't getting to the thing or something. I had seen that on a medical channel, so I knew leeches could be used to ensure proper blood flow. The doctor swore to me everything was fine, it was normal. I didn't believe a word of it, so I insisted we do something. What a mistake this turned into. He proceeded to cut with a scalpel from the tip of my finger to the palm of my hand on four sides of my finger and began to peel my dead skin off like peeling a banana. It didn't hurt until the bright pink virgin flesh, underneath became exposed to the air. The skin was so thin that just the mere bump, it would begin to bleed. I was sent home damn near in tears because I wanted to play doctor and question this guy's field of expertise. I would suffer another week or so of excruciating pain changing dressings that stuck to my now-raw finger. I am not sure how long those pins remained in my finger, but I do know I began riding my dirt bike again prior to them pins being removed. I purchased a set of hand guards to keep rocks from flying up within someone else's roost from their back tire from hitting my hand. The drive inside of me to ride was undeniable.

Several weeks went by, and the time came to have them pins taken out of my finger. I sat down in a sort of barber's chair and the doctor was all calm as a cucumber as he strapped my arms down to keep me from moving. I should've known better, he strapped me down on purpose to keep me from grabbing him by the throat from the pain he was about to inflict on me. He went for the smaller pin first; he grabbed it with a set of pliers and then yanked really hard. The pin came out without a problem. The pain hit me several seconds later as he grabbed the second pin. My finger was on fire with pain already, and he yanked the longer pin halfway out on his first attempt and then ripped the thing all the way out on his second attempt. I watched stunned as blood shot out of the tip of my finger like a squirt gun and drenched the front of his blue gown. I asked him if he was going to stop the leak after four or five squirts that coincided with my heartbeat. He told me, "No, it is better to let it flow out. You're lucky, son, it's not infected. That is a good sign actually; if it was yellow, then we would have a problem. I was beginning to get faint, and I had stopped screaming bloody murder from the pain. I asked him to untie me please from this chair; he slowly undid my restraints and damn near ran out the door when I hopped up all of a sudden and ran to his sink to let cold water run down my neck to keep from passing out. This was a very rough procedure to endure that is for sure. I wasn't even embarrassed when I left his office and the other patients looked at me stunned and scared themselves because they were next.

I had returned to this doctor six weeks later for a checkup and told him my finger wasn't bending enough to my liking. It was difficult to grip my handlebars while riding my motorcycle. He told me, "That might be exactly the way it will remain, I'm sorry, sir." I looked at him and just told him that's not happening. I screamed bloody murder as I forced it to my palm and snapped something. I didn't care one bit about the pain. The doctor was scared and a bit woozy as I left his office. I never returned to him again neither. My finger throbbed and remained swollen for several more weeks, but it certainly bends correctly now.

During all this chaos, my relationship with my cheating girlfriend had gotten a bit better and I decided to buy a house in order to own something instead of paying rent on a place. I purchased a fine two-bedroom, one-and-a-half bath with a detached garage in a quite area very close to Buttonwood Park Zoo. We got along fine for a while until I allowed a friend of mine to talk me into bringing home a pit bull who had been running loose in the downtown area, and it was going to be killed at the pound. I felt bad for this animal and took it in. I kept him in the garage for a week because I knew he was used as a fighting dog by some scumbag in this city and he was very skittish. It took a long time for this dog to trust me. I eventually worked him into the house and he became a pretty good friend to have around me. I never allowed company over unless I was around or my girlfriend was around because this dog was dangerous for sure. I would put him outside or in the basement just to be safe. Wouldn't you know it,? I went to help my brother for a day and left my house with clear instructions for my girlfriend not to have company over unless the dog was in the yard or in the basement. She paid no mind to my warning I guess because she left her fourteen-year-old and her sister's six-year-old in the house alone with this dog as they went to the store. It was a mistake on both their parts because this dog attacked the six-year-old and bit her hard enough to knock a few teeth out of her mouth and ripped a nice flap of skin up her scalp. I received a frantic phone call while it was happening from the older child, and I was rocked to the core. Just a simple miscalculation and a simple lapse of safety on these two women's minds and *bam*, this dog got this innocent little girl. When I arrived home, there was blood all over my living room and the dog was in the backyard covered in blood. I wasted no time calling the pound to have it put down. They put the dog down humanely and removed its head to send it to Boston to check for rabies. If not this poor little girl would have to endure somewhere in the neighborhood of twenty painful needles into her stomach. I remember this like it was yesterday. This was definitely a bad time in my life. My relationship with my cheating girlfriend ended not too many days after this occurrence.

I missed the dog because he helped me recover during a reconstructive knee surgery while I had him. He dragged me around Buttonwood Park and strengthened my knee rather quickly. It was all bone crunching and cartilage popping when the doctor told me after repairing it I wouldn't cause damage to it if I got up and walked after the swelling went down. This injury has been an ongoing problem with me since my football years as a kid playing fullback. My foot was twisted around backward at the knee socket when I was tackled. I just happened to hurt it again bad enough to show up to the hospital. Yes, this was another crash which happened on my motorcycle, and no, I'm not going to quit riding. I bought a knee brace to support the thing instead.

I was taking my HIV/AIDS medicine during all this, and the combination of breaking up and the side effects caught up with me. I fell into a pretty deep depression and began drinking in the neighborhood bars within the downtown area and the west end area. It was eventually turned into drug use once again. I would buy massive amounts of drugs and hide in my basement each weekend and just get high. I can't say it was all started after the dog incident, that would be a lie. I began using again right after I found out my girlfriend cheated on me. I was just able to manage it and not let it consume me. I was a functioning crack addict, if there ever was one. I knew it was time to quit when I no longer cared about anything or anybody. My dirt bike wasn't being ridden; my house was spotless because my weekend usage turned into weeklong binges. I barely came upstairs much other than sleeping or eating, so it remained very clean. If anyone came by to visit me, they wouldn't know I was a complete mess, on the surface

I looked very well put together. I remained locked in a mortgage. I no longer wanted because it kept me from doing something I loved the most, dirt bike riding. I also spent all my extra money on drugs, so how could I pursue any dreams or passions being a drug addict. I no longer wanted any responsibilities, I wanted to escape everything, and I became driven to leave it all behind to pursue a dream. I wanted my health back, and I wanted it back without medications, which drove me into deep depressions and caused me far too many side effects. I wasn't after any glory or fame either; it was pure passion and survival.

TEXAS

Without much thought in this at all, I sold my house and packed up my stuff and drove to Texas to begin again. I had met another woman living with HIV and figured what the hell. It was better than smoking drugs in my basement. I could leave my past in the past and just begin a new life. Nobody knew me in Texas, and that was fine by me. The girl I was heading to live with hadn't had a clue I was a drug-abusing fully addicted mess either. I told her I was a recovering addict, not I just stopped smoking three days ago, and here's Johnny! I kept it under wraps. I wasn't trying to remember my past, I was trying to be clean and ride a motorcycle back to health. I knew if I rode a lot, my addiction left me alone. The truth is, no matter where you are on this planet, your physical body and your mind follow and your addictions also. I was able to remain clean and focused for a long time actually. My shame left me and I was able to make history within the next couple of years while living in this fine state of Texas. Too bad it never became public while I was doing it. Here is how it all unfolded. This is a proud couple of years for me.

My house sold very quickly actually and the money I earned in profit during the sale I used to buy a new used truck and a new used 2000 Honda CR250R. It wasn't very difficult for me to stay clean once I settled into my new life actually. I would go to the gym five days a week for close to full year. My strength had returned, and my health was back on track. I thoroughly enjoyed being in my new relationship except for one spooky evening. I call it spooky, but it really wasn't. The women I was with had two sons. She gave birth to the oldest boy without having the

HIV/AIDS virus, but her youngest son was born while she had it. I think that's right, I'm a bit cloudy on that whole issue, but it was very sad to hear the story. Her oldest was very healthy, but her youngest son passed away regrettably at a very young age due to a heart defect at birth. He was only four years old. I never met him, nor did I see a picture of her late son. One night while I was sleeping, I felt a hand grip my wrist and it woke me up. I looked to see a little blond-haired boy looking at me. He got startled and ran into the next room. I thought nothing of it at the time and fell back asleep. In the morning I asked my girlfriend if her other son had a guest over. She told me no. I then explained to her my whole encounter. She was totally not shocked, which surprised me. She simply told me, "No worry, that is my baby boy, he came to say hello to you. Don't be alarmed, we see him and my grandfather all the time." She then showed me a picture of her late son, and sure enough, it was the same boy who grasped my arm last night. I found it to be pretty darn cool knowing I hadn't been the only one who was seeing spirits from beyond.

I checked into the veterans' department nearest to my location of Grand Prairie, Texas, and things went just perfect. The veterans' department Hospital in Dallas is one huge-ass place. I was impressed. I needed to get all my records transferred and be checked in with infectious disease and the dental department. I checked in without a problem. In fact the women in the infectious disease ward asked if I wanted a job. I told her, "Sorry, miss, I'm retired and my health isn't up to it, besides I'm going to be racing motorcycles, I won't have time for all that." She laughed because in her head she thought I was joking. For some reason no matter where I am, people of the AIDS community, especially the nurses and doctors, think it is a joke when I tell them I race dirt bikes. I guess in their minds I wasn't supposed to be able to manage that. I was supposed to be awaiting my death and resting on a death bed. I do have to rest yes, but I also need to stay active and get proper exercise. In motorcycle riding as a sport, it provides a full-body workout. In order to have the strength to race, you need to eat right, work out, and be a bit stubborn. *I guess these people will understand once I win a few times*, I thought. I filled my prescriptions of medicines and remained taking them on and off because I was nervous to stop actually. I was programmed to need medicine.

My relationship went as good as I could ask. My girlfriend at the time was very well educated and familiar with HIV/AIDS, in fact, she lived with it. It was a blessing not to worry about passing my deadly virus during intimate moments. I helped tear down a two-car garage in the backyard that had been built by her grandfather many years ago and it had fallen into disrepair and was neglected for longer than she could remember. I tore the whole thing down with the help of her father, her stepdad, and her son. I remember it was nice to bond with them all during some physical exercise outside in the hot Texas sun. Her father was a Vietnam veteran, a tunnel rat, and a helicopter pilot during his service time. We had some similar experiences, but he was a combat veteran and I was not. I always feel less than when I am in the presence of combat veterans, and to top it off, he was a retired Dallas policeman, but we got along just fine even with knowing my past issues with cops. I never really understood why I felt less than, maybe I am ashamed because I got sick, that is my curse.

I remember the garage had power running to it from the house. I shut off all the power within the house and was sure the main breaker was in the off position. With that checked and positive, there was no possible power heading outside. I chopped the wire with an axe in order to tear down the wall that ran through into the garage. I was going to wrap the exposed pieces of the wire with tape and keep them aboveground for later fixing. When I reached for the wires to begin wrapping them, the current grabbed me and I was stuck to the wire. My arms violently shook very fast and my fillings were getting hot, my chest began to really hurt, I was being electrocuted by more current than I've ever encountered. This was not your run-of-the-mill-house current at all. If it wasn't for her stepfather, I certainly would've been an electro-fried dead guy. He pulled me free with a very hard shove. I collapsed to my knees, and it was as if my lungs had been cooked, I could smell burnt flesh on every exhale. It turned out whoever ran the wiring from the pole to the breaker box had bypassed any sort of break in the current. It was a direct line from the pole just falsely run into the box and then right out to the garage. I got lucky to be with someone at the time. I mention this because it was just another bad luck moment.

Once demolition and cleanup was completed and I recovered from the burnt lungs, I built a nice gambrel-style shed to keep my dirt bikes in. I got rid of the scrap heap of a red van I had and transferred all my tools into my new storage area. I was proud of my new outbuilding. It had been a long while since I had any interest in creating something. I also cleaned up the yard and fixed the back stairs leading out of the house. My sobriety remained intact as long as I kept busy. During this cleanup, I was attacked by several large yellow hornets and bitten by a small snake. I found this snake while digging up a rotted tree stump. I remember letting the snake slither within my hands as I inspected it. I thought it was harmless enough because it was small. The damn thing bit me pretty good right on the wrist. It left two distinct holes after I yelled ouch, and it fell to the ground. I had to go inside the house to check online what kind of snake it was to see if I was in any danger of death. It turned out the thing was called a plains blackhead. It was light grey in color with an orange line running down its belly and had a distinct black head, hence the name. The internet information said its venom was toxic to arthropods. I didn't know what an arthropod was at the time, so I had to look that up also. I knew anthropology was the study of humans; I gave up looking around for information actually. There was no flashing red alert to seek medical attention right away, so I stopped. It was a rear-fanged little bastard though. I wasn't concerned at all. My wrist swelled to twice its normal size during my stubbornness not to go to the doctors. My girlfriend was worried, but I assured her I would be fine, the snake venom wasn't strong enough to kill me, so why bother with a big fuss. I wrapped my wrist and went back to my task at hand. I guess I'll suffer the pain. Lo and behold, I survived and continued on my quest.

I began riding at some of the local motocross tracks in my area to build up some strength and to just forget about my past. I ended up meeting a photographer who raced within the local areas cross-country circuit. We hit it off right from the start. He was a very nice guy, and his wife was awesome also. We pretty much hung out quite a bit; I went along with him to help out with his photography stuff. He was a racing photographer, so that was very cool. I got the pleasure of learning many different things about photography and also got to see plenty of motorcycle racing. He encouraged me to try out cross-country racing actually. This man was definitely one of my "angels." He saved me from myself. I had never tried it before, so what the hell did I have to lose? I remember my first race went decent enough. The race was about two and half hours total for me to complete. It was close to ninety degrees outside, and the trails were very dusty. I threw up in my helmet twice during this race but finished in fourteenth place. I was stoked, regardless of my place, I survived. He showed me a place for me to practice as well. It was behind a junkyard, I could practice there any day I wanted to. I now began practicing five days a week. I was still on medication like I said, out of fear as I began the 2003 season within the Texas cross-country racing circuit and never looked back. I began the season racing fairly decent with a determination. The races were every other weekend during the season if I remember correctly. I had kept my HIV/AIDS status a secret around my dirt bike racing friends just because I didn't want to be judged or alienated. I allowed them to see me, not my disease. I could remain hidden underneath my helmet also; I was invisible to everyone, especially the media, and press, but they weren't really looking. I also was letting go of the constant monitoring of my blood. I also brushed off the investigators who try to say I'm a fraud within my disability because quite frankly, this dirt bike racing is my form of exercise and I don't make any money doing it. So fuck you too, come wear my shoes for a while, buddy.

During the first six races, I was struggling. I constantly would throw up in my helmet, and on more than one occasion, I lost my butt mud into my riding gear, flooding my pant leg and my boots. I was racing, feeling very weak most of the time from nausea due to this medication, never mind the diarrhea. I was depressed because my results were very shabby considering all the gym time and practice I had been doing. It didn't take a rocket scientist to figure out the cause. I had to try something, so I stopped taking it. I was tired of finishing a race feeling sick the whole time and running to change my gear without anyone noticing my mess. It was embarrassing beyond comprehension. I would also turn down invitations to sleep in someone's huge traveling rigs also because I didn't want them knowing how badly I was sick. I stayed in a one-man tent and just stayed focused without using medicine. I certainly made the right decision. My stamina increased tenfold actually. All the practicing and gym time wasn't wasted. My body became one with my machine, and I began to have fun. I was absolutely in the best shape of my life for the remainder of this season. I practiced all the time and certainly motivated a lot of people to come on out and enjoy the feeling of freedom on a dirt bike. I was racing for my health and to ward off death, but nobody knew me at all. I never once let anyone into my pain other than my girlfriend. She knew my sacrifices and my injuries all too well.

I was riding so well people would point me out of the crowd as I went by them and started cheering me on. They were fellow riders from different classes and their wives and the children of the guys who raced within my age group. I had won eight races in a row actually; nine wins within the season and within a sixteen-race format. I remember the second to the last race I was leading by such a gap even with a broken rear shock and riding the remaining eight miles without any suspension and I still finished second. On the very last race, I let my entire class take off, and I followed for a complete fourteen-mile loop around, behind the very last guy. The guys from the motorcycle shop I rode out of made me a bet I couldn't get on the podium before the race ended in four more loops when I stopped to say hello. The owner of the shop screamed at me, "What the hell you doing!" I had won the season without needing to place at all during this race, but when they tossed out a few hundred bucks to put toward my bill owed them. I certainly helped that guy a lot during this time at his shop as well. I rode my wheels off and caught and passed everyone.

Some people called me a sandbagger, but I brushed that off because inside I knew it wasn't so. I wanted to scream at these people sometimes for saying such nonsense because if they only knew how much suffering I went through within this disease, they would clam right up that instant. I also cracked my shoulder blade during a bad crash during this season and I still pulled it off. Did they know I was dying and this was my cure?

No, I never said a word about it. I just kept my head down and focused on winning. I had an amazing season; it was unheard-of actually within the AIDS community to actually be possible, but in my head I remained silent out of fear. I had become the 2003 over-thirty amateur champion in the Texas Cross Country Racing Association on my eleventh year of my diagnosis of having AIDS. It was a huge accomplishment worthy of the Guinness book of records. I pulled off the impossible when you consider them doctors told me to get my affairs in order many years ago because I had so many opportunistic infections and gave me three years to live.

I certainly didn't want to be a public figure; we all know what happens to them. They get shot in the head for going against the grain. How do I begin to explain to the world how after all these years of illness, funky medications, massive drug usage during depressing times, and nearly being dead several times how I got back up and pushed beyond my own pain and illness beyond normal understanding? I also stopped using medications and never felt better in my entire career of having AIDS. You might think this is a great thing and people should know this about me. You would be wrong, I go against what these doctors say, yet I'm still alive, I'm also able to survive in better health without medicine. This is a very dangerous concept when you consider how much research is done and the money that is made by the pharmaceutical companies. I remained silent not by choice, it is fear, society believes in this whole scenario and has placed such a huge stigma on people living with HIV/AIDS, even I stay afraid. It also creates anger within me that I can draw on to prove them all wrong. It certainly would piss a few people off if they knew I say the medicine is a lie. I might possibly be assassinated just on principle alone. I had found my cure within riding motorcycles, yet I felt as if I was a criminal because I was collecting a disability pension while doing it.

My relationship didn't last the entire season either, but I did remain in it for over two years. I spent too much time away racing I guess, and she found another man. When could I possibly have screwed this relationship up? It matters not. I'm still friends with her and her son also. In fact her son just had his first little boy himself. I'm proud to have known them both and everyone I encountered within this time in my life. Maybe when I'm rich beyond my wildest dreams I'll stop by to say hello. We can go to dinner or something, it would be fun to see you all again. Even without visiting I can recall everyone in my mind and simply know it was awesome to meet you all.

A TOTAL MESS

After winning the championship, I really didn't have anyone to celebrate my amazing accomplishment with actually. I had done the impossible within the world of AIDS, yet no one took notice because I wanted to stay anonymous and I was ashamed of my life thus far. I had moved into my own apartment and was living alone once again. I had begun dabbling within drug usage once again. My loneliness and depression from my recent breakup caused this; I had reached my goal without a plan also. It began because I lost my ability to say no due to some innocent nights-out having a few cold ones. Each weekend I went out with a few fellow competitors just to break my isolation and loneliness. It was during my ride back home when I would pass through a very dangerous neighborhood, and it was only a matter of time before I copped some rocks. I only got high on the weekends in the beginning. I was still in semi-control actually. I was seen several times going in and out of this neighborhood copping drugs by the police and even pulled over late one night and searched. Good thing I was on the way to the bank prior to copping. This didn't matter though.

I was back under the watchful eye of the police once again. I noticed an undercover car parked at the bottom of my street. I know this because while I was at the motorcycle shop one day, a few officers I rode dirt bikes within this circuit asked if I wanted to make some extra money. I asked them how. They wanted me to where a wire and buy guns within the area. This was an odd request. So I asked them if I was able to carry a gun. They said no. "If I find a gun I like, can I keep it?" "No." "So how does this all work?" I asked. "Well, you get the buy money from us. We wire you up, and we'll wait down the street for you to return. We search you before you leave, and we search you when you return." I asked, "Why ask me to do that, anyways?" They said, "Because you're just the type of guy who can do this." I asked what the pay would be. They told me fifty bucks. I had to laugh at that request totally. You expect me to go into shady neighborhoods to buy guns wearing a wire, while you wait up the street?

You got to be stupid. Who the hell do you think you are? I thought to myself. I'm against all that sneaky bullshit, besides I don't need to do your damn job. I'm against guns. I don't even feel safe with you having one in your possession, motherfucker. You will watch on as I am shot in the head. I know the drug dealers around here most certainly know the gun runners. Besides I don't hold that fear of them because I'm not trying to tell them they can't own guns. I'm also not the guy trying to suppress a nation under the guise of a badge neither. I happen to like my life. I gave the hero shit up long ago. I may be crazy, but not that crazy. I also realized how absurd that was. I may be using drugs again, but I'm certainly not that desperate. I can't believe you would ask me to do such a Judas thing knowing I'm at an all-time low in life. Nice try though. Thanks but no thanks, pal."

I snuck into this neighborhood, copped, and bounced. Always knowing these cops were aware of my usage but never once stopped me. This remained my normal routine until some friends from up north came to visit and stay with me. Well, I can't say it's their fault entirely, but when they arrived, their own habits followed with them. They also brought the flu virus along with them also. It was okay at first. But within two weeks of them arriving, I was completely consumed with coughing, fever, puking, sweating, shivering, and the worst effects of this illness. I went to the veterans' hospital after two weeks of misery only after my friends suggested it. I definitely took their advice because my weak immune system was no match for it. It turned out I had contracted flu-A and flu-B. I'm not a doctor, but just hearing this was enough to know it was bad. I certainly wouldn't survive without help. The doctor gave me three pills actually and told me I should be fine. I'm sicker than hell and don't believe a word of his bullshit, but he assured me these pills would work. I was told that they were used for Parkinson's disease patients actually. Wouldn't you know it though after taking this medicine within less than twenty-four hours, I was up feeling completely normal again? I had been progressively getting sicker for over two weeks prior, yet this stuff cured me almost instantly. It was crazy to know as a person of semi-integrity that a few pills eradicated the flu from my body overnight and it existed. I felt weird inside because each year hundreds of people die from this virus. I certainly was confused on the whys of it all. Perhaps it was experimental in nature and the doctor was just trying something new. I don't really know the details; I was glad to be off my coach and healthy again and healthy enough to go riding.

We went riding quite a bit together actually. In fact my new riding partner was exactly what I needed to pull me out of my depression. I even got a visit from my younger brother and one of his friends actually. We all practiced together, and it was truly a great time showing these guys all the awesome motocross tracks I knew about within a thirty-minute radius of my place. We remained sober during the week while riding but definitely hit the clubs on Friday and Saturday nights. My sobriety slowly fell apart over the course of three months then I completely lost all control. A fall from sobriety would be an understatement. By the time all of them left to go back home to Massachusetts, I was within a twice-a-week habit once again. Once I was alone to deal with life on my own again I had no control whatsoever. I was using each and every night. My things were slowly pawned off for the drugs, and eventually I sold my championship winning dirt bike. I had purchased another motorcycle while my brother was in town, so it wasn't like I didn't have a bike to ride if I wanted to. As a matter of fact, it was my brother who initially bought the bike for me because my other bike was getting a new motor put in. He purchased it for me, and I made the payments. He arrived to go riding with me, not to wait for my bike to get fixed. My brother is a definite angel and a completely awesome brother to buy me a dirt bike for us to go riding while he was visiting. I am sad today that I sold my other bike for drugs; it was a nostalgic piece of machinery to me, but at the time I couldn't have cared less. My addiction was at the helm.

I had run into a couple of dealers who worked well with me. I would call and they would deliver. I would let them borrow my vehicle for a few days sometimes in trade for a block of crack the size equivalent to a cigarette pack. This would last me close to a week. I no longer left my house at all. I smoked morning, noon, and night for as long as I could afford it. I swear I was high each and every minute I was awake for several months. I even went as far as digging into my upper back teeth with the hook end of a fingernail file within nail clippers. I dug into them because they began to hurt and I certainly couldn't leave my house. Well, until I was visited by one of the older guys within this group one afternoon. I say group, but it was a well-known black gang actually. I mention no names. He arrived with my usual order and sat down across from me in my living room. He placed an ounce of crack on my coffee table on one side, and he placed a Colt .45 semi-automatic pistol on the other. He then pointed at the drugs and told me if I choose the drugs, I would die slowly. He then told me, "Quit being a pussy about it and pick up that pistol and shoot yourself in the head already." He told me he was no longer going to sell me drugs and wasn't going to allow any of his crew or the surrounding area to do so. He wasn't going to be the guy blamed for my death. He left my house with his gun, and I began packing my stuff. I no longer was welcome within my own mind. He hadn't threatened me in any way at all, but I understood what he meant. I had to get sober or die. This man's message reached me within a darkness nobody would ever understand.

Having guns in my presence doesn't bother me; I have had plenty put against my head throughout my life by police. The police do it out of fear and intimidation, nothing new in my world. Actually, my first experience was when I was fourteen while on a vacation with a friend's family. This wasn't a policeman at the time but it was definitely an indication on how much of a bastard I was growing up to be. My friend and I broke this Army Officer's balls that was traveling with us so much I awoke to a snub nosed .38 and him above me threatening to pull the trigger. He asked if I liked being a little bastard, I replied with you don't have the stones. He was then tackled to the ground by my friend's father who had just awoken to see this jackass threatening me. So like

I said, this man who arrived with the Colt .45 was a blessing not a threat.

I called one of the young black dealers I was dealing with and told him to have his mom and her sister to come by my place the next day. He was scared thinking I may rat him out for selling me drugs, but I assured him not to worry. When these women arrived, I told them, "Everything you see in this apartment is yours now, minus my own personal things." I helped them bring all my furniture to their home, including my dishes, television, surround sound system, a water bed, and just about five-grand worth of stuff. I even gave them a hutch I had gotten from my mother long ago. It was my parent's hutch while they were married actually—sorry, Mom. I did this because I wanted to feel like I helped someone who was poor and struggling in life. I had visited this woman's home in the past looking for her oldest boy to get drugs and noticed how poor she was living trying to raise three youngsters and her sister lived there with her two girls also. This family was very lucky to have a home, but the inside was very bare. I needed to help them in my mind because I had to do something good within my own selfish self-destruction. I wasn't going to need this stuff any longer, and they could use it. I was happy as I left Texas in that sense. I left to escape my own death called drug addiction. Nobody told me to leave, I had to leave. I drove thirty-two hours straight to make it back to Massachusetts, no sleep at all. I was smoking rocks the whole ride. I ran out somewhere in Connecticut.

When I arrived home, I was able to hide my drug usage pretty well. Truthfully my whole family knew I was a complete addict again just by my return home. I arrived with a broken motorcycle and only my personal stuff, clothes, some odds and ends, and my trophies from the dirt bike racing. They didn't mention a word about my drug problem, they were glad I made it home safely. I had gotten clean before and nothing would stop me from doing it again in their minds. My addiction slowed, but it didn't completely disappear. I was able to fix my motorcycle and begin riding with my younger brother and his son. I was healing from within, but it was going to take some time. I actually did really well in my first race back at home. I had come in third place in the amateur class at Jolly Rogers Moto-Sports Park. I had led for most of the race until two young kids passed me on the last lap. My riding skills were very good, and the entire cross-country racing experience had paid off. My stamina was very good considering all the drug usage. My failure to stop using drugs completely wasn't going to happen overnight.

I was also asked by some high school friends to track down their sister within the city of New Bedford who had been lost to drugs. They asked me because they knew I might be able to help her out. They also asked me because they were afraid to venture into them scumbag areas themselves. I risked my sobriety actually, the little I had, but it's always worth helping someone. When I found her, she was completely a mess. I was no better off than her actually, but my intentions were a solid, I want to help her out. I'm sorry to say this, but we got high together the night I found her sitting on a street corner awaiting a date. I really liked her as a friend, but I arrived addicted trying to help. I really would become a hypocrite if I told her one thing and turned around and did another. I think mostly it was because I wanted to keep her safe. The street is a hard place to live. I knew this from when I roamed them as a kid. I hoped maybe we could clean up together. I guess I was just pissing in the wind, shitting in one hand and wishing in the other. Two addicts don't mix whatsoever, no matter the good intentions, especially when I was drunk and already using drugs.

I remember about a month later a race was happening in Connecticut and my younger brother asked me to go racing with him. He always seemed to know I needed to focus on something else to keep me sober. I agreed to go along knowing full well I had just stop smoking crack seven hours earlier in the evening. I had slept for about six hours and figured sure what the hell. I was sober enough; I had come down, so to speak. I had invited a Spanish guy along who I had met during my drug travels within the fine city of New Bedford actually. He was another decent-enough person who happened to need a different outlook other than using drugs. I had brought him with me a few times when I practiced in the past and even taught him to ride a motorcycle. This trip may do us both some good actually. What began as a trip to go racing and to curve our addicted thought process had become a complete fucking nightmare beyond belief, and it was out of my control.

292   Gary J. Mello

I arrived at the track and went through the sign-up process for the race and also got my practice ticket. During motocross racing events, riders are allowed five laps prior to the first moto of the day. This time was used to figure out the track and to fine-tune your bike's suspension. I was feeling great actually once I geared up and started my bike. I warmed it up and headed to the staging area for practice. Awaiting my slotted time, I talked with some familiar faces from my area. When it came time for my practice, I told some younger kids from my hometown, "See you in the meat wagon." I was joking with them earlier about how every race held on this track someone gets swallowed up and they get hurt. I was just being funny because the jumps were very big on this track. I also said I'm going to hit them all. The young kids laughed because they didn't believe me. I assured them I was going to hit each jump, no problem, even the 110-foot spectator tabletop. They broke my balls a bit, that's why I told them it was either the win or the wagon. It's a slogan, my younger brother, I use, meaning, go big or go home in the ambulance. I told them "see you in the meat wagon" because I was trying to be funny.

My practice began very well; I had hit every jump actually. The reason I was able to commit to the biggest jump was because a pro-rider I knew had gotten in front of me and pointed at his rear tire, meaning, "Get on my ass and I'll show you the speed you need to carry the distance." I got behind him and matched his pace exactly. We approached a wall of dirt damn near twenty feet high. My heart raced and then stopped completely as I shifted into fourth gear close to wide open on a CRF450R four stroke. We were going very fast. If you want to know how fast that really is, go buy a bike and try it out. I had completely committed to this jump, and it was very scary as I lifted off the ground. I soared to at least twenty-five feet above the ground, and it felt awesome. I had preloaded my suspension prior to lift-off; and it was a mistake, my bike continued to climb higher, the landing had passed beneath me, and I landed in the flat. My suspension bottomed out, and my head smashed off the triple clamp pad. I was completely shocked from the impact, but I was elated by the actual fearless approach and commitment to jumping such a large jump. I owned this jump now. Each time I completed a difficult section or jump during racing or riding in general, I would never fear it again. I would master it and complete it without any hesitation.

I had completed four laps of practice and had one to go. The first lap I used to feel out the track's layout. The second lap was to hit all the jumps minus the 90-foot triple and the 110-foot tabletop. The third and fourth lap I had completed everything and was beginning to haul ass actually. The fifth lap was going great. I blitzed the whoops, turned into the inside sharply and passed someone through a rhythm section. He double-double-doubled the jumps within this section, and I triple-tripled it, making the pass stick. I jumped the next short 60-foot tabletop and pulled away from him nicely. I wasn't racing, nor was I showing off. I simply got into a nice pace at speed. I remained on the throttle around the next turn and was heading toward the 90-foot triple. This jump was big, and it took some speed and skill to pull it off correctly. As I was heading toward this jump, I noticed beyond the jump someone had gone down. There was also a woman rider just heading up the take off. I slowed as the flagger pulled his yellow flag out to warn us about the danger just beyond this jump. I doubled this jump according to the rules of racing and safety of others. The woman rider had done the same thing. As I landed and began to throttle up and over the third bump which was the actual landing if you were able to leap the full triple, the woman rider swerved toward me just a fraction of a few feet. I moved over slightly left about three feet and opened my throttle wide open to gain back my mock race speed and momentum. As I was heading down the third bump, *wham!*

Everything happened in slow motion. I knew exactly what was taking place as I was being hit. The rider I had passed in the rhythm section had hero-jumped the triple during practice under a yellow flag, and now he was coming down on my back. His front tire was over my left shoulder, and the bottom of his bike was crushing into me with all the weight of him and the bike combined from twenty feet above me. This weight was close to four hundred pounds actually. My body was sandwiched between the bottom of his bike and my own. I saw a bright white flash from the impact and then my body flew upward and forward. I watched as my body flew in front of my own bike and I hit the ground headfirst. I next had seen the sky then the ground several times before I came to a stop. My first instinct was to stand. I was scared to move at first because I had a weird feeling in my back. I was scared my spine had been broken and I was paralyzed. I began to kick my feet. I hesitantly looked down at my legs. I was afraid to see them not moving at first, but when I looked down they were moving. I wasn't paralyzed, thank God. I got up and stood and screamed, "What the fuck were you thinking?" in the direction of the guy who hit me. I turned to walk out of harm's way in case another rider happened to be jumping the jump again. I didn't need to be hit a second time. I took three steps, and then it was as if someone had taken several knives and plunged them into my chest. I collapsed to the ground on my knees and was on all fours. I tried to inhale, and nothing was coming in. I removed my helmet, and I coughed some blood and was able to take a very small painful breath.

As I was fighting to breathe, my younger brother reached me first. He asked if I was hurt or if I was injured. I told him I was unsure, but I was coughing blood and it was very hard to breathe. He laughed and said, "Look, so aren't I?" I looked over, and his mouth was full of blood. He had just crashed in that rhythm section I had just flew through. He asked if I saw him down, I told him no. Well, he had crashed in it and knocked three of his teeth out. So we were both hurt it seemed. As my brother was checking on me, the guy who landed on me ran over screaming, "It's not my fault, it's not my fault." I told him to get away. "Didn't you see the yellow flag, asshole?" I was able to breathe very shallow with blood trickling out of my mouth from within. I asked my brother for some water. I heard him scream he needed some water. Within less than ten seconds, I had a cold bottle of water in my hand. Someone from the stands had seen the whole thing and ran as fast as he could with the water as my brother yelled for some. I poured this water over my head and neck to keep from passing out actually prior to rinsing out my mouth. I then asked my brother to help me out of my chest protector and to help me remove my shirt. My body was beginning to overheat. This jackass brother of mine told me we needed to get off the track, other people wanted to practice. I told him I was injured and they could wait. Being hurt was just being a baby in our eyes, being injured meant you needed immediate assistance and the meat wagon. He helped me remove the stuff, and from what he told me, I knew I was in bad shape. He just witnessed my entire back turned purple on my left side before his eyes.

I could sense the panic in his voice as the medics arrived. They tried to grab me and roll me onto the plastic stretcher board. I yelled for them not to touch me, I was fine and to give me a few minutes to catch my breath. My brother wasn't having it. He told me, "Shut the fuck up and get on the stretcher, asshole. You need to get to the hospital." I screamed as I lay flat on my back. The knives were now being twisted inside me. I moaned and groaned the whole way off the track and into the back of the ambulance. As they closed the doors, I told them, "Look, I'm HIV positive, there is blood here, be careful." A rather large woman inside the ambulance said, "Thank you for telling us that in advance. I want you to remain calm and to focus on your breathing, okay?" I began coughing blood and kicking my knees upward to expel it in order to take a breath. I no longer could breathe at all. I was suffocating or was it drowning on my own blood. I could breathe out just fine, but in order to breathe in, I had to expel blood out of the way. Each time I did this, it hurt like hell and my oxygen coming in wasn't very much at all. The pain was completely unbearable.

This ambulance ride was horrible; I kept hearing this woman calling out numbers. She was yelling out my blood pressure or my blood oxygen level. I kept hearing her say, "Focus on your breathing, stay calm." Yet her voice was plagued with a sense of urgency. She then began a countdown it seemed. "Seventy-three . . . fifty-four . . . forty-one . . . He's going out . . . Thirty-four . . . twenty-two . . . twelve . . ." As she was calling out these numbers and yelling at me to focus on my breathing, I was slipping into sleep. I was dying. I began to see flashes of the day within my head as if it was a movie. It was as if I had pressed the Rewind button. My skepticism about people who have said they remembered seeing things while death approached was changed forever. I stopped hearing the woman's voice and the blaring siren coming from the ambulance. It all faded into the distance. I was away from the pain and was beginning to see darkness all around me. It was in that moment when a succession of images flashed in my mind. I saw demons, dragons, burning buildings, evil spirits, and lakes of blood and bodies all over the place. Death was with me; my specter had returned to me to bring me to hell. I heard no noise and smelled burning cedar chips again within my nostrils. I was being brought there against my will and couldn't do a thing about it. I got a quick flash of my mother's face within this dark place and was actually thrust back into the ambulance. Something had pulled me upward, I could feel the force of something else trying to pull me down, and I could feel both conflicting forces actually. My eyes opened, and the large woman was still above me yelling for me to focus on my breathing. I kicked my knees upward and forced some blood out of my lungs and took another desperate gasp of air. I remained without adequate oxygen for a very long ride.

We had come to a stop, the doors opened, and I was thinking thank God we made it to the hospital. I watched as someone else hopped into the back with us. The place the driver had taken us wasn't equipped for trauma patients. The new person in the ambulance was picked up because the trauma center was another twenty-five minutes away and he was a paramedic. We had already been traveling for close to thirty minutes already. I felt better knowing someone had gotten picked up to watch me die. I honestly wasn't going to make it. I heard them numbers being called out during the second leg of our trip. This time it didn't begin so high. "Forty-one . . . thirty-four . . . twenty-two . . . He's going out again . . . Twelve . . ." The pictures flashed through my mind of the day and quickly through my life. I was back in the darkness once again. I noticed a glow in the distance, very far off. My vision adjusted to the low light, and I noticed a mist in the air. It was very peaceful actually. Figures began to appear out of the mist and they began beckoning me to walk toward them. I then heard the siren and the woman yelling to focus on my breathing from very far off. The urge to continue forward toward the figures in the mist was easier to manage. I had begun to walk in their direction. I was greeted by several unfamiliar people and led toward the light in the distance. As I was letting go of the noise coming from behind me, a quick flash of my heroin-addicted friend came into my vision. A woman appeared from the mist; she was wearing a wedding dress and was looking very pretty with an aura surrounding her. I remembered how beautiful my friend looked when I attended her wedding long ago. This time she was exactly that and more. The softness of her hand was angelic as she caressed my face and she whispered, "It's not your time." I once again was thrust back into the ambulance. This time there was nothing pulling in the opposite direction to keep me within that peaceful place; all the pain had returned, and all the noise. My end was not to be. I was not wanted in heaven, and hell certainly wanted me back. I knew I wasn't heading to the Gloryland if I was to slip back off into the peaceful, painless, darkness again. I had to suffer this. I focused on the pain. I remember hearing if you focus on the pain, pain itself will keep you alive. I remained focused, and I kept conscious for the remainder of our ambulance trip. I was able to kick my knees upward and get a blood-gurgled breath each minute for the last twenty minutes of that crazy ride.

As we arrived at the trauma center, I asked them to wipe the blood off of me please. I didn't want to scare my brother's son in case they had made it into the place before me. I was wiped up real quick and then they rushed me into the emergency room. The entire trip took close to fifty minutes; I was unable to breathe, no air was coming in or out at this time. Actually for the last five minutes. My desperate attempt at kicking my knees to expel blood wasn't working. I kicked my feet violently a few times and ended up kicking the large woman right in the face accidently. I felt sorry for that instantly and just remained still and calm.

I looked to the right and saw my brother and his son. They both were waiting for my arrival within the double doors. They looked frightened, but I raised my hand in their direction in the hopes it comforted them. I knew if I held on long enough I would survive this once I made it to the trauma center. I knew upon arrival I stood a better chance than most actually. I survived the ambulance ride on sheer will to live, and not slipping out of the pain. Staying conscious was very difficult and painful, but it worked. I hadn't taken a normal breath of air for over an hour. My blood oxygen level was a steady 12 percent for a long time. Death was supposed to happen somewhere in the upper quadrant of numbers closer to 65 percent. I overheard the woman trauma doctor talking with my younger brother. She was asking him what my wishes were. He didn't know. He told her, "Listen, lady, you're the doctor, keep him alive." I looked to see my brother's face and he was crying. The tears were flowing as he looked at me. I felt his pain actually. He was watching his own brother die right in front of his eyes. She then told my brother he better call some other family members and get here as quickly as possible, I wasn't going to make it. "If your brother does make it, there will be significant brain damage due to the prolonged oxygen depletion. We need to know his wishes." Once again my younger brother told this woman to keep me alive, to save me. I could see the fear in my younger brother's face as he took it all in. I wasn't scared because I already knew I was going to survive. That angel in the mist had told me it wasn't my time yet.

I was quickly assessed, and within a brief few seconds, I was stuffed into an MRI machine. I was told I had multiple broken ribs, my lungs were pierced and both were collapsed, my spleen has ruptured, and your liver was torn, and oh yeah, I was bleeding to death inside. I was pulled out of there and watched as they all went to work on me. My hands were strapped down to the hospital gurney spread wide open. I wasn't given any pain medicine at all because my blood oxygen level was too low, it would kill me. The doctor told me I was going to feel some pain just under my armpits. I was told to breathe out the best I could. I couldn't breathe at all. That made no difference, they began to cut me on both sides simultaneously, and this incision was needed to insert two hoses to drain the blood from my lungs. They had cut straight through the muscle between my ribs to accommodate the hoses. These cuts were very painful, but what happened next was just medieval. The woman doctor told me, "Okay great, we are halfway there. Now this is going to hurt, but it's necessary. You will feel two pops, the first pop will be the hose traveling past your ribcage, and the second pop will be the hose entering your lungs." I looked at theses hoses and noticed they were clear and about as thick as your average garden hose with a forty-five-degree angle at the tip. I clenched my fists and groaned as they popped through my ribcage and screamed out in pain when they completed the second pop into my lungs. I watched as the two tubes filled with blood and headed underneath the gurney. I wasn't expecting this, but a catheter was rammed into my penis, and something very sharp was heading at my chest. It was very thick, like a pencil, with a very sharp tip. I tried to pull my body away and tried to sink into the mattress to escape. This thing entered my chest just about an inch below my collarbone and pierced through muscle and cartilage and was plunged into my heart's main vein. I screamed in pain and yelled, "Where the hell is the bedside manner? Jesus Christ, hold my hand or something, this shit hurts like hell." I heard the doctor say my blood oxygen level had climbed to 30 percent, and I watched as they sewed the heart catheter to my chest. They were expecting heart failure. I tasted the morphine as it entered my bloodstream, and then I felt a hand grip mine very softly, and as I looked to the right, it was my blond angel from the mist. I was next within blackness—no pain, no heat, no cold, no pictures flashing in my mind, no bright lights, no demons, no sound, no smell, no thoughts, no nothing, just blackness . . .

I awoke to see my mother sitting beside me holding my hand. My brothers were there along with the Spanish guy within my room. I felt thirsty and was consumed with massive amounts of pain. There were hoses still attached to my body and an oxygen mask placed over my mouth. I felt an itch on my inner thigh and reached down to scratch it; there was a small Scooby-Doo Band-Aid covering a small hole. I know my brothers were with me, but I honestly didn't recognize them at first. The only person I completely recognized was my mother. The rest of them, it was more of a familiar face without me being able to place them. I next was screamed at by that woman doctor. She yelled at me saying, "Why didn't you tell me you had cocaine in your system? I could have killed you." I was stunned at her behavior and told her, "Look, lady, maybe the cocaine kept my heart beating that whole time until I reached you. Perhaps it kept me alive." She calmed down rather quickly and explained how she had to insert a probe through my femoral artery in order to travel up to my spleen to insert an Angio-Seal within my spleen to stop me from bleeding internally. I wasn't going to be allowed any food or water for the next eight days to keep pressure out of my stomach. This seal needed to be undisturbed. Any pressure within my stomach could push against my spleen and jar it loose. I also realized I had a tube in my mouth which ran down into my stomach to keep it empty. There was yellowish bile within its center running into a pump above my head to the right. I was a complete mess, and

I was lucky to be alive. I was extremely thirsty, and after several hours, I began to beg for water. My pleas to them all weren't heard. I then asked my drug addict fellow crack-smoking Spanish friend to get me some water. He also told me no. I then begged for someone to piss on a rag and let it drip into my mouth please. Nobody allowed me a single drop of anything.

As time went on and days went by, the pain never left one bit. I was unable to sleep the whole time. I remember I got a visit from my father and his brother who happened to be my godfather. This was around day number 7 actually. I was allowed to have ice chips to keep my mouth and throat from hurting due to dryness. I would hide half of the ice chips given to me within another cup between my legs out of sight. I would sneak several swallows of water without anyone knowing. When my godfather and father arrived, I knew my godfather had a weak stomach, so I said, "Here watch this." I gulped down my little bit of stashed water and within a few moments the pump sucked the water out of my stomach and back out the hose running out my mouth. My godfather headed straight for the bathroom and began to gag. My father laughed along with me actually. It was something to amuse myself and to lighten the mood. When my godfather returned, he was smiling, calling me a little brat just like always. I found this new stomach-pumping machine to be rather entertaining.

I also was given a breathing testing machine to strengthen my lungs. I was supposed to blow out and keep a yellow ball in it at the top of the tube within. I was barely able to bring this ball up a half inch for like three seconds, never mind the full four inches I was supposed to. I tried every hour like I was told from day 3 actually unsuccessful in each attempt. I swore the thing was busted. My younger brother arrived, and I had him try it. Sure enough, he kept it at the top for damn near a full minute. My lungs were junk. When my doctor came in to see my progress, I placed clear tape over several of the air holes which were placed on the contraption to allow air out while blowing into it in order to force you to blow harder to bring the ball up to the top. I had to cheat in order to get these hoses out of me and get the hell out of this bed. If I was going to die from these injuries, I certainly wanted to do it in my own home. I remember my grandmother died in a hospital, and it just felt wrong in every way. I was nowhere near being out of the woods in this. When the eighth night came, they entered my room and removed all of my hoses. The most painful was definitely the heart catheter. The most pleasurable was the penis catheter, you would think it was painful but you would be wrong. As the nurse pulled it out, the itching I felt during its whole eight day stay was finally being scratched. The blood wasn't even a factor. It felt like heaven on its way out tearing the flesh which was stuck to the plastic tube and my itch was finally scratched.

It was on this night when I couldn't stay in the bed any longer. The pain had kept me up for a full eight days without sleep. I was barely breathing, and I knew if I lay down I would stay down. I reached out for the walker and lifted myself to my feet. I began to walk around the nurses' station. I had completed several laps around and began lifting my walker above my head to stop some of the severe pain within my chest. As I did this, I heard and felt a lot of crunching and popping within my chest. It hurt like hell, but it also felt good in a sense to be up walking and stretching my body. One of the nurse staff on duty told me I shouldn't be lifting my walker, it was too soon, she advised against it. I could cause myself further injury and I should go back to bed. I told her, "Look, lady, I have to do this. I can't take the pain anymore. If I drop dead, so be it."

I was told the next morning to call for a ride, I was being discharged. I was shocked actually, but was very glad I was going to be allowed to leave. I called my father to pick me up. He arrived and I was discharged. On the ride home, I asked my father to stop at a gas station. He asked me why, and I told him I needed a smoke. He protested at first, but I told him, "I'm quite possibly going to die at Mom's house, so please stop. This is my dying last request." He pulled over and bought me a pack of smokes without any further discussion. I lighted up my cigarette, drew in the smoke, and began to cough. The cough was very shallow because I controlled it. If I was to cough violently, my ribs on my chest plate would float around and pop out of place and it would hurt like hell. I knew this because I choked on some of my sneaked water back in the hospital. The simple pleasure of enjoying a cigarette was short-lived. I was only allowed two puffs because the pain was too much to bear within the controlled coughs. My father laughed when I told him that was a bad idea. I arrived to my childhood home driven by my father and accepted by no one. He helped me into the house and up the stairs to my bedroom. I lay down saying, "Thank you very much. I want you to know if I die, I love you very much." I passed out from pain and sheer exhaustion from not sleeping since this all took place.

I awoke to two puddles of blood the size of dinner plates on each side of my sheets from my chest. In fact each time I coughed, sneezed, or simply farted, blood would squirt out of the weep holes the doctors left under my armpits. I was within a nightmare once again. I was wide awake for a long time during a three-month battle of just pure pain without sleep. If I did sleep, it was very short and plagued by nightmares. Each and every morning I would be greeted by two puddles of blood actually for three weeks straight. I remember each night my mother would come into my room and light a prayer candle and she would quote some passages from the Bible. I sort of teased her about it because I had lost my faith long ago. "God doesn't like me anymore, Mom, what's the point?" She told me it helped her, so I should just have to get used to it. I cursed my mother for telling those doctors I was a crack addict and that she didn't want me to become hooked on morphine also. I was discharged with no real pain medicine at all. I was given a fentenyl patch and a prescription for an extra one. This stuff doesn't work at all for my injuries. She had one son already living as a heroin addict, she didn't need me to become one also. Within the first week of being on my death bed, I would get visits from my specter, the Grim Reaper, but I also got a visit one night from my dead relatives. These were all middle-aged folks that had passed away as elderly people within my youth. I had never known them in their middle age, but I knew them when they arrived surrounding my bed. This was actually kind of cool and a bit spooky if you think about it. My dead ancestors had come to be with me on my death bed to let me know it was okay to join them. I also was told I carry a message and a story that must be told. It was entirely up to me if I wanted to remain with them. I was visited by plenty of dead people within these first two weeks, and each time, I was allowed to remain within life itself. I was crossing over into death and speaking with the spirit world once again. This time everyone was my age. I was told many things about the world I was leaving and the world I was crossing into. If I stayed in the living world I would have to suffer pain far longer than need be and I was going to be shown a path to follow. I would be tested in my faith, and within my own mind, but the truth will set you free from bondage. You are the messenger.

I suffered for like three weeks before I took matters into my own hands. I could no longer suffer this pain. I crawled from my bed and crawled down the stairs of my mother's house. I crawled across the front lawn and pulled myself into my truck. I hurriedly started it and drove straight into the city. I stopped at a known crack house and shuffled into the place looking like Death wearing pajamas and slippers. There were blood patches under each of my arms and I walked like a hunchback, and the drug dealer was nervous selling me the crack, but I assured him I wouldn't blame him if I died. I purchased a large amount and wasted no time lighting up again. As I inhaled the smoke, within seconds the pain from my injuries were gone. I stayed in this crack house for two more hits and drove back home. I now had the perfect painkiller in my possession. I would only smoke it when I knew nobody was home during the day or very late night while they were asleep. I didn't feel much pain when I was able to smoke the crack, but sleep wouldn't occur due to one of the side effects of cocaine. I wasn't really able to sleep while I came down from the high, anyways, my ribs were broken and my chest plate was crushed. When I did manage a quick nap, I would be awoken suddenly by a sharp pain. My sleep did happen, but that time was very brief.

During this time my friend arrived to sit with me on my death bed. She was an angel sent from God in my opinion. This was the girl my friends from high school had asked me to go and try to help. I explained to her everything that had taken place during the accident and seeing her within my crossing-over into death vision. She was an angel, and she kept me in the living world. I no longer was alone within my own misery. This girl has had a rough go in life and people say a lot of bad things about her for being a heroin addict and a street girl in life. Her children had been removed from her care actually by the court system, she wasn't to be trusted. Personally I began to love this woman regardless of

Gary J. Mello

who she was in her past. I got to see her for who she really was. A kind, loving, caring, and beautiful human being. She stayed by my side through my very worst moments within this recovery process. I honestly was going through a massive amount of pain, and each time she came to hang out with me, my pain lessened and my spirits were lifted. In fact we bonded so well we stayed together as friends for over a full year every single day. We certainly cared very much for each other, but we had become completely addicted to drugs together. I started out using crack as pain management in the beginning, but it developed into an everyday habit for much longer than necessary. I had destroyed any hope of ever becoming anything within my mind. My drug addiction took on a whole new animal that couldn't be fed enough. I'm sorry that she was next to me during these times because I certainly shared everything right along with her. I most likely ruined some of her life in this process. I feel guilty in knowing I possibly kept her trapped in a vicious nightmare of plain old addiction that was out of control.

I was using so much that I would have to steal money from my own family to keep getting high. I had begun hanging out with all sorts of shady people also. I hooked up with a really nasty prostitute within the city and drove her around to stay getting high. She was nasty in the sex sense of it all, but she also was a solid friend from the past. This woman would go screw absolutely anyone and then rob them. I played as the driver within her craziness. It mattered not to me at the time because I was broke and needed to get high. Whatever she did for the money was her business. There was a few times I had brought along my friend when I would meet up with this crazy prostitute just to keep me company in my truck as the other girl went to work. I wasn't her pimp or anything; she just supplied me with drugs to drive her around. I would get high in my truck awaiting her return from whatever shady business she pulled. I just wanted my friend with me to get high and to have a few laughs. I won't tell you much more about this because it was a complete utter mess. I don't remember much actually. I guess the massive drug usage ruined those memory cells in my brain. I just know I was at the bottom again.

I was getting high so often that the city barely had a chance to resupply itself. I was buying from every different part of the city.

I knew where to find it at all times no matter which area I was in. The undercover cops sold to me plenty of times, but that is so they could follow me around I guess. There were times when I would go on huge binges alone without my friend because she need not know how bad my habit really was. I smoked close to two thousand dollars' worth of crack within a four-day period several times. I had already been high for five days when I purchased more. I ended up smoking methamphetamine, a.k.a. meth, when a dealer sold me a bag of it without me knowing. I remember this clearly because when I tried to smoke it, the rock gave off a dry sort of smoke. It wasn't the usual oily flavored melt-in-your-mouth candy flavor at all. I smoked close to an eighth of an ounce within twenty minutes, and it pissed me off because I had gotten ripped off. Each rock I smoked was the same, no flavor. By the time the high had hit me, it was pretty much gone. I smoked it all. I had no experience with this stuff in the past, so I didn't know how powerful it was. I was off the wall for damn near a day and a half. I should have died according to friends I've told this to. What happened was I drove toward the Cape Cod area early evening just after seven o'clock close to thirty hours later completely convinced I wanted to end my life.

I arrived in Chatham I believe, I wasn't really sure at the time. I followed Route 6 until I made up my mind on how my end would occur. I decided against driving head-on into a concrete bridge support doing over a hundred miles per hour. I didn't want to put the fire department cleanup crew at risk with my HIV/AIDS-infected mess while cleaning up my dead body and guts spread all over the place. I could've filled my cab with gasoline and lit my lighter prior to impact, but I didn't want to burn in the odd case I survived the impact. So I pulled into the parking lot of a public beach and exited my truck. I began to take off all my clothes heading toward the Atlantic Ocean. It was very dark out, and I entered the water naked as the day I was born. The water was a bit cool, but it wasn't really freezing, this was midsummer. I began to swim outward without looking back at all. I swam deliberately and strongly for as long as my body could handle it. I remained focused on a distant star within the horizon as I swam toward the end. I am unsure how far I swam, but I remained swimming for a very long time. I don't tire out very easily due to my endurance from racing dirt bikes in the past, and I was a very good swimmer. I swam until every muscle cramped within my legs, arms, and my back. My plan was working I figured because I wouldn't have the strength to return to shore.

My pace slowed, and I eventually wasn't able to go any farther. I stopped swimming and just tread water very slowly for a few minutes and asked God for forgiveness for not being able to carry this burden any longer. I asked for my salvation and asked him to watch over my family. I never once stopped myself at all. I was committed to this; I still hadn't looked back behind me to see where the shoreline was because it didn't matter. I had put it out of reach anyways, so why dwell on my past or my life? I then realized I wasn't going to simply drown from exhaustion and just began to float on my back for damn near an hour hoping a large shark or any shark for that matter would come along and take me down. I waited for the first half hour just praying for God to take me into heaven because I was unable to take my own life. I bit into my hands to make them bleed also. I knew the blood would attract a shark for sure. I floated and waited for another half hour, slowly releasing my blood into the water. I begged God to take me earlier, but I figured he wouldn't be able to stop the natural predatory instinct of a shark that smells blood in the water. I waited unafraid of my own death because I wouldn't be committing suicide in my mind. I would be eaten by a shark, a natural occurrence in nature. God would have to grant me my salvation.

When nothing happened within this half hour, I knew no matter how long I floated God wouldn't allow me to die in such a manner. I spun around to see how far offshore I had actually swum out. I was surprised to see land at all actually, but I did, it was beyond three miles if I was to guess. Most likely it was farther, but distance is hard to judge while submerged within the rolling seas. I cursed God again for not allowing me this death. I began swimming toward the shore very slowly in the hopes that the sharks would catch my scent and eventually I would be chewed for their evening dinner. I was being a stubborn bastard actually, I would stop swimming and just float and wait each ten minutes, but nothing happened. I screamed for the Devil to take me, I screamed for the souls living in Davey Jones's Locker to reach up and pull me down with them. Yet nothing occurred. The closest thing that came within any sort of harmful striking distance was a young seagull. It swam along with me actually. I began to look at this magnificent seabird and realized God had sent me a friend to keep me company as I made my laborious journey back to shore. I wasn't going to drown, nor was any shark coming to eat me at all. I'm unsure how far I actually swam, but when I hit shore, I was only a half-mile walk back to my truck. I retrieved my clothes and got dressed. When I hopped back into my truck and turned the key, my clock flashed on and read four thirteen. I had been in the water since somewhere around nine. So seven hours had passed within my attempt at suicide within the Atlantic Ocean. I was unable to die or so it seemed at this moment. I learned I was a pretty damn good swimmer, and drowning would definitely have to be an accident beyond my control. So as for the time spent in the water, that is a long time if you think about the area I was swimming in actually. There is always a sighting of great white sharks in this area due to the seal population. I think I was just cursed, even the sharks know my blood is bad.

I drove back toward home absolutely convinced I was going to die from overdosing. My head was pounding, my sight was beginning to go blurry, and I began to see white and purple orbs within it. By the time I turned onto my childhood road, my heart was racing in my chest and I couldn't stop hyperventilating. I decided against going to my mom's house and turned into her neighbor up the street's yard to visit my lady friend. I wanted to talk to someone who wouldn't judge me for being freaked-out due to all my drug usage for the past week. I drove into the driveway with my lights off in order to not disturb anyone who happened to be sleeping. This wasn't her home; she was allowed to stay there because the man who owned the house was a very generous man. He was a veteran, a special forces army soldier for that matter. This man allowed me to flop out at his home from time to time. I'm unsure if he knew of the massive amounts of drugs we were consuming, but it was very gracious of him to give her a safe place to be off the streets, myself included. I climbed up some staging that was set up to get to her window. The staging was set up to fix the siding on his house prior to it being sold. I had used it this early morning out of fear. I was afraid to face anyone within this panic and failed suicide attempt. I was embarrassed. When I knocked on the window, she let me in without hesitation. I began to cry and tell her I was going to die. I had consumed too many drugs this past week and my heart is going to pop, I'm going to stroke out I know it. She gently brought me to the bed and held me in her arms and rubbed my head and softly stroked my face, telling me it would be okay. I just needed to sleep, I had been up far too long, I was bugging out. I was lost in fear, yet this girl calmed me down with her touch and soft words. I fell asleep and awoke three days later.

You would think after a scare like that I would stop using drugs altogether, but you would be wrong. I just switched drugs. I had never used intravenous drugs ever in my life up until hanging out with this girl. It wasn't her fault at all; I had already been snorting the stuff with her in order to calm down, to take away pain, and to sleep. I also was trying to break my cocaine addiction using heroine. This eventually turned into me cooking my own crack, and while the cocaine was hardening from oil to rock, I would mix in heroine to create a mixture of crack and dope within my rocks. I now was chasing the dragon or so it is called. The shooting-up occurred because we didn't have much money one day and she was extremely dope sick and needed it. I just went along with the idea and allowed her to give me a shot. It wasn't much, but it was enough for me to get high off of it. She consumed the rest which was fine; I hated seeing her dope sick. I was more of a crack junkie and she was a dope junkie; she got sick, I got crazy. I remember telling her this was my first time ever to shoot drugs in my life. "It's your entire fault now." She actually cried. I had to calm her down because I could've said no. I was just breaking balls.

We still laughed together sometimes at the time I used too much heroin and decided to take a bath. I was nodding in and out and began to itch. I found a razor and began scratching myself with it. By the time she came to check on me, I had shaved my entire body. I was bleeding all over the place also. It didn't hurt at all during the shaving, and it really wasn't a big deal because I was out of it. When the hair began to grow back in several days later, that is when I really began to suffer. "I can't believe you left me in there so damn long, girl. Call me so we can catch up.

I know you bought my book. I hope you're allowed to visit with your children again in life. Tell your boyfriend I said hello. Also tell him it has been a long time since we had to jump bow to bow during that rough weather out scallop fishing at night to make it home. I was following his lead up until the point he told me to jump. Good thing I didn't listen or I would've been lost at sea long ago. Love you both."

I had become a total heroin addict on top of the cocaine addiction. I was a total loser in my mind, but nothing could stop my cravings. I went to the veterans' department and asked my doctor if he could prescribe me something for anxiety. I would always feel anxious beyond normal prior to getting more drugs. If I could stop the anxiety, maybe I would have a better chance in stopping. I never explained my intentions, but I did tell him I was anxious all the time. I also was fully depressed most of the time. He prescribed me trazodone to be specific. I tried using this medicine to shut my mind off and stop the never-ending voice in my head each day to go get high. The recommended dosage on this medicine was one pill a day, and it didn't help. I swallowed ten at a time so they would knock me out to end my cravings. This never worked at all either. I would pass out and wake up with someone different driving my truck around with me in the backseat passed out. I knew most of the people while I was in and out of crack smoking and being knocked out on prescription medicines. I was lucky actually; I could have easily been killed and dumped in the woods or a lake or the ocean or simply thrown into a Dumpster. This madness continued for a long time until I became consumed with guilt and fear. It overwhelmed me. I didn't know how to quit using drugs anymore. I no longer cared about anything or anyone. My life was far beyond fixing. My guilt came the day the repo man arrived to take my truck away. I hadn't paid any of my bills at all for over a year. My credit cards were maxed out, my family wouldn't talk to me, and they also didn't try to stop me from using drugs. I was alone with my drug addiction. I wasn't at home luckily when they came for my truck, or it would've been repossessed for sure. I had only owed like three hundred bucks on my vehicle before it was paid off, yet I couldn't manage the funds over the course of a year. What a shitbag I had become. My fear arrived knowing I was a hopeless cause.

I returned to the veterans' department and totally ratted myself out completely to my doctor about being a completely drug-addicted mess. He told me I could stay at the hospital in the detox if I wanted to. It wasn't mandatory, but once I committed myself, I wouldn't be able to leave for two weeks minimum. I wasn't ready for all that, so I left and told him I would work it out on my own. Yes, I did leave and continue to get high. My drug usage lasted a total of a year and a half after that accident. I also used for several months prior. I used day and night, as much as I could afford to buy. I couldn't stop but somehow, someway, I had to try.

I remember getting followed around by undercover police during this whole mess also. People tell me it was the drugs causing me to be paranoid, but when you're high as long as I have been, you come to recognize their vehicles and their tactics. I also noticed the surveillance from the odd vehicles and the flashes from a camera one night from a tower next to the downtown exit in New Bedford where the police like to take pictures from. I was tired of all the sneaking around also. I have been a recluse for too long within my addiction, and I was pretty much living in my truck just driving in circles. I had gotten high with lots of different people also, strangers at times. I don't consider fellow crack smokers strangers though when I'm using, they become needed friends. Getting high alone sucks. I remember one of these undercover guys followed me from Fall River all the way back to New Bedford. I sped up within the narrow streets and quickly pulled ahead and out of his vision. I then spun my vehicle around and headed straight for him with my pedal to the floor doing close to ninety. I then smashed my brakes and skidded sideways, blocking the road. The guy panicked braked and stopped. I was already out of my truck and running to his window. I opened his door and grabbed him by his shirt collar and swore to God I was going to smash his head in. I asked repeatedly, "Are you following me, motherfucker?" He got choked up and he cried and swore he hadn't been. I let him go because I knew it was true, and I was at fault for being a drug-using maniac for far too long. It was in that moment I knew I had to stop or someone was going to be killed within my drug-induced mania.

I stopped using drugs on a whim actually, or at least I tried to. I met a new HIV-positive girl who lived in Whitman, Massachusetts.

I stopped using the night before we met in person actually. She found out I was full of shit when I told her I hadn't used drugs in a while after about a week when I told her my past. It didn't matter to her. She didn't even care that on the night we met I showed up with two freshly broken ribs from a sledding accident earlier in the day with my younger brother and nieces and nephews. We set up a huge ramp at the bottom of a steep hill. Sure enough I hit it at speed and did a full upside-down flip and crunch. I felt my ribs snap and just crawled to my brother's truck. When I arrived to meet this girl, I had her go to the liquor store and buy me a pint of Jack Daniels. I guzzled it down for the pain and passed out within a half hour. I woke up and threw up out her bedroom window actually. She was a strong woman to accept me. God bless her.

I had tried racing again in 2006 with her encouragement actually, but I became spooked beyond belief. I was riding looking behind me constantly thinking someone was going to hit me again. I got back into the gym and worked out for the whole off season and sold my accident bike along with all my gear. I removed the bad karma completely and began again: a new bike, new gear, and a new determination. I ended up winning the over-thirty-year-old-novice motocross championship within the Middleboro series called NCSC in 2007. My younger brother won the expert class, and his son won his class also. This was an awesome year for all of us actually. The season was very cool, and I got a lot of encouragement from my fellow competitors to keep pushing for my dreams of becoming a professional within dirt bike racing once again or to simply keep racing. Everyone was very happy. I remained clean from drugs the whole season. This whole moment in time is etched in my memory as amazing. I was blessed to be alive and blessed to witness my brother and his son win their own championships within the same year as I had done. I was feeling very good about myself once again, but something happened within my mind.

The residual effect of all them medications and drugs certainly had me in a state of fear beyond my understanding. I remember going to my doctor at the veterans' department and telling him I hadn't been sleeping very well if at all. I had been off drugs for quite some time but couldn't get any sleep. I was back taking my

HIV/AIDS medicine, and my health was just fine. I was back racing again and even won the title. "Things should be okay, Doc." It may have been caused by a post-traumatic disorder from my accident or maybe the stoppage of drugs. I was told to expect a chemical imbalance within my brain juices; a psychosis was supposed to happen within a few months or possibly a year or so longer once I had stopped using. I honestly don't know why I couldn't sleep. I told him it was like I was on watch, waiting for someone to break down the door and kill me. I think in this doctor's head I was still using drugs actually, but he never asked me. I would later find out that this drug was a new experimental drug being tested to stop the cravings of cocaine. I was never told this at all at the time, I found this out a year later. If he had asked me if I was using, maybe this outcome could have been avoided.

He tried to tell me I was bipolar first and prescribed me lithium. This stuff created a headache so severe I had to return within a day. I was then given Imitrex because I might suffer from migraines. This stuff caused me to go into a semi-anaphylactic shock, I remember not being able to breathe very well and I scared my girlfriend and her mom when I told them what was happening. I told them I always knew I would die from a lethal injection; I just never knew I would be giving it to myself. I joked with them to calm them down. I refused to go back to the hospital; I tried to fall asleep only after saying if I die, I die. It's in God's hands. I knew if I closed my eyes to sleep my body would calm down and breathing would happen naturally. Being in this sort of anxiety can definitely be managed if you remain calm. I awoke a few hours later to them both still weary and a bit scared. I returned to the doctor's the next day on their request.

He then prescribed me gabapentin, the experimental medicine, to help me get some much-needed rest. I thought nothing of it and gladly took this stuff without hesitation at bedtime. I increasingly got more and more agitated and started to become manic beyond belief within a few days actually. I had a massive pounding headache behind my eyes and almost plunged a screwdriver into my skull to end my suffering. This was the worst feeling in the world. I have never in my life ever wanted to kill any of my family prior to taking this medicine. This stuff had me believe everything I had ever imagined or made up within my lifetime. I had become a wanted man within my own head actually. The bedroom me and my girlfriend shared was bugged, she was some undercover federal agent sent to observe me and to monitor my actions. I now began to believe I was some sort of serial killer or some mob hit man. My mind raced into my childhood up to the present moment; I profiled myself actually. The cops were always following me, they must know something. Jesus Christ, I was a serial killer, I had all the background to prove it too, and they were constantly watching me. I was cruel to ants and insects when I was a kid, I was sexually abused, I had drug usage and high sexually addictive tendencies, I abused alcohol, I had violent past, I was in midthirties, I was under surveillance, and I'm a fully trained disgruntled Marine, my delusions were real. I freaked out and began tearing our room apart looking for the hidden microphone and began screaming at my girl to call out for backup or she was going to be killed within the next twenty seconds. "Who is your handler?" I kept saying while thrashing our room. I was straight nuts. My girlfriend's mother calmed me down a bit, and I decided to go visit my own family. When we arrived, my mother had cooked us dinner that afternoon, so I sat down to eat. I had calmed down a little bit and felt safe among my own family until I found a small sliver of glass within my food. My mom had broken a glass while cooking accidently, and it ended up in my plate. I flipped out screaming, "You're all in on it." I jumped up and threw my dinner plate across the dining room, and it shattered against the wall. I left that instant without one more word spoken. My family was actually pretty scared at the time because I had told them prior to my arrival something was wrong in my head.

I returned back to my mother's home the next day embarrassed by my actions, but in my mind it was real. They wanted me dead. I remember helping my mother chop some onions for soup or something this day. I couldn't believe in my heart my own family wanted me dead, which must be delusional. What happened next scared the hell out of me. I flashed into some weird dimension. I looked down, and my hands were covered in blood and the whole kitchen was soaked in red blood. I followed the trail of blood spatter into the dining room, and there lie my mom dead in a pool of blood. I then went through the house and realized I had killed my youngest brother and cut my oldest brother's throat damn near severing his head completely off. My two nephews were both curled in their own blood pool dead as well. After seeing this, my mind flashed back to reality, and I was standing back at the cutting board chopping onions. I had wet my pants actually during this hallucination and almost collapsed on the floor when I realized it was just a weird vision.

I left my mother's house without saying good-bye and drove back to my girlfriend's house. My mother called me when I was en route and asked if everything was okay. I didn't want to scare her, so I said, "Yes, Mother, everything is fine. I just felt ill all of a sudden." She told me it would have been fine if I lay down on her couch, I didn't have to leave, but I knew in my head I had to get away from them before I hurt them. I returned home and just shook in a sort of convulsion for the rest of the evening and didn't sleep a wink. I swore in my head that I was going to kill them all. I was going to begin my killing spree, and it was going to start with the people I love the most. When morning came, I was in my girlfriend's basement holding a kitchen knife positioned in the corner waiting on my attackers. I swear to God and on my own soul this mania was far worse than any paranoia that I have ever encountered during my life—smoking crack was far less, trust and believe that.

I drove back to my mother's house after I called my father and told him he needed to be at my mom's house along with all my brothers. I walked in and went straight into my younger brother's room to tell him what I was going through. I didn't even start to talk; I began crying like a baby. He was like, "What's wrong, guy?" I couldn't speak at all for close to ten minutes actually. I ended up in the breezeway of her house sitting in a recliner just crying and not saying a word. My mother got scared and rushed to get my oldest brother from the basement. He came upstairs and tried to ask me what was wrong. I watched as they were asking my girlfriend what the hell was going on. She tried to explain the best she could, but she didn't know about the death vision. I hadn't told her because it scared me to madness. I couldn't speak until my father arrived actually. I then told them exactly what was going on. They were scared when I finished telling them everything and suggested I get on the phone with my cousin the doctor.

I still trusted my cousin even though I lost a testicle with his expert advice. I also consulted him several times about my double hitched breathing during my accident recovery when that dirt bike landed on my back. He had told me I was lucky to be alive back then, 98% of people who sustained my amount of injury die on the way to the hospital. He broke my balls about having nine lives, and said someone upstairs must love you kid. The awkward breathing was caused by the blood still in the base of my lungs. He had offered to aspirate with a long needle but I told him no thanks. I'll deal with the pain. He recommended on this occasion that I just relax for the evening and to come see him in the morning only if I promised not to hurt myself or anyone until then. I was completely exhausted and wigged out, but I assured him I wouldn't harm anyone. I don't think anyone slept that night except me.

The next day I went to my cousin doctor's office to explain everything that was happening. He told me it was a reaction to this gabapentin medicine. I should stop taking it right away. He also was going to prescribe me Seroquel, which is used for schizophrenia, it would calm me down. I was completely manic, and he assured me it would stop my mind from racing. I reached out to get the prescription paper and read the fine print. It mentioned something about the federal government, and my mind snapped. I screamed at my cousin and threw some stuff around his office. He was all part of this whole fucking mess. "As a matter of fact, you were in on this mind fuck the whole damn time." I stormed out of his office and jumped into my truck with my girlfriend in tow. She was absolutely petrified because I was driving very fast toward the New Bedford Veteran's Department to get my prescription filled. When I arrived, the place was closed. I was completely enraged, screaming, "I'm going to kill everyone, I swear to God. If I don't get some answers soon, you're going to fucking die first, woman." My girlfriend was crying for the whole ride into Providence so I could see a doctor at my usual veterans' hospital. I noticed three black SUVs along this ride. There was one in front of me, one behind me, and one just on my passenger side following along with me doing close to eighty-five miles per hour. They must be state police or the federal crew escorting me. My cousin must have called them because I was irrational to the max.

I arrived to the hospital and pulled right up to the front door. I jumped out of my truck and entered with several police and security guards awaiting me at the doors. They didn't say a word to me; they just followed me into the building and remained at a safe distance actually. I walked up the stairs and headed straight to the psych ward. When I reached the doors, one of my younger brother's childhood friends was at the doorway. I didn't recognize him at all. He tried to say something like, "Hey, man, it's me, your brother's friend." I told him, "Get the fuck back away from me, I don't know you." He stepped aside rapidly, and I opened the doors to the crazy house and shut them behind me. The doors shut and locked automatically. I told the women at the desk I was absolutely nuts, I wasn't leaving until I was better, and I needed to lie down. She told me to go into room 5. I hurriedly got into the room and just crashed out. When I awoke, they told me I had done exactly the right thing by coming to the hospital. I was thinking, *Yes, no shit.* I was about to kill my own family due to this fucking medicine. I had come into this place under my own power within the good side of an evil I wouldn't have been able to stop once it began. I remained in this place for five days until I considered it safe to leave. I refused to talk to anyone other than my doctor and his nurse practitioner. I knew I was being completely fucked with mentally when this nurse asked me inadvertently if I was scared yet. How dare these people play with my mind like this? I was prescribed Seroquel for the next six months to quite my mind. This stuff completely knocks you out for days at a time. I had to cut back on it slowly because my mind was very fragile and the residual effects of this psychosis were present the whole time until present day actually. My whole medicine side effect list caused this also. I should have a lawsuit within this whole entire mess of my life somewhere, which medicine should I blame, which company. My pension wasn't enough for peace of mind, I'm not a lawyer, so why bother?

I had tried to confess my sins to a Catholic priest at my mother's church. I remember setting it up with my mom because I was certainly thinking I was going to stroke and die very soon. I figured since I was semi-religious, this wouldn't hurt. I drove to the local church with my mother on the day this priest would hear confessions. Now here we go, more delusion. My mom said inadvertently, "Oh, it's Father What's-his-nuts, and not Father So-and-so." I asked what she meant. She told me it wasn't the normal priest who did confession.

I watched as this man exited his car and headed into the church with a tape recorder in his hands. Right in that moment I was off my thoughts of my own issues. I certainly wasn't going to confess to this guy anything I considered an abomination to God. I am an abomination. I started getting flashes of how the Catholic dioceses allowed a known child molester priest to roam free among parishioners' children. They kept transferring the sick bastard from city to city. I also remember coming to this building when my younger brother's son was born. I was supposed to be his godfather. The priest told me I wasn't a true Catholic. I was like, "Listen, guy, I went to Catholic school, I'm baptized, had my first communion, and I'm confirmed, and even my dog tags while being in the Marine Corps say I'm Catholic." He wouldn't allow me to stand in as my own brother's second according to the faith in the event of my brother's demise. I guess I'm not Catholic because I have AIDS. "All you want is an envelope with money, fuck you, pedophile motherfucker. I don't give a shit what costume you're in, I am a believer, I believe in everything and nothing at the same time. Yes, this did happen. Go tell the pope, how since I'm on the fringe of society, an AIDS-infected person, an outcast now, a leper, that they won't even allow me to do my penance properly or to be my own brother's child's godfather." I was so all set with their lies and deceit also.

I was fully enraged and not focusing on what I wanted to say. I certainly don't want my confession recorded. This was a holy sacrament between me and God, the priest was supposed to be bound to silence according to my faith and how I was raised within the Catholic school system. I simply told this priest I needed to be forgiven by God because I had been abusing myself for too long. I had been a total drug-addicted mess, and I needed to be cleansed in order to have peace. I didn't know how to begin again, I was here for forgiveness. I wanted the promise given by Jesus that if I accept him into my heart, I would be saved. I had prayed plenty of times, I'd seen too much in my lifetime, I'd been among the spirits, I'd seen demons and dead relatives, I was haunted by a specter. I was God's plague. People condemned me without knowing me. *Bless me, Father, it has been far too long. I was drawn into hell, not accepted on earth, and heaven is closed for me now. I was told I carried a message, and I don't know what this all means. I feel possessed, I hear voices in my head, and I see visions. I'm not sure if it came out like that or not,* I was thinking it at the time, so that counted as confession in my eyes. I guess we could ask for the tape recording. What a pile of heaping, wet, steamy dog shit in my opinion.

I was told to say a few Our Fathers and toss in a few Hail Marys and everything would work out. "God works in miraculous ways. Follow your heart. I bless you in the name of the Father, the Son, and the Holy Spirit. Amen!"

"Thanks, Father."

NEW DIRECTIONS

As you can see, my life has been a total and complete shambles beyond repair. Drug addiction had me by the balls once again because I couldn't deal with my medicinal paranoia. I have considered that suicide has become once again my only escape from this never-ending nightmare. I was faced with my ultimate decision within this suicidal thought process, and it didn't look good for me at all. Instead of being selfish about it all and leaving others devastated within my wake, I considered a new direction. This direction was not something I was comfortable with one bit. It was called asking for help. Now if you have done drugs or have been addicted to something so strongly that it had consumed your every thought each and every day just like I have done for the past year and a half, well, you should know this is the worst feeling in the world. Owning up to your ultimate flaw, guilt, fault, loser feelings, and lowlife acts within your life to anyone outside of close relatives or friends is strongly forbidden within our weak minds. Most of the time, we don't even allow family into our lives at all when I think about it. It's not that we are weak individuals with childlike minds; it's more that we have become so powerless against our cravings we are no longer in control of normal thought processing. I had resisted this course of action completely until the course of this mission was completed. Each and every time I seek out drugs, I call it a mission—you never know what will occur. Or what you're willing to do to keep it coming. Once again after the year and a half of being clean, I slipped up and let myself drive into the city to score. I was possessed by my eight-hundred-pound monkey once again. That evil little bastard had slipped into my mind because of a few extra beers and a few too many shots at a party for my girlfriend's brother or something along those lines. I don't really remember the details of the how I ended up within the clutches of the all mighty crack rock again, but if I was to point out the cause of my relapse, I would have to say stress from a relationship, drinking, and the thoughts of my past which haunt me every day. I also was considering who I really was in life. I was answering, or maybe it was justifying, the *why* to myself. I am nobody, no one cares, what does it matter anyways? I'm supposed to be dead already, who gives a flying fuck, I'm getting high, I will never amount to shit anyways. My escape from reality has always been to chase the high instead of anything worthwhile within life. I have always considered myself unworthy of anything especially an education leading to a well-paying job. Hell no, that is way too much effort; besides, who wants a diseased, rotting reformed drug addict around their workplace anyways? It's better if I just allow the thrill of the temporary fix to take over at the helm. Once I allow it in, the thought patterns shift entirely out of anything that has bothered me from my past completely during my chase for the rocks. My mind is so consumed with where I can get my glass dick, my pipe, my Choy-boy, a pusher, and a lighter on top of grabbing a few fifty rocks that no other thoughts, I mean absolutely nothing else is allowed in. No one on this planet can stop this process once it begins. Forget about some bullshit intervention because it will only compound the crackhead mind and make him or her become hateful toward anyone who gets in their way, no matter what their good intentions were. I know this from experience and from the events that transpired on this night and the following two days. You're thinking to yourself, wow, only two days, that's a short relapse when you consider that I have gone on three-month-long binges without much of anything else within my life other than copping and smoking every hour of the day. No sleep, no food, only water is necessary. But you would be wrong in thinking it was small in nature. This was a huge moment for me. So pay attention, fellow junkies, crackheads, drunks, pill poppers, sex fiends, and shitbags. I found the key to the sobriety door we all have longed to find our entire lives.

    I remember stopping at the usual scumbag streets within the city of New Bedford and grabbing two or three fifty pieces bright and early in the morning. If I was to guess, it was around 5:00 AM. This could have been anywhere on this planet which I chose to have copped my drugs, so the place is of unimportance. As I had hoped, my first copping of the rocks went unhitched without any bullshit drama attached to it. I always hate when things go wrong while you're copping looking to get high, especially getting beat, ripped off, shot at, stabbed, bamboozled, cheated, or any other ugly drama shit that can be attached and happens or has happened to me in the past, but whatever, that is all part of the game when you care to partake in drug use. I always seem to get my first bunch of rocks without any drama attached usually. It was an awesome feeling of relief on this transaction. After copping my three-fifty pieces which were about the size equivalent of three peanut M&Ms, I hurriedly got back into my truck and stopped at the store for the rest of my works in order to get that sweet candy-flavored, melt-in-your-mouth, makes-you-cream-your-shorts first hit. It is always the first hit which is the best for me, all the rest of the hits just don't seem to match it no matter how big or how powerful the shit really is. Nope, I've done crippling fall to your knees, puking brown foam hits in the past, and it just never matched the first hit after being clean for a while. I'm not saying all the rest of those hits sucked because that would be an absolute fucking lie of major proportions. Every single hit I have ever taken of crack was pure pleasure regardless how big or how small. It's just the romance of the first one which I can remember most of all within my mind. Maybe I have had too many of those so called first hits, that's why I'm an addict today and every damn day until I wither away within my casket. But let's not lose focus on my story of this day's events. Truth be told, while writing this section of my book, I have had several trips to the toilet to shit because I have spoken about cracking it up. Weird how when a crackhead talks, thinks, reads, writes, whispers, or even secondarily hears the mere mention of its sweetness we all run to the hopper to take a damn shit. Perhaps it's caused by the use of baby laxative as a cutting agent to lessen its purity so someone can turn a profit. Yes, I've encounter this and several other additives over the years, and it still triggers the shits. It also can be said that while copping all the way through to the moment, we light that rock we have to shit. This happens a lot but not always. I have shit my damn pants within this time frame before, but this wasn't one of them times at all. Maybe it was because I had been clean for a while and the mind-body thing was in control. Thank God for small miracles because I didn't want to be inconvenienced with a stop to take a shit anyways. I gathered up my supplies within the one of many convenience stores on our great country's landscape and paid the attendant who gave me a look of disgust, fear, loathing, sympathy, and weirdo amusement. I disregard those looks because they are so common to me it's not worth my time. Who is he to judge me anyways, fuck him, and "Give me my change, fuck head!" Out the door I went without a word spoken between us at all. It's just my thoughts playing tricks on me anyways. I have brief moments where reality can pierce through my crack-possessed mind telling me not to get high, it's a mistake. But those thoughts are very fleeting at best once I have everything within my grasp.

I made quick work of assembling my pipe and placing my first hit on it. I didn't even leave the parking spot I was in at the store. I didn't care who was watching at all. I lit up and inhaled for as long as I could. I listened to the rock melt with its familiar pops and fizzes. The smoke went in very smoothly and the smoke took on a familiar yellowish tinge while traveling through the glass. Yes, this was the good stuff, and I was happy about that. I had consumed a complete half of a fifty piece within one hit and held it in. While I was holding it in, I placed the other half on the pipe before the drug took effect completely upon my exhale. It's always the exhale where you completely flew off into outer space. I didn't want to be fumbling around as I drove, so I began placing my next hit on the pipe. This was definitely the time to take care of it. I used my lighter and half-melted my next hit so it wouldn't fall out when I placed it down to leave the parking lot. Everything was scripted and rehearsed plenty of times in the past, so it's almost as if I was on autopilot while I blew out my first hit. Only this hit was a big one that fried my mind and had me temporarily go blind. Ears ringing and my stomach wrenching, I opened my door and puke out everything within my stomach including the green bile. *Holy shit, that was good,* I thought as I closed my door and shifted into drive. I left my parking space and headed for the highway. This highway thing had become commonplace lately because it was easier to keep getting high driving in a straight line rather than using the back roads. I hadn't even completely made it around the on-ramp and I was already burning my second hit. That's how crazy this drug is, you want it rapidly. I think less than five minutes had passed since I was puking out the door in a shitty gas station convenience store parking lot and I was after seconds already. So without even merging into traffic, I was ablaze again, sucking in that sweet poison once again. I didn't go blind on this hit nor did I puke.

What did happen was everything sort of slowed down around me and I instantly became hyper aware of my surroundings and became borderline paranoid. No longer did I care where or what I have become as a person within society at all. The other motorists alongside me didn't have a clue they were sharing the road with a crack-fueled crazy behind the wheel. I viewed everything and watched everyone very closely while I was high. If you have ever been around drug users long enough like I have, we all eventually get stuck—stuck, meaning no talking, semi-paralyzed, and just totally immersed within our own minds. Each person I passed or I was passed by had now become part of the secret club of informants to the police within my mind. It becomes absolutely mind consuming at times, and the fear is just a chemical imbalance within your brain brought on by the drugs. The world around me has become once again filled with followers and people who are looking to have me arrested and locked away within a cage. I locked my doors and rapidly shifted my vision from each mirror looking for the attack that never came. It becomes almost laughable now when I think about it, but there is nothing funny about tweaking to the point of immobility. The only thing worth doing is to keep feeding the addiction and to keep driving. I drove and smoke all morning to the point of running out of gas. I had completely finished all of my stash around 10:00 AM. It lasted a long time do to the fact I was completely paranoid and needed to be sure I had proper distance from each oncoming and traveling-with-me vehicles. It was completely insane to be worried about someone seeing me getting high from the other side of the highway, but it's also something I had no control of. It's always the fear of being caught that frightens the hell out of crack users including me. It is like the world will stand you against a wall and throw stones at you until you're dead or something. I had become so paranoid that the mere thought of stopping for gas was totally not conceivable until I came down a little.

During this coming-down stage of my high, I began to Jones something awful. The word *Jones* is exactly how it sounds. This is a very bad time for the crack users of the world. These are the times when crimes will be committed to add more food to the pipe their monkey is craving. For me in the past, I would most likely be up to something shady to score the next fix, but I didn't need to worry because I still had money with me. Nope, I was within the pick-at-the-floor stage looking for some miniscule crumb I might have dropped. I had pulled off the highway on to a side street for this task. This was comical to see if I was observing someone else doing it, but this time it was me. My only concern at that time was not to be seen acting funny on the side of the road with my door open looking under my seat for the magical rock I never seem to find. I know it's not there, but the compulsion to look overwhelmed me so I had to look. While I was searching, I was able to stow away all the evidence of me getting high. I tossed out the leftover Choy-boy copper wool and stashed the pipe which had been scraped clean with my makeshift pusher which was the inside ink cartridge of a pen. Those last few scrapings were consumed also within my crack ride. I always push my pipe to clear the resin which if added up properly can pretty damn near send you to the morgue, but it's primo stuff. I also grabbed the coconut spray out of my truck's console and gave my truck's interior a good dousing to eliminate that burning plastic smell. What took me about two minutes to complete, actually felt a lot longer in my mind. My body was so shaky and nervous at the time. Each time I would reach to do something, I would have to have my head on a swivel to check around to make sure no one was coming up on me. I could just sense that someone was actually in the trees also watching me. The whole scene was bad, and my heart began to race a bit faster than it was already beating within my chest. This was definitely a full-on panic attack happening, I was going to be attacked from behind when I wasn't looking, or my heart was going to pop in my chest. I got back into my truck and locked the doors very quickly and sped the hell out of there. I quickly lit a cigarette to calm my nerves, and it helps a little. My eyes were glued to the rearview mirror, thinking something was following me just out of my vision. Each time I looked into it, I saw something but then it's gone. I was now in the hallucination stages of my high, but this was a mild episode for me and it took a little bit of coaxing, but I suppressed it and quickly returned to normal thoughts. It was very easy to turn that switch off when I needed to these days because I've already been far worse in the past. This also allowed me the presence of mind to look at my fuel gauge which had been below empty for at least ten miles.

Once I had stopped my mind from racing and rid myself of the phantoms that weren't there, I found a gas station. I pulled into it knowing full well I was high as hell and it was obvious to anyone who happened to be looking in my direction for any extended amount of time. I jumped out as quickly as I could and fumbled for my wallet and pulled out my credit card. Good thing I was clean for a substantial amount of time because my bill was actually paid. I didn't have to enter the store at all and face the clerk while being high and on display. This was certainly an easier task to complete or so you would think. My card worked once I looked around several times and positioned myself perfectly while pumping to view all angles of anyone who might be hiding behind the pump itself. I slipped the card into its slot and waited for confirmation. Lo and behold, it worked. I nervously stood with my hand on the pumping lever to keep the fuel flowing, wishing it was an older pump that actually had the locking mechanism that allows you to pump hands free. At least this way I could hide in my safe space which was the cab of my truck. Anywhere else would have been just fine. I started to think that whack job DC sniper within the trunk of some rusted old car might have me trained within his scope. My panic was in full tilt again, and the sweat running down my back and my twitching hands reminded me of it each second as I stood there looking around with my big freaked out eyes. I needed a lot of discipline to keep from stopping the pump and from running away again. I focused on the numbers running before my eyes on the display screen of the gas pump. I watched as gallons climbed and dollars added up. I actually was thinking to myself if I owned one of these gas stations myself, it would be very easy to skim money from it. Think about each person who pulls into the station to gas up on a daily basis. If

I added two or three cents to each gallon, I would most likely make an extra twenty to thirty bucks per day. That's if one thousand gallons were sold in a day. Even if it were half that amount, that's still ten or fifteen bucks a day. On an average of one hundred bucks a week gives or takes a few dollars. Within the course of a year I could be looking at, oh well, let's see. There are fifty-two weeks in a year, so if I multiply weeks times one hundred bucks it comes to fifty-two hundred dollars. That is a worthy pile of cash to have lying around. Now just imagine for one moment if you controlled the whole East Coast, let's say five hundred stores. If you do the math on that, you have got my drift on how lucrative the gas scam put on the citizens is, by our government. Whenever they need to fill their pockets or to fill the coffers again, they can just squeeze the nipple of the unsuspecting motorist.

Click! My nozzle stopped in an audible rush. I was jerked out of my mind and back into reality. It was nice to drift off into my head and just relax my paranoia for a moment. It was also nice to think about numbers and how the government controlled it all. For some reason, numbers are soothing to me, and the government corruption is a no-brainer. I hung up my nozzle and replaced my gas cap, and when I shut the little gas cap outer door, suddenly I was normal again. I was back in the peep show so to speak. All eyes were on me. I hurriedly got into my truck and exited this gas station and headed for the highway. I wasn't really sure how far I was away from the city I originally left from, but I knew my Jones was in full effect and it hadn't left me at all. My monkey was still hungry. I needed to make short work of discerning where my location was, then deciding on the direction toward the closest guy with more rocks for me. I figured out I hadn't really gone far at all. Actually I was only ten minutes away from my medicine, the almighty crack rock. I had traveled nearly two hundred and fifty miles only to find out I had gone in a complete circle. Kind of crazy, but it was pretty much normal because I have done this plenty of times before in the past so I wasn't shocked.

I drove the ten minutes without a problem or a care. I was once again on the hunt, and it felt good knowing I had a few hundred bucks to burn in my pipe. I pulled up on the corner of Holly Street and North Front Street. I was on Holly Street facing upward toward the avenue. If you're familiar with New Bedford's

north end at all, you would know my location. If you're a brave
soul who hasn't a clue where I'm talking about, be adventurous
and go there some late night and take a walk around. Be sure to
bring some cash with you because the muggers like that aspect
and they could most likely use the money for something. Well,
anyways, I hopped out of my truck and headed toward a few
choice spots I had already known about to cop my drugs. It really
didn't matter the location like I said in the past because I have
found drugs in every damn state I have ever lived in. This just
happened to be my old stomping grounds so to speak from my
youth. I have traveled throughout the whole city on foot or on a
bicycle in my younger years to cop drugs. So it can be said there
is definitely a drug problem within its limits. I just happened
to choose this area. While I was walking, I noticed a few people
lingering around outside of one of the houses I frequented quite
possibly a thousand times before. It had been up and running
since I was a teenager. Many a fools have been caught up around
here. There have been raids, shootings, robberies, stabbings,
bashings, arrests, assaults, loads of police brutality no one hears
about, and a whole bunch of drama. Yet the crack dealings keep
flowing and it was fine with me. I wanted my nasty little demon,
and none of that concerned me.

It didn't take very long for someone to approach me as I was
walking in this area. I had asked a few regulars who had the
rocks, and they said they didn't know. That was a typical answer
to expect because who really wants to say they know. It was a
trained response learned over the years I am sure to avoid that
pest called the police. I wasn't the pigs, the man, the popo, or
the narco, but they have to be careful whomever they speak to on
the streets. After that ritualistic banter ended, a woman wearing
ripped jeans, a dirty coat, and a bandana told me to go up into
a certain house. She also asked me for a ride to the far side of
the city. I agreed to give her a ride if she would go up and get
me a hundred piece and I would share it with her. I didn't feel
like going up into some trap or to be set up by this chick just in
case she was a cop. It was a normal thing around here to have a
prostitute go and retrieve your drugs and it's not really a big deal.
For the most part, women of the streets are pretty honest when
it comes to getting high and getting a free ride. She agreed but

also spit out a twenty piece from her mouth into my hand and asked where I had parked. I told her right around the corner. It was pretty simple, and I felt okay with handing her my hundred bucks. I watched as she hurriedly went up into the house, and I retreated back toward my truck. Under normal circumstances, I would put the bag she gave me in my mouth also, in case the cops rolled up. It was to ensure you didn't have possession charges put on you while they searched you. It's very easily swallowed. For some reason on this day I just slipped it into my pocket.

Here's where things just fall apart for me. I had made it back into my truck and was sitting waiting for the chick to return. I had locked my doors upon entering my vehicle just out of sheer habit. I have been in some shitty parts of this world, and it was always good practice. This came in handy at times before. I'm no lucky tough guy who has never been robbed at gunpoint before, so why not lock your door. It may save your life. So that's my safety tip for you fellow motorists of the world. Lock your damn doors. I was not really looking around all paranoid, nor was I at all in a nervous state of mind. I was actually pretty comfortable. I had done this exact thing nearly a hundred times before within this same area. I watched as a car pulled in front of me and parked. Two guys got out and walked past my truck on either side of my windows. I really didn't pay much attention to what they were up to at all. They looked rather dirty looking also, not uncommon to see two shitbag junkies rolling together in this neighborhood at all. They were most likely going to get their morning fix. It was ten in the morning according to my clock, and a lot of junkies get a late start within their day. Who knows what the fuck they were up to, I was getting my stuff and that's all that matters. Meddling in other people's business will get you stabbed, shot, beaten up, or even killed around here, so fuck them. I think I was too damn comfortable on this day or I was just so possessed with getting high and I didn't watch these boneheads or look to see what they were up to. I should've been more aware because while sitting there, everything was quiet and calm around me and I was actually in a good mood.

Then *boom, boom, boom*—both windows were being pounded on at the same time. It was as if they were trying to break them with their fists. I snapped up like, holy shit, what the fuck! I was startled and my instant reaction was they are trying to assault me or they are trying to rob me. Not wasting any time, I rapidly opened my door to confront my would-be attacker on my side of the truck. I knew if I made short work of this guy, the other one would be nervous and shocked at first and it would give me vital seconds to have this guy on his ass and be able to face him with his back jump tactic which he surely would capitalize on before he had a chance. The door flew open hitting the guy's legs, and he stumbled backward a few feet. I exited very quickly and closed the distance on this guy very rapidly. As I approached him, I noticed he was reaching into his shirt for something. *In a moment I am going to be shot,* I thought as I grabbed his arm and neck at the same time. I screamed, "What the fuck, you trying to rob me?" I was cocking back my arm to smash this guy's face in when his other hand pulled on a chain wrapped around his neck. He was trying to release my fingers from his throat, and he got lucky and hooked it around his thumb. When I reached back to punch, he revealed a shiny gold badge attached to this chain. Instantly I knew he was a narco pig undercover cop. I raised my arms up and took a step backward telling him, "That's a surefire way to get fucking hurt, asshole. Next time approach me with some decency."

I just had the feeling a fight was exactly what they wanted. They wanted their chance to pummel me again in the streets or to just shoot my ass and say I went for their guns. That's the mentality of the New Bedford police; they are so scared out on the streets that they shoot first and ask questions later. I had just watched a news clip about some guy who had a knife and a screwdriver in his own home coming toward the police in a threatening manner. Two cops had shot this prick from close range and put several bullets each in this guy. He was shot multiple times and killed. What happened to nonlethal force? Are you fucking joking me or what? How about a leg wound first to drop the guy and then arrest him. They wear vests, don't these cops of our city? Knives have a hard time going through them if they can stop bullets. So with that in mind, I retreated knowing full well I have a record of violence and several charges of assault and battery on police. I wasn't giving them an excuse today. Besides, I was not doing something I hadn't done hundreds of thousands of times in my life. I was getting high, big deal.

The other guy behind me must have panicked because he was still twenty or so feet away when I turned to see where he was. After my hands were up, he closed on me and tried to play tough guy, but I knew, he was a pussy. I just let them cuff me and then search me. Oddly enough they didn't find a thing. I had gotten lucky I guess. The pocket I had the twenty-dollar rock in was searched by the officer behind me who panicked and then covered his girly man behavior with macho talk toward me while he searched. It definitely serves that prick cop right not to find any drugs on me.

I was sat down on the tailgate of my truck as they searched through my truck looking for my stash all the while it's in my pocket. I was also thinking, *Well shit, I hope you do find something because I've already searched that fucking floor for what seemed like an hour looking for a crumb much less a rock.* The skinny red-headed cop who was scared to the point of pissing himself while I had him by his neck came back to talk to me. He gave me the same old routine: "We know your holding, we just observed you purchasing drugs, and we had you under surveillance with a camera, tell us where it is and we will help you out." "Yeah sure, buddy, you'll help me into a fucking cell I know, thanks but no thanks." I didn't speak to this guy, but I was thinking about his helping me out, yeah okay! It's better to just shut up and let them run their mouths and play tough guy. It makes them feel special I guess. So when he was sure I didn't give two shits about what he was saying, he stood me up again and began looking in my pockets again. I had squeaked by on the first search, and I was hoping they would just get frustrated and let me go. This had happened before in the past many of times. It is very common to get harassment from the police. It starts early in life and never ends when you're a drug user. Being stopped and questioned for no reason was very common only to be let go, only after their violation of my rights has ended. So I was thinking, *Damn it,* when he began turning out my pockets again. He actually got lucky this day and found the crack rock I had in my right front pocket. He wasn't the cop who searched that pocket originally, so I took the opportunity to ask him if his partner put that in there. "Was that so you guys could bust me?" He didn't like that question one bit I guess because he reached up and began to choke me. How very easy it is to provoke a response of violence from a cop. Where is the training these days to handle words or questions that may offend their delicate sensibilities? I had to laugh, but I turned my laughter into a look of just pure hatred into this man's weak-limp-wristed skinny pig's eyes and told him, "Typical cop move, to choke a man while cuffed, you're a pussy!" He faltered and swallowed nervously and let go of my neck. I wasn't combative, nor was I being disrespectful when I asked my question about his partner planting the drugs on me during their botched search. He lost control and broke his composure when he choked me. He knew he fucked up, and he also knew he was a scared little girl in a uniform, hidden behind a badge and a gun. So when he saw my look of total disgust toward him, he must have thought twice about possibly losing his bowels in front of his partner or possibly his job. If he was correct in saying I was observed and videotaped buying drugs, quite possibly his act of police brutality was caught on tape. Most likely not, but hey, I can have my wishes also, right? I sure as hell didn't have any rights as an American citizen when I'm in the company of these yahoos. Either way I was caught with alleged possession of drugs and placed under arrest. I guess being abruptly startled and then handcuffed wasn't the official arrest. He had to say you're under arrest after the fact. I don't recall hearing my Miranda rights either; I guess those weren't available to me during this process.

As I was sitting there completely disgusted, another unmarked police car pulled up and I was placed into the backseat. My truck was locked by the two arresting officers and my keys were given back to me. My truck would just have to sit there unprotected for however long I would be detained. If any scumbag happened across my unattended truck, they could smash my windows, slash my tires, spray paint it, piss on it, steal it, or whatever else they wanted to do without anyone even caring one bit in this neighborhood. While sitting in this cruiser, I was thinking to myself what a damn shame. I had once again shamed myself and everyone who had stuck by me during my commitment to stay clean. Self-pity would creep in very hard at times, and this was one of them times. I blocked the guilt out of my head and focused on our drive. We weren't heading to any station at all. I was driven behind the mills at the very bottom of Sawyer Street. This was a surprise to me actually. I was sure they were just around the corner waiting with their sticks and Mace again, but that didn't happen this time. Instead of the police beat-down, I was shuffled into a waiting paddy wagon equipped with my own metal seat and cage for my comfort. Once inside, I was greeted by another stray dog of the streets that had been collected up by the human dog catcher. I didn't know his name, but he was someone I had gotten high with in the past so we had us a little chuckle about getting caught up. We both were sad souls, but when you have fallen this far in life, your only option is to laugh or cry. We chose to laugh and enjoy ourselves. The truth is I was so bored with my life of just sitting around for days and weeks and months that this was a welcomed field trip to me. Maybe that's why I was surprisingly upbeat once my reality check came and passed. All of this was just part of the ride within our city's finest grand tour. The travel guides at the beginning of this shitty tour weren't very nice, but what the hell, it's still better than what I was doing.

I had begun to lose my taste for this field trip when hours ticked away just sitting handcuffed on a cold steel bench. Every so often the doors would open and new people would be let in. The police were running a sting operation in the area I was scooped up at. I learned from the new arrivals that the police were actually inside the house selling the drugs and then arresting you on the way out. Sounds a bit like entrapment, but hey, I guess cleaning up the city was a good thing. Maybe it was all prearranged for all of us to realize there is more to life than to get high. I'm sure that wasn't why I was arrested, but for some, it might just be. I still believe the police department holds a sour, biased opinion toward me because of the record they see in front of them when they identify me in a known drug area. Truly that is exactly the reason why they come strong and fast and on the surprise kick with a whole lot of attitude during my apprehension. When you have any sort of assault on police officers on your record, they certainly don't fuck around, who can blame them really. I guess I could say for myself it was a bullshit charge that was attached to my record a long time ago that remains the first red flag waving above my head. I could also understand both sides of the argument, whatever though, all I knew was I was back around the shitbags within this paddy wagon and the phony tough guy pigs, and I wasn't too pleased. I had remained clean for almost a full year, only slipping or relapsing three times, which was very good considering how much of a junkie I had become the prior year after my dirt bike crash. I had also restrained myself when provoked during my initial arrest—that all looks good in the eyes of the judge and jury. I really think I was arrested because it was just my time to be taken in. None of the other stuff mattered at all.

My frustrations grew bigger after three hours ticked by. The police had a good morning I guess because eight of us were crammed into this paddy wagon. Including a female dog, an ugly bitch in the kennels, but she was funny when she talked trash through her four-toothed mouth. I had lost all my patience when they tossed in our ninth dog for this morning's roundup. This guy was young, loudmouthed, and a complete jackass in my eyes. He got in, and when the cops closed the doors behind him, he started running his mouth loudly about how Billy bad ass he was. Tough talk never impresses me when spoken like a defense. He started whining he had swallowed his stuff and was nervous because it might break open in his guts and fuck him up. I could tell he was young and scared, he must've been new on the block also. Any self-respecting street dealer in this city wouldn't have his whole stash in his possession but very close by him. He made it sound like he swallowed his whole stash. The person next to him was certainly not amused when this kid asked him to put his finger up his throat as far as he could while sitting sideways and cuffed. This kid put his mouth over this guy's finger to gag himself so he could puke up his rocks. I was not at all amused with the smell once he began vomiting on the floor. He shuffled through the puke with his feet looking for baggies. He had found one so far, and he said there was more. So in went this guy's finger again and this kid gagged and gagged and drooled all over this poor guy's hand before he vomited again. This time one more bag was found, and the kid said, "Okay, that's all of them." I had to laugh, so I began cracking up at this fucking kid. Everyone else knew he was being a pussy about two tiny little rocks. I told him he should just shut up and sit there and hope one of us didn't kick his ass for stinking up the place. He sort of looked away ashamed of his behavior and just went limp. His loudmouth, cocky attitude was gone, and he was just a heap of useless pussy juice attached to some skin and bones. I didn't feel bad one bit for calling him out on his actions during a panic. I also had to tell him a few rocks are a joke; mostly everyone in the paddy wagon agreed. We were some hardcore drug users by this time of our lives, and a few rocks are just twenty minutes' worth, and they definitely weren't going to kill you if you swallowed them. You might get high, you might shit yourself, or you might enjoy knowing you're high while you're locked in a cage. What he didn't need to do was panic and show that yellow streak running up his back for all to see prior to being locked up. What a dumbass!

This wasn't my concern at all, but it was pretty disgusting just sitting and waiting for countless hours with the smell of fresh vomit wafting into my nostrils. These police had never cared one bit about the comfort of an arrested individual in the past, and this was a normal expectation. If I expected anything more than nothing, I would definitely be disappointed. Finally after they decided enough people were in the paddy wagon, we headed to the new west-end station to be booked. It wasn't new, but it was the newer one built after they tore down the downtown station. I was arrested at ten in the morning, and I was finally booked in around six o'clock or so. That was by far the longest stay in a paddy wagon I ever had. The idea behind that was to definitely fuck with us for being lowlife crack smokers, nothing more. Perhaps it was a tactic used to let us Jones in a confined stinking space to lessen our cravings and to be sure we weren't in a drug-induced psychosis that makes some people violent. Whichever their plan was, it definitely sucked ass and it pissed me off.

We were escorted in through the back of the station under darkness within the sky above our heads. The only thing worth taking notice of was how bright the light was around you. It seemed bright because our light perception was off from the dark caged-in paddy wagon from hell ride. My eyes adjusted quickly as they were leading us inside. I started noticing nice dark areas within the distance of makeable odds, if you decided to bolt to freedom. All I need to do was pick the handcuff keys, which was definitely not going to happen without that shitty key the pig, a.k.a. policeman, had on his key chain. So if you're smart, you'd purchase one of those things ahead of time. Possibly get one cheap on eBay or Craiglist. Maybe you can feel lucky punk; I'm not James Bond tonight—goes ahead, picks lock, runs for the darkness feeling brave and confident in your decision making process, shots multiple times in the back by not one but two officers? That wasn't an option for me at this particular moment in time, but hey, it's cool to daydream about worse-case scenarios prior to some suicidal attempt at freedom over a twenty rock of crack allegedly on my person.

Nope, I shuffled into the backdoor just like everyone else, attached on our human string line, securing us together with the silver bracelets. These pieces of jewelry are never on sale, you got to earn them I guess. We kept stopping and going along the way kind of like an inchworm. All this stop and go was caused by a couple of the heroin junkies who are coming down from their high, so they were semi-being dragged along in and out of their nods! Who knows, maybe they consumed their dope on the ride. Nothing would surprise me. Once inside, we were unshackled one at a time and given a new spot to sit and suffer.

I found myself shackled to the steel bench I was sitting on to another anchor point at the back of it. Actually it was two sets of handcuffs: one set used on my left arm linked to the other set which attached to the bench. High-tech equipment put into place to keep your ass stuck without much room to reach out and grab someone possibly walking by. As I'm thinking this wonderful thought of bashing a cop, the whole sting operation crew walked by us all giggling and smiling, talking trash to each other about us. I just laughed and pointed out the clown who grabbed my throat to one of the fellow shackled crack fiends next to me. I like to share my story of how they are fucked-up-scared police in a society of whack job crackheads, heroin junkies, combative drunks, killers, rapists, fight club members, all sorts of miserable bastards of the world who they get to process every night. Not my idea of a good time at all! But I'll always point out the ones who like to misuse force during an arrest and have it backfire into building him a reputation, make him feel proud, and someone along the line of assholes in the world will take heed and correct his behavior eventually. Maybe they will just dot his eyes up raccoon style from a couple of combos. Quiet possibly could do him some good before his use of force escalates and he mows down some kid while firing his weapon on some sociopath perp, and misses. The stray bullet finds its way through someone's home, the bullet rips through the walls and directly hits a six-year-old right in the head. Has happened in the movies, and I'm sure it's happened somewhere in America. So yes, I am a cop hater in that sense. But for me at this time in my life, I'm having a good time shackled, talking shit myself, I'm on vacation. So thanks for the tour.

I even throw out the ultimate rip to these guys, just to bust balls, "Who's the highway killer? Have you found that out yet? Or is that just a myth? It's possibly a corrupt cover-up, huh? I know why too, because it is one of your own, huh? What about that lawyer guy? Oh yeah, he's close to you guys too, my mistake. I will be sure to tune in to the six o'clock news to hear the breaking story. Honestly, were all your recourses necessary tonight to arrest a few drug users? Oh yeah, we commit crimes, sorry!" This always gets them in a tussle. Their panties get ruffled even! One of them asked, "Who's this guy?" pointing at me. The cop at the booking desk said my name, and then I heard another one say, "Oh! He's connected!" I was now a mob guy according to them, or I was part of some underground illegal drug operation, perhaps I'm a mob hit man. Leaping frog testicles, Batman! These guys were definitely drinking way too much of their own city's water again. Someone should test it then test them for hallucinogenic properties within their hair follicles.

I was brought over to the desk first in line, that's always a plus, sets the tone for how it's going to look for the rest of these guys.

My next question was, "What gang do you run with?"

My reply as always was, "The only gang I've ever been a part of is the United States Marine Corps. But you wouldn't call a soldier a gang member, perhaps you could write down *veteran* in that square, Officer?"

"You got a lot of tattoos, we need photos."

"You have those on file, I say, from the last time I graced your doorsteps, sir."

The cop at the desk laughed and kept asking the questions. I gave my name, rank, serial number, address, and phone number. Not sure if my phone would ring, but I'm sure they got a laugh out of my conversations when they illegally tapped into it from time to time. Oh well, it's the information age anyways. If you want to listen to my rants when I'm in them, feel free. Don't get too offended about what I'm saying, it's just an opinion. Maybe I'm just a gifted bullshit artist just like you. Who gives a crap? One good thing happened though, I was allowed to use the restroom unshackled after his questions were answered. I wasn't searched, possibly because they have their planted evidence from within my pocket. I was all set with these puss wads anyways. I gave them a bone, anyways. Philosophy moment, reader! Pay attention! It's better to be caught small! Than busted big! No need to do the big-time for more than personal use. Although a quarter-ounce rock is my use amount in a day when I have money to sustain such a habit. That amount can have you do a fine-amount time in the hoosegow according to the drug laws. How this sort of habit occurs, it happens when you stop paying for hobbies that are healthy and divert funds to strictly drug usage. My disability pension is no longer a blessing at all, it becomes a curse. No matter what, the money keeps coming every month regardless if you're using it for drugs. Only I wasn't using on a regular, this was only a slip in my sobriety. I was clean three months or longer prior till last night. In walked a ratty-dressed woman who approached me and recuffed my hands then led me back to the waiting bench of pain I started out in before I spoke to this clown.

Hey, hold the damn phone. It just dawned on me that the chick that was getting me the crack was part of their sting. "Shit on a shingle, Willis! She's a narco also." I began laughing to myself while thinking, *Shoot, this woman dressed the part pretty good there, shit flap.* Surprisingly enough I was duped! I'll give her that, the whole white trash wanted to be whore, get up and look convincing. Strange to think of you as a policewoman now! You had me fooled; maybe I should ask you for my hundred bucks back. Nope, you keep that, consider it a tip, sweetie. You looked nice to me. But I was not a whore master anymore; all their uses to me now were to hang out with them just to get high with, a drug-using partner. No sex needed when I'm using drugs anyways, my sexual interest disappears. Not meaning, that's all a street-walking prostitute is trusted in doing with me, but most of them I know or have met me along my travels within your fine city. I also could call them friends, could you say the same, Miss Devious Officer? Your life has become so phony you began lashing out as a child toward the bully in the schoolyard. Now it showed up in your job. Thanks for the taking back of your school change from my pocket and not your nemesis's. You harbor so much hate that it's followed into your private life at home. I bet you like to beat your man, huh? The whole bondage thing has given me wood already, just thinking about it. I promise not to say anything about those huge moles on your neck and chest with the black hairs poking out. As you unleash them butch, lesbian-wrapped, flap jacks you call tits and they drop to your bellybutton before our very eyes. I won't laugh, I swear. God knows the smell alone coming from the harbor a mile away smells better than you do at the moment. Funny how that money wasn't in the police report, as it eventually will make its way to the prosecutor's hands. No worries, girl, I'll deal with that prick tomorrow morning. I'll let you worry about it if I will canary your little sleight of hand with my cash to the judge, for pocketing evidence in a case. That cash was proof of the drug transaction, I get it. It was an officer, so that's a frame-up, and not really evidence against me. It wasn't to line your pockets, was it? So how much money did you rattle lose out of all the drug users who crossed your unit's path today? I guess you guys needed more money for something. With all this knowledge of how shady this whole system is, you should be asked where my money is, right out here in public within my book. I wouldn't even begin to bother asking at this time among your friends and fellow corrupt boys in blue. I wouldn't get nothing but denial and possibly a stick bashing in the adjoining room on my way to your new play toy, the restraint chair. I can only imagine what goes on in there.

I only asked one question in reality though, "When's the bail bondsman coming?"

"He'll be at Ash Street jail. When we finish booking all of you guys and ladies, we will bring you there for further processing," she said.

Oh great, longer wait time before I can be away from you people. Your hospitality has been nothing but five-star services so far. I sat back in my original spot shackled to the bench once again. Time just seemed to drag on by as I looked to the left and right out of sheer boredom. I could care less if anyone says a word if I was looking in their general direction. I no longer worry about what the police were up to at all. It's time to associate with others in my presence in this shithole environment. I recognized the two junkies in our group and realized they were young kids out getting high in the streets in the area I was picked up near. I'm quite sure they were kids like I was and a few of my friends at the time, a couple dumbasses causing trouble because of our youthful rebellious years in life that just happened to start using drugs. Most definitely these kids need help also. I began to ask them, I was wondering how well they do, being Latino within this city once they're in courthouse. I know most of the Latinos around here seem not to understand English when it's time for questions and answers with the judge. They clam right up and pull the classic "No habla English," allowing someone else to explain what the asshole judge is saying to them. That sort of scenario is just funny to me the first time it is done. After about the third guy in the line, it's just something that makes your day in court longer. *You know what, fuck you, two clowns. You don't deserve my time just for that reason alone,* I thought to myself. But I included them on my thought as I said "what's up" to them. They laughed their asses off and called me crazy. I asked them, "Hey, I also always wanted to know what in the hell the interpreter rep says to this guy." Mostly in my head I make up the commentary. I finally drifted into it with my head crooked against the concrete wall with my sweatshirt as a pillow in my best Spanish interpretation:

"Well, look here, Julio Hernandez Garcia Ramone Quadlupei Cruz, what the judge is saying is that he has to take a hot wet shit this morning because he was drinking all last night and snorting long rails of coke off some strippers' ass then decided to get some late-night tacos from some other Latino related to you on this planet and wants to take it out on you because of his cooked rear end from the fire shits he's got. He also says your last bag sucked. It was mostly baby laxative, he knows because when he cooked it up, it came back small. Then he mumbled some legal shit at you, asked did you understand. Of course you didn't, everyone knows we speak a bunch of lies in here in English, so just say yes. He also wants to know what you plead!"

They both started laughing, nodding, saying "Si." They knew that the jokes was on us; no one had a fucking clue in the room because we were all too fucking lazy to learn Spanish in school and blame them for not speaking our motherfucking language when they crossed the border. Everyone has a dumb look on their face, even the prosecuting attorney up front on the left of the rule maker when you're facing the judge looks dumbfounded, even the judge looked like a bonehead dumbass.

The Spanish guy acted as though he was so freaked out with his reply back to the interpreter rep, "Eh no! Tell him I was out on my rounds digging through the trash cans minding my own business. Me poor man, I have four generations of people living in my house. I collect the cans to buy my beer because my wife doesn't allow me to drink in the house anymore. I accidently tripped over my son's low-rider bicycle with a bottle and stabbed my neighbor with the steak knife I was trying to open the bottle with. They said it was an accident and I was trying to celebrate being released from prison a few years back. My wife was pissed because the bottle smashed on the ground, total waste of fine tequila we smuggled across the border sixty years ago. I didn't even get to taste it. I took a shoe in the head for that move, and then she freaked on me and went all religious saying it was a sign from God. No drinking is allowed. So now my drinking has to be done on the down low. The whole neighbor stabbing was because he owed my fifteenth cousin Chi Chi money, so he really doesn't need to hear that, but the effect will be perfectly placed in this old prick judge's lap. Who is he to pass judgment on me anyways? Tell him I won't tell his wife if he won't tell mine, this is my last chance. She already caught me twice sleeping with my second cousin Maria. I don't want to have to be the guy who drops dime on him, we know the whores he paid for with us last night. As a matter of fact, that gringo owes me money from the last eight-ball he fronted last night. Remind him of that! The other girl he was all hot for and was banging in the ass was my second cousin's fifth wife! We shouldn't get him involved at all. So let's just call this even."

The interpreter told the judge in reply, "Yes, he understands his rights."

The interpreter couldn't say all this for us to hear in the crowd, so he carried the little secret to the side bar with the dumbass prosecuting attorney in tow in side bar. The judge looked nervous already, or so it seems, maybe it's because he was already feeling the ass mud leak into his pants from them fucking tacos and clears his throat aggressively.

The judge replied back, "Second call."

Now during second call the prosecutor sticks his pointy-nosed ass into the whole bartering system in the front lobby of the courtroom.

"Mr. Cruz, you still owed fifty-eight dollars on your probation agreements, because when you pleaded no contest in this so-called accidental murder beef, the judge went light on you and called it manslaughter. That's not just an accident, you was paroled early on your two-to-five stretch and was supposed to pay restitution to the victim witness protection program for the next ten years during probation plus we are adding another thousand bucks just 'cause we can."

He added on another hundred bucks, making it $1158 total and threatened to sentence him for five years' conspiracy to violate drug laws, because they found cocaine on his person. *Mr. Cruz is fucked now,* I thought to myself. He was left stunned by this whole situation, and the look on his face was classic, he deserved an award for how cool he was under the pressure to look scared at a moment's notice.

They returned from second call, and the judge entered his high-backed chair filled with the new knowledge of his adversary's wishes and just blatantly gave the quick nod to the bailiff. As the bailiff is heading over to Mr. Cruz, the interpreter quickly converted the conversation.

"Take Mr. Cruz into custody please, he has other warrants for public intoxication, bribery, assault, and some other stuff that we will fabricate as we go. He's in default, unless he can come up with $1158 to pay his fines off and bail for his new crimes. We will hold him on bail, until then, we need time to build our case against you because quite frankly, no one will believe otherwise Mr. Cruz. Oh, and by the way, sir, I call the shots here."

I just happened to understand their game of cat and mouse in my head, I told these two junkies as I sat on my bench shackled down with a cuff digging into my wrist remembering and using my mind to unlock the physical world around me to keep me from going insane from being locked down. Anything is better than here. I slipped back into the story as I shifted my weight on the cold bench.

"I can't believe that pincha judge," Mr. Cruz did ghetto sign language with his hommies behind him to make sure his car gets flats outside the courtroom today and every window gets smashed.

I remember seeing Mr. Cruz at the donut shop just the next afternoon after the judge got wind of his car. He told me the prosecutor wet his leg when three psycho-looking Spanish guys met him on the stairs and threatened to machete murder his whole fucking family if he wasn't set free today with no fines. We got a good laugh over a few donuts and a coffee together.

These two junkie kids were in stitches along with a few other cops who were in earshot of what I was saying. So I just laid it on thick to these kids. I began talking, staring straight into their eyes and into their souls in a soft, barely audible, creepy voice.

"As a matter of fact he says he sent me here to find you two fuck ups and tell you he's not going to allow your family or anyone to pay your fucking bails."

They both were shocked because they actually believed my bullshit. I told them, "It is going to be all right now because these cops have a way with dealing with punks like you once they get a hold of you and have permission from good old Uncle Cruz to fuck you up. Oh yeah, I heard all about it right before they arrested your ass. I heard them on the paddy wagon radio joking about it. I also know because I'm here to make sure it happens." Now these two kids were really bugging out thinking holy shit, asking me, "How do you know my Uncle Julio?"

Now I knew I had the both of them hooked in good. New fish are easy to catch. I had no clue that their family held a Mr. Cruz or not, I made that shit up, but I wasn't telling these idiots. I got lucky with that dangling piece of bait and landed a ten-pound bass with Julio as the winner.

"He used to be my dealer back in the day, now I'm playing messenger boy for him out of the kindness of my heart, and the fact I was you when I was younger. You see, I robbed your uncle at gunpoint for cocaine when he was a street dealer. I have paid my debt back years ago on that issue when I got clean many years later and realized the error of my ways and honestly gave him his money back. He told me thanks and wished me a long happy life. He also knew I was an honest buyer of drugs in the past with him. He never pursued me to collect because he knew it was the crack Jones that made me steal from him. He didn't want the money back, but I was compelled to give back anyways. He had done me a favor back then, so I owed him one, and now he called me for my help and a favor after all these years. A few days ago he called me about the both of you and if I would deliver the message clearly. Smarten up I say, pointing at my chest or feel my wrath. The beating you get later this week is from your uncle, not me. You definitely don't want mine. This is your chance to start a new life, use it to your advantage, don't come out till you're cleaned up."

I turned my head away and didn't answer another question that these kids had asked me for the remainder of our stay on the steel bench. I held my tongue even when they called me a crazy crackheaded white boy. That's all they needed to hear from me. Someone along the way will test these two fools and beat them up within their first week in the gray bar hotel. I'm sure my story was bullshit in my own head because I changed the name of the real guy I actually made amends with but added in the rest about them being related. In their minds, it's definitely true for the moment. Perhaps I would allow them this small gift of fear, let them sweat it out on their way to prison tonight. It would be a long time before they got to use the phone to verify what I made up anyways. Besides they surely won't ask their uncle about me. Even if they do ask, they'll say yep, that dude's totally loco because I'm sure I know someone in your family from this area. Old people seem to know when someone is trying to help their fucked-up relatives when they get hooked on drugs. They will back me up on it for sure, because to them, I am the chupacarbra!

Who knows, maybe it was a wasted story, but by the slim chance it helps them out, it was well worth it. Maybe these kids will get clean after my little speech. What they will never know for sure in their heads is if I'm telling them the truth. It's always fun to mess with the new young fish, even if it's only in a shitty police station chained to a bench. It helps to pass the time. Getting into someone's head is easy. Making the message land firmly planted within their tweaked drug-induced memory banks takes a special skill. It may take years for them to hear me again in their minds, but they will remember when they finally reach the bottom. I was there to help. Maybe I should've taken the time to actually do all this. Instead I woke up with a sore neck from the wall. I dream very vividly these days.

After what should've taken an hour ended up being four hours later. We were finally shipped to Ash Street Jail. We were once again up on our feet aligned in a row shackled from wrist to wrist again making our way out the door into the awaiting sheriff's office van. We had upgraded from the previous paddy wagon I guess. They unhooked every third guy, and we found our available seat, with the back row being filled first. I was first on my three-guy string, so I got a window seat. That was a treat actually. I could take in some scenery on our trip, I thought as we pulled out of the brightly lit area and on to the street. We blew through the Route 6 red lights with the flashers on and a burp from the siren. We took a left and headed toward Ash Street Jail. I recognized the whole neighborhood as memories from my past crept in. I savored them and just went for the ride. I had been to this place before visiting my older brother and have graced the lockup here on one occasion prior to this one for a drunken disorderly, or a disturbing the peace. Maybe it was an assault charge, nope, it was possession. Quite possibly, it could've been all of them charges together, but who gives two shits?

I had a few weeks to wait for trial on a case without any bail money in here before. I remember I was too embarrassed to call anyone at that time for help and to pay my bail, so I suffered this cockroach-infested shit hole. I deserved to be punished mostly because I knew better and got high anyways back then, just like this time. Only this time I have bail. I would be leaving when that crusty old bastard, bails bondman, showed up. I'm not in any mood to try and punish myself for getting high like I did on that occasion to see if I could break the pattern of destructive behavior. Unless perhaps they let me stay in Lizzy Borden's cell tonight just for shits and grins. But I was sure that's not going to happen, so I was getting the fuck out of here as soon as possible. It's always better to go home and shower before court anyways. Way better than being brought up on the chain gang, bright and early in the morning looking all stumble bums and cuffed. That always looks like you're guilty before the show even begins. Yes, court to me is a show; it's all actors in a play in my mind. Guilt or innocence means nothing anyways; it's all about who puts on a better performance or it means you're willing to pay for your freedom because—guess what?—the court system loves to collect your money, when you're fucking up in life, it's called asshole tax. No, you didn't pass go! You're not collecting two hundred bucks! You owe us, motherfucker! Maybe when we deplete you of all your walking-around money, you might learn a lesson. I know I learned the hard way too. It's nothing new on the walk of courthouse shame. It's an ugly place. "Fuck you, pay me!" This is a classic judge line if he or she had the grit, the sand, the balls, or maybe even the total asshole personality trait required for their position of honor to mutter these words aloud.

So I was heading toward the cells, and the officers segregated us by race right away. I guess that helps to keep things to a dull roar. Who knows what's up within the group of people being held already and those of us coming in? Lots of gangs around the world, don't let shit fool you if you happen to be uneducated and on your way inside. I stay out of that whole fucking mess. I have resisted joining any of that gang shit. I'm only responsible for myself and those who I hold dear to my heart. I guess that includes more than 98 percent of the people who walk this earth. Not that I'm going to be the one who keeps you in check. I will let you police up yourself or give you the tools to start with. Someone else gave me the skinny long ago. I am inspired by you all. Watching someone transform their lives is amazing to witness. The other 2 percent consist of (a) family and friends, (b) the people to the left and right of me. I hold no loyalties to anyone anymore, nor will I answer for anyone other than myself. My life belongs to me. But I will fight by anyone's side to save their life. Maybe it's the Marine in me, the Christian I am within my own head, the protector, and the guard dog. I guess I'm a stand for others no matter their plight. I believe all can be taught to obey and follow some sort of civil structure within their existence with other human beings or maybe that is what I strive to do in life.

Knowing that simple fact of life about myself allows me to not show any fear whatsoever when I enter a shithole place like this. My battles are fought in my own head just to stay upright on my wheels; my feet, my sticks, my bum knees, and my skinny, AIDS-infected, lowlife, crackhead, drunken ass. I really don't have time to get involved. My own struggle consumes me. I am just trying to get back on my bike so I can go riding. I can only offer advice on how to not catch what I caught back in the day if you're on the attack coming after me to take me out.

Unless it's on the sneak, you won't get me, because you're a pussy who needs a knife to stab me in the back or slit my throat while I'm asleep. All I can say is good luck. Make it quick. Be aware if you fuck it up and I'm able to get lucky and survive, you will most certainly die when I see you again. Or someone who holds me dear will visit you because I happened to have made him laugh or made him feel free by telling him a kick-ass, in-your-face, God-given-right-to-do-so story to lift his spirits one day when he needed a friend. Maybe I knew enough to listen to them talk for a day and offered them a sympathetic shoulder to cry out their problems. I actually do care about what they have to gripe about. Sometimes I don't need to say a thing, just wave hello. A few of those people just might like to kill for fun. They will definitely make it painful. I can almost guess who it might be who gets you. I have an imagination. I would paint the picture very grim for you to consider prior to your piss-weak action. I would hope they cut your fingers off first and work their way upward in chunks no bigger than a swordfish filet size, keeping you quiet in your cell because your tongue was cut out and all your teeth removed with a set of pliers borrowed from the maintenance shed. The guard conveniently walks away from any vantage point because he wants you dead too because you're a coward. He doesn't want to be a rat either in this place, so he understands the need to walk away when justice is served cold. Perhaps you underestimated yourself and tried to install a fear-me attitude toward me and others within your immediate area. My fear is only for your safety. Like I said, I have an imagination.

I would much rather we do it this way instead; I'm no easy win first and foremost, but this is what I would consider first before a life is taken or possibly both our lives. I say we go bare hands, kid, out back or in the yard. I prefer the sandbox pit I was trained in during boot camp. A three-foot-deep hole five feet by five feet square with a screen surrounding the upper half to hold us inside till the business is finished. Let them place bets. Give them prisoners something to feel excited about. Announce your intent, call me out, and pick me. I promise I will yell as if I was ten again wanting to play on the weaker team by far and still find the power to rally myself to a victory. But the reality is I would much rather talk to you and possibly hear something worthwhile about your travels, which may enlighten me. But if pressed, I am willing.

I do love reading or seeing a story about some lifer who trains every day and wins some interprison championship. I see both sides of an argument before I commit myself to warfare. Truly you can dig that. I might possibly swing this idea by the warden's office so we can embark on the fair fight journey together. Whoever wins doesn't matter, but you will hold your honor intact. Once the victor is declared, that's one cat that is all right in my book. He holds respect just by his determination and discipline to remain outside the troubles and focus on a freedom planted within him. I guess I would help him train or train with him to ensure he wins the much-sought-after Massachusetts finals against another prison somewhere else in Massachusetts. That really doesn't happen in this fucking place at all, but one can dream, right? I love to throw hands. Careful of my blood though, because when I bleed, I like to cause some of yours to spill out also. According to the doctors, my shitty venomous blood may mix into your open wound and may kill you if you don't have a solid mind.

I just hope at the start you don't knock me out cold. I have been hit far too many times in the head by shit much harder than somebody's fist and stayed awake, but feel free and try. My chin has been checked plenty. In fact, when I was sixteen, someone I consider a friend today—God rest his soul, another drug-addicted person of the earth who overdosed before he had a chance to fix his wrongs and get clean—broke my jaw with one hit. Granted I jumped up to punch him in the face first and split his lip with a quick right hook. He got his wound, I got mine. My jaw broke because he was twenty-eight at the time standing six feet tall, double my height and weight, and he threw a heavy fist. I wasn't letting him off for stealing my pot plant and my stereo while I was out on a trip scallop fishing for two days. No fucking way. If it were today, I would most certainly be able to cause more damage than a child's spaghetti arm, which I possessed as a pubescent youth fresh in the world, which had been indestructible at that time. In my head I said fuck it. He deserves a punch in the mouth for that shit-bag junkie desperation. That was the excuse I heard. We were in the Jones, man. No apology. No nothing. One of my brothers took part with him. I remember I asked who else was involved, and without hesitation, I marched right up to this oversized, mismatched to my weight class by far idiot's ass and yelled out, "You stole my shit." He warned me not to swing, but fuck the consequences, I did anyways. Then I watched as my brother ran the other way prior to the bone-breaking downward smash to my face as he grasped my long hair at the time for more leverage. I only took one hit; he knew he smashed me good. I had seen the white flash and staggered back from the impact of the blow. Some of my hair was in his other hand because it had torn out at the roots as my head jerked out of his grasp. I was staggering a bit, but I was still upright. I looked him dead in the eye and called him a pussy; I turned away and we left it as it was. It was a punch to the mouth for a punch to the mouth. We happened to be sort of friends. I drew blood, he broke my jaw. No words spoken, no jive talk, and no winner or loser, just a message learned on both sides.

I'm fearless in his eyes at that moment, and he also knows I learned not to care about pain when I'm wronged. He will second-guess treating me like a punk and strong arming my stuff again. Hence, he will be getting hit again. I guess I earned his respect or something because he only hit me once but never took another thing from me ever. Truthfully I earned nothing, and didn't get my stuff back either, but I did learn a few things. I learned not to fall and to never trust a junkie with anything valuable of mine in their possession when they are using ever again. I didn't know my jaw was broken till the next morning until when I tried to open my mouth and it didn't open. Learning that little fact was no prize, but it was also something learned. It did require my mouth to be wired shut for six weeks and a molar removed because that broke in half also. But that's a whole different kind of pain you might not be accustomed to, believe me, it sucks. That fucker hit hard I guess back then. I'm pretty sure people said, "Thank God Gary shut the fuck up during that time," but it's all good. Years later before he passed away, I called him out for round 2 in a disagreement, and he declined my request. He told me to fuck that shit. He thought I was crazy then as a kid; now that I'm an adult, he wanted no part of it. So take a look at friendship first, okay? Let's not fight again. You're a stand-up dude. He also said I would most certainly kick his ass. He didn't want the beating. I respectively left it alone. We actually got a good laugh at some of our shenanigans we had done together prior to that fun-filled day of punches. To tell you the truth, he was all right, he had my back if asked to do so and vice versa. I had heard him say to me and others he respected my stand for living loud about having HIV. His younger brother had given up on himself and overdosed years ago. People knew and the word got out he had the ninja, and sometimes back in the early years, people decided to check out instead of living it. I can honestly in my heart say I miss them both now that they are gone. I can still hear their laughter and see them both young thugs when I was just a pup. Always quick to break balls and make you laugh. They died, my friends, even though we only hung out for several of my rebellious years.

With that knowledge already infused into my being as a kid, I recommend we box. I can only hope we become friends afterward because fighting is a part of existence within these walls. I don't want you to be dead. I enjoy the company. It will build sportsmanship among the fighters. Who knows maybe if you win the title, they might consider a work release program for you and get you the fuck out of this fucking place? All I can do is just live my life, allowing you to be you and me to be me. In any environment, learn the system, change the rules, but follow simple guidelines. Don't fuck with me, and there will be no problems. I don't need the hassle. That is exactly the sort of thing I carry around in front of me on my way to my cell. I wear my honor badge well and demand it of others. Maybe people are a bit intimidated by that way of thinking, but fuck them too. I'm at the bottom anyways. I shuffle along looking ahead at the cell I'm due to be put into. I notice a good-sized white kid in there, he's got a few tattoos and looks like he's in good shape, might even have some scrap. That was how I sized him up and rated him on my level of threat meter. I was wrong in giving him level 6 on a 1-10 scale. This guy begins to yell for the other officer to be removed prior to them even opening his cell doors to let me in. I had to laugh at the scene he was causing over his fear of me I guess. I wasn't threatening him or anything. Shit! I just got here! This guy doesn't even know me, and he's running scared. That is definitely a pussy in my mind now. He doesn't even rate on my scale anymore. Who knows maybe he knew me and got spooked because of my disease? It's sort of funny how that happens to people who know confined spaces are dangerous. It's like falling asleep, well, in my case, passing out in an elevator in a real tall hotel. Waking up after God knows how long and having to find your room. At least someone was nice enough to toss you in a cab and deposit you in the hotel lobby's elevator that you're staying in. Well, maybe that wasn't such a great example of fear. But I'm sure there are plenty of people who hate elevators with an extreme passion. My sort-of-twisted mind would place me in a buried casket with no air to breathe rapidly approaching. Waking to the sounds of a wild animal in the box with me, panic takes hold a bit quicker when you compare the two scenarios. This guy most certainly has seen a wild animal when he looked at me. I guess I couldn't blame him for being freaked out. I sometimes put off a bad vibe when angered by the system for interrupting me getting high.

Wouldn't you fucking know it? Just before they swing my empty cell's door shut, I think about getting high. Even after all that time and bullshitting around from being cuffed at 10:00 AM and all the way up to this moment in time. The power of crack never stops to amaze me. I step inside and hang my head as I close my eyes. I step backward and push my hands up toward the tray. I'm uncuffed now and step forward away from the door; they didn't take my boots, which was a plus. I open my eyes and soak in my confined space. Not much has changed down here in holding. Same blood on the walls painted over. Names scratched in the wall, also painted over, but it still remains because it's gouged into the concrete beneath. A metal bench totally enclosed at the bottom. It was a steel box actually. Wasn't very long either, it was only enough room to lay in the fetal position, no blanket provided or pillow. This wasn't the Ritz Carlton. This was jail. *I so hate this fucking place*, I thought while staring at the wall with my back turned to the cell door. I was at the entrance to this crusty place and almost within its grasp if not for my restraint during my arrest. No extra charges, just an alleged possession charge. I was glad to know that in advance of seeing the arrest report. This charge was a bailable offense, I had no outstanding warrants, nor were they looking for me in any unsolved crimes which they happened to have at the ready if anyone resists, including me.

Cops love to add charges and question you about other shit. Believe me when I say, "Just go with the flow, it's much easier." Tell them about the time you were riding your tricycle when you were a dumbass kid and a car hit you but you survived. It was a cop who saved you. Cops love to hear heart-wrenching stories about heroism and how one of their fellow boys in blue saved the day. Don't you know they are other humans just doing their job? They like to be super cock, I mean super cop, and they all have Superman costumes at home. Loosen up the attitude in here. Lighten the fuck up, everybody. Laughter is much better medicine. That's always a surefire way to move things along. Be aware though, each and every word you say can and will be used against you in the court of law. I totally believe that happens in any conversation in any building or structure these days. Our whole society has gone soft, we have bowed our heads and said, "Let the man's will be done." I did that today, and that's why they called me next to be booked in. Tapped cell phones, tracking devices, listening devices, odd vehicles parked in observation areas, traffic cameras, video surveillance, undercover sting operations, unmanned drones floating around above people looking for targets to unleash their deadly arsenal for those who resist. My word, is all this shit necessary?

Sometimes it's best to drift away into your own mind because the outside world has passed all sense of order. I relax myself within my new environment and await my turn to be processed. As I'm waiting, two new guys are placed in my cell. I just respectfully asked these guys if they didn't mind sitting on the floor due to my back issues because of my accident. They agreed with no problems at all. I listened to their story of being arrested and how one of the police officers drew his gun during their apprehension and actually fired a round into the ground accidently. I told them to make sure they mention that little mishap to their lawyer because that was a gross misuse of force on two unarmed citizens. Their lawyer would definitely find a way to discredit any and all words this policeman had to say about what went on. Obviously he was in a panic and not thinking clearly once the apprehension process began. How could he possibly be taken seriously within a courtroom? I left them with a reasonable doubt in their own minds about the whole ordeal, which was a good thing to have within a jury trial. So I offered them a gift of freedom in payment of my comfortable steel bench.

Time clicked by very slowly waiting on the bail bondsman to arrive. I always find a way to entertain myself no matter where I end up. Whether it is in a small confined space like this one or is it out in the jungle during Marine Corps survival training in Japan, I will always occupy my thoughts with anything to remain from boredom. Boredom in and of itself is a slow death. When I was a kid locked up in Plymouth house of correction, I entertained myself with a cockroach which happened to scurry into my cell. I tapped two pencils on the concrete floor to make it run back and forth for several hours before letting it run off. My philosophy at the time was maybe he wouldn't return this way again. This kept me entertained during a moment of sheer boredom back then, and now was the time to begin some sort of drama before my mind snaps and I end up a dribbling drooling zombie. So without any hesitation, I yelled for the guard. He came over, and I began asking him some questions about what time am I getting out of here, when is this bail guy showing up, I need to take my medicine, that sort of bothersome banter. While I'm asking him these questions, a fat black guy is yelling from his cell louder than need be over my voice to get this guard's attention. I found this to be very rude and insulting. I excused myself from the conversation with the guard and turned toward this rude fat-ass mother and just screamed at him, "Hey, shut the fuck up or when I get out of this cell close enough to you, I'm going to smash your fucking teeth down your throat, you fat motherfucker." He stopped yelling at his cell door and retreated back to his spot on his bench without one word back to me. He knew me and I knew him, I wasn't a guy to mess with nor was he, but the simple fact remained, he was out of line and knew it. This was a definite display of respect, and he would certainly be getting his teeth smashed if my bail doesn't go through on principle alone. This was a moment he definitely knew when to withdraw. In prison, rules change—you're no longer a human being, you're an animal, and respect is greatly guarded. People lose their lives over disrespect in here. I was glad he withdrew actually. If he didn't, I would have to walk up to him in a public place, like the yard or the chow hall, and just kept punching him till he stopped breathing or the guards intervened. If not done this way, I would be labeled a bitch, and that's not a good thing at all. Everyone shits on you when you lower yourself to that level. I turned back to the guard and apologized for the interruption and my language. He told me to hang tight because they were going to start pulling people out to process very shortly. "The bail bondsman is here, it should be less than forty-five minutes and you'll be out of here if you have the bail money." I thanked him and lay back down on my cold bench feeling a bit more relaxed from that initial I-need-to-get-out-of-this-place-already feelings. Sometimes my anxiety caused by boredom will get me into trouble, but this time I just told someone off instead of just punching him in the face and causing a shit storm. I've done this plenty of times just to feel alive in the past.

I waited and watched as they called the first person to process, wouldn't you know it, and the fat black guy got called first. He strolled by all jive walking and said to everyone, "That's right, motherfuckers, I'm out of this place first. You all can kiss my fat black ass." He was looking in my direction, and he winked after he was done spewing out his line of bullshit. I looked at him all smiling and happy with that shit-eating smirk on his face and just nodded back at him with the look of "fuck you." I think I even laughed at the whole irony of it all. The stare down at dawn right before the gunfight at O.K. Corral is exactly how it seemed. He didn't disrespect me by directly screaming his joy and putting it in my face that he was getting out first, but he did make it clear to the rest of them they were all suckers. It was just him trying to save face for being put in his place. I understood this and brushed it off. About ten minutes went by and he was escorted back to his cell. I had to be a bastard and just started laughing at him for all that carrying on. He was totally bummed, and it showed when he sat back down. All his joy and smiling were ripped from him. He was a child who just dropped his ice cream in a pile of dog shit.

No freedom for you and no gloating allowed. The guard passed in front of my cell and gave me a shit-eating grin. I guess he didn't appreciate this fat asses interruption either. It was classic. Wish you were there to witness this firsthand the way I got to.

I was called several guys later and cuffed up then escorted into the processing room. My fingerprints were taken along with my picture holding the black sign. You know the one, it's always in the movies, or on some gossip channel when some celebrity does something stupid to boost their image. I was able to bail out for twenty five dollars and be on my way. The guard escorted me back through the holding cell area, and I made it a point to stop at this black fat bastard's cell. I told him I apologized for screaming at him and calling him a fat motherfucker. I also explained to him that he was out of line. I also told him, "Look, we are in this shithole together and we both want out, we are both bored. So next time, just go with the flow and keep his trap shut." I also asked him if he was going to get out anytime soon because I needed a ride to my truck. We could share a cab or something because I know where he lived. I said this in a way like I may show up and get him, but with humor attached. He laughed and said he was sorry about that; the boredom had gotten to him too. He wasn't going to make bail tonight, but he wished me well. It was, "Go easy, white boy, you're all right." We had entered this place enemy, by environment, but parted as friends once again on my departure. I knew he was glad to see me go because he asked me to say "what's up" to a mutual friend of ours. It was crazy how this all unfolded, but sometimes you just got to be human with another person. Take this as a message, young one, never underestimate the power of forgiveness.

I headed out the door and was on the sidewalk once again. I was free of the clutches of this shitty place, and it felt good to be free. I took a moment and took several breaths of the clean free air; it just tasted so much better outside than on the inside. I was a bit disoriented when I looked around because they had me exit on the side of the building, and it took a few moments to orient myself to my surroundings. I was facing the familiar United Front housing projects, so it meant I needed to go left to get to the closest phone. There was a phone at the front entrance to this place if I'm not mistaken I think as I turned to head that direction. I walked pretty quickly due to the euphoric energy I had gotten when I realized I was free. I reached the phone and dialed up the number to the only cab company I knew off the top of my head. I had remembered it because I used it plenty when I lost my license for eight years. It's kind of tough to forget those days of beating my feet due to my stupidity. I knew all the taxi drivers by name back then. I even knew who the undercover police were when they drove the taxis in our fine city off and on back in the day. I sat down right on Ash Street Jail's front steps and just waited for my ride away from this horror house. The night wasn't over yet, but it was getting close to dawn. I could smell it and hear it in the air actually. The smell was very subtle like sweet tea but very heavy. The sounds of several early rising birds had already begun their morning songs. It was very peaceful actually.

My cab arrived and brought me back to my truck before the sun poked its head up and said hello. I am not sure what triggered me to do this, but once the cab pulled away and was out of my sight, I walked past my truck and continued on to a known crack house. You could call this pure defiance, stupidity, being a straight junky, or you could just call it crazy. For me it had gotten into my head within that jailhouse holding cell and never left me. Yes, I had lost control of my senses so to speak. The draw to get high was still alive and very hungry; my eight-hundred-pound gorilla screamed "feed me." So without hesitation I was within the sweet vapors of cocaine smoldering within my glass pipe once again. I smoked it until 8:00 AM and then left for court. I was totally high as hell when I went through the court process. Waiting for my name to be called was the worst; I was sweating like crazy and fully paranoid. I could tell people were staring at me, all twitching and shaking looking all freaked out and dangerous. If they were people who knew me, they kept their distance; if they didn't know me, they were afraid to approach. My name was called, and I was sent home with a further date, my pretrial was set and a public defender would be appointed to me. I didn't care, I wanted out of this nightmare, so I accepted whatever the judge had to say and ski-doodled the hell back out the front door. I was certainly thinking at any moment as I walked to my truck I would be attacked by the police and hauled back in. This scenario was real but never happened. I honestly think it was all prearranged for me to get caught in the city with drugs in my possession by the veterans' department. The police who banged on my door were undercover officers from Rhode Island. I had told my doctor about wanting to stop using drugs; maybe he dropped dime on me and informed the police. I think it's a bit farfetched, but I will never know for sure. The fact is however they arrived to stop, my own destruction was a blessing and a gift. I will have to thank them all someday.

As I drove home to my mother's house, my high was wearing off and depression was sinking in full force. When I got home, I asked my mother to come into my old room, we needed to talk. She came in and I collapsed to my knees in a gut-wrenching full-on snot-flowing sob. I had hit rock bottom again in life. I begged her to give me her permission to die. I gave her all my reasons also. I had no wife, no children; I was a failure at everything I do; and I couldn't live this life no more. I had suffered enough, I was back using drugs, and I'd been prostituting myself to keep staying high and out of my own pain. I wanted my whole nightmare life to go away. I could barely function in normal life, nothing meant anything. "Please, Mom, I ask you to release me from this life. I am tired of all those pills, tests, probes, strobes, visions, hallucinations, fevers, chills, broken bones, thrown stones, headaches, muscle fatigues, vomiting sessions. No matter what I do I can't find peace. I get called nigga lover, fag, tranny lover, AIDS victim, ninja carrier, crackhead, junky, loser, useless motherfucker—constant fucking miserable shit goes on that I can no longer take from people, and their dirty fucking looks just makes me want to kill them. I don't want to hurt anyone, all I want to do is end this suffering. I have visions of crazy shit all the time, even without using drugs. I believe the government has stolen my mind just like a couple of crooks. The doctors don't know what the fuck they are doing either, I'm always on some new ass busting give me the shits till I bleed medicine and they tell me it's okay, to keep taking it. I fall into massive clinical depression and use drugs all the time after taking them medicines for too long. Just please let me have your permission, Mom. If you love me like I know you do, you will grant me this one request. I only ask this of you." I cried and cried for damn near an hour in my mother's arms telling her how much I had failed in life, I had slept with more women than I could count,

I had had sex with men, I robbed people, I robbed from my own family, I'd been in to many fights, I'd stuck knives to people's throats, bashed people to a bloody pulp, I'd been bashed to a bloody pulp, and to top it all off, I failed as a Marine. "I am an embarrassment to this family. To tell you the truth, Mom, when I left for boot camp, I never wanted to return. But look, here I am once again back fucking hooked on drugs again, my bills haven't been paid in months, the repo guy came for my truck, you paid him even though I stole from you and my brothers to get high. I'm a complete loser, and I can't keep faking I'm okay. I want to die. I had my chance to give up in that fucking ambulance ride after that dirt bike hit me and I didn't take it. It could have been a perfect way to check out. Just think all that pain and suffering for what, a lousy crackhead in life again. Please, Mom." I whimpered. I had confessed all my wrongs to her, gripping her waist like a small child. For the first time I allowed my mother to see me on the inside. I was very skinny, weighing fifty pounds less than normal. She cried along with me, and it rocked her soul I'm sure. Somehow she knew this was her son crying for help in his own way. I had reached the absolute bottom in my life again. My mom lifted my head and talked to me by looking me in my eyes after clearing my tears and told me, "No!"

She told me she would never give me permission to take my own life. She loved me and enjoyed having me around. She told me, "You will find a way just like you have always done in the past. You're my strong one, Gary, I'm so proud of you. Your brothers all love you, your nieces and nephews love you. We all miss you when you're off somewhere else." She also told me she knew about me not wanting to come back when I left for the Marines, but it was okay. "Trust me baby, you can do this."

I felt bad laying this all on my mother's lap, but she was all I really considered worthy to ask permission from to end my own life. She gave birth to me, so it was hers to decide. Her answer had saved my life. If I was given permission on that day, I would have been dead that night for sure. I wasn't just crying for help, I was crying to say good-bye. She knew I was a mess, yet held me close in her heart and kept me alive. I have completely surrendered to my life and my addiction in this moment, her words and loving touch kept me in this world. I love you, Mom.

Several months went by, and my court date was upon me. I would have liked to have met my appointed public defender more than once, but I guess a quick briefing was okay. Ten minutes before I'm called was what I got. She was busy on my scheduled appointment a few weeks ago, whatever. So I arrived and met up with the woman. All she kept repeating was I'm going to jail. "Look at your record. Look at your record." I think she was a bit nervous or something. I just told her simply, "Never mind about my record, lady, I'm here for a possession charge. My past has nothing to do with these charges." I asked if she represented me, or did she represent this fucking building. I told her, "Stand up for something for once in your life, lady. You're supposed to zealously represent me in this case. You're bound by what is blind to you. This building and these people have poisoned your mind to think we all are guilty before we are proven innocent. Pull yourself together, lady, please." She got all offended and pissed. She yelled at me telling me she wasn't going to allow me into the courtroom talking like that. I told her, "Let's just not speak about my case until we get in there, okay, lady. Obviously you're against me anyways." Nothing more was said actually. She looked away and went into bitch mode.

So we walked into the courtroom together when I was about to be called. They called me, and we approached the bench. The court recorder read my charges against me, and the judge asked, "What's going on, Mr. Mello?" Now this bitch public defender tried to chime in saying things to the judge about my record and my past, like she wanted me to go to jail. How dare this women spilled that deformation of character about me. She was playing judge, jury, and the hangman to this judge. The judge looked at her and said, "I asked Mr. Mello, not you, so let's hear it, son. What's going on?"

I spilled out a river of my life to this man for like ten minutes: my accident, my drug usage for pain in the beginning, living with AIDS, almost dying several times, being an addict since I was a kid, serving in the Marine Corps, being attacked by police, going to prison. I told him I had never asked anyone for help to stop using drugs. I had always worked it out on my own and managed to clean up and move on. "I can't do it alone anymore, sir. I don't need a prison cell. What I need, sir, is help from you. I need a program to follow. Can you help me, sir?"

He looked at me with an open mouth in awe the whole time I was telling him what's going on. When I was finished, he asked me one question, "Who did you get the drugs from?"

I could've said the police set me up and that lesbian bitch undercover cop rifled a hundred bucks out of me. But I replied with this instead: I got the drugs from Leroy. "Who's Leroy?" he asked. I said, "I don't know because they're all named Leroy, and nobody knows who that guy really is." The people in the courtroom started laughing at what I said, but it pissed the judge off.

He said, "I'm not going to put you in prison, Mr. Mello. It seems you're already in prison, son, in your mind."

Those words cut to the bone; he wasn't fucking kidding when he made them assumptions. I was locked in a vicious recurring nightmare, there was no escape. Thanks for reminding me I'm a whack job. So he said, "Piss tests once a week, mandatory drug treatment once a week, probation for one year." I asked him if it was okay to switch my probation to Brockton. "I would love to follow your program, sir, but if I do it within this area, I'm bound to run into some other drug addict I know and I will say fuck your plan and get high anyways, sir." He agreed and wished me luck, and out the door I went. Thank you, sir. I laughed at the public defender on the way out of the door also. Not a rude laugh, it was more of a "see I told you, honesty is the best policy" sort of laugh. I was later questioned by a whole lot of other people on how I remained out of jail. They were convinced I must be some sort of rat or something. I simply told the judge the truth, I had had enough, I needed help to stop using drugs, and I was willing to be directed on a new path. My path didn't lead anywhere anymore. If I plan on surviving any longer on this planet, I better allow him to give me a new path and to follow his recommendations. Truthfully I didn't care what anyone had to say about me being a rat; I wasn't sworn to anyone but myself, nobody owns me.

I did my drug treatment meetings at night in a very dangerous area of Brockton actually. Main Street is no joke sometimes. Plenty of shootings and assaults each and every week was in the newspaper as I continued this path to recovery. I figured if I could come to a neighborhood like this for drugs, I certainly could find help also. I met some amazing people within this Catholic charities meeting house. Hearing them speaks and being able to share my own battles helped me out. I was blessed to know each of them. I hope the young brother, about eighteen, who got stabbed on his first week to the city of Brockton, has a better outlook on life. His mom moved them from a seedy neighborhood near Boston so her son could have a better chance in life. Nice, warm greeting he arrived to. I felt bad and ashamed at how fucked up this whole planet has become. I just listened to him seeing myself at that age also and thanking God for all his protection over the years just to be privy to share something with this young kid about myself in the hopes he turns it around now. He still has plenty of life ahead of himself. Don't you end up completely lost as I have been.

I reported to my probation officer each appointment without missing a beat. The guy in the seat across from me watching over me for the court system was a troubled teen himself, drug user, the whole works. He went to school and got this fine job. He wasn't concerned on month 3 of the piss testing, which I decided was time to stop wasting eleven bucks a week. I asked if that was okay, he replied no worries. How's the program going? I'm clean; things are well, thanks for asking.

My relationship ended with my girlfriend due to me being an absolute nut case. I didn't blame this girl for not wanting me in her home no more. I could've done without her smashing a glass picture over my head while we got into an argument over her sneaking my medications without my knowledge. It was probably because she didn't want me hanging around with another girl, but I'd blame it on her stealing my medications. She was taking them one evening and was completely out of it. She swan-dived down her mother's stairs and broke a few ribs in the process several days prior to this confrontation. I had to bring her to the hospital the next day because I karate-chopped her in the ribs to see if they were just bruised. Sure enough she wailed bloody murder. I barely bumped her ribs, so I knew they were broken. The hospital personnel were totally thinking I beat her up at the time, typical.

On the day of our argument, I was escorted by five policemen actually as I gathered some of my stuff. They arrived and asked me to come outside. I was super pissed off. They tried to tell me I had to leave without my things, and that just wasn't going to happen at all. I told them, "Let the chips fall where they may, I'm taking my stuff." I ended up being allowed to remove my things from the house. I carried everything outside and positioned it all on the street. I called my youngest brother to bring his van and explained to him what was going on. He told me to calm down because the cops were most likely going to shoot my ass if I got violent in any way. I remained calm and muscled all my stuff out the house. I even heard one of the policemen say, "Jesus, I wouldn't want to tangle with this guy, he's got stamina for days. I still talk to this ex-girlfriend all the time." We remained friends even after all this madness. We actually laughed our asses off when we talked about the stuff we did together. She was an angel also. In fact she had a tattoo on her shoulder to remind her each and every day. She supported me with racing like nobody else had ever done. I'm sorry we parted within such a crazy fashion. "I hold you close to my heart and pray for you and your family all the time. I hope I explained things close to what really happened while we were together. If not, I'm sorry. My memory sucks. I will say thank you for taking care of me while that tumor was cut out of my neck, or was it a tracking device?"

I didn't move back home to my mother's house because I was still spooked from the vision of me killing them all and the delusion of them wanting to kill me. I remember my mom walking me into her basement to show me that the woodstove wasn't filled with bones from that girl I thought I killed years ago within a medicinal nightmare. In my head it was real. I was so convinced of this actually being reality that my mother had to walk her full-grown, adult son by the hand like I was a small child into her basement. We walked together toward the far end of the basement. I was a bit rattled, but she assured me I had made it all up. My mother's heating system was being upgraded, and the woodstove was all broken apart. I searched visually half-expecting to see some bones or maybe even a skull. Then I sifted through the pile of concrete blocks and ashes because I was certain this had all been real. I was left confused by all this; my mind was warped. The medicines caused this to happen to me, nothing more. A sense of relief washed over me. I told my mother, "Thank you, and yes, I am fine now." I had asked her to keep this a secret between us because my brothers would laugh at me if they knew I was a complete pussy. I needed my mommy to show me it was all a delusion and made up in my mind. I really truly believe if it wasn't for having a solid family structure, I would be dead already or locked up in a crazy house. I didn't want them to suffer my delusions any longer, so I moved into a friend's house that he had just purchased. He lived one town over from my family home, and it was just close enough if I had to get over there because I was wigging out. I was completely honest with this guy about being a mental case and confessed to him everything prior to moving in. He accepted me regardless. I would lay my life down for this guy in a heartbeat. I had never been so lost in my life at this juncture, and I was greeted with open arms. This guy was an angel to me and he didn't know it. This is one of my truest friends, his older brother is also actually. My whole community of friends and family are all my life support.

I had found out after a good six-month-long battle with fevers, headaches, and a botched lumbar puncture at the veterans' department that I had hepatitis C supposedly. I say botched because the guy doing the procedure poked that thing in and out of my back eight times and couldn't get the job done. I had to return the next day for a different doctor to complete the task of getting some spinal fluid from me in order to run some tests. I am pretty sure this occurred while living with my ex-girlfriend toward the end of our relationship, but it matters not—well, actually it does. I had been exposed to hepatitis C, and they gave me massive doses of Interferon and Ribavirin. During this treatment, I was told I had to have a psychiatrist appointed to me because at the dose I was on, I would have homicidal and suicidal thoughts for sure. I know I began this therapy after my incident with the gabapentin medicine. I would be subjected to more of the same issues, so they needed to monitor me for forty-eight weeks of therapy. I didn't care because it was pretty much the normal thing when it came to medicines within my life so far. I also told the doctor, "I don't care if you have to strap me down to a damn table for forty-eight weeks. I will die if we don't eradicate this hepatitis from my body. My liver will not be able to handle the HIV/AIDS medicine of the future if it was diseased."

So that was exactly what I did when I arrived at this guy's house. I injected a full syringe of toxic medicine into my stomach once a week. I was totally and completely crazy as a shithouse rat the entire time. Needless to say, I didn't commit suicide, nor did I kill anyone. The thought was there every damn second though, no doubt about that.

TRANSFORMATION

"The definition of *transformation* is the act or an instance of transforming, the state of being transformed, a marked change, as in appearance or character, usually for the better."

I would have to say this was the most important step I undertook within my recovery process. I had asked for help and even stayed clean for short intervals with my mom's help. I had her become my payee within my finances also. I was no longer to be trusted with my own money; I surrendered all my credit cards, my checkbooks, and all of my money to her.

I knew she would take care of all my bills, and I fully trusted in her to not steal or swindle me out of any funds. I only allowed myself twenty-dollars-a-week spending money within my possession at a time. Any extras would certainly have me thinking about getting high. This allowance stayed in effect for close to six months before I had paid most of my debts back to family members who I stole from and caught me up on bills. I would sit with my mother each month and watch to learn how to balance my checkbook; I had forgotten how since the accident actually. I could grasp the concept quite easily but couldn't actually follow it. I felt like a child, but this needed to be done.

During my times away from home, I would spend time with my girlfriend at the time and we would play Yatzee over and over again in order for me to get my numbers back. My girlfriend never knew at the time, but I clued her in on it after the fact. If I was to regain control of my life and simple responsibilities, I needed to have a grasp on simple math. After six months had passed, I had proven to my mom enough that it was going to be okay. I got all of my finances back under my own control, and things had been going well since that day actually. Well, not really, I still don't have enough, but who really does?

I remember when I first tried to stay clean actually. Every time I wanted to get high, I would have this overwhelming urge to go get something. I sort of tricked my mind by running to Wal-Mart and purchasing a movie and coming home. I would get the same satisfaction as copping drugs. This worked for a very long time actually prior to my last slipup. I actually ran out several times in a day and purchased two or three movies in one day to curve my craving to use. I have a pretty good collection now, actually. But those were just things to stop drug use and to occupy my mind. My slipups were farther apart, but I wasn't free of the grasp cocaine had on me.

I was still locked in a very bad depressive state which would come and go very rapidly without warning. I would find myself crying for no apparent reason sometimes. Listening to Johnny Cash for too long has that effect; it was a good tool for me to let out some pent-up frustration, allowing myself to cry. Other times I would be so bored all I could do was think about all the things I ruined along my path of life up to this point. It was around this time I received a phone call from one of my mom's neighbors. This man entered my life through the heroin-addicted girlfriend who sat with me after my accident. We were both heavily into drugs together for almost a year and a half actually. I remember he tried to get us both to go to this educational program a year earlier while we were flopped out at his house. This program wasn't based in drug addiction or recovery at all. I remember we went to this thing on a Friday; we both sat and listened through complete drug-induced minds actually. During each break of this seminar, we would head out to my truck and consume copious amounts of crack only to return into this program all sweating and shaky. It was supposed to be a three-day seminar, but we only made it till Saturday afternoon before we split from that scene. I was shocked to hear this man's voice on the phone asking me a year later to give this program a try again. I figured he would be pissed because he had found remnants of our drug usage in his house, the burnt spoons, a few pipes, and a cooking test tube in one of his spare bedrooms closets. In my mind, I couldn't wrap my head around why he was helping me. I honestly told him, "Thank God you called actually. I have been clean for a full year now, and now would be a good time to get into something healthy before I fall again." Boredom was getting the best of me. I hadn't mentioned any of my depression at all. But I admitted I didn't want to blow it and start using drugs again. With that, my journey to redemption began, perhaps.

I arrived at this weekend meeting early Friday morning. I walked into a room filled with people, about 180 I guess; there is one guy at the front of the room with a microphone. He's blabbing on and on. I wasn't hearing a thing; I was thinking I needed to ask this guy the answer to my problems. I wasted no time to get up and quickly rambled off twenty-five minutes of my life to this dude and even tossed in the usual desperation plea, "If I don't get some answers, I am prepared to get in my truck, pull out the suicide letter prewritten to my mom, a nice nickel-plated .45-caliber pistol with a gold hollow-point bullet made from a melted-down crucifix she gave me when I joined the ranks of fellow Catholic school confirmation graduates and just simply pull the trigger and blast my fucking brains out!"

Oh wait, I don't have those things. Does somebody out there have one? I gave up my weapon when I was asked to leave the military. You know what? I don't need it, neither do you, go give it back to the gun store, or return it to some policeman. Live your life without them, it is much safer.

He told me to stay the course, meaning, all three days, and I would get the answers I so desperately needed.

I was satisfied with that answer, and it felt good to vent. The bad feelings about myself changed I guess when I began to speak it out. Perhaps I needed a larger audience to get a grip on myself mentally.

I began to listen to others for the first time without hearing my past. So my past was completed according to them. They had given me nothing. The great part is, from nothing, everything is possible.

So what did I learn from this course? Absolutely nothing, which was fine. Let's reprogram my mind to think different thoughts, speak differently, something. I had no future yet though, you should take our next course. I agree to do the next course because, hey, I like it all so far. I certainly have the time. It's got to be better than chasing my own tail in circles like I have been doing all this time. I also learned about how the leader of this course I was in happened to be a battle of Kaison survivor during Vietnam. They were surrounded on a hill with enemy closing in around them on all sides. If you look up some history of Marines in combat during Vietnam, you will see how listening to this man was important to me. His words were a gift. He also had become fully addicted to heroin for many years afterward and is completely clean and sober living an amazing life. I wanted what he had.

During the second seminar series, I learned how to get related to people. Somehow I think I already did that quite well with the people I know and people I absolutely haven't a clue who they are, because this guy right over here happens to be a homeless person. I try to run across all walks of life without malice in my heart. But the truth was, I was still a mess. I was a mess emotionally, but the simple fact remains I'm off medicine and cocaine. I'm starting to see the light, and I'm having fun. I feel like celebrating. I had a few drinks with my girlfriend at the time and prepared for the next course.

Yes, they were keeping my interest; finally, I got something to do. I wanted to be racing or riding my motorcycle somewhere, but without knowledge on how to get sponsors, it becomes difficult to afford on a pension. I was meeting a lot of new people; I always enjoyed doing that anyways. Plus my riding needed a break. I was broken; I needed self-healing.

The third course was to find your own voice again.

Scary thing to do, but somehow it comes alive in me, hence the continuation of this whole book and all of my rambling sentences.

I even tried to spark my hometown's interest in holding a charity cross-country dirt bike race within our surrounding forest and a few connecting properties. It was a decent-enough idea that never came into fruition. The way I felt was alive and inspired while doing it, and that's what mattered most. I still would like them to consider hosting a yearly AIDS awareness benefit race. What the hell does the town lose? I asked. People love participation to a good cause, raise money to expand the school, give kids a chance to enjoy the outdoors, allow troubled youth in the nearby forestry camp in Plymouth to come and design the layout and be in charge of cleanup when the race weekend is over. A twenty-mile loop would be sufficient, throw in a few checkpoints, a start line and a finish line, a few simple ribbons, and directional markers and we are off. Let the police block roads that need to be crossed during our entertainment and pure peace on two wheels. The fire rescue crew actually does something within the forest. Remote locations are quickly accessible with helicopter rescue from nearby Otis Air Force Base. Those guys love racing and doing that kickass hero stuff, allowing access to certain sections of the course for them to land near in case a bad crash happens.

This allowed the high school to be in charge of video production, kids need to learn how to master their own crafts and skills. Let them have memories of doing something really cool for someone else.

Bring in a few live bands to play. I had the whole plan written out to where everyone gets paid, and millions are raised to find a cure. Maybe it will happen when I'm dead, because nobody had the time to listen while I was alive. That's why writing this book is so cool also. It remains permanently planted in your head and then your kids' head; I was here to help with their own future. But guess what, I want 10 percent off the top. It was my original idea.

On to the next course—oh wait, I had to be cleared first.

Proper business casual attire was required, more hassle.

This was a leader course which led me to New York in front of six hundred people who got to hear my tale of woe for thirty minutes. The reaction I got from the people wasn't one I expected. I was thanked for my words, some said, "I wish my father, uncle, brother, sister had heard what I was saying, and perhaps they would still be alive today." They were lost to drugs, AIDS, drinking, and everything I was dealing with, but they threw in the towel. I was hope to them and comforting to them. All I did was spark a memory for them to bring back a happy thought about their lost family member. I carry the burden, like a soldier wearing a pack in a far-off land to keep you safe. I shook off any fear within me to purge my soul during these times. The courses have lasted in my mind since going through them. The people I met along this journey were difficult to deal with at times, but I remain true to my cause. Below is the formula I have always used for redemption. Your course was very thought provoking, and it was nice to have a structure worth following at the time. It also got me present to my own self-worth and the impact I could have on others in a good way.

- Confronting my life
- Confessing my sins
- Asking forgiveness
- Forgiving myself
- Creating new ideas
- Getting inspired
- Living my life
- Helping others

I wrote out a letter to my close friends and relatives; I called each person individually and read my letter.

You know I went into this program to find new hope. I needed a reason why I should not just give up and accept death. What I am accomplishing is the ability to express myself more openly to possibly all of you without regret, pain, blame, or just plain old "you suck and so what." The possibility I have invented for myself and my life is the possibility of loving myself once again and sharing with you freely and openly, as just I do with my brothers, my mom, my dad, and my friends. I would like to let you know I'm done with holding you responsible for my misery. You are actually my biggest strengths and that I want to just be involved with your lives without my hurt and shame. I want to invite you into my life as just friends again. I keep selling the idea that my AIDS status is who I am and it defines me in everything: relationships, love, happiness, and it shackles me from my dreams, in which I desperately want. I do have a reason for being here; I'm still alive. I'm realizing I'm gifted with a powerful way of presenting myself to others that inspires them also. These are definitely new and amazing discoveries about the power I posses which I deny myself from living an extraordinary, amazing life. I want to thank you for that wonderful gift of a new me. You are allowing me to reach out from my darkest, loneliest void. You have rejuvenated me immensely. Thank you!

I was brought back to peace of mind. If you happen to want this information about this course, feel free to ask me; I'll direct you accordingly. I'm no longer involved directly with this program, but it does help in a quest to remain clean from drugs. The application of your mind into another task will always deter you. I lost interest in them when I was told I wasn't allowed to wear short sleeves; my tattoos were intimidating. I considered this a total insult, reacted negatively toward it, voiced my opinion and moved on. Like it or not, I became an introduction leader in their business. I don't get paid, I travel all around, no reimbursement for fuel or any costs I may incur to faithfully show up to required meetings. Oh, and guess what? No prize, no parade, no medals, no more cocaine usage. I guess it was a fair trade. I got to be inspired and to inspire a few people in the way.

We were allowed to do shares within a certain conversation designed to enroll others into living a life they love. We coach them along and get them to register, pay a fee, and walk into their own life created by them. It was cool; I shared a story about being confronted by fear as a child.

I was four years old at the time. I remember we raised chickens in our backyard. We had three hundred of them if I remember correctly. My parents ran a breakfast joint, and this was a source of income to feed us five children. For some reason they abandoned the whole idea, and the day came to slaughter the chickens. I didn't know the politics of it all. I was four. I was just asked to go fetch a chicken. My aunt told me to pick out my favorite actually. I came back all innocent and said, "Here, Auntie." She reached out and held the chicken in her arm and wrung its neck. It squawked once and then dropped to the ground flopping and flapping all over the place. I was paralyzed; I screamed with no noise and then cried. I had lost my cute brown-and-beige chicken friend. My aunt was a mean, evil, and wicked woman. I can't trust her with anything precious of mine again. I guess I carry that fear into life all the way back from when I was four. It stops me in life and my future. It has to be that. It turned out to be a really cool share; it even brought me an animal rights supporter next to me and says,

> "I can't believe those factories slaughter them! They should be shut down!"

I had to laugh this off; I couldn't rightfully rip into this woman about how I happened to like the little tasty bastards in my dinner plate today. It was fun to stand up and talk creatively about the past. I would later find out from older brothers my fear didn't last long at all. They said I would laugh each and every time after I calmed down from the initial shock. My hands went to work catching chickens like I was told to do so. We even chased them while they were flopping around all crazy. It became sort of cool watching and learning the process of slaughtering a chicken in your own backyard among your family, old world techniques being passed to the next generation, no machines needed. All I need is a sharp knife, a pot to boil water and provide steam, then they are hand-plucked, gutted, and packaged for the freezer. I learned by watching and participating hands-on. I've never been to a factory, so to speak, I just go to the grocery store now. No need to comment on some other guy's method; simple is always the better. I just hope he keeps the meat fresh from factory to my pan.

Somehow I have lost that ability to raise my own food to the machines. Too much hassle feeding the suckers till they are ready for consumption.

I remembered a rough life growing up. It was lots of hard work to keep from starving as a child. My parents were very strict, but they provided us with knowledge, on sustaining your family in the woods of Rochester. No real frills, a stick, a few rocks, and some trees to play around in. The garden was for work, so get your ass in there and start weeding or planting or hoeing or picking. It was truly awesome in that garden, wild even. Tomato worms were great for fishing, the wasp nest was cool every year in the raspberry bushes, and the garden spiders were fat, black and yellow spotted with really cool web designs. I would catch other insects all the time to watch the evil spider spin its web around them and suck out the juice. Catching fireflies in a mason jar, keeping them as a night-light in my room, but of course they all got free because the holes we poked into the lid were too big; eventually they were free floating around my room. There were garden snakes and black racers cruising around, which scared the holy hell out of my mother only. We used to put them in our pockets and carry them to her all innocently to watch her bug out. It was fun times in my memory.

I even shared a yellow jacket encounter when I was around the same age.

My brothers were up in a tree messing with a really big nest; it was beach ball-sized anyway. Well, here I am, prancing around in my new winter coat I got on my birthday which was in July. It was a fake fur one actually. The '70s were brutal in fashion. I watched as they reached with a stick to pry it loose from the branch it was secured to. The nest fell from the tree and exploded on the ground. I was cheering our victory and running around like a normal four-year-old. I was then swarmed on by the entire nest. I guess I looked like a bear or animal to them because they stung me repeatedly all the way to the back door one hundred yards away. I entered the house covered by them. My father was swatting them off me and getting bit by them in the process. I ended up covered with bites inside my mouth, ears, head, arms, legs, and even down my back. So a lot of dried baking soda and water spots on me for this week.

I'm not sure what exercise I used in the program to tell this story, but it was a very cool one to tell. My family laughs when I remember it with them. Only a few things happened for me that day; I no longer fear hornets, yellow jackets, wasps, or any stinking flying insect. I know not to mess with them wearing a fur coat anyways. I would tempt fate plenty with them all the time. The purplish black mud wasps packed the best hit, pound for pound. I have been stung plenty on my adventures.

I also created a Web site, I even wrote this book, began racing again, stopped using drugs, and also stopped using medications for that matter. This program allowed me to find my voice to inspire other people. I share my tale today because it was in my path to follow.

END STATEMENTS

The purpose of writing this book was to open up other people's eyes to a world unseen by many. So basically it's a warning to all who read it. I was in no way looking to encourage anyone to follow in my footsteps or to live their life with such reckless decisions. The truth is, I am just like you, stubborn and independent and have been for a long time. My stubbornness has kept me safe through plenty of life-ending moments within my existence on this planet. My independence has cost me plenty of real loving relationships. I was unable to feel or to accept anything given to me if I couldn't get it myself. That's exactly why I don't accept handouts or sponsorships for my racing. I am totally selfish within that. My life works or it doesn't work, and I have become content within it. I have given away all my possessions in the past just to rid myself of bad memories and bad karma or to escape my drug use knowing a new environment helps if I move to a new spot several states away. I also moved because being monitored by the veterans' department all the time wears on my mind. The constant blood draws and psychiatric appointments make me feel like I'm a criminal being investigated. I have to run and leave stuff behind in order to stay sane. Material things had meant nothing at all. I have learned that it's life experience, new places to explore, and new faces to meet that have become the truly important things that matter to me. I am what you call a self-taught person. I learned how to survive within a very destructive thought process and just barely was able to make it out alive. I honestly could say that all of my travels have taught me some harsh realities about life. I have become a successful failure or maybe I'm a success in someone else's opinion. But like the old saying goes, our future is not written in stone, so I will make the proper changes to become something I am proud of. I will reestablish self-worth to myself. I will always judge myself far worse than anyone else could or can, so don't bother judging me, it's a fruitless task. I am also in the religious sense a believer of God and his teachings. There is a quote in the Bible which reads, "Judge not unless ye be judged." So let's just get along, it's easier that way.

You may have been irritated or upset about some of my writings and thoughts along this journey, but my intentions were to rid myself of my past. This was all written as a form of therapy, so to speak, for me. Once again it's all about me. So I thank you for following along. I may have ripped into your soul or tapped into your inner being and caused it to stir just a bit; maybe I was successful, or maybe I wasn't. Perhaps you're actually alive inside and want to consider changing your view toward others in a good way. My hope is just that. Perhaps you could send your copy of my book to the president and tell him to read it. We could start a whole new resurrection of revolt toward our constitutional rights being taken away. This could just end up in your trash, but either way, at the very least, you used my words to speak out against war, a police state, a dictatorship, and our freedom of speech. You also helped me to be able to continue on with my dream of becoming the first-ever cross-country dirt bike racer living with AIDS to become a professional or to just continue on competing wherever on this planet I wish to let it rip on two wheels. You can help me by sharing my tale with others and showing them where to buy this book. Sooner or later I may add up all the funds allotted to me by the citizens who pay for my disability as a United States Marine veteran and pay back every single cent wasted on me to survive a disease and possibly save some lives in the process of taking experimental medicines which might save me and possibly give future generations a cure and a firm grasp on what to expect if they don't take heed to my warning.

I also would like to become a role model or a reference that you could use on how not to begin using drugs or how to stop because it is a very difficult life to live. Use my story to shock your children when they begin the experimental phase of drug use. I can say for sure there is no denying the fact. It only takes one hit, and *boom*, a lifetime of regrets and lost dreams occurs, and time will fly by. If drugs weren't presented to me at such an early age, I honestly think I may never have gotten sick and quite possibly would be well into a promising career with my master's degree tacked on my wall within my office. I would have children of my own and a loving wife. That possibility could now be within my radar because like I said before, our futures aren't certain. We can change the outcome no matter how bad it seems. There is always room to grow and to learn new things within our lifetimes. I feel as if I've been blessed just to be alive to share my story. I hope you enjoyed the ride and look forward to the reactions and actions you pursue in a life created by you. Make your stand for yourself and accept others in with open arms. Just remember, this was my vision; I wanted to discern between basic survival instincts to live, or was it something else? I have noticed my survival has always been dependent upon my "angels," people who have shown up at critical moments, and I was able to recognize that fact and held on. As for the basic survival instincts to live versus something else, the paranormal, it still remains unknown to me. I know what I've seen and know what I've done; I try to make use of my visions in a good way versus the evil I see within them. I wanted to tell my story and be remembered and not to just vanish from this earth without passing on my knowledge to those who need it the most during their critical moments. I completely wanted to inspire you, to make you laugh, to make you cry, to piss you off, to make you question things, to make you simply feel. If you can experience the whole spectrum of emotions during each day, that's awesome, don't you think? You're living life! I have seen and witnessed this while speaking to others firsthand; this book is the delivery system for those I don't get to meet. In time I would like to hand-deliver this book to veterans in the hopes it helps them in their own battles while recovering, perhaps to motivate them to get up and begin again. That goes for anyone in this world who just needs a little stir of emotion to press through their own issues. Remember, we are all connected; your happiness and peace is mine also. I may not speak this outside of my house or outside at all, but every so often I get down on my knees humbly before God and thank him for giving me just *one more day*.

So love too much! Love many! Love too often and never enough! All the time . . . every day!

I am a free spirit roaming this planet looking for a place to land. I fully respect and welcome others with open arms and love. I expect the same in return. If I don't find this in a certain area and it falls short in any way, I'm back on the breeze.

I find myself today befriending everyone I encounter regardless of my paranoia and fear. I will forever question in my mind whether or not they are truly friends, but I have learned to accept living as a paranoid, sometimes delusional schizophrenic. Years of abuse by my own doing and years of experimental medicines have put me in this position. I can only go along with what people tell me about themselves and keep focused on, everything is okay. It doesn't matter if they are working for the government or not. I just pray they will work with me within my trials and tribulations in order to find a cure. Keep diligent in knowing I carry a divine spirit, and most of the things I am petrified of are nightmares I have had during delusional thought and dream states or simply when watching the television or playing video games and listening to music. I must remember I voluntarily accepted everything that has happened. Everything that has occurred in my life up to this point has been of my own doing. I have moved beyond blame. I stand strong in not knowing what will happen in the future for me. It is the unknown which drives me to stay healthy and to do whatever it takes to survive a disease which should've ended my natural life a long time ago. The power of my mind over matter is and shall always remain stronger than my situation. I held the keys to the gates of hell fully prepared to enter, and heaven sent me angels to guide me within my choices. I can look back now and laugh or cry or just simply know a life is far more interesting when you have fallen from grace and then to allow others to show me that paradise still exists, within my own existence, by allowing myself into their lives.

DELUSIONS

In reality and not in my past, I wasn't going to add this, but this one is a whopper. All my control is lost once again. Just when I think I may have some control—fwaaaapp!—I was hit in the head by a huge fish, like the scene in the cartoon square in the funny papers.

I haven't used drugs since 2005, I would guess; others may tell me different, but sometimes getting high to find or help a friend out of drugs happens in my lifetime. Honestly, I can say this. To the best of my knowledge, my approximate year of remembrance of the said—actually being off drugs—was 2005. I'm unsure why this occurred within my head and I allowed it to become all consuming. I completely feel powerless over some weird conspiracy that floats into my psyche, and I'm unable to vocalize it in a way that may not frighten others. Not to say you're going to be scared, but in my head, I lost it. Yeah! No doubt in my mind whatsoever, I was on the brink of insanity.

I wasn't sneaky at all; in fact I was quite the gentlemen. The other party involved somehow took on a sneaky character created in my delusional mind and just wigged me out. I feel bad I didn't complete the prior full-month commitment I had given my word to. I am usually a man of my word when people request my help. I was to care for a friend who just went through knee surgery. Simple request I wanted to fulfill and have a breakthrough in actually being of service to another. I jumped at the chance actually. This friend works in the HIV/AIDS field, plus various other nasty biological, viral, and crazy diseases for the government. For me it was a chance to swap chairs so to speak. I was helped by these people earlier in life with their biohazard gear on back in 1992; it was so ironic, me an AIDS survivor after all these years lives long enough to help a medical researcher who quite possibly could save his life in the

378

future. I think I may have saved hers just a little, but like I said before, she transformed into a sneaky idea manifested within my mind. I can't pinpoint the actual misfire in my head, what sort of chemical imbalance has happened within my brain juices, I wonder. I haven't even been on medicine for over five years give or take a few months. I can't blame the medicine, so what caused this? Oh, great one! I ask?

Everything became scripted as if it were a play or an investigation of novel proportions. It was downright dirty, sweaty, and very tiresome, but exhilarating and quite amazing until my fucked-up brain confused me. Call this delusional if you want, but for me it was real and very sneaky. Let's face it, everyone is dirty or sneaky about shit, especially the Feds. Well, here goes, live, present in 2010, a warped mind becomes cracked once again in paranoia.

Everything goes just fine. I got semi-permission to go from my current girlfriend, so off I went visit for a month to help this woman. I arrived to a completely amazing example of a human being just waiting to be discovered. This wasn't her view of herself when I arrived, but transformation took time. I wanted to help, but also learn. She was one week out of surgery when I stumbled onto the scene. The leg was twice its size of normal, swollen to the point of burst. All the blood would have come out of her foot if it was poked with a pin and did pop. Damn thing was purple and doubled its size around the ankle, that's for sure. Her bandages were too tight underneath a straight leg brace. It looked painful. So anyways, I'll get to the point. Within the first week, I massaged the swelling down for her to keep the blood flowing within them muscles to keep atrophy of the leg to a minimum and to reduce that swelling. We were sure to ice that leg constantly. This was another fun task of fetching ice and using a cool machine to flow ice water over her fixed ACL and meniscus repair job. That area was the most painful and definitely needed ice to stave off swelling also.

I ate, slept, and totally immersed myself into this woman's life. She resisted at first because the familiar "she could do it on her own" arrived along with me. Quite common when someone is independent, which she was. I was honored to be of assistance and drove her to the store, went to the gym early in the mornings with her, went for walks, listened to her, learned some things along our journey of getting her back to independent as quickly as possible again with that bum knee. By week 3, she was two weeks ahead of schedule in her recovery, swelling almost completely gone and well into the physical therapy prior to even beginning those visits.

My healing hand and heart still worked I guess—learned that from my relatives, mainly the grandmothers, older aunts, and definitely my own mom. Just glad to see you recover so quickly actually.

She had a really cool convertible go-cart-sized sports car with six gears. I had to make it chirp through the gears when I was alone after she began to go to work again, and I dropped her off, of course. I reached about sixty in a flash within redline and totally enjoyed the smell of burnt rubber. Hey sorry, that car needed to be punished and shown some love. I even went and hand-washed her car and detailed it with my own two hands just to stay busy on one of my off days. I say off day because it really wasn't. I swear, if I knew that she was moving to a new place during this recovery, I may not have come. Well, wouldn't you know it? I carried all her shit from one house to the next alone, minus a few boxes, her late steal-all-the-glory boyfriend showed up to carry after the fact. But it was all good. The gym was cool; I showed her a good upper body workout to help with her fighting. She is a kickboxer actually. Cool chick, huh? I had an amazing time, regardless the work involved. Wish this didn't happen but it did, and now I'm embarrassed by it.

Several bad things occurred during this trip prior to my mind losing its grip. I got a parking ticket when we went to the movies the first week. During the second week, I spent far too much money on a chiropractor due to the intensity at the gym and carrying them heavy ass boxes. My body needed to be cracked loose, nothing new in my world. Rigor mortis set into me when I slept I swear to God after all that activity. I parked at a metered spot outside his office, went in. He did his magic—snap, crackle, pop ripped me off, kick in the ass out the door. That's one great fucking guy, n my eyes. I came out, and my truck was gone. I was towed for parking in a signed No Parking area between the hours of 3:30 to 6:00 PM. Total fucking rip-off by the tow company and the city. City charged me $105; tow company cost $130 to tow one block to a lot just around the corner. I argued to no avail, even knowing I still had money and time left on the meter. What's the point of having the fucking meter if you can't fucking park there? I didn't see any sign.

It was up the street, fuck, you pay me!

Not a happy camper one bit. They suck, and so doesn't this whole fucking place.

Within this rage state of mind, my mind shifted to something was out to get me, or someone. I began questioning in my mind what my new friend's intentions really were. I no longer saw the amazing woman in the world; I saw she worked for the government. They were planting a research scientist next to me to observe me as if I was an animal or a sideshow freak. I no longer enjoyed her temper tantrums or emotional moments due to the healing process of her knee; I wasn't able to get her to laugh much less myself when I would talk her out of it on prior occasions. I no longer viewed her creative writing style as unique and pretty; it took on a writing of code only she understood, and I thought it odd. It was innocent on her end, but to me, I viewed it odd. I was under surveillance and a microscope once again. There were too many questions in my head, and no way to communicate these feelings to her without hurting her feelings or quite possibly smashing some stuff in a delusional rage.

The constant note taking, requests not to answer my phone, questioning me about family and friends, wanting me to read my book to her but only the getting sick part first, maybe to discover something that may deny what actually happened to me in that hospital, telling me to write knowing I'm angry, asking me to go into my head but to allow her to follow, wanting my secrets to life, wanting my ability to speak to anyone, the isolation, copying all of my music—all ways to profile me, it is all tactics used to interrogate in my mind. I didn't want to show this woman my weakness called delusional rage when she viewed me as a strong, powerful person who was in control. I get extremely angry when my mind twists on me.

Here I am within the nation's capital, well close by anyways, with one of the top researches of her job place and I go schizoid. Was I schizoid, or was this a conspiracy? I couldn't tell. I took her attitude as ungratefulness for all I had done for her. I hooked up my trailer and bounced. It was a simple bad vibe I was given that had me boil over in the gym. My mind was already twisting prior to her crab-ass attitude. A small grouchy reply stated, coming from a healing, tired, working woman who happened to not know what we were doing next for an exercise; she snapped at me and said something that sparked a response within me. I instantly allowed everything to take on conspiracy.

She had asked me, "Don't you think the feds and the cops are afraid of you?" during a discussion of my mistrust of them from my dealings with them in the past, so it wasn't out of context within our discussion as we had been driving home the day before. I picked it out of the hat and placed it next to some other weird things I heard or felt and came up with bad karma. I simply left that day with a good-bye note written and left it on the counter. I apologized for not being a man of my word in staying the full month and only managed two weeks, also for not pursuing a business venture with her. My sixth sense told me otherwise. A few simple phone calls to get some other opinions on the goings-on around me, and that was that.

I vented my weird, freaky delusions to some friends and family on my drive back home, eleven hours straight. No break necessary when my mind is cracked and being fed by delusional thoughts. I'm back at home, away from stress, which must be the cause of all this. Perhaps it's not stress at all; maybe someone slipped me a chemical to get me to sing like a canary about all my bad deeds, like I might be hiding something. Maybe the protein she let me have contained something. The water maybe or them smokes I bought on the military base. She might have drugged me? All sorts of crazy things entered my mind as the cause. I was also away from the auditory hallucinations, the voices that I began to hear. It was one voice actually, a small child called my name while I was awaking from much-needed sleep. No one was in the house at all, but I heard it clearly. I even began to see the ghostlike figures within my peripheral vision; they started to appear once again. All this was enough to know I needed to leave.

I really liked the company of this woman, and she might have enjoyed mine also. There was no sex involved at all, but the feelings of love were very strong. I certainly managed to feel remorse for leaving early. Maybe I do have a heart. That's a breakthrough. I miss her terribly and hope she is well.

I also hope prior to me becoming silent and spooked out, she learned something of importance that she can apply to her own life and greatly enhance herself to the riches and happiness we had dreamed together for each other's futures. One day soon I hope we get to visit each other again. Maybe it will turn out better; maybe I'm not as strong as people think; maybe I'm absolutely crazy. Just know you're loved by me regardless of my disappearance from your field of vision. Perhaps I was one of your angels during a critical moment in your life. I will always remember good versus evil. Just wanted to try it on, doesn't fit well on me, but transformation within myself to help another is what the world needs more of. I managed to give without prejudice; pure love for another human being caused this occurrence. Pass it on, my love! Thank you for all the pleasant moments prior to my own issues. If ever asked how I survived so long within this disease, it was all the emotions, the biggest two being love and hatred. Hatred of the ways I was denied my human rights by my own countrymen, but loving them enough to try anything to find a cure for future generations of their children's children.

I missed my fiancée; my practice in love shall carry into my relationship within my own life and the future of my marriage. Use those exercises well and get back to the ring. Boxing is a wiser choice; save the legs for walking and not kicking. Each and every exercise I demonstrated to you and as I walked you through will most certainly increase the power of your punches. I should've stayed more focused on teaching rather than on conspiracies, but I am also missing my dive knife from my camera bag; I guess someone needs it more than I do. Funny how it disappeared into thin air while visiting. God gives, and the sneaky government takes away.

I'm still in your corner if asked to be, and I would love to see you win the Olympics like you wanted to. Just go, become whoever you wish. Speaking of a wish, remember this?

Your words are divine
I cherish them because they were mine
Our friendship has grown stronger
wishing my stay was longer
In my heart is where you are
as I wish upon a star
aching for your touches
wanting for you to be off them crutches
to gaze into your eyes
to stop asking the whys
cradle your face in my hand
Finally I take a stand
my nervous feelings removed from this
My craving heart healed from your kiss
Long have I dreamed since we joined forces
My emotions are running strong just like galloping horses
Perhaps you will know on this day
my feelings for you in this way
your skin. Hair. Touch. Smile. And your lips
are etched in my soul as my heart sings and skips
Truly and forever I shall love thee
Want you to know you have set me free
my sweet love
You are my peace
the symbol of a dove
Another angel sent to me by God's good grace

*Your feelings are quite apparent as well, it is written all over
your face
Find the courage if you can
Anytime you wish I am your man
I long for you to give me a try
I promise I will be there when you cry
So take a chance
Let's the dance
Two new lovers are in the making
I am so ripe for your taking
I wish, I wish, I wish some more
Forever and always will I adore
the waves and crashes in orgasmic bliss
all within reach. It begins with our kiss
Being flattered is truly what mattered most
Your generosity is pure as my host
No matter the physical act
We form a bonded pact
my longing for play
of which you say
has already been started
Regardless if our bodies stay parted
I'm letting you see for yourself
You are a porcelain doll placed on my shelf
I stare in awe and appreciate your beauty
Know in your heart you are a cutie
release your ugly view
Any guy would be happy to be with you
I spin you this yarn and my twist
rocking together in a boat with a list
travel the world and the seven seas
I bow humbly at your knees
You are a fragile flower
reaching to the sun to gain its power
Relax n knowing it's just a wish
I shall cast a line to catch us a fish
let's work this plan you put in motion
One day soon we will greet this ocean*

So what did I really learn from my whole life and this encounter? Drugs played no part within my delusions. I create them in my mind. Test medicines have driven me nuts. I truly believe my cure has been realized within this statement. This whole concept of having a disease that is going to kill you is a myth, and a way to suppress, enslave, and discriminate against me, and others who are told they have it. This disease is created by an outside source of information within my mind. I can easily disregard all the scientific research and predictions of how it all looks through a microscope within a slide magnified to the millionth power. I will also remember how angry people became when I would state propaganda statements like, maybe that entire crack binge was my cure, and you couldn't deny it because there is no cure. Maybe I brought enough cocaine into my body to kill it. I certainly was at toxic levels but was in no danger of death or thinking of killing anyone until I took their medicines.

Unless it's lived, the truth will never be found on how the human body can heal itself through the power of our mind, proper diets, exercise, and a hobby, a loving God in which I trust, a dirt bike, and people to lean on and to allow them to lean back, some fresh green buds, help from the spirit world, and from heaven and hell. It definitely isn't found in a magic pill or a combination of pills. I am sorry, but the recipe to life is simply to live it and have a good time in the process. Learn everything, experience it all, talk to anyone and listen to them all, and most certainly, shed some tears of pain and joy equally. Perhaps my next book will include my diet and exercise program for the world to see how someone with HIV/AIDS does not need medicine to survive. I need the money to go racing my motorcycle, so yes, I'm going to write another one about my nutrition, and it will cost a fee, just like this one—nothings free it seems.

I also realized that the question, "Don't you think the feds and the cops are afraid of you?" goes deeper than what we had discussed. I am quite certain they are. I have been repeatedly harassed, followed, and profiled for something I haven't done. I certainly hope they are ready to apologize for all they have put me through over the years. The craziness all of them think about me is all absurd and a gross fabrication based on their lies and imaginative delusional outbursts I have said aloud on poison called medicine. I wish they would own up to their mistake. I don't deserve to be treated as a suspect or as less than human. I will certainly be on the lookout for a subpoena to meet them in the supreme court so we can discuss the secrets behind all this.

Bring your best, because I know my own truth, and that is what matters most. You tried to fry my mind with powerful drugs and even told me to leave the past in the past, but I will not be silenced until God takes me home. My freedom is already established within my mind. Bring along a big checkbook also because I will not lose this fight and I need the money to keep on riding; I expect compensation. I also noticed that every federal building, courthouse, and police station around our country has metal detection devises and we are all searched prior to entrance, yet you're allowed into our homes with or without a warrant armed to the gills. You act like you're a friend sneaking among us hiding in wait like a rat waiting for an opening to steal the crumbs. Who is the one living in fear? I ask.

I also realized I'm in love with my soon-to-be-wife. Well, maybe? She may get angry about my time spent away in my head or on the road, but in my heart, she shall stay each and every day for the rest of my life.

I also got to experience indirect contact with my nemesis, the government—well, at least in my mind anyways.

Stop the madness please. Enough, back to the Constitution, as my bumper sticker now reads.

I crossed its path on my way out of that area and back toward home, words written in the past by great men. They too knew when to say no way; we aren't taking this bullshit no more. I was filling my truck with gas when I commented about a man's choice of bumper stickers. He handed me a brand-new one to have for myself, I proudly display it. Let's get back to the American principles. All freedom lies within this document. I defend those words till death. My hand raised, and I accepted the challenge as a young Marine—once a Marine always a Marine as the slogan goes. My mission to survive took on a form of an unseen enemy. Not an actual bullet that entered my body during combat against another human being, but a microorganism planted within my bloodstream and my mind.

My enemy is me and those who support the lie.

My war is this.

My sense of power lies at the heart of America, its people, and its allowances within her borders. Read the Constitution prior to all those added twists of the truth. I think I will read it again myself. My main focus stays on the opening line.

"We the people of the United States!" I then skipped over the lies and directed my attention to the first nine amendments. No need to discuss further. Those are ours. Habeas corpus, semper fidelis.

I love this part prior to the Constitution.

Drafted by Thomas Jefferson between June 11 and June 28, 1776, the Declaration of Independence is at once the nation's most cherished symbol of liberty and Jefferson's most enduring monument. Here, in exalted and unforgettable phrases, Jefferson expressed the convictions in the minds and hearts of the American people.

DECLARATION OF INDEPENDENCE: IN CONGRESS, July 4, 1776.

The unanimous Declaration of the thirteen united States of America,

When in the Course of human events, it becomes necessary for one people to dissolve the political bands which have connected them with another, and to assume among the powers of the earth, the separate and equal station to which the Laws of Nature and of Nature's God entitle them, a decent respect to the opinions of mankind requires that they should declare the causes which impel them to the separation.

We hold these truths to be self-evident, that all men are created equal, that they are endowed by their Creator with certain unalienable Rights, that among these are Life, Liberty and the pursuit of Happiness.—That to secure these rights, Governments are instituted among Men, deriving their just powers from the consent of the governed,—That whenever any Form of Government becomes destructive of these ends, it is the Right of the People to alter or to abolish it, and to institute new Government, laying its foundation on such principles and organizing its powers in such form, as to them shall seem most likely to affect their Safety and Happiness. Prudence, indeed, will dictate that Governments long established should not be changed for light and transient causes; and accordingly all experience hath shown, that mankind are more disposed to suffer, while evils are sufferable, than to right themselves by abolishing the forms to which they are accustomed. But when a long train of abuses and usurpations, pursuing invariably the same Object evinces a design to reduce them under absolute Despotism, it is their right, it is their duty, to throw off such Government, and to provide new Guards for their future security.—Such has been the patient sufferance of these Colonies; and such is now the necessity which constrains them to alter their former Systems of Government. The history of the present King of Great Britain is a history of repeated injuries and usurpations, all having in direct object the establishment of an absolute Tyranny over these States. To prove this, let Facts be submitted to a candid world.

He has refused his Assent to Laws, the most wholesome and necessary for the public good.

He has forbidden his Governors to pass Laws of immediate and pressing importance, unless suspended in their operation till his Assent should be obtained; and when so suspended, he has utterly neglected to attend to them.

He has refused to pass other Laws for the accommodation of large districts of people, unless those people would relinquish the right of Representation in the Legislature, a right inestimable to them and formidable to tyrants only.

He has called together legislative bodies at places unusual, uncomfortable, and distant from the depository of their public Records, for the sole purpose of fatiguing them into compliance with his measures.

He has dissolved Representative Houses repeatedly, for opposing with manly firmness his invasions on the rights of the people.

He has refused for a long time, after such dissolutions, to cause others to be elected; whereby the Legislative powers, incapable of Annihilation, have returned to the People at large for their exercise; the State remaining in the mean time exposed to all the dangers of invasion from without, and convulsions within.

He has endeavored to prevent the population of these States; for that purpose obstructing the Laws for Naturalization of Foreigners; refusing to pass others to encourage their migrations hither, and raising the conditions of new Appropriations of Lands.

He has obstructed the Administration of Justice, by refusing his Assent to Laws for establishing Judiciary powers.

He has made Judges dependent on his Will alone, for the tenure of their offices, and the amount and payment of their salaries.

He has erected a multitude of New Offices, and sent hither swarms of Officers to harass our people, and eat out their substance.

He has kept among us, in times of peace, Standing Armies without the Consent of our legislatures.

He has affected to render the Military independent of and superior to the civil power.

He has combined with others to subject us to a jurisdiction foreign to our constitution, and unacknowledged by our laws; giving his Assent to their Acts of pretended Legislation:

For Quartering large bodies of armed troops among us:

For protecting them, by a mock Trial, from punishment for any Murders which they should commit on the Inhabitants of these States:

For cutting off our Trade with all parts of the world:

For imposing Taxes on us without our Consent:

For depriving us in many cases, of the benefits of Trial by Jury:

For transporting us beyond Seas to be tried for pretended offences

For abolishing the free System of English Laws in a neighboring Province, establishing therein an Arbitrary government, and enlarging its Boundaries so as to render it at once an example and fit instrument for introducing the same absolute rule into these Colonies:

For taking away our Charters, abolishing our most valuable Laws, and altering fundamentally the Forms of our Governments:

For suspending our own Legislatures, and declaring themselves invested with power to legislate for us in all cases whatsoever.

He has abdicated Government here, by declaring us out of his Protection and waging War against us.

He has plundered our seas, ravaged our Coasts, burnt our towns, and destroyed the lives of our people.

He is at this time transporting large Armies of foreign Mercenaries to complete the works of death, desolation and tyranny, already begun with circumstances of Cruelty & perfidy scarcely paralleled in the most barbarous ages, and totally unworthy the Head of a civilized nation.

He has constrained our fellow Citizens taken Captive on the high Seas to bear Arms against their Country, to become the executioners of their friends and Brethren, or to fall themselves by their Hands.

He has excited domestic insurrections amongst us, and has endeavored to bring on the inhabitants of our frontiers, the merciless Indian Savages, whose known rule of warfare is an undistinguished destruction of all ages, sexes and conditions.

In every stage of these Oppressions We have petitioned for Redress in the most humble terms: Our repeated Petitions have been answered only by repeated injury. A Prince, whose character is thus marked by every act which may define a Tyrant, is unfit to be the ruler of a free people.

Nor have we been wanting in attentions to our British brethren. We have warned them from time to time of attempts by their legislature to extend an unwarrantable jurisdiction over us. We have reminded them of the circumstances of our emigration and settlement here. We have appealed to their native justice and magnanimity, and we have conjured them by the lies of our common kindred to disavow these usurpations, which would inevitably interrupt our connections and correspondence. They too have been deaf to the voice of justice and of consanguinity. We must, therefore, acquiesce in the necessity, which denounces our Separation, and hold them, as we hold the rest of mankind, Enemies in War, in Peace Friends.

We, therefore, the Representatives of the united States of America, in General Congress, Assembled, appealing to the Supreme Judge of the world for the rectitude of our intentions, do, in the Name, and by Authority of the good People of these Colonies, solemnly publish and declare, That these United Colonies are, and of Right ought to be Free and Independent States; that they are Absolved from all Allegiance to the British Crown, and that all political connection between them and the State of Great Britain, is and ought to be totally dissolved; and that as Free and Independent States, they have full Power to levy War, conclude Peace, contract Alliances, establish Commerce, and to do all other Acts and Things which Independent States may of right do. And for the support of this Declaration, with a firm reliance on the protection of divine Providence, we mutually pledge to each other our Lives, our Fortunes and our sacred Honor.

*This is the fine print.

Go reread this entire section and then look up the nine amendments I'm referring to. Take a look at habeas corpus while you're at it. I plant the seed, not the work, never the work of opening your mind. Make a decision of your own free will to understand each section. I'm not a lawyer or a lawmaker, but I can read and write also. I should thank that judge who asked me like a wise ass if I could. You as a citizen are required to know this; we are free from bondage. This document also belongs to the American people, not just the government.

These words echo from the past within the hearts and minds of each and every one of us Americans. Our government needs to change; there is no denial in that fact. A government built on corruption needs to be abolished. New guards need to be established. Good luck, President Obama. You're the new guard. Rewrite history further and bring these pharmaceutical companies to justice. They poison our minds; countless numbers of people have been maimed and killed during the HIV race for a cure. Bring government itself on trial, that whole past administration before you needs to be on trial also, all the way back to the Reagan era. I have no trust in my government whatsoever. Our government has become so twisted and corrupt that the enemy resides in its own house. Create me an American dream for future generations without this disease of hatred. Think global, but remain true to the people of this country. I chose a cause and plan to keep fighting till my demise, but I refuse to idly stand by when I know citizens have been shorted. Part of that Declaration states this also. He has erected a multitude of new offices and sent hither swarms of officers to harass our people and eat out their substance.

He has kept among us, in times of peace, standing armies without the consent of our legislatures.

He has affected to render the military independent of and superior to the civil power.

We do that in our own country and overseas. What did you think was going to happen? Of course someone is going to attack us. How blind are you? The arrogance of you all frightens the hell out of me. Yet after you caused the problem long before I was born, fed it weapons to help them defend their own freedoms, they secured it, but put people in possession of them who couldn't be trusted. Decided it was a mistake, our armies were sent to fix it. You stopped short of the objective, they sent predictable hornet attackers in return, and then you call it their entire fault. Blind America screams, "Oh my god, they attacked us," as the towers fell. I tried to join the military because I was pissed off too. You said no. I called my cousin's husband Jim, he's a fireman, and thanked him for all he does. I watched them towers fall as did everyone else. I cried for all the families who lost their loved ones. I still cry for lost loved ones because I see families burying children at home. People protested in their funerals, yet it was that asshole holding the protest sign who called for war in the first place. Bush didn't know what the fuck to do; he's fucking retarded. We let the royal Arabs fly home. Wake up, people. Admit you're sorry and shake fucking hands already. We stuck a stick in a hornets' nest, we got stung, so you committed all forces as per usual. How many more lives need to die? I ask. I also admit they are crazy fanatical people, but who are we to judge? Consider it a punch in the mouth for a punch in the mouth just like I have always done. We hold freedom in a higher sense than any nation on the planet, but we keep feeding the monkey with its fix, more of the same self-destruction.

I am an avid golfer myself; perhaps we could discuss a change in policy while you invite me to a game. I am a supporter of change also. I am sure this won't happen, but it is the thought that counts, so think about it.

Also think about this, I am a fully trained Marine who was denied many times from entering the armed forces again even after 9-11 happened. I can only say it hurt me to watch scared, impressionable young kids enter combat knowing full well I should've been there also, or in the place of at least one of them. The excuse was I have a preexisting condition and I would put people at risk. Thanks for the vote of confidence and the propaganda of fear. You know what, I'm glad I didn't get the nod to rejoin the ranks because this war has many conspiracies behind it, and that is all I got to say about that. Bring my brothers and sisters home.

About the medication.

Somebody would bring this point up, so I'll save you the trouble.

Nobody put a gun to my head to take these medicines.

Yet in my mind, the pharmaceutical companies and the Center for Disease Control has done just that, including the veterans' department. I feel that they have scared a population of people who happened to catch the HIV virus into the same scenario. The outright blatant propaganda has definitely sent a bullet into our minds to take whatever the government allows them to deem safe for human consumption. Has the FDA lost its fucking mind also? Do they not oversee these poison pushers?

Here's a prime example, Atripla, a once-a-day pill, a drug deemed safe for human consumption which hit the market a few years back. This medicine has three parts which is the new normal combination therapy for those of us living with this disease. What the public fails to hear is that this medicine has a hallucinogenic property within its chemical makeup. I was given one of the main ingredients to this combination therapy, miracle drug prior to its release several years earlier. I know this for a fact from my experiences, and this is my opinion and so are the government's and these companies' who manufacture this. Have they actually believed it necessary to mix in these compounds to keep us believing the lies? I was told these were normal side effects and they would pass over time. Obviously they haven't. I hold each and every one involved responsible for holding a gun to my head and leading me to believe if I didn't take this shit that I would waste away and die without it. How about a lawsuit against this manufacturer for pumping dangerous drugs into unsuspecting patients only to have them at a state of belief so they will keep consuming their product? Sounds just like a drug dealer to me and a cult. I remember Charles Manson used LSD to gain control over his followers, and we all know the outcome of that scenario. I have to question the motives quiet honestly. Is this all about money, power, and control? We all know the

CIA has done extensive studies within the use of LSD to create assassins, patsies, and the much-sought-after Manchurian candidate. They also do extensive studies within hypnosis, mind control, and intimidation interrogation. What the fuck is going on? I ask.

Here's another fact I discovered about the leading developers of these drugs during my quest for possible sponsorship for racing dirt bikes. This too is my opinion. I researched several different companies in order to find an in, so to speak. While poking around on the Internet, I came across several ad campaigns about how taking their medicine was the way to go if considering or searching a course of therapy. I noticed the ads had very healthy, vibrant, in-shape, muscular people with nice teeth on their billboards. This was obviously an at-first-glance trap for the uneducated individuals. The truth is these companies use models, not HIV-positive people, to promote their poison. Why do I bring attention to this? I believe it is to cover up the absolute fact that the medicine they are promoting causes deformities. Examples are fat displacement, skinny arms, skinny legs, sunken faces, swollen stomachs, accelerated osteoporosis, tumors, high blood pressure, neuropathy, heart problems, anemia, and the all-too-common camel hump, never mind the problems with tooth decay. I found this to be a slap straight in the face to all who have believed the lies that these ads project.

Here I am, a true athlete who has won several amateur motorcycle titles in search of some funding to help out with my travel expenses from huge pharmaceutical companies and they don't even use HIV-positive individuals within the ad campaigns. Oh wait, Magic Johnson popped his head up once in a while on flyers for you, another money grabber, who happens to be famous already. What bullshit! Yes, I am pissed, and I'm totally biased against them. But the fact remains they are providing the public a propaganda campaign. Where are the casualties to your horrors? I know plenty, in fact I'm one of them myself. I had even lost one of my testicles due to your medicines over the years and had a tumor cut out of my neck. I have pissed and shit blood, puked till I was coughing blood. Yet I wasn't even considered even after receiving a well-thought-out and planned course of action for you to take in promoting a real HIV-positive person in your advertisement campaign. I guess I'm only good for testing? Fuck you!

END THE WAR!

Start over.

We need to provide jobs for each and every one of them returning soldiers and veterans.

Rid our government of them old relics who have become stagnant minded and resemble furniture, much less a leader of men. Institute a new draft system, not for war purposes, but for educational purposes, rebuilding the infrastructure of our own country. A good time would be right after their eighteenth birthday and let them pursue college afterward. Quicken the education system up and teach practical life skills, survival skills. No child slips through the cracks and ends up lost in a sea of uncertainty. End this doctrine of hate.

Demand three years of military service upon its new citizens and the youth of our nation. Make it mandatory to all though, no privileges to the rich. Empty out some of these prisons, and put them to work in those foreign countries, rebuilding another's home. Let them have no reprieve until the long laborious day has ended. Reinstitute the chain gangs of the past if need be, but bring back the best of our youth and put the worst against the worst in these hot spots around the globe. The people of our prison systems unite because they have to, in order to survive. Send them with tools not weapons on their missions of mercy. Have them plant crops just like the pilgrims did. It wouldn't be long after the enemies of our country would lay down the weapons also and pick up the tools alongside of us, for that I am sure. I am sure we have plenty of willing, able-bodied men and women who would love the chance to be free again even if it meant giving up their own life in the defense of the full meaning to the word *freedom*. Give them an e-tool and tell them to dig in next to that grunt and learn by doing. After they have a firm grasp on their situation and job duties, make them complete double the required three years of service to allow them return back into the country. Use the illegals the same way if need be. Locking them up and sending them into our prison system clogs the pipeline so to speak. Nobody is above public service. Nobody's job is less important than another. Start regulating these senators, congressman, and even your own spending of American tax dollars. Put an end to so much foreign aid for a while. Let some relief happen on our end. Once we rebuild the roads, bridges and secure our sewer treatment facilities, and clean up our own mess for a little while, provide homes and jobs to our people, feed the hungry of our borders, send aid to America before her dream is lost, maybe there would be less thought on going to battle if we were more self-sufficient. We have the knowledge and the resources to make it happen, just put it into action.

Secure this problem down Mexico way by tearing down that useless fucking wall and integrating that whole place clear down to the Panama Canal into Mexican-American soil, most of them live among us already. There are massive killings going on down there in this moment in time. Send some help closer to home, they are our neighbors, yet we send massive amounts of food, fuel, and troops to countries around the globe. Let's not talk about the price tag on these endeavors, offer free passage, but we will send the resources to rebuild your nation and stop the flow of illegal drugs by giving you a better plan to sustain your economy without the bloodshed by making something illegal and all-evil within our own hypocritical nation. Let's face it, drugs are a huge business; supply and demand needs to be regulated not be illegal. I would love to have free trade of medicinal marijuana, especially in my hometown in Massachusetts. I would love to build a medical treatment facility and distribution center there. No weapons are needed to make this a reality. Growers are needed, and distribution centers need to be established—plenty of job opportunities within this idea. Farming of plants for fuel, peace of mind, medical care, and just plain old get fucking high needs to be a solid foundation of principle.

Allow more water to flow downriver into this Mexican nation for farming on a larger scale. Lots of food are needed to feed the world. I know people living in Africa where the AIDS population is huge could use food more than medicine when I know this from my own survival. Don't tell Oprah that though. She will steal my idea and use it as her own if she could pull her own self-righteous hand out of the cookie jar herself. I would much rather see my own countrymen and women benefit first. Where do these celebrities on television get off asking the American lower classes to send money to foreign aid when they make millions each year themselves? Send your own money. The cure is based on proper nutrition and exercise. Sending medicine which is poison helps to kill them quicker. I also know that the disease will never be cured because it is too much of a money maker. I also know that if doctors continue trying to kill a virus within a patient's body, it will eventually kill the patient. It is not about HIV/AIDS virus killing people; it is the secondary, opportunistic diseases that need to be stopped. I have been running on fifty-two T-cells the last time I allowed them to be checked. I stopped caring about the numbers and just started living. My immune system may be very low, but it is still working just fine as long as I eat a proper diet and seek medical attention when I get the flu, hepatitis, bronchitis, and pneumonia. They all have the potential to kill me as does the common cold. But I will survive.

How about you skim some of them water companies who charge us to bottle up free water and sell it back to us. Oh, I forgot, our water supplies are filled with pollutants unsafe for consumption, hence the bottling. Ask them for permission to let a few trillion gallons to wash through their countryside. Pipe that shit south. Let's get to work feeding these people, clothing them, rebuilding their towns. Allowing them to freely come and go as Mexican-Americans or just rename them all to North Americans. South Americans begin below the canal. Allow access to free trade agreements within these barrios, hamlets, and remote areas also. Do your fucking job! Light a fire under some people's asses! Inspire them to make a difference in the world. I wouldn't mind having a legal Havana cigar once you make peace with that island of peoples.

As for the stronger so-called drugs like cocaine and heroin, these need a regulation system as well, but not to be condemned or illegalized. It's a total waste of time and money to try and deter a population of free Americans from using drugs, never mind the rest of the world. Drugs haven't killed me just by simply doing them in search of a cure and to regulate my own pain. It is the whole lousy illegal status that has caused the whole fucking mess and has made it dangerous. The legal drugs I was told to take for my so-called health issues make me far worse feeling than the illegal ones. Truthfully, I have become convinced the medicines make me dangerous and delusional; this is exactly why I refuse to take them.

Prohibition of alcohol is a prime example of how a mess was created when a simple pleasure was taken away from its people. Americans love their vices; we are free to explore any endeavor we set out to accomplish. This does include self-destruction of our own bodies, as long as you're not causing harm to others, it's all good. Nobody twisted your arm. Well, maybe some of my friends would like to twist mine completely out of socket if I was picking up a crack pipe again, but I won't twist yours. Nor will I encourage people to stop taking the medicine they think helps them.

I have to question the validity of HIV medicine actually doing anything good in the interest of health as should you. I have countless amounts of side effects experienced during each and every experimental medicine documented within my medical records held by the government. My blood has been drained countless times in the search of this phantom called cure. Give up this bullshit and stop the madness. I hereby decree to all who have read this story that my words are true. I am sure big business, meaning, pharmaceutical companies and our government will try and discredit my claims of their denial of basic human rights. This genocide has to stop. I hold them accountable to lost lives and many deformities caused on nations of people and your relatives. I held nothing back within my story to give you the truth. If I withheld any information about my life, I apologize for not including whatever they pull out of their own ass and try to use to smear my credibility. That fact is I gave you my best while living the worst. I am a simple, broken, medicine-tested, delusional man living on a disability pension with a payment dictated by the government. I risk losing all my financial freedom, but in my mind, it is a way to silence me. So fuck 'em, let them take it all away. I will quietly disappear into the forest and reunite with all your ancestors within the spirit world when my life expires anyways. The fact is nobody can touch my disability monies allotted to me; it is protected under the disability act, and it was established by the veterans of the past and the people of our country within our government long ago. Isn't that ironic? I know plenty of veterans milking the system sitting on their asses because that is the easy way out. I have fallen and risen from death many times, I have rested for many days, yet I still get up and do something physically demanding and very dangerous, all the while living with AIDS.

Truth is within the listening of the people. I wanted to share my experiences and my mistreatment within the hands of capitalists who think of money before the welfare of its citizens. I loudly request all of the HIV/AIDS diagnosed and those who have lost family to this disease to stand with me in the hopes we shut down these poison factories protected by our own government. Their need to see our suffering and pain hasn't been in vain. They make billions upon billions of dollars peddling false hope, and it destroys our bodies along with our minds. Guess what, motherfuckers, they still haven't given us a cure. The cure rests inside of you, proper diet and exercise kept me alive all these years. I chose another course of treatment without believing the medicinal lie. I refused to follow their directions when I knew this medicine was poisoning me. I believed half of what they said and began to question it all.

As you begin to understand the words I have spoken to you while reading about my life experiences, remember this also: this is not a fucking movie or some shitty-ass talk show. You're getting it spoon-fed from a survivor, an HIV/AIDS-positive Marine since 1992, proof of a life filled with amazing accomplishments since, a guy who isn't afraid to say he has had sex with women, men, and a few very hot transsexuals. All races are equal. All sexual preferences are the individual right of each person who walks this earth. Just don't be touching kids, stay in your own age group, you sick, twisted fuck.

I never had to use a weapon that killed another human being within my lifetime. I thank God and everyone for all their help during my journey through hell. You walked beside me and kept me safe. I also thank the people he sent within my path who kept me from destroying his wondrous gifts me and my neighbor. Remember my tale of misery, pain, and discovery, and apply it to your own life as I had done each time I fell. I found a way to get back up, dust off, and begin again. Try it out, and then pass it on. I plan to stay exactly that, 100 percent hands clean, and my soul remains within heaven and totally disconnected from causing another's inner fire to burn out. I remain, maintain, and fight within my own pain. I am quite sane; it is everything else going on that's insane. I can say now I'm content in knowing this fact as well. I have enjoyed the company of plenty of people. However, I arrived innocent and curious about the world around them and joined in their games. I have had intimate encounters and enjoyed plenty of wine, women, songs, and occasionally a few T-girl dongs.

I was unable to continue on with the new test medicine I mentioned in my first delusion chapter. The drug called Intelence was its name. It was supposed to help other combination drugs which grew resistant to the virus over the years. The theory behind this medicine was sound in its plan. I was also told by my doctor to send them my resume within sponsorship for racing. I tried to take this stuff as directed along with two other powerful medicines I had taken in the past with decent-enough results according to my blood counts. I wanted to be honestly taking something and collecting my pension at the same time reestablishing my prior commitment to finding a cure for others in the future. I'm sorry to report that this medicine had me pissing blood within a short period of time. I can't idly sit and be poisoned all over again, can I? How convenient it seems they come up with a medication which can now boost the medicine someone has taken in the past that has grown resistant to the virus. This is definitely going to make someone a lot of money in the future. The times when I felt fairly decent after suffering close to a year to adjust to medications of my past which you told me had lost their ability to kill this virus are all available for my usage once again. I knew it was a lie each time a new medicine came out, and doctors told me my health status suddenly turned for the worst according to my blood counts. You needed side effects data for your new poisons. Thanks, but no thanks. My only true regret is that I actually fell for my doctor's hype about possible sponsorship. How easily I was lured by possible extra money to help with racing expenses. They had done their homework, I was reeled in very quickly, and money is always good bait to me. So aren't sex, drugs, and rock and roll? This will not happen again.

I went into the Marine Corps in 1991, and it is now the twenty-year mark. Twenty years is the usual term of service needed to fully retire from the military. I was in actual service till the end of 1993 when you told me to leave. I gave up working to pursue a dream in 1998. In my mind I was still connected regardless the honorable discharge, because I was monitored since. My mission had been changed, that's all. I would love to say my term of service is completed, but this virus still exists within me. I will consider my debt of service paid in full to the American people, and I refuse to take another medicine manufactured for this disease. I also apologize to the American people also for crying Uncle when it hurt too much to bear.

If God has made me, then I'm not yours to pass judgment upon. The truth is I am your brother, your cousin, your uncle, your friend, and quite possibly, I was a stand-in as your dad. I don't need their medicine no more. I will not partake in this medicinal madness anymore. My constitutional rights and my civil rights have been infringed upon enough.

This lower section is just because I can.

Within my dreams or hallucination episodes, I wander into the woods and come upon a whole community of people. There are many tents and many different groups of different tribes here: Apaches, Mohegan, Cherokee, Zulu, Navajo, Vikings, Mongols, and any other group you can name living in peace long removed from the natural living earth. The forest is quiet with a soft blanket of snow covering the ground. The air is crisp; it cuts through me to the bone, and my hospital gown is no defense to the icy winds. I pass several unfamiliar warriors and their children. As I get closer each time, they smile and just point to keep going. I finally reach the tent I am meant to enter, and Squanto opens the flap for me to go in. He pats me on the shoulder and says, "Welcome, please sit by the fire." I wait for several minutes desperately trying to warm my body from the heat of the flames. I feel the touch of a warm blanket being placed over my shoulders and thank the man responsible. I was shocked to learn that this old man who sits with me now was a great chief when he was alive. I am sitting within the tent of Metacom, King Philip, who is puffing on a peace pipe and watching the fire dance before us. We speak of simple pleasures and not of world domination or a capitalist society. It's once again peaceful within my mind, and my inner spirit settles into the comfort of the warmed buffalo skin wrapped around my body. He tells me the fire is warming to an old man's bones, and I agree. I laugh when he breaks my balls about needing the whole tribe to come to my aid after a simple puking, shitting, feverish mess I had created in my youth. I ask him if he knows he is dead. He tells me he lives on within my spirit. He also thanks me for only calling that one time when I desperately needed a friend. He inhales deeply on his pipe and blows out a huge cloud of smoke. He begins to chant and tells me to peer into the flames. I see myself as a young boy reaching for booze, pills, crack pipes, medicines, guns, knives, and anything that would get me high or get me off. I have come full circle. Everything that has happened was exactly the way it was supposed to happen. I am by far the winner in my battles so far, but I can't find peace and happiness. I have journeyed plenty of times here in my lifetime. I am in the spirit world again looking for answers I already know about surviving.

He tells me how his father before him kept true to the laws of nature and listened to the four winds and the earth. Squanto tells me of his own travels during the time of his own capture long ago from his own family. His tale is similar to mine. "Man is but a simple creature in comparison to the hawk, the fox, the bear, and even the wolf. Without coexistence, we don't exist. We have watched over you for a long time, little sick, crazy Mello man! Oh yeah! That's what we call you within the Indian nations. In heaven they call you Gabriel, in hell they call you Judas, in Davey Jones's locker they call you the Tempest, in life they call you Uncle G.—a Marine, delusional, crazy, and a fucking fag. Some may say you're Odin from the Viking era, the Hindus call you the Ganesha, in Japan they call you Jizo Bosatsu, the Chinese P'an Chin-lien is heard to live within your spirit also, and even

Buddha laughs because he was you in another life; but truthfully, you are yourself.

"You are Gary—the name is a short form of all the Gerald names and a well-known family name. It is derived from the sixth-century Anglo-Saxon *gar*, meaning spear, and *wig*, meaning battle, or the man using a battle spear."

Shaka Zulu arrive, and he was impressed with my life also. Being a stand for freedom against foreign and domestic oppression within your heart takes courage worthy of his buffalo formation.

I thanked him and grabbed my Johnson and shook it. They always told me I liked to use a big stick to stir up the shit just to make it stink when I was a kid. We all laughed together because it was funny.

"So what does all this mean?" I asked.

"Am I dead? What of my family, my mom, my dad, my brothers?" I asked. "I hope I can see them again. Can they see you as I can see them?"

"We're in the spirit world, asshole. They can't see us." *(Classic line from the movie* Young Guns, *I had to use it.)*

Squanto laughs and tells me to relax. "You are among friends here, and your own family is just fine. They can't see us because they haven't made the journey yet. You are the messenger. Carry peace in your heart, and tell them of your travels and visions.

"You have many gifts to share with others who are ready to listen. Sit with me, Marine. You have lost your path. Here take this peyote tea and swallow it, you will see your path. Be aware, there is a lot to learn from your vision. Go in peace, my friend. Give yourself a purpose which benefits all."

Oh yeah! Release my medical file, and that federal investigation on me to the public for them to study upon my death, use anything to give them peace, if only for one more day. Also, in case you think I'm telling my story because I think I'm Jesus or a prophet or something, you're wrong. I was concerned myself at one time, but I made it past thirty-three years old, and I don't wear a long robe with sandals carrying a staff. I certainly don't need to wear a shirt and tie to feel important either. You also won't see me carrying a gun on my hip to install fear into another either. You also won't see me bobbing my head toward a wall in Jerusalem either for that matter. You won't see me throwing a rug on the ground and bowing repeatedly either. I won't be wearing a pointy hat in Rome either. I will never bow to the madness in my head either to take another's life. I will certainly beat you into submission as I have been trained my entire life by all of you. But I will not kill you. I certainly wanted to be like Jesus, but even he had his own cross to bear as do I. You may see me riding a motorcycle within the forest from time to time, I'm also tattoo covered, I wear bandanas, I'm proud of my scars and I play golf.

I'm nothing more than a leper among the rest of you; we all are sheep not worthy of his grace.

I now know this, and it totally bummed me out too.

Armageddon can be stopped by us. It's not too late, and the prophecy points to December 21, 2012. Some believe the Second Coming will happen. It would be better to actually be living peacefully upon his arrival, don't you think? God have mercy on us all.

I guess transformation could exist . . .

I have accepted my life sentence, and it's calling . . .

Lance Corporal Mello reporting, sir . . .

From my blood, find peace . . .

Remove this ban on gays/lesbians in the military also, it's bullshit!

I remain U.S. Marine awaiting your orders . . .

Never mind . . . my time is drawing to an end . . . as is the enemies . . .

POEMS

Near Death

Body cramping, muscles tighten, sight dimming.
No air provided to your brain.
Slowly slipping out of the pain.
Moments of life wheeze by fraught with your guilt.
Scary, quick flashing pictures of the day racing through your head from the past.
Flashes of bright light coming into your vision.
You try to hold on, but drifting off seems peaceful.
The struggle goes on forever and ever to stay alive.
Strange people yelling in your mind from a distance.
Memories of youth and dead relatives come out of the brightness.
All seems right.
You want to stay, but your time is not now.
You're back in that ambulance whisking toward hope.
Time flashes forward three months.
You're back on drugs—no dreams and no memories that feel happy or are worth remembering.
Time has stood still.
God turned you away, your time is not up.
Cast down back to earth among the mortals.
More pain to suffer, fix your wrongdoings, sucker.
Not wanted in heaven or down here.
Nowhere to go, nothing to do.
Live without fear because the end is not up to you.

Dust

Clouds gather, thunder rumbles while lightning strikes.
Fear grips and chokes you.
Pick up your swords and grab your pikes.
For the enemy approaches on this field of morning dew.
Gather your courage and suppress your fears.
Screams of pain and whimpering tears.
Long live the King and his court.
They have turned war into a televised sport.
Forever remembered with honor and glory.
I am here to tell that story.
Draped in a flag and lowered slowly into that six-foot hole.
No worries, mate, I'll remember the life that they stole.
A brother, a sister, a mom, or a dad.
How wonderful the thoughts and times we all had.
When the field is cleared and the steel is left to rust.
Keep this thought in your mind, we all become dust.

Processed

Buying and using too many drugs.
Wish Momma would have given me a few more hugs.
Under surveillance, cops watching everything you do.
Arrested, arraigned, and sent off to the human zoo.
Racked, stacked, and aligned in a row.
Stripped of your belongings standing naked from head to toe.
Lift your feet, lift your balls, open your mouth, and say ahh.
Check your hair then your ears
Bend over and spread your cheeks, in goes a few fingers
How dare that guard reach in so far?
Feeling violated and quite ill.
Should've thought twice about taking that pill.
Fucking piece of shit cop, I should've smashed out your grill.
Thoughts of naked strippers dancing in my head.
Ass stinging and leaking, wish I were dead.
Pushed out a door, given a bright orange suit and some flip-flops.
Pissing and moaning about how much my life sucks, blaming
the cops.
Shitty lawyer, asshole judge, and that fucking jury.
Entering a place filled with fury.

Battle Cry

Light your torches, light your flames
We will not take part in their games.
Throw of your moments of doubt.
Rally together and push them out.
The beast is coming and that's right soon.
Stare at the sun, but howl at the moon.
Night's air is calling you out tonight.
Scream and holler because you know it's right.

Stop the enemy who twists your mind and makes you not care.
Don't play fair.
Crush their will with knives, sticks, bats, and broken bottles of rum.
The time has come.
Strong hearts don't run.
Stand together, and we shall win.
Lop off their heads and watch them spin.

It's the way of the warrior who deals out death.
Never stop swinging or kicking until your last breath.

See them scurry.
See them run.
This night is ours.
Do it quickly, we only have hours.
Smash the enemy till they're all gone.
A new world order comes at dawn.

Just Business

Strolling outside down on the block.
Out for that release, they call it crack.
It comes in the form of a rock.
Hustling home to smoke and feel better.
Killing my dreams and writing this letter.
Lessons learned and lessons taught.
Crazy nightmares and crazy visions is what I got.
Planes crashing into buildings.
Soldiers fighting and coming home in metal boxes.
Starving people living in boxes.
Lost our will.
Feeling quite ill.
Swallow another pill.
Wash it down with nice sour mash whiskey.
Smash that computer and your TV.
Laugh at the government; be careful, that is quite risky.
Patriotic act is in effect, you may be judged as a terrorist.
Never mind that corruption because justice is always on their list.
Pointing fingers and their guns.
Judgment day is coming; it is then we shall see who runs.

Ode to the Shotgun

Woke up this morning without a damn clue.
Watched the television until two.
Really have no purpose in life now that I have become a rotting
diseased,
Infected, drug-addicted, wasted squirt of man goo.

Slowly slipping into a dark abyss.
Sweat covered, shaking, and stinking of piss.

Why don't I just release myself from this misery and pain?
Let the coroner deal with the gray matter flung about the room,
Causing that stain.

Sorry, Momma, I couldn't take it no more.
Sorry for the mess I left on your floor.

Forgive me if you can see *fit.*

I was tired of all those pills, tests, probes, strobes, visions,
Hallucinations, fevers, chills, broken bones, thrown stones,
Headaches, muscle fatigues, vomiting sessions, and their dirty looks.
Government has stolen my mind just like a couple of crooks.

I was tired of running to the hopper because I had to *shit.*

For God has granted me a one-way trip for that never-ending
rebel yell.
I'll say "howdy doo" to all the lost souls on my journey to hell.
Wonder if the devil has set up my room?

Load, pump, squeeze . . . *Boom!*

The Tale of Two Socks

Worn for comfort to stop the blisters from forming,
To keep my feet warm.

Walking for miles with no destination in sight.
Someone save me from my plight.
Circling buzzards fly around my head.
The smell of bacon in their nostrils as I fall over dead.
Gathering boldness as they swoop down and peck at my skin.
Thoughts of angels and long-lost kin.

Awoken on the sidewalk in the middle of the day.
Must have been dreaming is what I can say.

Slip off a sock and wipe my swamp-covered ass cheeks.
Thank God it was only a hallucination brought on from the shits
I've been having these past few weeks.

Drunken Delight

Out at the club drinking beers and shots.
Music is banging, honey's looking fly, giving me the hots.

Stepping and fetching, trying all my charms.
Nothing works to bring one into my arms.

More shots and shooters.
Guess I won't be playing with them hooters.

Night ends without a number or name.
"Christ almighty" is screamed after puking on the sidewalk.
I have lost my game.
Staggering around, bouncing off parked cars for at least a block.

Into a cab I hop, depressed and defeated, I'm to blame.
Stop uptown in the city for some crack to ease the pain.

Several hours later, broke and tweaking.
Head to the corner for what I had been seeking.

Hustle some ho into spending the night.
Crash out in a cockroach-infested shitty motel, what a fright.

Wake up several hours later with my ass hurting so much I'm on the verge
Of tears.
Turns out her name were Manny.
The neighborhood tranny.

The mother of all fears.

Casualty

A kick, a punch, a bullet, a tank, a bomb, and another dead body.
A kiss, a hug, a smile, a greeting, a fond farewell, and best wishes.
Sending peace and love to your neighbors from afar.
These things are common in this moment in time.

Don't let me rant and rave or protest or even care,
Because these thoughts are not mine.
They are only from years gone past.
This hatred and misfortune cannot last.

Put away your evildoings and your bad deeds.
Eventually we all will be planted within the weeds.
Flies and maggots will help this process along.
I would feel safer without the bullets, the tanks, and that bomb.
For a kick or a punch is what I long.

Coward-ass people use weapons that kill.
Show true strength and resist that delusional pill.

The choices are yours and yours alone.
Throw punches and kicks until you break a bone.
Don't be coerced though in causing others harm.
I would hate for you to return home missing an arm.

Corruption

Traveled the country from Boston to Maine to Texas to Florida
to South Carolina, all the way across to California.
Seeing poverty, pain, suffering, and a sickly, drug-infested,
diseased population
Living in fear and paranoia.
Struggling to keep myself disconnected and unaffected.
Try as I may with no avail for I have become totally infected.
My mind races, and I have wild nightmares of what we have become.
Stand back if I'm bleeding unless you want some.

Killers, rapists, drug dealers, corrupt politicians selling their *wares.*

Liars and deceivers answering to no one for their crimes.
Shocked, frightened people within their phony-ass borders.
A line, a parallel, a divide.
Laying claim to land that is rightfully ours.
Dying for nothing more than their greed.
Someone has poisoned his or her thinking.
Ask your mayors, your judge, and your senate, even ask the Congress.
Fuck it, ask the president what is wrong.
You'll get double talk and brushed aside like all the rest.
Questions unanswered and left confused.

All you get in return is their hollow *stares.*

Just Life

Allowed to live on medication.
Born, beaten, broken, bashed, burned, and brainwashed.
Conspiracy-filled mind.
Screams fall silent from within.
Stumbling, stupider, stinking, stuck on a shit pot, slurred speech.
Drunken, drugged, diapered old-ass motherfucker.
Lost, loser, lowlife, with no life, leaving a legacy of suffering.
Hurry the fuck up and die.
Take this gun and shoot.
Take this pipe and smoke.
Take this bottle and drink.
No need to think.
Death is calling.
His name is George.
Follow him into the ninth circle of hell.
Or don't follow and get more of the same when you return home.
You must be crazy your thoughts are all whack.
Should we all line up and give you a facial smack.
End the bullshit.
No more denial.
Put him on trial.
Add him to the pile.
Fuck his lies and deceit.
Just be sure he pays his victim witness fee and give him a receipt.

Born Free

Innocent child enters this world. Taught to read, write, and speak.
Once these are learned, he is told how to speak.
Hold your thoughts in because it's not polite to speak your mind.
It's against the rules.
The child is given so many rules that his weak developing mind loses
Interest and rebels against being told how to act.
The adolescent takes pleasure in going against what is perceived
to be the
Right way.
Follows a new code:
Live your own life.
Let everyone else be victims of the closed-off mind.
Break all their rules and regulations.
Perhaps within this new form of living, there lies a freedom.

A world of people left screaming for their human rights.
The politicians not listening during the day or the long nights.
Gasoline costing way too much money.
I'm sorry, child, there is no food to eat; it went to the gas, honey.
Millions starving and left in the cold.
Wake up, people, it is getting old.
Greedy rich people not giving a damn.
They get breaks from good old Uncle Sam.
Send the poor off to fight in their senseless war.
It leaves the rich with that much more.
Rewrite the Constitution I shall say.
Let them go fight for at least a day.
Rally the resistance and stand tall together.
Stand ready and we will use old tactics such as the tar and feather.
See if the system will crack from us dropping out.
Our inheritance is written, so get up and shout.
Teach them what it means to be of some worth.
Fuck these rich fools, we are the meek of the earth.

So it is written, so it shall be.
Never a wasted thought, forever and always I shall live free.
Take up your weapons and go fight, soldier boy.
Uncle Sam needs your worthless body, you're his new play toy.
So keep watching their propaganda flicks and believe their lies.
They show no concern when one of you dies.
Sooner or later you will make the six o'clock news.
Kill your enemy 'cause you're left all alone without any clues.
Death is coming for you, so why such the rush?
Drop the weapon and let them others fight who keep it all on
the hush.

It shall be written, dearest young soldier boy, for your family to see.
They will see you in a fine picture within the obituary.
You'll look so fine in your uniform with all your medals glinting.
Straining their eyes from the sun, they will even be squinting.
At the bottom in fine print the caption shall read Born Free.

Once it's read, you may get some comfort in knowing this one fact.
Some politician from our government will thank you for your
life being
Given up, they will call it a selfless act.
No worries, soldier boy, you're now a star.
The world was watching even though it was brief and disregarded.
I even heard their speech while driving in my car.
For it is a soldier like you who keeps us all safe.
I only wish mankind would wake up and stop all wars.
This poem should reach the White House if I carry it to them myself.
I'm sorry, soldier boy, they wouldn't open the fucking doors.
It now grows dust sitting on my shelf.

Perhaps my thoughts of you were enough on this day.
Perhaps I will remember you before I sleep tonight when I drop
to my knees
And begin to pray.
Thank you, soldier boy, you are an unsung hero who is entitled
to my praise.
Watch over me from heaven throughout my days.

I shall meet you in heaven when my days are through.
Be sure to come over and greet me so I can meet you.
A simple handshake together, if you would be so kind.
Your memory shall live on, at least on this day, through my mind.

Pleasure

To my sweet little Tommy girl,
we met in such a rush
yet I hold an immense crush.
Time will tell if my feelings are true
all I want is to be next to you.
Struck in the heart by Cupid's little arrow
I feel like the pirate Jack Sparrow.
I watched as you left my vision when we parted
feeling very sad because our relationship had just started.
I long for your touch and your soft lips,
My loins are aroused while I watch the swing of your hips.
You are a gift sent to me in this moment of life,
I totally was flattered when you said to marry you and have you
as my wife.
You're a perfect match to me
hopefully in time we shall see
the winds have spoken when we got together
I will lift you into my arms 'cause you're light as a feather.
Holding you close in a warm embrace
kissing you softly on your pretty face.
Gazing into them big brown eyes
my heart is alive in the midnight skies.
You have a great many powers
all I had was a few simple flowers.
Yet you took me for quite the ride
Allow me your hand and walk by my side.
We shall dance to the rhythm of our own song
the gods put us together, they can't be wrong.

Sealed with a Kiss

^^The clock was ticking within our heart and mind^^
^^We needed someone to fill the void and to be very kind^^
^^Years have passed without a hope or prayer^^
^^Thoughts of loneliness and pain, did anyone care^^
^^Along came a message on my Facebook wall^^
^^Wasn't expecting it to be you after all^^
^^Could it be true^^
^^Was it really you^^
^^After twenty years of waiting for the right person to arrive^^
^^My heart skips a beat and reminds me I'm alive^^
^^The stillness of my life awakens anew^^
^^Our first call, heard your voice, and knew it was you^^
^^Drop everything in such a rush with meeting you in sight^^
^^Pack my truck and take off in the night^^
^^Drive half-lovestruck and so excited I must have reached 144^^
^^Rehearsed this in my dreams many a times before^^
^^Arrive in your town and then on your block^^
^^Quite nervous with flowers in hand, you hear me knock^^
^^You open and our eyes lock on to each other's and we both
smile^^
^^My arms reach out and we embrace for a long while^^
^^I feel your heart racing inside your chest^^
^^I think it was mine, your stunning beauty nearly drove me to
cardiac arrest^^
^^As each day passes that we are together^^
^^Nothing seems wrong and my problems are as light as a feather^^
^^I promise you this^^
^^I will love you forever, and its *sealed with a kiss*^ ^

I had my fiancée open the dictionary to a random page and close
her eyes and just point at the page. Her finger came to rest on
the word *filth*.

FILTH: foul dirt, obscenity, dirt, dung, feces, contamination, corruption, pollution, foul matter, sewage, muck, manure, slop, squalor, trash, grime, mud, smudge, silt, garbage, carrion, slush, slime, sludge, foulness, filthiness, excrement, dregs, lees, sediment, rottenness, impurity.

I laughed because it's exactly who we are. What that means to me, nothing. But for some, they would really have them words attach to me, and attach them to others, instead of themselves. Not a good idea, it keeps you from being pure. God grants life and death, not us. Throw down them weapons and start living without the hate and the filth within you.

Insights
The Missing Link to Peace

There are stronger forces pulling at your soul to make a difference and to be heard. With words the difference can be first listened to, within time actions will be taken for people to see and become inspired. It is within this new inspirational way of displaying true, authentic equality that civilization will begin to work together. This in turn shall teach others how to communicate on a level of fair play. It is through honesty without any deception that progress is made. The longer you are able to spread a message of peace, the more ears will hear it. The longer it is heard, eventually mankind's hearts will be more opened up and they will see that destruction, oppression, and pure disregard to human life is not a foreseeable future for anyone who wishes to prosper. True aggression shouldn't be used to convert, change, or take away someone's right to live their life the way they see fit to do so. Their beliefs should remain their own. The only thing need be done is let them see how with unconditional cooperation anything is possible. It takes a stronger person to reach out their hand in friendship than it takes to stay close-minded to new possibilities and ideas to be constructed together as a unit.

A True Journey

Slipping from dream to reality eventually intertwines itself and becomes a way of existence. Following a pursuit of happiness and tranquility within one's lifespan will take you to the ends of the earth. If it is pure peace one seeks, they will not find this in a physical place, time, or group. Pure peace is developed from within oneself. It is in that moment when you will be truly transformed. All that traveling around would not be wasted though. You would eventually come to understand this simple fact. Lots of wonderful things would be seen and lots of horrible things as well. A journey into your own mind and body would reveal the same things. You must learn to look past our existence and understand that our divine spark within flutters like a candle flame in a soft breeze. There are no reasons to fight the fact we are all connected in one way, shape, or form. Is there a rush to cause anyone's flame to be extinguished? You must ask yourself this. The only true peace made is within us. Once reached, life truly begins together. So drop your weapons and shake hands.

Flashback
A Plea to God

I was jerked awake from a vivid nightmare. I was sweating, shivering, head throbbing, stomach turning, and vomit spewing from my mouth coming out of my nose, and I was unable to breathe. I was covered from the waist down lying in my own piss and shit. I was seeing men in biohazard gear surrounding me, poking me with needles and talking in medical terms sounding very alien to me. Have I been abducted?

Nope, soldier boy, this has become your reality. You must get better and get free of this place. They are all crazy in here. You have become a piece of mold in a petri dish, a white lab rat being given funky injections to see what will happen over the course of their experiments and time. Someone has to be told of what they have been doing to me. My mind is mush. I have lost the ability to care. Let me die, God. An old woman enters the plastic-covered room on the fifth day to console me. No gear on, unafraid. God's answer came in the form of an old woman.

Praise the Lord.

Here is something to consider. When I was overseas, I drank habu sake, which is snake venom and the entire pit viper within wabushu. Wabushu is an awamori-based liquor distilled from rice which is mixed with herbs and honey then placed in with the pit viper and its venom in a jar until consumption. This has been considered to have medicinal properties. With this being Okinawa, the proper term used for this snake, which is *Trimeresurus flavoviridis*. I used it because the local Japanese people who lived in the rural areas told me it would lessen the effects of the actual snakebite itself and could possibly save my life. I didn't want to go through the fear as I had done when a timber rattlesnake sunk its fangs into me during the North Carolina training.

Now with that said, who is to say that when I drank this stuff, it wasn't the cause of my esophagus rotting away over the course of a few months? I also had acute mononucleosis at the time I was finally brought to the hospital. I have to question this whole diagnosis of having AIDS actually. Perhaps you have made a mistake, and after all these years, the government is unwilling to admit the wrong diagnoses and just keep me in the state of belief I'm dying so they can pump me full of medicine and get their side effect information. They no longer will have that opportunity because I just confessed all my wrongs to the world. I no longer harbor guilt, but I am forever remorseful for prostituting my body and mind to them. I allowed you to tap into my reptilian brain to create a weapon to do mortal combat against other human beings. You made a mistake in doing this because I am not that easily swayed. My lessons learned as a small child among the nuns of St. Francis remained stronger. I pretty much destroyed most of the rules given, but killing another wasn't going to happen. It was my faith that kept me from such evils. We are all children of God. This is heaven, and the battle continues among his angels, us.

I know good from evil.

This would definitely be a kick straight to the balls. How do you give me my life back, or my mind?

This also puts your back against the wall because I can prove reasonable doubt in the eyes of a jury if the case ever went to court. I don't need proof when I have the truth. I will not allow another drop of my blood to be taken again either. Now because of all this medication, depression, and a horrible state of mind, I have completely lost my concept of reality. Like I said before, be willing to question things in your own life and how you learned them from others.

Love them all, but . . .

Trust no one. Have faith instead.

Perhaps I should look into politics. I will actually do what I say, unlike the jackasses we got now. They are all double talkers, but we allow them to run the show anyways because we are too lazy to take any responsibility ourselves or make a stand for equality. I guess acting is a better gig; they get paid more. I think they are all one and the same in my opinion, but at least an actor can create a character and return to normal. Politicians remain confused and close-minded. The filthy rich get richer, and we idolize them for being on our television screens and listen to their bullshit as if it were the truth. I like competition on motorcycles, playing golf, going to the gym, going swimming, watching movies, lots of movies, all the movies, including the wars, the crime, and the documentaries. I hold no office. I hold no title. I hold no authority over anyone. Nor does anyone hold authority over me. I was born free, yet beaten, crushed, arrested under false pretence, brainwashed, and still I march on, keeping the peace.

Psalms 6

O Lord, rebuke me not in your anger, neither chastens me in thy hot pleasure. Have Mercy upon me, O Lord; for I am weak: O Lord, heal me; for my bones are vexed. My soul is also sore vexed: but thou, O Lord, how long?

A letter written by my fiancée in response to my question: Why are you with me?

"What's forever for?"

You may ask yourself, Gary, why I am with you.

When I ask myself that question, this is what I come up with.

When *God* created you, he created the most perfect ideal-giving soul, and that was *you*. You have courage and strength of a boar and a face of a million man war, *strong* and fierce. You are built like a perfect mountain. When lost, I can look into your eyes and feel wrapped in a deep blue sea of blankets. I truly believe *God* has favorite angels that are by his side. When he released you to the earth to make a difference, he knew you were strong enough to handle any challenge you are given. Being with you causes my world to be lit up like tiny fireflies. Before I was with you, nothing seemed like it seemed. Since I have been with you, everything seems as it seems, perfect and full of sense. Very fine silk and precious threads were selected when *God* constructed your heart. He has woven with favor by hand. All bond together with angelic, courageous lace. When *God* felt your heart was perfected, with love and all that he knows, he himself with his glowing hands held your heart and kissed it and placed it into your supreme vessel. Gary, *God* shines down on you from the heavens. I am with you because you are my forever mate. You make me happier and fuller of life than I have ever felt! As a result of being with you, I feel hopeful and full of life and I know *our love is forever.*

Another fine creation for the cause, a movie, and all could happen. It's just a piece of real paranoia for you to consider on all sides of warfare. Since I believe AIDS and war are linked, I will say I'm a constant soldier for one, and hopeful about the end of the other. Let's just say I want them both gone.

I wonder sometimes if I would make a good father to my own children, and most certainly I would have to say, yes. This will not happen within this lifetime for me, perhaps in my next life. I most likely have been chemically sterilized by now. I have accepted that, but in the odd case God grants me a special gift in the future, I will cherish that child. I would protect most diligently within their safety. I am not fearful of my disease passing into my child. I am fearful of the burden and the disease they would encounter within our society, because war and AIDS are infectious diseases. We all want it to end.

So this is what I propose.

If you consider me an enemy in any way, shape, or form or a traitor, I will gladly arrive to Washington DC to the capital of my country and be nailed to the cross. Just let me know so I can get my affairs in order, just like I was told many years ago when I was told I had AIDS and was no longer effective. Yet I have managed to do all those things for mankind during and afterward. You gave me back to the world because I wouldn't kill for you. Then you labeled me a plague. You gave me poison to trigger me into killing others. You have made a mistake in your judgments. I still stand fast. You starved me and denied me water; you send my children to their deaths, because they are all my children and yours. I love them all. Position the cross right in front of the Lincoln Memorial where all the liars of my country like to preach from nowadays.

I'm willing to die for peace and equality, to end this disease, and to feed the hungry, nothing more. I do not need a weapon for this. The pen is mightier than the sword.

Let the world see with all cameras rolling on December 21, 2012. Let your hatred end in my death. If you think this is a threat, well then, you live in fear.

I love my brothers and my sisters on this Earth from all regions and all tribes, including the ones who you told me to call the enemy, because my disease has no borders. I now know we are all connected. I would like to meet my ancestors and theirs again in the promise land as Martin Luther King graciously proposed. President Kennedy said, "Ask not what the country can do for you; ask what you can do for your country." I would rather we try another approach, but if that's what is necessary for peace, equality, to end this disease and to feed people, so be it. I will remain nailed till the twenty-fifth; then I would like the executioners, meaning, all of you to fear the Almighty's wrath.

Anything short of that is definitely a conspiracy and definitely means someone assassinated me and they were too close-minded for change. Let there be no interference, I ask this of all, because I can hack it till the chosen date. Believe it.

Burn me in flames and offer me back to the God whom you think wants war.

Who will be crucified beside me? I ask.

I only need three, because that has always been what has mattered to me, the person to my right or my left. I walk beside them always to keep them safe as they did me, as they do for you. I haven't passed this AIDS disease to anyone either with or without protection. I challenge the person who claims otherwise.

They must hold the rank of colonel or higher, and they can also be politicians, religious leaders, warlords, and the judges because those were the ones who judged me and considered you expendable also—the higher the better.

I want true believers of war beside me. I await the names from the warriors of this Earth. I suggest the soldiers all hold a vote in each country who are willing to fight and die for a cause in battle because it is the warriors who decide, not the leaders who are governing them and sending out orders to kill for them as they sit back and scratch their own ass. So if you're a soldier of any military or you have killed in battle for someone else because you were ordered to, or you thought it was justified on this planet, choose those men wisely. I hoped and prayed we could get all their names on my list. I was not allowed by the rules given me in the spirit world. One will be sufficient within this game, from all the nations of the four corners of this Earth.

Unless you like war and you're obsessed with killing, your vote won't count, you crazy fucker. If you're unable to choose peace, well then, let the whole world be annihilated in one final push of all the buttons to nuclear holocaust on this day. Let the whole shithouse go up in flames. Nature will find a way; a new heaven and a new earth will begin again.

They also must be in control of you as we speak. They also must not offer themselves as I have done. You must be chosen by those who serve under you that they order to do thy bidding. This will take away your fear of your enemy because your enemies will be doing the same thing. This includes the gangs of this world as well, one each, motherfuckers. They must not be aware of your choices until a week prior to allow time for transport, no one will stop you, and it has been seen in my vision.

Bring one each from your country in chains to my country and we will spin the wheel of death like it is a lottery to choose the other two out of 195 countries recognized by the United Nations and the 70 or so independent nations. Only one soldier is allowed to bring the chosen per country. I accept all tribes to my game. This is the only way to force them all to come out from behind that curtain of lies and false doctrine. Become a true warrior of your own God. Hurry up and decide, the clock is ticking. I will await your decisions while I'm riding my motorcycle. When the final three are chosen, allow the remaining warmongers to nail us three to the crosses. Then shoot each one of them in the back of the head. Pitch all the weapons into the sea and begin again. That means all of them. I will even stop smoking cigarettes until the last day. Feed us a last meal, offer us a smoke, and let peace begin.

If all of them are unwilling when we ask them to die next to me, it proves my point; we can live together in peace.

I will not die by my own hand, and God wants me to live in our garden called Earth peacefully. There is food and water for all to share. This does include you. This also includes your neighbor. Where ever you live.

I suggest if you think this might be you within our country, or within your own country around the globe, start changing the policy today. I like my life, and I love all the people, so get to work to stop your own death, asshole!

Ticktock. Ticktock. *There is only one death needed to end all war with me.*

Ticktock. Ticktock. *Should've questioned those orders sent out.*

Ticktock. Ticktock. *That's dude's fucking nuts.*

Ticktock. Ticktock. *Should've tried harder at my real job, providing for the people.*

Ticktock. Ticktock. *Somebody save me from this madness, somebody save me. Put him in prison, throw away the key.*

Ticktock. Ticktock. *Could this all be real?*

Ticktock. Ticktock. *He's been delusional, he's been a drug addict, he's been among thieves, he's been a fighter, he's been crazy, he's been to prison, he's seen it all, he's an AIDS carrier, he's a Marine, he hears voices, he is one of us, he's a test subject, he has many friends, he's been to the land of the dead, he's not afraid, he's a dirt bike racer, he has been to the valley within the shadow of death, he lives in it every day, he's a survivor, he loves all creatures, he loves all races, he accepts all religions, he's been through the worst yet seeks no revenge, he's a leper, he has no enemies, he's a peacemaker, he's one tough motherfucker, he's my friend too, he has walked with all the worst, and he's been with the best, and he's been a fucking fag, he's also sent the invisible after me.*

Ticktock. *Peace and equality stops this clock!*

He's also honest and speaks of truth.

Shit!

He's also right!

I am an asshole!

Give up what you hold most dear and be set free, just like I have just done by writing it down for all to see. You can put down your weapons and live in peace, just have faith and believe. Nobody will call you a coward either, especially me. I will have walked this earth twenty-one years prior to this disease, and twenty-one years without it on this chosen day. I haven't come for any other reason. No amount of money will be sufficient. Sounds like prophecy.

It only takes one life each from all nations, the lowest sum worth paying to end all war and bring peace to your lands. That is the price to open the gates. I'm the messenger and the light of the world. Take action, or we remain in hell. I will remain riding my horse, a motorcycle. This all depends on you. I have been chosen by the dead. I will await them all on the steps on this day. From sunup till sunset, I will remain at my post. I will not abandon my post until I'm properly relieved.

Will you vote me in?

I'll try anything for one more day to save you and myself.

I'm not even a terrorist, yet I have them all scared.

We call that checkmate! Assholes!

Let the new world order begin today without any more killing.

Consider this my run for vice president nomination if he'll accept me by his side. I will try not to swear in front of the kids. I refuse all interviews. I will await the people's vote. Just write it in magic marker right over that ballot filled with liars when they bitch and whine about one another's faults and point their fingers and guns. I gave you my worst deeds so you can know them ahead of time. I no longer hold secrets and tell no lies.

Keep Obama at the top. He's the only guy making any sense thus far, me in the middle, and I'll watch over the warmongers and play Uncle G., your brother, your friend, and the cure. Let me be the chosen one, we the people's choice. I have heard enough bullshit, haven't you? So when you vote, say you're voting for Uncle G. regardless the choices. I will overcome and adapt like a good Marine should in my new job. Once the prophecy is fulfilled, you will need him to start over without weapons on your missions of helping one another out. Just as I have done for all of you. I will surrender my life over to you.

Now I have the world's attention.

This wool has now been pulled from over our eyes. I was given safe passage throughout my travels and the ages. I was handed this key because it has been hidden. Throughout the dawn of man, we have gone to war over everything. If we plan on surviving as a species, the human race, all nations have to come together as one. We are sacrificing our young for all the wrong reasons, love and hate. All the great war chiefs of the past know this and have sent me to change the path. The one thing I was told was, there is no enemy. They all agree that they themselves were also blinded from it. Even Sung Su had agreed. This is the truth behind war and HIV.

If there is no enemy, there is no need of weapons. The battle ends; peace is restored. In the world and in your own mind and body.

You can join my fan page and watch a video I created on Facebook at http://www.facebook.com/pages/Gary-Mello/337064332762.

You can also check out my Web site at www.GaryMello.com.